The kitchen in the Hannibal, Missouri, home, which Sam immortalized through Tom Sawyer. Photo by permission of the Becky Thacher Book Shop.

The parlor in the Clemens home in Hannibal. Photo by permission of the Becky Thacher Book Shop.

E. S. Gowdy, Fredonia, N. Y.

A portrait of Jane in later days, which Sam, in the adjoining letter, calls "admirable work."

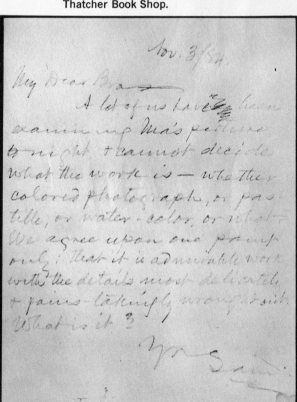

Nov. 3/84.

My Dear Bro—

A lot of us have been examining Ma's picture to-night & cannot decide what the work is — whether colored photograph, or pastille, or water-color, or what. We agree upon one point only; that it is admirable work with the details most delicately & pains-takingly wrought out. What is it?

Yrs
Sam.

Varble, Rachel
Jane Clemens

Jane Clemens

The Story of Mark Twain's Mother

BOOKS BY RACHEL M. VARBLE

Jane Clemens—The Story of Mark Twain's Mother

A Time Will Come

JUVENILES

Three Against London

Beth and Seth

Pepys' Boy

Romance for Rosa

Julia Ann

Jane Clemens

The Story of Mark Twain's Mother

by RACHEL M. VARBLE

Doubleday & Company, Inc.
Garden City, New York

To

Doris Webb Webster of the Clemens family

and

Ruth Paull Burdette of Adair County, Kentucky,

right lovingly—

ACKNOWLEDGMENTS

Grateful acknowledgment is made to the editors of the Mark Twain Company for permission to use the unpublished letters of Jane Clemens, Orion and Mollie Clemens, and Pamela Clemens Moffett—a permission made more valuable by the criticisms and advice of Frederick Anderson, assistant editor of the Mark Twain Estate.

To Harper & Row, Publishers, Incorporated, and the Estate of Clara Clemens Samossoud for permission to quote from *Mark Twain's Letters,* arranged by Albert Bigelow Paine.

To Doris Webb Webster and the late Samuel Charles Webster for permission to quote from *Mark Twain Business Man* by Samuel Charles Webster. Little, Brown and Company. Boston, 1946.

To the State Historical Society of Iowa for permission to quote from *The Palimpsest,* October 1929 issue; Iowa City, Iowa; five biographical essays devoted to Orion Clemens, written with rare insight by Fred W. Lorch.

To Houghton Mifflin Company for permission to quote from *Sam Clemens of Hannibal* by Dixon Wecter: Boston, 1952; a reference to Ella Hunter Lampton and Dr. John McDowell.

To the University of North Carolina Press for permission to quote from *Mark Twain, Son of Missouri,* by Minnie M. Brashear. Chapel Hill, North Carolina, 1934.

To Annette Patton Cornell, co-editor of *Talaria, A Quarterly of Poetry,* for permission to quote the beautiful anachronism by Isabel Fiske Conant titled "Eternal Event." Winter Issue, December 1938. Cincinnati, Ohio.

A special measure of gratitude is hereby expressed for the kindness of the late Dr. Dixon Wecter, editor of the Mark Twain Estate from 1946 until his death in 1950. He encouraged me to write the life of Jane Lampton Clemens, and, in turn, honored me with requests for Lampton-Clemens minutiae during the writing of his popular yet scholarly book —the first of his intended series on Mark Twain—*Sam Clemens of Hannibal.*

"—there's a contribution in him from every ancestor he ever had. In him there's atoms of priests, soldiers, crusaders, poets, and sweet and gracious women—"

THE AMERICAN CLAIMANT
Mark Twain

1 ❖

The baby whose birth had just occurred would have various superlatives to contend with. Her father, Benjamin Lampton, was the handsomest man at any local gathering. Her mother, Peggy Casey Lampton, was perhaps the frailest girl on the frontier. ("Peggy looks to break like china," people said.) Her maternal grandparents, Colonel William Casey and his wife, were the community's most revered characters. And when the baby should have become a woman of middle age, her son would be called the wittiest man in the world.

The babe was born in the Casey farmhouse where the Lamptons were staying that year. The location was Adair County, lately cut from Green, in southern Kentucky. The date was June 18, 1803, of a Saturday. Although the weather was hot, every leaf and bloom being lush with summer, the big log house had a cavelike temperature, pleasant to the folk assembled there.

Benjamin Lampton had left home at daybreak to oversee some road construction, a civic duty; and though his young wife had been tossing fitfully because of her burden, she was not yet in labor. At Benjamin's return in the late afternoon he saw signs of a convening of neighbors and presently learned that his first child had been born. He heard it from a slave woman named Nancy who was gathering greens for supper.

"You got a gul, Mistah Benjy, pretty lil gul!" Nancy sang out. "She was borned foah five hours atter you lef'."

"Ho!" Benjamin shouted. He dismounted hastily, gave over his horse to a stable boy and strode to the house.

Dusty, but properly cravatted and carrying a noticeably fine riding crop, he made a cyclonic entrance into the bedroom, greeted his wife with tender formality while the neighbors watched, and confronted his offspring.

The baby, from the midwife's arms, seemed to fix her eyes on him—one dared not say she focused them—giving him look for look before the lids resumed their newborn squint. A number of persons in the room noticed it and informed the young mother, who accepted the oddity with wan composure.

Neighbor women of various ages had begun to arrive while the baby was being bathed, for the news had got around, and now that the afternoon was well along, everything had been said several times. "A mighty active baby!" was the opinion that recurred oftenest.

"When she's seventeen," Benjamin said to them, "I'll marry her off to a Lexington planter with silver toddy cups!"

Some of the women exchanged disapproving glances, but others laughed in appreciation. The Green River settlers envied, till it rankled, the prosperous Fayette Countians, and sometimes it was a relief to hear a person own up to it.

Lampton was a man of medium size with mahogany-red hair that curled riotously and a proud way of holding his head. He was thirty-three years of age, more than a dozen years older than Peggy, his wife. He had called several places home: Virginia, his birthplace; Clark County in Kentucky, whither his parents had migrated; the Cherry Creek region of Tennessee where he had pioneered youthfully; and now Kentucky again, between the Green and Cumberland rivers.

Mrs. Casey, his mother-in-law, born a Montgomery, entered the room in time to hear his frivolity. "Well, Benjamin," she probingly asked, "is your highest concern for this little girl that she marry a rich man?" She paused for his answer, though overly busy.

"No, ma'am," Benjamin replied, "wealth's a mere addendum. My first wish is that she be a comfort to her mother. My second is that she ride well and take pleasure in it."

"All the Casey girls ride well," came the answer too quickly.

2

"Jenny and Polly and Anne do, ma'am. But your daughter Peggy doesn't. She sits a horse poorly."

"Did you never ask her why she sits a horse too rigid?"

"No, ma'am. Ought I have asked her?"

"It gives Peggy a pain in her side, that's the reason. Must you criticize her on the very day of her lying-in?"

"I'm sorry, Mrs. Casey," Benjamin said contritely, and the friction ended. This was disappointing to some of the women. They wanted to see Lampton get a dressing down.

He was not a typical pioneer, for all that he so robustly tried to be one. A few generations ago an ancestor of his had foregone the heirship of Lambton Castle in England's County Durham to come to Virginia and buy a little plantation and allow his name to be misspelled. This abnegation appeared the greater now because vast collieries had since been opened on Lambton land, and the lucky incumbent had got an earldom.

Benjamin, to do him justice, rarely referred to Lambton grandeur; but he had some tiresome English ways, the Montgomerys thought. At the Christmas season he preferred carols to fireworks, and he would ride miles to find holly and mistletoe to decorate the house. He thought foxes should be trailed on horseback in the orthodox manner, hounds to the fore for the kill. (As Thomas Montgomery once said to his sister, "I doubt if your son-in-law would shoot a dam' red fox in Colonel Casey's own chicken yard.") In the matter of clothes, Lampton wanted a ruffle too many on his shirts and doted on silk neckwear. While these oddities annoyed the Montgomerys, there was another fault of his more grievous to them: his inability to make money and his cavalier attitude toward that failing. Benjamin often joked about his poor credit. At such times only his father-in-law was amused. But then, Colonel Casey was Irish.

Benjamin left the room and returned with a glass of cold well water for his wife, fetching it in a chipped goblet he admired, though a stoneware mug would have been more suitable. Peggy thanked him.

"Make people go home," she begged wearily.

They had all left except three elderly cousins and, at Peggy's plaint, those tied their bonnet strings. Mrs. Casey came forward to bid them adieu. She accompanied them outdoors and watched them ride away, now and then waving her hand absently.

The babe's grandmother—Mrs. Colonel Casey, as she was called now—was forty-two years old, erect and somber; her face had a listening look. Her hair was severely knotted under a black lace cap. Only her eyes, violet-blue and serene, lessened her stern mien. She had, as the saying went, lived hard. General Benjamin Logan was her brother-in-law, a royal connection in wilderness circles, though the Montgomerys had never leaned on Logan. They had left his fort to build their own station twelve miles distant as the crow flies—four cabins without stockade—and they held it even after the Indians bloodily depleted them one spring morning in 1781. Soon afterward, Jane Montgomery's hand was asked in marriage by Captain William Casey, a young veteran in ragged buckskin about to found his own settlement. Jane accepted. She wed William Casey in the clearing whose grass had lately been stained with the blood of several reckless Montgomerys and two faithful slaves. There was a wedding supper on a crude table covered with a wide-loomed linen cloth, enlivened by a jug of Scottish whisky of which only the men partook. All was sedate. Montgomerys and Logans were not addicted to shivarees. The honeymoon was a watchful horseback journey southward into Green County, where Casey and some comrades had built a cluster of cabins. It was a locality not frequented by the red men, being off the beaten warpaths and somewhat bereft of game. But eventually the Indians spied them out and pestered them with spiteful, bloody little raids. Three times Jane Montgomery Casey helped her husband hold his station against them. . . . This very spot, it was; but now covered with the big comfortable house that was sealed with plaster inside, and had china dishes in a corner cupboard, and cherry bedposts towering toward the ceilings. Being made a grandmother today had caused Mrs. Casey to think backward. And for a little while, standing there in the dog run that had not yet fashionably become a breezeway, the dangerous past was more real than the quiet present.

Little Peggy Lampton, glad to be alone with her husband, contemplated their child and said, "We must name her after Mother, mustn't we?"

"By all means," Benjamin answered, for it seemed inevitable that Mrs. Casey should be so honored. His own mother had never molded a bullet or held an Indian at bay; had even thought it suitable that Lamptons should refrain from snapping at royal hands during the late unpleasantness. A cheerful woman, born a Dutch Schuyler and not caring that the name was turned to Schooler in the Shenandoah Valley. She had never met her son's formidable in-laws.

Benjamin looked at his baby daughter and said experimentally, "Jane Lampton." He noticed that her eyes were wide-spaced, her little chin exquisitely shaped, her hands flowerlike. He sent his rollicking laugh around the room, the laugh that the child would imitate almost before she could speak.

"What are you laughing at?" Peggy asked tiredly from her pillow. Dutifully, she wanted to laugh with him. She saw him take a frayed newspaper from his pocket. "Read me a funny tale," she said.

Benjamin unfolded *The Farmer's Library,* printed in Louisville, searched a moment and read in a resonant drawl:

"Run away from subscriber some time in November last, a Negro woman called Kitty, about five feet, six or seven inches high. She was enticed away by a Mulatto man called Ned, tall and well made, an artful cunning fellow, owned conjunctly by Mr. Estell and Charles Quirey of Beargrass. He procured for himself and Kitty forged papers of freedom, from a person not prudent to mention. Plays upon the violin, and is an excellent blacksmith and gunsmith. Took with him a bay mare, the owner not known. A reward of fifty dollars will be paid for the woman's delivery at—"

"When we build our house," Peggy interrupted drowsily, beguiled by the daring of Kitty and Ned, wishing them well as they made for the Ohio River but not concerned with the larger issues of servitude, "Father's going to give us two slaves."

"So he mentioned yesterday. It's very generous of him."

5

"I wish he'd come home," Peggy fretted. "I want him to see our baby. He likes a baby even more than a colt."

She was anxious for her father's approval. He was a gentle, dark Irishman, almost without human fault except that of over-eating. His spoken word was as good as his signature, and he supposed all men to be as honest as himself. When a person failed him, he seemed to forget it. When a person did him some little courtesy, he never stopped finding ways to repay him.

Colonel Casey had a pink bulging forehead, like a saint's, with black and silver curls falling over it, and he spoke in a per-suasive voice that had a far reach. There were paradoxes in his behavior, for he had once shot dead an Indian chief who was drinking water from a spring, and another unaware Indian from ambush, and those blots must always smirch him till he resemble any other pioneer. But it was during a time of warfare, when the Indians were bent on exterminating his settlers and had killed some of the more helpless of them. He never boasted of his dis-patched Indians and he buried them decently.

Casey's early life had been expended in soldiering on the frontiers. Right gladly he hung his rifle over the mantelshelf when peace brought an influx of settlers into southern Kentucky over the Wilderness Road. He become founding father to two county seats—Greensburg and the newer village of Columbia. He could effect beautiful compromises; and in the assemblies where the laws were being drawn and the policies shaped for the new com-monwealth, he could make even the quarreling Scots pipe down. He was never ambitious for wealth or social honor and declined to sit for a portrait. But he had a thirst for learning. Only half educated, himself, he was a seeker of tutors for his settlements, a founder of schools. As for religion, he tempered the stern Calvin-ism of the Montgomerys to his needs. When he had caused Shiloh Chapel to be built on his plantation and had called a minister, he saw that the pious man was well housed, well mounted, and well fed.

"Here comes your father now!" Benjamin exclaimed to Peggy, for there was a commotion in the yard. White children and colored could be seen running to open the gate for a towering horseman

6

who was bareheaded and carelessly dressed. "They're telling him about the baby, dearest."

But Peggy was asleep. Exhaustion had overcome her.

Lampton, immured in his own vitality, looked down at his spent wife in surprise. Now that she had got through the worst of her day's work, it was disappointing that she could not enjoy her prestige. He bent to the bed and kissed her forehead gently. Then he gathered up his child, cocooned in wool, and carried her outdoors to meet her ancestor.

"Bless my soul!" Colonel Casey exclaimed above the hullabaloo, "What have we got here?"

He was awed that a matter of such importance had happened, but not dismayed at becoming a grandfather. Though but forty-seven years of age, he had carried responsibility so long that he thought of himself as an old man.

All that summer and autumn the young mother remained lackadaisical, breast-feeding her baby but not otherwise handling her.

"Peggy's delicate," was a comment heard so often by young Mrs. Lampton that she accepted it. She also overheard another thing, a prophecy that upset her. "Peggy will die before her time."

The babe was passed about like a doll, for she had three aunts and an uncle under twenty, and the slaves found her enticing. When her father was at home and unoccupied she often rode in the crook of his arm. She watched the waving branches of the trees with evident pleasure and, if held indoors, seemed pushing to get out. When reddish curls appeared on her head it created a diversion. Soon it was evident that she would not have the Scottish Montgomery eyes, nor the cornflower blue eyes, black lashed, of the Caseys. The irises were darkening, and an auburn tint appeared in them. "She favors her father," every one conceded.

Perhaps never a child born at the ancestral hall in Durham had carried the Lambton look more exclusively.

Overshadowing this domestic idyl was a national tension that played on the nerves of Kentuckians until they threatened to break, like a loom's warp, drawn too tight. Spain had ceded Louisiana to the French; Napoleon Bonaparte would take over when he had time. The Port of New Orleans was being kept open only by strepitous backwoods pressure and the light, swift stepping of Mr. Jefferson.

A closed door at the mouth of the Mississippi was the western nightmare. Desperate frontiersmen negotiated shadily with Spain for short-term rights of deposit at New Orleans. One Benjamin Sebastian, a prominent Kentucky jurist, was a go-between, alleged to be on Spain's payroll. General James Wilkinson, though not a Spanish pensioner, was a manipulator. You depended on those men to treat for you if you lived in Kentucky or Tennessee or the Mississippi Territory. But the West was tired of backdoor diplomacy, it was fed to the teeth with uncertainty. That Napoleon might land his seasoned troops in Louisiana and dictate trade was intolerable.

The definite talk had begun, even on the steps of the Greensburg courthouse, even in Columbia's taverns. Questions were fired, inviting reckless answers: Why not pack the powder, jerk the beef, fill the old canteen, and move on New Orleans? Barges would cut the overland effort, the bolder ones stated, and barges were easy had. President Jefferson was trifling; he argued to buy a port for two million dollars that could be taken with a few rifles; he lived in his big house on the favored side of the mountains, else in Washington; had the Rivanna and the James and the Potomac to serve him. Did he suffer if the westerners' tobacco and grain and hemp rotted at Vicksburg?

Some of the New England Federalists, to rattle Jefferson, were writing editorials to egg them on, reminding them of their former dream of a trans-Allegheny empire. Aaron Burr too was watching, his own plans still undefined, filing this knowledge of the western temper for future use. The West, wavering, was asking where allegiance was due, where repaid. "We could do it," went the talk. "By God, yes! Just the Kentucky and Tennessee outfits could do it." Certain facts were evident; Bonaparte was busy in the Indies, had an eye on England too; not even the backwoods was ignorant of that. One quick slash now at those lazy Spaniards before the French took over, and New Orleans was theirs. Then more when they were ready. They could run up a flag. . . . What flag? Chins rubbed, heads scratched. It sounded like treason, but here was their destiny. How could they get the produce out except by the rivers? . . . There were always a few deliberate voices to say wait, though. They might foul up Jefferson, said the thoughtful ones; Jefferson had Robert R. Livingston in Europe, and he'd sent James Monroe to help Livingston dicker. Such things took time, took a little cajoling and banqueting. The French were a mannered people. John Breckinridge said wait. Colonel Casey said wait. . . .

Jane Lampton did not begin life at a dull time or among listless people. Her neighbors and kin, though rustics short of specie, were the nation's first expansionists. Had she made her entrance a few weeks later she would have been named Louisiana, like a score of other girl children born west of the mountains that year. For Monroe came home with all of Louisiana in his traveling case, "875,000 square miles of territory at three cents an acre," and the West was beside itself with joy.

Benjamin had a strip of land within sight of the Casey place, and he soon began to build the dwelling he had promised his wife. There were available some carpenters who had just completed the Columbia courthouse. They were a covey of young men who had been apprenticed to builders in the older settlements. They could have built Benjamin Lampton a better house than he ordered, for they knew how to fit an interior with cupboards and paneling, such as found in Bluegrass houses, and would apply mouldings as fancy as pie crust if a person so desired.

Benjamin so desired, but he could not pay. He ended with something ordinary and humble: two large rooms on the ground floor, two above with sloping roof, all very plain. But he saved face by using clapboards, painted white, and by having a pretty pair of chimneys. He built his own chimneys, for he could lay brick with old English precision. He had inherited a critical appreciation of well laid walls and chimneys, and had, somewhere in his wanderings, got the hang of it.

To the rear of the new residence, at conventional distances, were the outbuildings, and one of those was the double cabin where would dwell Christina and Toby, the pair of slaves allotted

9

by Colonel Casey. There were no plantings as yet, and everything seemed raw.

Benjamin said contritely to his wife, "I meant to provide us a better home than this, I'm sure you know that, Peggy. But my money gave out." They had moved in.

"It's a sweet place," Peggy assured him. She was hanging calico skirts around the great bed, for underneath it was her only storage space. The room's other furnishings were a chest of drawers, little Jane's cradle, a sewing table, and some settles.

"We can add a room when we must," she reminded him. "The house is big enough now." She was a gentle girl, easily pleased, not accustomed to making decisions.

Colonel Casey arrived, bringing a pair of brass candlesticks that he had ordered sent from Louisville. His daughter cried out with delight and embraced him, saying he must come without a gift sometime.

Benjamin agreed. "Yes, you must, sir." But he was wondering when the papers for the two Negroes would be forthcoming. As matters stood, Toby and Christina were a sort of princely loan, subject to recall. Was this absent-mindedness on Casey's part, or was it deliberate conduct, perhaps rooted in a pledge to the Negroes themselves? Lamptons had been known to use their slaves for legal tender if hard pushed.

"A bad thing has happened in the East," Colonel Casey announced, his voice large and formal. "Vice-President Burr killed Alexander Hamilton in a duel. It's hard to believe."

Benjamin shared his wonder, tried to imagine hating a man to the point of dueling. Yet he had no love for Alexander Hamilton, the man who had thought up banks and a tax on copper stills.

"I saw Nathan Montgomery in town," the colonel continued. "He was mighty callous. He said Burr killed the right man."

"I wouldn't go that far," Benjamin said. "Hamilton had some admirable traits. There's this to be said for him, too: he was in favor of annexing Louisiana."

"Another thing's being talked about," Colonel Casey stated. "Napoleon's had himself crowned Emperor."

10

"Good God!" Benjamin exclaimed. "I ought have gone to town!" He seemed to imply that he would have witnessed all this panorama in the public square, but Colonel Casey knew what he meant. A man can picture events more vividly when he rubs shoulders with his neighbors and hears them talk and answers back.

The child came toddling from the kitchen and diverted them. It was her second summer, supposedly a bad time, and she was teething. She wore a bib to protect her ruffles. Her grandfather swung her aloft, and she laughed.

"Her cheeks are so bright," Peggy said anxiously. "Can it be a fever? Must she have a hard August?"

"No, she mustn't," Benjamin retorted. "And she won't die till she's an old woman. I've spoken to Heaven about it."

If the child throve in this climate of optimism, so did the new town three miles distant. A dozen streets were dotted with excellent houses, and even alleys bore such highfaluting names as Adams, Monroe, Washington. Stores had been stocked with goods to tempt townspeople and plantation folk. Taverns offered board to families not yet domiciled and to travelers passing through. But the very heart of the place was the courthouse, and that heart throbbed audibly when County Court was in session. The big, bare courtroom (as throughout pioneer America) was regarded with reverence. The justices, the clerk of the court, the lawyers were held in esteem; and even jurors gained an awesome stature when they removed their dusty hats and took their places.

Into this courtroom in 1805 was brought a scandal that was considered local; but it was hardly so, for the west coast of Africa had produced its substance. A Negro woman called Pat came to trial for feloniously murdering her infant child, to the outrage of her master, a prominent citizen and landowner. The slave declared herself not guilty and put herself "on the mercy of God, Country, and the Attorney for the Commonwealth."

Though Pat said few words in her own defense, she could not be shaken from the guarded, sullen few that she had spoken. Right gravely the jurymen filed out of the courtroom to deliberate. What weight of social guilt they balanced against the woman's

11

crime is not known, for she had killed her child to save it from slavery, and thereby they were trapped. Through their reserved utterances, their silences, they arrived at Pat's acquittal, and she was "discharged of the premises, to go thence without delay." She went out into the bright May sunshine (some persons long remembered), walking alone, her own race not yet drawing near her, her face secretive, anguished.

It was a case the white folk rarely mentioned. They had been shown a brown-skinned slave, a piece of property worth about four hundred dollars, with a capacity for suffering and revenge greater than they cared to think on.

2 ❖

Peggy Lampton presented her husband with a second daughter on March 22, 1807, little Jane being almost four years old. Now it was time to remember the other grandmother. The child was named Martha, to be called Patsy, in the tradition.

Benjamin wrote and told his mother so. In replying, she brought him up to date on the family news. Clary, widow of his late brother William, had kept his land and his stud horse—a beautiful black stallion by Brilliant, which she let out for a fee. John had a farm in Clark County and six or seven slaves; he grew tobacco. Wharton, now twenty-three, had bought a little land and was courting Miss Diana Duncan. As for Joshua, he was given over to horses. Reading his mother's letter, Benjamin recalled Joshua with affection rather than pride: large, noisy, hearty, concerned with the latest thing in rolling stock and harness; not able, now at twenty-eight, to write his name legibly. Joshua was opening a livery stable in Winchester.

Mrs. Lampton concluded with Lewis, the literate one, the airy one, who had never found any work to suit him. Lewis had gone to Philadelphia to look around, she reported. Benjamin could count on it, he would put up at the best places and would boast of Lambton Castle as if it were his own. He would bring home gifts for everybody, most of them too fancy to use.

Benjamin folded the letter thoughtfully. He regretted the smallness of the family farms. Lamptons must play second fiddle to the big landholders though on a par with them socially. And no Lampton shone in the professions, even in the backwoods, for none had applied himself to learning. They must look sharp, or they would go to seed. Benjamin mixed himself a toddy and drank it, sitting under a hickory tree in a rush-bottomed chair, and presently felt complacent again.

Mrs. Casey, who had been calling on her daughter and the new baby, came out of the house and joined Benjamin, accepting a proffered chair. This surprised him, for she rarely took time to sit down. She asked, "How does Peggy seem to you?"

"Not very strong, Mrs. Casey. But she was like this after Jane's birth. By fall, she'll be fit again."

"Never wholly fit, Captain Lampton, you may as well face it. I doubt if Peggy ever bears again. I doubt if you ever get a son by Peggy."

Benjamin looked at his mother-in-law in surprise, saw that she had a very melancholy expression. He waited.

"Something's out of place in her body," Mrs. Casey stated. "She suffers unduly. I've seen displacements happen to women now and then. It ends their bearing."

"She'll be just as dear to me," Benjamin answered gallantly, but he poured himself another drink from the demijohn.

"Peggy's always been our weakest child," Mrs. Casey said. "She was the first one. I'd not gotten over the Montgomery massacre, I think. I didn't sleep well for several years after that thing happened. I couldn't digest meat, or hominy, either. There'd be a burning in the pit of my stomach. Milk was my salvation."

"You don't eat much now," Benjamin remarked.

"But I'm strong," Mrs. Casey said. "Those other Indian disorders I took as they came. Like a day's work, you might say. Living with Colonel Casey has given me a good deal of composure."

Christina appeared, carrying little Jane, making a tour of the yard for the child's entertainment. Within the fenced area was a pied calf, separated from the other stock, and the nurse bent to

13

let child and beast touch. Jane's small hands caressed the calf's head, explored the budding horns, the silky ears until the animal sprang away.

"Let Jane walk, Christina!" Mrs. Casey called out.

"Hurts her feet," the woman objected. She laid her cheek against the red curls, triumphantly disobedient, and ambled away.

"Jane should get used to walking," Mrs. Casey said to Benjamin. "We must put soles in her moccasins. You've got two very pretty little girls," she added, as if to atone for the bad news she had brought him.

"Thank you, ma'am," he replied, politely standing while she went away. When engrossed with thinking, his drawl, his Tidewater manners were always pronounced.

When visiting weather came in April, Mrs. Casey invited the kin to a family dinner in honor of her husband. Colonel Casey had had a county named for him—a stunningly unexpected thing—and a celebration was due.

At the long dinner table, flanking the colonel and his wife, were their children: Peggy and her husband Benjamin Lampton; Jennie and her husband Captain Robert Paxton (soon to die at New Orleans); Polly and her husband John Creel; Anne, too young for marriage if not for romance, and young John Montgomery, her cousin, who was courting her. Green, the youngest Casey, the son and heir, sat next to his father. Then, several Montgomery men were there with their wives, and several Montgomery women with husbands of lesser name. Children impatiently awaited the second table, now and then entering the dining room to check the diners' progress.

Benjamin Lampton was unstinted in praising Colonel Casey's new fame. His affection for his father-in-law was evident in his words and in the tone of his voice. "Think of it, sir! The Commonwealth named that county for you before it honored Meriwether Lewis the explorer! Casey County is several weeks older than Lewis County."

Thomas Montgomery cleared his throat and addressed a cousin across the table. "I don't need to remind you, Nathan, that there's been a Montgomery County in Kentucky for ten years?"

14

"So there has been," Nathan responded. "And so large it's already being whittled away. Mighty good land, too."

Lampton then made the speech that assured his unpopularity with some of his wife's kin for all time to come. "I was living in Clark County when that area you're referring to was cut away from Clark and dubbed Montgomery," he said. "I remember it well. It wasn't named for your family. It was called after a Revolutionary general, that New Englander the Kentuckians admired so much—General Richard Montgomery."

"Tom and Nathan are apt to forget that," Mrs. Casey remarked. "We all are. It's well you've reminded us, Benjamin."

Young John Montgomery showed his surprise, though he was so in love with Anne Casey that he addressed her exclusively. "Doggone it, that's news to me. Ain't it to you, Anne? I always thought that county was named for us."

"I reckon I did," Anne answered. "Anyway, it ought've been. Our folks were such Indian fighters."

Colonel Casey spoke up, transferring the weight, reducing the tension. "I venture to say all Montgomerys in America are kin," he said. "An honor to one compliments the whole clan. But in my own case, I've been recognized beyond my worth. I'm mighty surprised and touched. Casey County has not got rich soil, I grant you. Its hills are numerous. But, like the finest, it will have a courthouse where men can patent their land, redress their wrongs, get their marriage papers and record their wills."

"True, sir!" Robert Paxton called out. "Long live Casey County!" He raised a mug of hard cider as a toast, and the Montgomery men responded courteously.

Little Jane Lampton came and tugged at her grandmother's skirt. "Why are they taking cider for Grandfather?" she asked.

"Because Kentucky's got an Irish county, Jane," Mrs. Casey said with a laugh, "and it pleasures everybody."

It pleasured people all the way to Maryland. Some say the Catholic migration thence to the new county was accelerated by the grand old name of Casey, worn by an unchurched man.

Here and now (we speak from Adair County in 1808, the underbrush being disturbed by fox hunters) we come upon the

15

bleached bones of a twelve-year-old boy in a ravine in the woods. Certain things (a buckle and bits of cloth) identify him as John Trabue, the manly little son of Captain Daniel Trabue, from one of the region's leading families. The Trabues are of Huguenot stock by way of Virginia. Five Trabue brothers served with Virginia troops in the Revolution, after which three of them married daughters of Colonel Robert Haskins—a family they evidently found irresistible. The Trabues were an exceptionally gay and lighthearted family before their sobering ordeal a few years ago.

Jane Lampton, though but five and a half years old, hears in detail the grim story of young John Trabue, for the finding of the skeleton has revived it, and the community talks of it with a sad compulsion.

Such are the facts of the Trabue ordeal. One ill-fated day toward sunset the sturdy little boy set out on horseback from his father's gristmill to take a sack of meal to a neighbor who had requested it. On the way, his path crossed that of the Harpes, a pair of bandits known as Big Harpe and Little Harpe, unequaled for hideousness of face and character and marked by a lust for senseless killing. The Harpes, with their two evil women, had broken jail that week at Stanford in the county beyond Casey and were cutting south on the most bloody foray of their career.

John Trabue's fate could only be conjectured, for no signs of a struggle were found. Horsemen, hastily called and led by Daniel Trabue, followed the Harpes beyond the Tennessee border but lost them in the cypress swamps of the Mississippi. Some blank years followed. The Harpes appeared like evil lightning now here, now there, leaving their signature of murdered families with each robbery and always escaping. Daniel Trabue was made Sheriff of Adair County that he might cope officially, and the bitter miles he traveled on his lathered horse, with a posse or alone, were more than he himself could remember.

It was supposed that young Trabue had met his death in one of the Harpe haunts, possibly with torture. It was also rumored that he had been retained by the outlaws and forced into a life of crime; though when the Harpes were finally captured in western Kentucky there was no boy with them to verify this awful

16

possibility. . . . But now, at little John's funeral, there is tranquillity. Those who loved the boy are at peace, knowing how long he has been in Heaven, and how speedy, apparently, was his going thither. Trabues and Haskinses and all their friends rejoice as they raise their voices in the singing of hymns and as they lower the lad's walnut coffin into the good earth of the family burying ground.

Jane Lampton will never forget this funeral, her first. It is dramatic beyond anything she has ever known; it is tender with soft tears and the condolence of pressed hands; it has been, in its way, a triumphantly happy gathering.

Jane began to go to town at an early age, sharing her father's or her grandfather's horse, and by the time she was six years old she was calling howdy to a number of persons. When engaged in conversation, she was articulate but not forward. She knew many saddle horses by sight, and if an unfamiliar one attracted her attention she would study the beast as if it were a human stranger come to town. She would ask its name, and when she saw it again she would recognize it. Once she said accusingly to a man coming out of the courthouse, "Your horse Tramp has got a saddle sore under his blanket. I saw it when I went to pet him. I've put some lard on it."

It made her face brighten with happiness to see horses drink at the public watering trough. Dogs and cats too. She would assist the smaller animals if they were unable to reach, and she began her annoying habit of carrying home cats with prominent ribs. When Colonel Casey or Benjamin objected, she could throw a fine tantrum wherever they happened to be.

There was a reason to spoil Jane, and for a few weeks this was done too abundantly, because she had one day slashed herself in the eye with a sharp knife while helping Christina peel sweet potatoes. Hastily called to treat her was a young doctor who had lately moved to town from North Carolina, Nathan Gaither. He was skillful beyond the average. Dr. Gaither's clean compresses, soaked in some virtuous brew, warded off infection. Afterward no scar remained, and the eye appeared normal. Only the child knew

17

how things were: a blur there, forcing her to turn her head with birdlike quickness to catch the vision through the other eye.

Her loss was only a baffling inconvenience to her, a dimness that she tried to wipe away with an impatient little hand. She could not explain that she had almost ceased to see through the hurt eye, for the mechanism of sight was still uncomprehended. Besides, she had already acquired that admiration for the stiff upper lip which was held in such esteem by the Montgomerys, Grandmother being the high priestess of this cult.

Jane's trips to town were not always ahorseback, for the farm wagon was sent often for supplies and she was allowed to ride in it. The vehicle was driven by a slave named Silas and staffed by Green Casey, Jane's uncle, ten years her senior. Green tolerated her. Silas treated her kindly. In cold weather they spread straw on the wagon floor to keep her feet warm.

Going to town with Silas afforded Jane acquaintanceship with many colored persons in Columbia, for he was a gregarious man. As he toted supplies from the stores and loaded the Casey wagon his hooting voice and carefree laughter announced his presence; the male and female servants of other folk, errand bound, were drawn to him, as bees to clover. Jane, listening in the wagon, was enthralled by the gaiety of their persiflage.

Then, suddenly, all that was stopped. Silas was replaced on the wagon by Abraham, a very taciturn man. Perhaps Colonel Casey restricted Silas to the farm at the request of the town trustees, for local mores were being corrected; henceforth, Negroes would not be allowed to congregate. A severe jolt had come to that complacent community by way of murder. A prominent farmer had been done in by his own slaves. Joseph Chapman, not regarded as a hard master (though God alone knows the facts), had been attacked by three of his people—Peter, Nance, and Robert—bludgeoned with a handspike and thrown into a log fire.

There was irrefutable evidence of the Negroes' guilt, and though Peter, the well-spoken one, was permitted to testify a second time, the trial moved swiftly. By nightfall the three were sentenced to be hanged one month hence—that sentence common to criminals of both races. Before being remanded to jail the condemned ones

18

were appraised, for the Commonwealth must prepare to repay the Chapman estate for what it destroyed. Peter and Robert were estimated at four hundred dollars each. Nance, through some strange whimsey of the appraisers, was evaluated in the sedate currency of an earlier day; a hundred pounds was Nance's worth, said her estimators.

From the time of the murder and its implacable punishment relations were not the same between the two races in that place. The Negro had replaced the Indian as a symbol of danger, and the African's attitude became of as much importance as his ability to turn out work. If a Negro grew sullen, his owner suspected him of planning some savage reprisal for his captivity. A morose houseservant, though acceptable in her work, might be making voodoo or sprinkling arsenic. On the other hand, a jolly field man, albeit lazy, was "a good Negro" in the new scale of values, and an amenable nursemaid was a prize to be coveted.

The slaveholders tightened their grip. County patrols, always active on the roads against highwaymen, were advised to take on espionage as well. They were urged to watch for slave uprisings and investigate any plantation gatherings that seemed secretive.

The townfolk were more methodical, leaving nothing to chance, and Columbia became one of the first towns west of the Alleghenies to put its fears on record:

> *Resolved, that all the male inhabitants of the town of Columbia, and those on the donation lands adjoining, above the age of fifteen years, be compelled to patrol the said town from ten o'clock in the evening until daylight. Citizens will be classed in seven classes, with a Captain in each. . . . It shall be the duty of the patrollers to apprehend any Negro or Mulatto who may be strolling about, or who may be from his, her, or their lodging, and give them any number of lashes not exceeding twenty, unless said Negro has a pass from his Master which specifies the place where he is going, and said Negro using pass is not to remain more than an hour, except at his wife's house.*

Soon the tension eased, and so did the harshness of the patrol, but a feeling of rectitude was not regained. Possibly, some argued,

19

the drafters of Kentucky's constitution should have put in a clause for gradual emancipation. Editor John Bradford had urged it in his *Gazette;* Henry Clay had spoken out for it, quoting old George Wythe, chancellor of Virginia, to whom he had been clerk and disciple in his salad days. Look at Ohio (went the arguments), forging ahead without slavery, about to outstrip Kentucky in commerce; and every man there slept better at night for having an easy conscience, and no fear of a vengeful black man hanging over him.

Meanwhile in Adair County the estate of Joseph Chapman was appraised, and local thinking became practical again.

Chapman, they saw after reading his inventory, was a man who needed slaves desperately, for how could he have been expected to clear his two-thousand-acre plantation if he must depend on itinerant white labor? Would white Americans spend a hot day grubbing stumps? Not except for themselves, certainly. Not on your life. And if land could not be speedily cleared and planted, how was the United States to raise her foodstuffs, and her hemp for rope and sailcloth that the young Navy was yelling for?

It all seemed to add up, they said, to this: slavery was essential to an agrarian civilization; destroy slavery and you destroyed the black man along with the white; for had you ever known a Negro who could stand on his own two feet?

In the pulpits now all was quiet; Father Rice, the frontier Presbyterian missionary who had lashed at slavery too early for audience, had gone to his rest.

3 ❖

Adair County had a far-reaching romance that year.

Simon Hancock, a retiring bachelor, a wistful surveyor of other men's felicity, no longer came to town in an empty plantation wagon. With him now were a new wife and five attentive stepchildren. He had summoned them from Mason County in western Virginia, and they had come gladly. It seemed miraculous to him.

20

He told his friend Robert Trabue, who went on his marriage bond, that he should have done it sooner.

Hancock's eldest stepchild was eleven years old, an obedient boy, observant, helpful. His name was John Marshall Clemens. His habitual expression was one of downright sadness. Persons who tried to make up to him found him unresponsive. His mother, the new Mrs. Hancock, explained it simply.

"Marshall hardly knows how to laugh and play," she said. "He was seven years old when his father died. From that day on he felt responsible for the children and me."

The children she referred to were her younger four, like stairsteps: Pleasants, Betsy, Hannibal, and Caroline.

Everyone knew that Simon Hancock had courted and lost this woman a dozen years before in the Shenandoah Valley of Virginia. She was Pamela Goggin then, called "Permelia," the prettiest girl in Bedford County. His friend Samuel Clemens had won her. Afterward, the rejected suitor came out to Kentucky. Now and then he would hear news of Permelia, for some of her kin were living in Adair County. One of those was Thomas Goggin, her brother, whose farm adjoined Simon's. Another was Mrs. Alexander Gill, her sister, liltingly called Polly Goggin Gill.

The Clemens idyl had ended in a frontier Virginia county where the Kanawha River enters the Ohio. There, near beautiful Point Pleasant, Samuel had purchased land and established his young family. (One child had been born to Permelia as they crossed the high Alleghenies; and Samuel, being of a classical turn of mind, had named the babe Hannibal.) Two years later Samuel was killed at a houseraising for a neighbor, struck down by a falling log. He left Permelia and the children scantily provided for. She found herself with a small plantation, several slaves, a library of books, and a handsome sideboard that was a Clemens heirloom. Not even the slaves were practical to the widow's needs; three women, they were, with some children as young as her own.

Relatives came to the rescue, but not handsomely. Her father, back in Bedford County, was a Revolutionary veteran with a wound and a houseful of younger children. Her mother's people, the Moormans and Clarks, prosperous Quakers, were inclined to let her struggle for the good of her soul. Samuel Clemens had been of the Established Church, not one of their own.

With her five little children and her slave women, the young widow stayed on at the lonely plantation, doing the best she could. The place had a bloody history, for here the forces of Colonel Andrew Lewis and of Chief Cornstalk had battled each other savagely; the very owls that hooted at night, it sometimes seemed to Permelia Clemens, told of that carnage of three decades ago. At other times the owls seemed to lament a young husband and father, struck down while helping a neighbor. But the soil was congenial to tobacco, and the crop was easily got out to the broad Ohio. Neighboring settlers were kind, and her emergencies were met.

In the first summer of her widowhood Permelia had visitors from home, two Moorman cousins who were going out to Ohio. They brought her a little money from her father, and his sympathy. When she lamented poor Samuel's death, reciting all the tragic details as the bereaved are wont to do, they could only sigh in confusion. When she asked, "Why did Samuel have to die so young? Why was he taken when doing an act of kindness?" the two Quakers admitted their bafflement. "But it was God's will," they declared.

Marshall, a sensitive yet literal boy, dwelt on his mother's rebellious "Why?" and the reply of the comforters: "God's will." He began to think harshly of God. He developed an aversion to the Bible, though he ploddingly read other books in the house.

Permelia and her son lacked time for grieving. There were Pleasants and Betsy and Hannibal and the baby Caroline to be looked after. There was the farm. Marshall thought of himself as his mother's mainstay, the head of the house. He helped the women slaves with the tobacco, greatly exceeding his childish strength. One summer day he fell down in the humid field, unconscious. They carried him to bed, and he lay ill with sunstroke for several weeks. After that he could do no field work in hot weather.

The tobacco crops were doing poorly, for the land had not been virgin when Samuel bought it, and now it was depleted. Fresh clearings should be made, an impossible task. Permelia said that

22

was why a person needed a big plantation, so the old fields could be abandoned and new ones planted.

The boy thought about this a good deal. He concluded that his father had not acquired enough land. He took for hero one Mr. Peter Hogg, a neighbor who had eight thousand acres and was a lawyer besides. The Honorable Peter Hogg had formerly been prosecutor general of the Colony of Virginia, and his legal prestige had followed him to the wilderness, matching his vast acreage. Whenever the courtly old gentleman talked to Marshall Clemens, the boy touched the hem of his greatness and was gratified.

In the hardships of those early years there flourished the roots of John Marshall Clemens' adult motives and limitations: his hankering for vast acreage; his admiration for the legal profession and his need to identify himself with its formalities; his cheerless atheism; his "sunpain," recurring every summer, forbidding him to undertake the manual labor that ennobled other pioneers in the expanding West, and pushing him, against his better judgment, to accept slavery as necessary and inevitable.

When Simon Hancock wrote to Permelia early in 1809 and asked her to come out to Kentucky with her children and marry him, she accepted without coyness. Leasing her farm, she gathered up her children and slaves and boarded a clumsy "broadhorn" bound for the Falls of the Ohio. She took only some trunks of clothing, the children's rush-bottom chairs, and the Clemens sideboard. Her brother was waiting at the Louisville landing with a hospitable wagon to take them to Adair County and security.

On the jolting ride southward, Permelia and her brother talked away the years that had separated them. Now and then she would ask a question about Simon Hancock. Had he changed in looks? Had he grown stingy in his bachelorhood? Was he patient with children, black and white? Tom Goggin gave satisfactory answers. He added that Simon was prosperous, was buying a second large farm.

While the Negroes and little Clemenses laughed and sang in the back of the wagon, Marshall meditated on what he had heard.

23

Those plantations would be his heritage, he may have thought. And it would hardly have occurred to him that there would be a Hancock son to shut him out. His own mother's child.

The new Lampton dwelling burned down without having time to age. The family was away from home at the time and so the little girls were spared the terror of the conflagration.

Patsy would remember only the talk of it in years to come. Jane would recall the news being brought to her parents; the consternation; the return to the scene; and there, where the house had been, just a shocking pile of charred timbers, and one chimney standing like an untidy sentinel.

"When I build again," Benjamin told his wife and her kin who were gathered there, "I'll not use clapboard. I'll build with brick. We'll have more rooms, too."

But Peggy, remembering the difficulties of getting even this modest structure, laid her head on his shoulder and wailed.

No one reprimanded her. Colonel Casey said, "There, now, Peggy, you must all come home again!" And Mrs. Casey added in a decisive voice, "Yes, there's room, daughter. Come now, before the little girls get upset."

If Jane was disturbed, it was not deeply. Afterward, when she would tell someone, "Our house burned down when I was a child," there was no horror in her voice or in her face, only a sort of "too bad," entirely dutiful. A love of leaping flames had been born in her, and it would not abate in the years ahead.

The return to the Casey house was a happy interval for Jane. Benjamin's house had been in "Lampton's Lane," as the site of the standing chimney was afterward called, and Jane had not liked its remoteness. Grandfather Casey's house stood near the main road on a fine rise of ground, and a child could see people approaching by wagon or gig or horseback when they were still a distance off and could race to the gate and call a greeting.

Company came often, for persons who knew Colonel Casey felt a compulsion to talk to him if something good had happened to them, or something ill. Mrs. Casey was likewise sought, though for practical purposes rather than companionship. She could set a bone if the doctor was out of reach, and would go dutifully to lay out the dead. She was a ready nurse. The request to sit up with a sick child, sharing the mother's vigil, was a call she never declined. Her Bible, notated, laid those charges on her.

But not all who hallooed were in emergency. Many persons came to the Caseys' for purely social reasons; like the Stotts from the next plantation, a family who outdistanced their neighbors in replacing their log home with a brick manor house. . . . Paxtons and Creels did not confine themselves to calls on the Caseys, being part of the family, but came for days at a time, sometimes without warning; bag, baggage, and babies, they came.

In this splendid confusion little Jane put down her roots, her talent for sociability already promising to be a genius.

There were the horses, too. Nothing was more diverting than to see a big black man in a leather apron lift a horse's hoof and put a shoe on it. The horse hardly minded, but stood patiently, and afterward seemed satisfied and sure-footed.

Green Casey began to let Jane ride his horse alone, shortening the stirrups till she could reach. When he was reproved for this by Peggy, he held his ground.

"She'll outride any girl in Kentucky if you'll give her a chance," he told his sister.

Peggy said that was not her ambition for Jane. "I just want to keep her alive and whole," she explained to Green. "Poor little child! Sometimes I think she can't see out of both her eyes."

"Well, the horse can," Green replied shortly. Like the rest of the family, he considered Peggy strangely timid. He very well knew that Jane had one dim eye; he had seen her favor it. All the more reason, then, that she learn the quirks of horses.

Benjamin noticed his daughter's progress with approval and he soon took charge. When he thought Jane was ready, he coached her in making low jumps. It was a pretty sight to see the thin little creature with the flying hair bend low and easy to her horse to take a jump. Though one hardly spoke of it. It was considered better form to praise the horse.

While they were living at Grandmother Casey's, little Patsy (to be enshrined in literature as Aunt Patsy Quarles) shed her

baby ways and blossomed into a human being. Jane was enthralled. She talked to her as freely as she talked to adults and
animals. Jane claimed to understand Patsy's responses, her patois
and her moods, and she always interpreted them favorably. Their
mother, who had feared the little girls would never be compan-
ionable because of the disparity in their ages, was reassured. Some
charming affinity existed between the sisters. Each thought the
other choice, amusing, and adorable; and so it would ever be.

Patsy Lampton was a well-formed child, tall and lushly rounded.
Her blue eyes were heavily lashed in the Irish way, and her skin
was creamy white, resisting freckles. Every one considered Patsy
to be the family beauty, especially since Jane was long-legged and
losing her front teeth. Jane wholeheartedly agreed. She would
feast her eyes on Patsy maternally, and if the little sister's face
became smudged, Jane would not hesitate to lift a corner of her
best apron to wipe it clean. Whatever Patsy wanted, Jane strove
to get for her; and on those occasions when she lost patience
with Patsy and slapped her, she would weep in remorse.

4 ❖

Only Anne of the Casey girls was now unmarried at home, and
she was betrothed; romance abounded, like an obvious perfume.

Her wedding to John Montgomery, her cousin, occurred October
24, 1810. The day was golden in every way, for maples and
beeches show their finest colors at that time in southern Kentucky,
and the air is as tender as a caress all day till sundown.

After the bride and groom had gone away to their new home
in town, where John Montgomery was in business, the plantation
seemed unduly quiet. Colonel and Mrs. Casey were indebted to
the Lamptons for staying on.

It might be said that Mrs. Casey tolerated Benjamin for the
pleasure of his family's company, but Colonel Casey valued him
for himself. He liked to hear Benjamin's baritone voice raised in
song of a morning. He enjoyed the absurd twists that Benjamin
gave to stories at the supper table. Some easy camaraderie in his

son-in-law's nature answered a need, too often suppressed, in his own. He had never had enough laughter from the Montgomerys; he was glad to get it now from a Lampton.

"Don't think of building till spring," he advised this favorite son-in-law the day after the wedding, for Benjamin had dutifully spoken of getting some timbers hauled. "A freeze would likely catch you in December."

"That's true, sir," Benjamin readily agreed as if wanting to be persuaded. Green joined them, and they went hunting.

Whatever had been going on in Benjamin's mind took form that winter. His mother died over in Madison County in January, and he came into his share of her property. This he soon sold for ready cash. But he did not use the money, as the Caseys supposed he would do, to buy mules, cattle, pigs, and seed.

Farming had become bad business recently. Plantation owners and small farmers were settling down to wait it out.

The reason was England's Orders in Council against Napoleon, and his retaliation, a condition that closed too many ports to American trade. In the East the manufacturers were afflicted, while in the West the young agricultural states and territories were suffering their own peculiar pains. Not only were the vessels of the United States (an underrated little newcomer) excluded from trade; such ships as ventured out were searched, stripped of seamen, and badgered at the whim of the British Admiralty. Now, even Benjamin Lampton and his brother Lewis with the elegant ways were boiling mad at England.

Mrs. Casey observed this with excusable malice.

"I've heard that none of the Lampton name fought in the Revolution," she remarked to Benjamin and their house guest Lewis. "I must say I've often wondered about that."

The Lampton brothers were silent. They had been little children during the last war, and if their father had even breathed wrath at England, they had not heard him. They had lived in Virginia's Spotsylvania County, off the beaten tracks of the contending armies. A painting of Lambton Castle had hung over their dining-room mantel. In the hall was a crayon drawing of the Lambton Worm, a water dragon reputed to live in Wear River, every bit as

27

ugly as the Loch Ness Monster. Perhaps Benjamin and Lewis were thinking now of those cherished relics of their childhood. How could their father have taken sides against England without disclaiming Lambton Castle and the Lambton Worm?

When Lewis was packing his saddlebags to leave the plantation he asked Benjamin, "Is your mother-in-law always so harsh?"

"She has a sharp tongue," Benjamin said, "but she's well-meaning and just. One good jab at you, I've noticed, will last Mrs. Casey quite a while."

Early in April, Benjamin startled Colonel and Mrs. Casey with an announcement. He said he was about to become a building contractor in Columbia; he had pledged himself, in company with one William Diddle, to build a Clerk's Office for Adair County.

"What does a farmer know about that sort of thing?" Casey asked.

"Diddle has confidence in me," Benjamin replied, "and my inheritance gives me a little capital." He was striding about the big family room of the farmhouse, his red hair rumpled, a bright gleam in his brown eyes. Now and then he would whack the chimney piece or a doorjamb with his riding crop. Drama radiated from his person, and his little girls fixed him with fascinated stares. Jane thought she had never seen a finer sight, even on court day. She hastily removed a sleeping cat from the hearth so that his swing around the room might be unimpeded.

"Try your hand at town work if you must, Benjamin," Mrs. Casey said quietly. "You'll come back to the soil, I expect." She was mending some garments piled in a basket. For such work she wore a starched muslin cap, almost as imposing as her black lace one. "There's no certainty away from the land."

"The world moves, Mrs. Casey," Benjamin answered her. "I'll move with it. Our county needs that Clerk's Office. We can't continue to operate from William Caldwell's parlor." He turned to Peggy who was sitting in a straight little chair, clasping and unclasping her hands. "Get ready to move to town, Peggy," he instructed her. "We'll go as soon as I can find accommodations."

"Are we moving to town?" Jane shrieked, thrilled and somewhat horrified.

28

"No," Mrs. Casey replied. "Only your mother and father are."

"The children too, ma'am," said Benjamin, stopping before her. "I'll take them as soon as I can find suitable rooms. Diddle himself has an ordinary out beyond Fortune Street. He expects to enlarge it. Just now, his spare rooms are taken by carpenters. Mrs. Diddle has a good cook and sets an excellent table."

"Your two little girls in a second-rate tavern," mused Mrs. Casey out loud, not lifting her eyes from her needle. "You'll dine with Diddles," she said, like a gadfly. "You'll live a new life. In time, Jane may catch a carpenter's apprentice."

Colonel Casey came and laid a hand on her shoulder, warning her that she had outdone herself. Her head bent a little in submission. The touch of William Casey's hand reminded her that it was suitable for every man, even an eccentric Lampton, to be the master of his own family.

Diddle and Lampton built a sturdy brick Clerk's Office for Adair County and received pay for it January 6, 1812; three hundred and sixteen dollars, but every dollar counting triple because of the hardness of the times.

With Negro Toby to tote the hod, Benjamin himself had laid the brick. His shapely hands were often bruised, but his enthusiasm held, and his singing was a treat to his fellow workers. Harmony of tone, harmony of conduct blessed the undertaking. Diddle and Lampton agreed to continue in harness.

January 1812 brought to Columbia more than the new Clerk's Office. There arrived in town by carriage from Clark County, Lewis Lampton, complete with bride and baggage, the baggage being numerous leather trunks and hatboxes, the bride being the former Miss Jennie Morrison of the Bluegrass. Lewis was Benjamin's favorite brother, a kind and sensitive man, physically fragile but courageous, vulnerable to every wind of chance. Historically, Lewis Lampton was to have one abiding use: when he had produced his second son, James, he would have produced Colonel Mulberry Sellers of *The Gilded Age*. He had come here to open an upper-class tavern to be called the Eagle House, having decided that innkeeping, for a sociable citizen with a few slaves, was the most agreeable and least arduous method known to man of making a living.

That he chose this rustic village, a town doomed to early decline because of its need of a river, does not argue him stupid. America was on the move, and southern Kentucky was a crossroads of passage. Columbia, midway between Louisville and Nashville, offered pause to north–south pilgrims. And to those moving from Virginia and the Carolinas toward the growing towns of Glasgow and Bowling Green, it was an acceptable haven. No innkeeper need fear empty rooms or ennui.

Lewis's first concern was for a large stable. He bought Lot 43 on Merchant Street for the site and requested the town trustees to clear Adams and Monroe alleys of debris, to insure easy access to his stable. This, they did do. The other alleys of the town also came under scrutiny, and a general clean-up was ordered for all those littered little arteries. The Lampton request was a boon to sanitation.

With a brother in the contracting business, he lost no time in getting his stable built; and soon its clean, brick-paved court and other conveniences were the talk of the roads. He had anticipated stagecoach service for Columbia; here horses could be changed with ease and dispatch.

A large brick house on the public square was available for his inn, and he protected himself by a long lease. He decorated in the pleasing mode of scenic wallpaper and white paint. From Louisville by wagons came adequate furniture, for Lewis was accustomed to the niceties. Had not his father, old William Lampton, brought a wig stand to the wilderness before 1790? He had, indeed, while the settlers laughed. Lewis purchased lamps in plenty; light, he said, attracted people of good will at nightfall and repelled the furtive. The windows of Eagle House shone cleanly and were curtained wherever curtains were expected. The bedrooms, with whitewashed walls, boasted mirrors and bedside rugs; washstands were equipped with decorated bowls and pitchers and chamber pots.

It was inevitable that Benjamin and his family take up residence at this stylish new establishment.

30

Here they were living, Jane a wondering nine-year-old, when war against England was declared.

The town reacted almost festively. Rifles were fired in an excess of patriotism, and bonfires lit the streets at night. The Adair and neighboring home guard outfits, mounted to a man, had recently filled their ranks; they were united in anticipation of this glad day. And now came the laying on of hands from Frankfort, making them the 52nd Regiment of Kentucky Militia. Cavalry drills made the roads interesting if perilous.

Benjamin Lampton was commissioned Lieutenant Colonel with duties of adjutant, and the uniform that he ordered tailored in Frankfort had braided epaulets and became him well. Peggy and his little girls were awe-struck. Mrs. Casey remarked pointedly that Robert Paxton was still a captain, and Green was a mere private; but perhaps Benjamin would consent to wear a muffler, such as she had knitted for them?

Benjamin thanked her, overlooking the acidity. He took his rank for granted, as something due him, as something suitable to a Lampton. And no doubt it was; why, else, had it fallen to him? He had never been a man to wrest and push.

Little Jane may have put her finger on it when she said, "Maybe the governor saw my father in the saddle."

Travel increased, and the Eagle House turned away as many guests as it took in. At the dining table it was agreed we would take Canada in sixty days.

Too many local troops volunteered for a go at Canada. You would have thought it was Kentucky's private war. Of the 52nd Regiment that rode northward from Adair County, only a few were accepted. Among the officers chosen were hard-riding Lieutenant Robert Trabue and Captain John Butler, the latter a dedicated Indian fighter who had helped Colonel Casey settle, a man so fascinated by his archfoe that he always wore his hair in a pigtail.

This prelude to war was known as the Illinois campaign, and it went badly. It was brief. "Old Hopkins," the eastern brigadier commanding the mounted Kentuckians, treated them disdainfully and scorned their advice. His troops, mistrusting the Indian guides he had hired and noticing the prairies to be here and there on fire, mutinied just beyond the Wabash River and rode homeward, sweating harder than their horses.

Nineteen-year-old Green Casey was among them. He found his mother's raised eyebrows and his father's grave questioning more disconcerting than the prairie fires.

Patriotism had cooled, but it took stock, refueled, and went forward. Enlistments resumed, if more thoughtfully. The lightly garrisoned forts in Ohio and Indiana and Illinois must be frequently supported. There even came a time when unaccustomed Kentucky feet walked the decks of a ship on Lake Erie. At the River Raisin in southern Michigan half a Kentucky regiment died with their youthful colonel, John Allen; and this was a piteous story to carry home, because Procter's Indians massacred the wounded.

Benjamin Lampton, after his rebuff, made no further attempt to meet the Canadians, but he remained in uniform and was available for state guard duty, wherever summoned. When free, he was a contractor, building and repairing houses in Columbia to earn his family's keep at the Eagle House. Almost every one in town and county called him Colonel Lampton.

Thus he conducted himself for more than two years. But on October 4, 1814, he tried again for active service, taking an oath which Kentucky now required of her officers. He swore that since the first day of April 1812 he had neither given nor accepted a challenge to duel, nor had he carried a challenge for any other person. He was responding to a frantic call for help in the South. The war rumors put General Sir Edward Pakenham at Jamaica; reported him assembling thousands of troops there; foretold his moving this force in British battleships and frigates against New Orleans; predicted that unless General Andrew Jackson and a deluge of volunteers hasten, Louisiana and the Father of Waters would be captured.

There began to assemble at the Falls of the Ohio a great muddle of detached militia from Kentucky counties. Benjamin, complete with sword, was among them. This time he was adjutant of the

32

green 93rd; John Warfield Shirley was its commander, Dr. Nathan Gaither its surgeon.

Boats for conveying the rendezvoused troops were lacking. So were tents and food and winter clothing. Frustrated officers looked upriver in vain; the United States Quartermaster at Pittsburgh was totally unprepared for this emergency.

While barges were being sought in all the rivers, the generals appraised their volunteers and dismissed such as seemed unfit for hardship. Out went the 93rd as a unit, though some of its tougher stock was culled and attached to other outfits. Lieutenant Colonel Lampton, who must confess to the age of forty-five and had never seen action, was dismissed. The rejection was the more embarrassing to him when he learned that his brother-in-law, Captain Paxton, was retained; and his youthful nephew, Jesse Lampton; and young Isaac Caldwell, assistant clerk of Adair County, and several young Montgomerys, hardly dry behind the ears.

Enough decrepit boats to carry two thousand men were procured, loaded, and started downstream. And so, into the miasmic delta country right tardily went that unpaid army in leaking keelboats to meet the British. Whoever had a blanket shared it. Whoever had a greatcoat thanked God. They arrived four days before the battle and went into camp without tents; even without straw for bedding. On January 8 they stood beside the Tennessee Volunteers, the Mississippi Dragoons, the Louisiana Militia, the Lafitte pirates, and the rest to serve Jackson creditably at the bloody, quick battle of New Orleans.

The encampment then, through the winter and into March. After a spell of cold there would come mild days when swamp birds sang, and myriads of insects awoke to harass. Many fell ill. Some died of pleurisy. Some from wounds that had seemed trivial but festered. Others from a bilious fever that produced agony and delirium.

Among the casualties was unassuming Captain Robert Paxton, Jennie Casey's husband. His sergeant, William Pitt Montgomery, sat beside him in his last hours. Tell Jennie so and so, he would mutter. Or he would repeat the names of his six little children,

33

wonderingly. Once he asked for his father-in-law, Colonel Casey, perhaps to put Jennie and the children in his charge.

"He's not at New Orleans," Sergeant Montgomery reminded him gently. "His joints were too stiff to come to war."

Robert Paxton died on February 28, 1815. When he had lain a short time in state and had been looked on by his men and fellow officers, he was buried in a place allotted to the military. Then a bugler sounded farewell for one more soldier who need not have died. For now it was known to all that a treaty between the United States and Great Britain had been signed on Christmas Eve at Ghent, two weeks before the battle.

"This will be hard news to send the Caseys," William Montgomery said to Jesse Lampton who stood beside him at the grave. The young men were as thin as scarecrows and they felt strange and lonely without their captain. It was decided that Isaac Caldwell should write the letter. And so young Isaac, ever quick with words, dipped his pen in clotted ink and wrote the news to Colonel Casey.

At mid-March Captain Paxton's Adair County men started their return journey. To Natchez by boat in the laborious hand-propelled manner. Across country then by the Natchez Trace to Nashville; then on to Kentucky, living off the land as their fathers had done in the old war. Late in May they reached home, footsore, bearded, ragged, emaciated, articulate. While whisky jugs were hoisted in the public square they told what had happened to old Pakenham at New Orleans.

Benjamin Lampton was on hand to greet them, as were the rest of the men who had failed to warrant boat space in the crisis. Some took it hard that they had been excluded from the great adventure. But Benjamin bore it philosophically—indeed, almost as lightly as his grandson would accept his Civil War chagrins a half century later. Benjamin observed that by being twice turned back at the Ohio River he had missed an excess of mud, hunger, swamp fever, dysentery, chilblain, and horror.

Besides, he was not greatly incensed with the enemy, anyway, now that he had mulled it over. "Most wars are a mistake," he said one day to a surprised group at the Eagle House table.

34

"How's that, Lampton?"

"The first war was a necessity, I grant you. But take this one. It ought've been avoided. A good many men around here are dead that needn't have died. Englishmen too—decent chaps who had wives and little children they never got home to. England wanted her lost colonies back. We wanted Canada. All that either side needed was a free sea. We might have talked things out, I think."

One man at the table cursed. Another threw down his cutlery with a clatter and left the room. But most of them concluded the meal in silence, looking thoughtful.

Jane, sitting beside her quiet mother, saw then how it was. Your enemy this year might not be your enemy next year. Her father had been furious with England and had tried to die for that anger, but now he could hardly recall it. . . .

Right or wrong, and without so intending, she would carry this strange and unpopular knowledge with her into adulthood and would pass it on to her sons.

5 ❖

Now came the era of the Pink Cottage.

Benjamin had built this house for Joseph Patterson, who presently found it too small for his increasing prosperity. Benjamin's prosperity had not increased and his family needed a home, as Peggy kept reminding him, so he bought the place with its adjoining lot. He liked its central location near the public square. Besides, he had been enamored of the little house with the fanlight ever since he had laid the brick.

Only the color of the bricks displeased him. They were liver-colored, from an unfortunate local clay, so he attempted to have them painted the warm, rosy hue of Virginian brick. Because of his overshooting the mark, the shade he concocted was startlingly gay. Before long the house was referred to as "the Pink Cottage" and became a landmark for the guidance of strangers.

Peggy was blissfully happy there for a few months. But as 1816 came in, Benjamin found himself out of work and he leased the little house, furnished, to one George Davenport. He explained to Peggy right firmly above her sobs that they must spend a half year in Winchester; he had contracted to build a livery stable extraordinary for his brother Joshua. Peggy was appalled. It meant living in a tavern again. Jane was twelve years old. Patsy was eight. Both were too pert and worldly, she thought.

"Let the little girls go to the plantation," she requested, and he agreed.

And that is the year in which we have no further record of Benjamin and Peggy Lampton. Until December, that is.

But of the plantation, there is record enough. Colonel Casey's famous last days were at hand. He was confined to his chair, sore in all his joints. Lately he could not unbend enough to go to bed at night but slept upright in his chair. He was made wonderfully happy by his granddaughters coming to stay. Jane especially diverted him, for she had a strange Irish genius for communicating with animals. Patsy pleased him with her beauty and coquetry.

Actually, the plantation was never more lively than now. Green had married at twenty and was the father of a baby son named John Allen, after the hero of the Raisin. His wife was eminently pleasing to her mother-in-law. She was Janie Patterson, whose background was Montgomeryish.

A special stir at the plantation was due to plans under way to build a new manor house. It would be of brick and would annex the big log house as a wing. The new rooms would be five in number, including a parlor twenty-seven feet long and fifteen feet wide. Wood was being cured for flooring and other needs. Wainscots would be of polished cherry plank, waist high. Colonel Casey wanted this house for Green, his beloved and dependable son. Other prosperous settlers had enlarged and refined their houses. It behove the county's founder to do as well, or shame to the name of Casey.

The colonel's rheumatism created wonder. It kept him rigid, yet permitted him to remain corpulent and ruddy. The family room became a salon for visitors. Stephen, a colored boy, attended him.

In the fight to limber up Colonel Casey, Jane Lampton was allowed to take an active part. Her textbook that year, replacing a whole course of study at Robertson's Academy in town, was her grandmother's scrapbook, a pharmacopoeia of remedies interspersed with Bible verses, mournful poems, and rules for taking out fruit stains. The ledger also gave directions for delivering the young of human beings and animals.

Mrs. Casey encouraged Jane to take her turn at mortar and pestle and brewing kettle. She helped concoct liniments and blisters to ease pain; became familiar with the medicinal foxglove, yarrow, licorice, yellow jessamine, ipecac, and rue. She knew that flaxseed tea was loaded with strange nutriments (Mrs. Casey often reminded her, "It has kept your mother going!") and when they served it to Colonel Casey they would flavor it with wintergreen, to make it bearable. A brew of wild cherry bark was considered a fine sedative. Fern sweet was marked "tonic and alterative." Pokeberry bounce was as gaudy as a sunset. Peppermint could hardly be overdone; and if you wanted a really exquisite hue, add flowers of sulfur to milk. (It caused Grandfather to sweat.)

There is something about the last day of summer, especially to an Irishman. When August ended, Colonel Casey seemed sad and withdrawn, as if he had come to a significant milestone. Dismissing Jane and Patsy, he listened to the intermittent rifle shots that came from the back of the farm; for Green had opened the hunting season, taking three friends who wanted to use his bird dogs.

"I'm moved to make my will, wife," he said. "Get out the tools for it. When Cyrus Walker comes back from hunting, bring him to me without fail."

"Nonsense," Mrs. Casey protested. "You're only sixty years old, William. Four score and ten is your due." But she saw the determination in his face, and she set out a great stand of brown ink, a new quill, and some foolscap paper. She was vexed, for this was Saturday. The household was in the midst of a mighty baking.

At the men's return, Mrs. Casey waited for them to quench their thirst at the well and inspect their soft limp feathered kill. Then she summoned Cyrus Walker, the young lawyer Colonel Casey had asked for, the husband of her kinswoman Flora Montgomery. "It's his whim to make a will today, Cyrus," she said.

"I'll ask you to do his pleasure. Draw up the will, however he wants it."

And so the document was written and witnessed and signed by the three hunters: Cyrus Walker, Thomas Gilmer, Isaac Caldwell. . . . Two of those signatures would turn up in far places. Isaac Caldwell would make his splash in the South and die dueling. Cyrus Walker, after teaching law to the stripling John Marshall Clemens and holding offices of trust in his county, would denounce the practice of slavery and go into the free state of Illinois; he would tangle with Stephen A. Douglas before Lincoln did; with most of his old friends he would keep contact, but between himself and his former law pupil, John M. Clemens of Missouri, the shades of slavery would fall, obliterating friendship.

As the autumn progressed, Colonel Casey played a more startling card; he ordered his grave made in the family burying ground. He instructed that all brick on hand be diverted to the purpose of lining an underground vault which would accommodate a great square coffin. "I'll be buried in my chair," he said, "and will need attentions out of the ordinary."

He looked at his wife and son levelly and saw them receive the unnatural idea rebelliously. He let them think it over, saw them come about in the circuit that was now a familiar one to him; namely, that his body could never be straightened out without violence.

"Then you must have a tomb in the side of a hill," said Mrs. Casey out of her composed sorrow.

"Like General Washington? Never, wife. I'm only an ordinary man. I'll be buried as such."

He gave further instructions, ordering that the project be started at once while good weather prevailed. He did not wish to have the coffin made before his death, he said, for that would be depressing. But plenty of hard wood must be kept in reserve for it. "Have the planking put by," he told Green. "Have it ready. I may not last the year out."

After the news got around that Colonel Casey had made his will and was having his tomb built, old friends came from a distance to see him; some to bid him farewell, in a manner of speaking, others to dissuade him from dying.

William Casey was right about going out with the year. In December he died triumphantly, having no fear and committing his soul to God without ritual.

In electing not to be buried like the Father of his Country, aboveground, Colonel Casey had laid a stupendous hardship on his pallbearers. To get the mammoth coffin from the house to the family plot, and then, without mishap, down into the brick-lined grave, was a task that tested nerves and brawn. Afterward, in the counties of southern Kentucky or in other states, Green River men who had not met in years would refer to Colonel Casey's interment as a landmark of experience. Fifty men, all told, must have taken their turn at the ropes.

The Reverend Samuel Robertson of Shiloh Church delivered a funeral oration at the house; but at the graveside his prayers were short and final. Spectators as well as pallbearers were exhausted, though none departed till the grave was filled.

At the plantation the fires glowed cheerily, for hospitality was part of the rural funeral scene. Many persons stopped for an after-funeral call. Jane Lampton was pleased to help serve refreshments. Soon she had occasion to pass cake to Mrs. Simon Hancock's eldest son, Marshall Clemens, tall, important looking, and almost handsome. He was eighteen, an Olympian age, and he took the cake without noticing her.

Marshall was talking to Henry Hatcher, telling him about an adventure just ahead of him. He said he was going to take his sister Betsy Clemens to Bedford County in Virginia. They might be gone a year.

"To Virginia!" Mr. Hatcher said nostalgically; in Virginia he had married Colonel Haskin's fourth daughter, the one who had not married a Trabue. "You're sure to get married in Virginia," he told Marshall. "You can hardly help it, the girls are so pretty. Are you joining Kelsoe Walker's party?"

"Yes, sir," Marshall answered. "Mr. Walker's niece, Mary Patterson, is going, too. That's Mrs. Green Casey's sister. She and

Betsy will be company for each other on the way. They're having their riding habits made now."

"What will you do with yourself all that time in Virginia?"

Marshall Clemens seemed glad of the question. He said he expected to work in Lynchburg, keeping books at an iron foundry. "One of my father's relatives has asked for me," he said with obvious pride. "A Mr. Langhorne."

Mrs. Simon Hancock joined the group and she noticed Jane loitering near. "Howdy, Jane," she said kindly. "I see you're being mighty useful." She was a remarkably pretty woman for her years, with a breezy, impersonal manner.

"Yes, ma'am," Jane answered. "My mother had to take to her bed when she got here from Winchester. Grandmother needs me now."

Mrs. Hancock veered the talk from Jane's mother (of whom it was being predicted: she'll never get out of that bed, mark my words. Peggy's mortally sick!) and sought a more cheerful topic. "You favor your father, Jane, with your red hair and all . . . Don't you think Jane Lampton favors her father, Marshall?"

John Marshall Clemens looked at Jane at his mother's behest, but the inspection was cursory. After all, she was only thirteen years old, and she was bedraggled from the day's ordeals. He was not to remember her, at least consciously, but she would remember him. He was at his pinnacle: a young man visioning fulfillment after the disappointments of his childhood; a youth about to go on an exciting and dangerous journey through Cumberland Gap and along Wilderness Road into Virginia, riding a good horse, entrusted with the care of a sixteen-year-old sister, slated for employment on arrival.

Jane, carrying her cake plate, followed in his wake as he made a formal tour of the rooms to bid people good-by. She had not fallen in love with him—God pity her, she never would—but she was impressed by his looks and manly bearing.

One day in early autumn, Peggy Lampton slipped away. Her children would hardly have known the hour except for Christina's carrying on, for the languor of anemia was hers at the last.

Benjamin was far away when it happened, occupied with a new business venture. Not realizing the trend of Peggy's illness, he had bade his wife and children good-by at midsummer and had set out for the East to buy merchandise.

But it was not Benjamin's absence in Philadelphia that had mattered to Peggy in her last days; it was her father's absence in his long home. Colonel Casey's passing from that house had smitten her with a loss and a wonder too great to be borne; she had thought of him, even in his great chair, as indestructible.

As Peggy's invalidism had crept upon her, so had her social inadequacy. She could no longer ride with the gay crowd in Winchester. She could not change frocks or meet new friends with any art or pleasure. Benjamin's energy wearied her; his romantic affection reminded her of her shortcomings as a woman. She became an unsure child again, yearning for her parents and the neighborhood that had been her safe little world. Leaving Benjamin in Winchester, she had returned to the plantation a few weeks before William Casey's death. There she had nestled down, to the puzzlement of a daughter who would never nestle.

Mrs. Casey had offered to take Peggy to Dr. Ephraim McDowell at nearby Danville. That craggy physician, five years ago, had cut into a woman's abdomen and relieved her of a great growth—an operation that was becoming the talk of the medical world. He had performed several similiar miracles since then. No doubt Peggy needed some corrective surgery that this strange and daring man could administer. But Peggy had declined the experiment. She had even evaded simple measures. Instead of sipping, thrice daily, the solution of iron filings that Dr. Gaither had made for her, she had stealthily poured the tonic out of a window because it darkened her teeth. (The hydrangeas beneath that window prospered.)

41

Mrs. Casey, though not burdened with sensitivity, had seen the case in its true light: Peggy had fled from wifehood. To those who came to commiserate she said simply, "I couldn't wish her back. She'd lost her health. The will to live had gone out of her." But Peggy was her first-born, her most amenable one, and the loss of her took its place beside her widowhood.

Patsy became a problem, fretting tryingly for her mother. To meet this emergency, Jane grew up. Through Patsy's need of her she was elevated emotionally to a sort of adulthood. She made definite plans to keep house for Benjamin on his return.

At the plantation the steady decorum of mourning prevailed. Mrs. Casey had become more majestic, more religious. She was not so much the Widow Casey as the Widow Montgomery-Casey, for dominant traits were reasserting themselves. She knew how a widow should act and should not act: even while grieving she should be alert to her land, her purse, and her household. She remembered seeing when she was a girl (1783 was the year) twenty-three widows who owed their titles to the tomahawk or the arrow, all assembled at Logan's Station. They had journeyed there for the settlement of estates. Her own mother, General Logan's mother-in-law, had been one of them.

Twice daily Mrs. Casey spread the great Bible across her knees and read it aloud to as many of her descendants and slaves as she had been able to call together.

Over and through Jane's head rolled the sonority of Joshua, Samuel, and Daniel. Presbyterianism flowered best in the soil of its Judaic heritage, and Mrs. Casey conformed, adroitly skipping such passages as were unsuited to innocent ears. Genesis and Exodus were thrilling narratives to Jane. Job was pitiful. The Psalms dirged and sang. Isaiah told a spellbinding story and laid down the law, after which he became a sort of gangplank that led Mrs. Casey to the tender comforts of the New Testament, led her even to St. John. . . . Actually, Jane would never be a Bible reader, but she would complacently think of herself as one, having got its grandest passages by ear at the altar of her grandmother or from the pews of frontier churches. And, thus equipped, she would one

42

day urge her children to read the Bible from cover to cover as affably as she told them to wash behind the ears.

Just before Benjamin's return from Philadelphia, Mrs. Casey summoned Jane to her room and said they must have a talk. "Close the door," she murmured discreetly.

"What have I done, Grandmother?" Jane asked, for she was often called on the carpet and supposed this was such a time.

"You've done nothing wrong, child. But there's something that needs to be talked about. Your father knows, by this time, of your mother's death. He's gotten the letters. The shock and the sorrow will wear off somewhat while he's in strange places, while he's over the mountains buying stock for his store. He'll come home all but reconciled." She studied an engraving on the wall, General Washington drinking his breakfast chocolate, and continued stoically, "Your father is apt to marry again in a short time. Most men do, it's their nature."

"Oh, mercy," Jane said.

"If he does, I advise you not to set yourself against it, and don't set Patsy against it. Rebellion worsens things."

"Heavens!" Jane said. She was really shocked.

"I'm giving Christina the same warnings," Mrs. Casey told her, "though I reckon I'm wasting my breath. But I count on you to have the right attitude. If somebody replaces your mother, she's apt to be a good woman. Try to accept her. Try to set the right example for Patsy."

Jane said, "Yes, Grandmother," though guardedly. She was thankful that not once during the interview did Mrs. Casey speak the word stepmother, for that was a term that could raise a rash on a girl's neck if her father happened to be a widower.

Several friends of the Lampton girls had stepmothers whom they resented, possibly in imitation of Cinderella. Among those were the Caldwell and Patterson girls. William Caldwell (a man of rectitude and acumen, destined to foreclose on the high-flying Lampton brothers) had wed spinster Ann Trabue, a lady of property, a year and a fortnight after his first wife's death. And widower Joseph Patterson had been just as importunate in securing Mrs. Nancy Johnston to run his house. In such menages the first crop of chil-

43

dren seemed impelled by tradition to rebel, and they were abetted by the servants. Rare was the cook or mammy who received a new mistress with co-operation.

After young Mrs. Lampton's death, Christina's attitude was not exceptional, for she had been devoted to Peggy and had dominated her. At the funeral she gave a lavish performance; afterward she elevated Peggy to sainthood. She treated the Lampton girls as a heritage, calling them her orphan lambs and in various ways mixing true sympathy with wile. She declared that she and the girls could take care of Master Benjamin very well, and she built up Jane's importance with a pleasing deference. To Patsy she made herself invaluable. Her biased backing of Patsy in any squabble between playmates was as soothing as a piece of maple sugar, and the child could count on both.

One day Patsy, no fool, said to Jane, "Stepmothers won't let you eat sweets between meals, will they? Mrs. Patterson won't. She locks the sugar chest and hides the key."

Jane remembered her grandmother's warning and evaded a direct answer. "Sugar makes your teeth ugly if you keep nibbling at it," she observed.

On Benjamin's return to Adair County he brought his children to town to live with him, and it was as Mrs. Casey had predicted: he was reconciled. He had loved Peggy tenderly, but he was in no mood to sit grieving. The wonders of the cities still dazzled him. So did the prospects of his new store on the public square: LAMPTON AND MONTGOMERY—DRY GOODS AND HARDWARE. He had bought recklessly to stock it, pledging himself by note to Augustus Cushing in Philadelphia. (John Montgomery was startled to hear of it.)

While he sat drinking his evening toddy Benjamin would speak to Jane and Patsy right yearningly of their mother. "Dear little Peggy!" he would sigh. "Sweet little love. She was this world's gentlest soul." But presently he might describe the warehouses of Philadelphia, or the excitement of stagecoach travel.

With great enthusiasm he established Christina and Toby in quarters in the yard. Colonel Casey's will had given the slaves

44

to Peggy, but now they had become his property. Toby would be useful at the store as well as at the cottage.

Three brooms swept clean at the Pink Cottage, the girls and Christina being determined to prove their efficiency. Though Jane managed to keep her head, she was exhilarated at having become a housekeeper. A girl of fourteen is but a prophecy of herself; she strives to cast a fine shadow toward the future.

Jane functioned outwardly, and she was in many pleasant ways a typical girl of her era and station. But she was not quite standard. A dash too much of energy, certainly; an overflow of imagination in identifying herself with other human beings and with animals. Excursions into the vegetable realm, even. A forgotten house plant, wilting for water, was exhorted: "Poor darling, don't die! Drink this!" A mulberry tree, shivering under the first blows of Toby's ax, because unwanted and dropping wormy fruit on the bricks, found reprieve in a breathless shriek: "Let it alone! It *wants* to live, can't you see?"

Jane had odd and exotic streaks but she was not morbid, for she compensated in ways as practical as rain water: food carried to a stranded family at the edge of town, and Papa's extra ax slipped to them, and the neat roll of knitted stockings that had been Peggy's. No sentiment about the dear dead at such times, because it's the living who suffer with cold feet, isn't it?

And a fondness for the sensational. A bonfire at High Street and Jefferson Alley was a pleasing event one November evening. Oh, the smell of the burning leaves in the cool dusk, and the laughter of boys and girls, gathered there. Jane exerted herself without stint to make the flames leap higher. It brought the volunteer fire department on the run, and the next day she was able to write to a friend in Greensburg: *We have got to be more careful. We almost burned down the town.* Anyway, there had been sparks on Dr. Gaither's roof, and the Craven boys had gone up with a bucket of water to put them out, so the story was not utterly without foundation. In Greensburg, however, word got around that Columbia's public square was a blackened ruin.

"They jumped at conclusions," Jane said regretfully.

At this point in her life Jane Lampton's looks foretold the young Sam Clemens'. She was lithe and too thin, crowned with a tousle of red hair; her skin was milky white, her mouth a scarlet line. She had plenty of nose.

The year of 1818 was not an unhappy one for the Lampton girls. Every one was kind, and they liked living in town. Peggy was a sweet memory, still fresh, dutifully treasured. Sometimes, reminded of her too poignantly, Jane and Patsy would hold each other tight and rock with weeping, wanting her greatly. But presently they would be diverted, and the pain of longing would go away, and when it returned it would be a little more bearable. Their father never took them to Peggy's grave, nor went himself, and if he recalled her birthday, or any other anniversary in connection with her, he refrained from speaking of it. Apparently he was aware that such things are the time-honored javelins for lacerating the heart.

But Peggy's miniature stood on the mantelshelf, and Benjamin mentioned her naturally whenever there was a reason to do so, and never with a long face. Sometimes he told an anecdote that had her in it, and they would laugh, seeing Peggy at her demurest. He reminded his daughters to emulate their mother's virtues in brushing their hair to a sheen as she had brushed hers (a habit that appealed more to Patsy than to Jane), and in putting sachets amongst their handkerchiefs and always being thoughtful of others. Such practical references to their mother suggested life and continuity instead of death, and did not stir up their emotions any more than a memorandum from him to borrow a newspaper from Uncle Lewis or take daffodils to old Mrs. Wheat.

Benjamin did not require his daughters to observe a given period of mourning. If they were invited to a picnic or a spend-the-day he would give his consent to their going. "That will be jolly," he would say enthusiastically. As for their wearing crepe bands, he would not hear of it. And when they were given a doleful book titled *Young's Night Thoughts,* the gift of a Shiloh deacon's wife, he put the volume on a high shelf.

Thus, it was from her father that Jane learned how to depreciate a time of mourning and get through a death with the least possible pain and devastation. An achievement that would cause wonder in the years ahead, and no little criticism.

7 ❖

The heady year passed; four seasons of it, with Jane managing herself and Patsy and their father's house. Christina was an active partner, watchful of her charges, protecting them to the best of her abilities, but hardly curbing them. Her own costumes and head-dresses were as flamboyant as the girls' new clothes. Jane chose striking materials from the shelves of the family store, and when she had cloth snipped off for herself and Patsy, she always remembered Christina in one way or another. A dressmaker came to the cottage and sewed for the three of them. Christina was the envy of every servant in the county, and the Lampton girls were becoming noticeable.

Among their more interested observers were Grandmother Casey and her daughter-in-law. Green's wife Janie went often to town to mingle with her family, the Pattersons, and when she returned to the plantation she always had irrefutable stories to tell Mrs. Casey of the goings on at the Pink Cottage. "Your oldest grand-daughter has a calico print that cost a dollar and a half a yard! Think of it, when you can buy an acre of ground for ten dollars!" . . . "Jane and Patsy were at the race course last week. They went with some of the Tuckahoe crowd." . . . "Christina buys beefsteak almost every day for their dinner." . . . "They say Toby has sold two hams from the plantation to one of the taverns, right out from under Mr. Lampton's nose." . . . "Patsy is noticing boys—just eleven years old!"

Mrs. Casey finally sent for Benjamin. They had a talk behind closed doors.

Afterward, Benjamin seemed to ponder a great deal and to display a curious interest in what went on at his house. Jane uneasily noticed the change in him. She was conscious of no wrongdoing on her part, yet her father's attitude toward her had become critical, his admonitions sharp.

"You and Patsy are on the street a good deal," he said crossly one evening. "My attention has been called to it. I want that sort of thing stopped. It's unseemly."

"Yes, sir," Jane replied in surprise. She began to devise intricate ways of getting from one place to another without crossing the public square. It caused her a good deal of bother.

Just before Christmas, Benjamin came down on Jane's purchases at Lampton and Montgomery. He had examined the books and was surprised at how much was charged to his account; it far exceeded the purchases made by John Montgomery's family. He told the clerks to sell nothing more to his daughters unless they paid out of pocket. When Jane encountered this roadblock her pride was hurt, her plans were altered.

The old clerk who waited on her was embarrassed. "I must decline to charge anything to you, Miss Jane," he said. He was a kindly, courteous soul who had once owned a store in Virginia and failed. "How much cash have you, Miss Jane? Forgive me, but I am forced to ask."

Jane confessed that she had less than a dollar in her purse.

"In that case, sad to say, I can't let you have these articles you've picked out. You'll have to consult your pa before you buy. Try him tonight after a good supper, that's my advice." The old clerk regretfully restored to a cabinet a tortoise-shell round comb that Jane had chosen for Patsy, and a silk handkerchief for Uncle Lewis, who was about to take a trip.

Early in January, Christina shared some ominous news with Jane. It was after supper, in the kitchen. Christina was ironing. Jane was cracking hickory nuts and picking out the meats. Patsy was in bed with a cold, upstairs in the dormer room she shared with Jane. Benjamin had just departed from the house wearing his best clothes and not naming his destination.

"Master's courtin'," Christina said. "Everybody in town know it but you."

Jane was so startled that she dropped the hammer and upset

48

the basket. When she had collected the rolling nuts she steadied her voice and asked, "Who is he courting, Christina?"

"Miss Polly Hays is who."

"Oh. That one. . . . She brought us a cake last week. She put it on Mama's cakestand."

"Sure did. Mr. Benjamin et hearty of it. If Mr. Benjamin favors any food in this worl', it's a fine poun' cake."

"We could make him one tomorrow."

Christina shook her head. "No use. Everybody's done pick out Miss Polly Hays to take over this house."

Mrs. Casey, people said, chose the second Mrs. Lampton, but that was hardly the case. She merely told her daughter-in-law one day that Polly Hays would make Benjamin Lampton a good wife. The reasons were obvious. Miss Hays had turned thirty. She was healthy, reliable, handsome, agreeable, and neat. She could sew, cook, trim her bonnets, and hitch up a buggy unaided. The English Hays blood in her veins was outmatched by the Scotch, for her mother was born Mary Campbell Walker in Virginia's Rockbridge County. One of the Alexander Walkers, one of the everlasting Campbells. Thus, Benjamin could be saved from marriage with a Tuckahoe woman who would make a careless and extravagant stepmother.

The biased diary of the Honorable Hawkins Taylor of Illinois tells that:

> In 1792 my parents moved to the Green River country of Kentucky from the Shenandoah Valley of Virginia. Three of my mother's brothers, the Walkers, soon followed and settled in what is now Adair County. Our settlement was Scotch-Irish, about twenty families of us. Near by was a large settlement of out-at-elbow Virginians, all claiming to be related to King George and descended from the First Families of Virginia. They sent their eldest son to be educated in Virginia; the others went without education. These Virginia Tuckahoes looked upon their neighbors as poor whites.

The Honorable Hawkins Taylor's comments cannot be ignored historically, except the final charge. The Tuckahoes did not look upon their clannish neighbors as poor whites; merely as stiff, pompous, and reserved.

The diarist might have added that the Tuckahoes rode for pleasure and hunted with hounds. They had not established their church, the Episcopal, in that area as other denominations had established theirs, though they treasured their well-worn prayer books and used them at weddings and funerals; they attended any church service that seemed lively and diverting, and afterward they assembled on the church lawn as if for a party. They regarded the institution of slavery as inevitable, never trying to justify it by Scripture as the uneasy Scots did. They entertained hospitably at suppers and balls, borrowing silver spoons and plates from one another to replace the lost and broken. They invariably served punch that was potent. They wore out their land with tobacco and moved on. Their Tuckahoe appellation indicates that some of them claimed descent from William Randolph of Tuckahoe plantation on the James River.

Benjamin Lampton, by every standard, belonged to this Cavalier remnant. As a bachelor he had lived among them, and he still retained some worn-out land in their midst. Mrs. Casey hoped to keep him from reverting.

It would seem that spinister Polly Hays had already set her cap for him, for he became engaged to her almost immediately. He married her on the second of February, the day after purchasing the marriage license and misspelling her name. Right rakishly he signed himself Ben Lampton, perhaps because he remembered that his age was forty-nine and his bride's was thirty-one.

They went to Lexington in a buckboard behind a spirited horse for a fortnight of honeymooning.

On the day set for their return Jane Lampton dropped her mother's cherished cakestand on the kitchen hearth and broke it into a dozen pieces. Patsy, who saw it happen, was puzzled and shocked by Jane's awkwardness. Christina, who also saw, laughed softly in approval. It was such laughter as might be heard in the forests of Africa when a rite is accomplished on schedule.

Jane and Patsy were instructed to call their stepmother Aunt Polly, and they did so. They were docile from the moment she entered the door of the Pink Cottage; but they were on guard, braced for collision.

There was no doubt in anybody's mind that the second Mrs. Lampton was in love with her middle-aged husband. She wished to please him in every way. She would be a good stepmother to his daughters if it killed her. She would tame them, weed out their wild tendencies, teach them thrift, piety, and needlework. And she would cure them all of the broad A, a Lampton ailment which she found especially annoying. After Benjamin or the girls used that offensive pronunciation she would contrive to repeat the word and "stomp on it," as Jane said, "to flatten it out."

Jane could divert Patsy in the privacy of their room by taking off their stepmother's conversational quirks: the folksy Scottish nasal drawl, the "land's sakes!" and the "well, I never!" and the "more's the pity!" with hands lifted to imply astonishment.

But while Patsy was amused she was not stilled. "I can't abide Aunt Polly!" she declared to Jane within a week's time. "I can't see myself getting along with her."

"I can," Jane said. She had already decided how. She would circumvent her. She would lead her a chase, a pretty chase, through the fields of their contentions, throwing a little dust in her eyes. She conveyed her plan to Patsy and then gave her a simple demonstration. "You know very well, Patsy, I can't see to work this sampler. Cross-stitching makes me squint."

"Tell her so," Patsy advised. "Tell her loud and clear."

"Do you think I want the woman to know I'm half blind?" She took the valuable needle (all the stores were out of them) and dropped it down a crack in the floor. "Now I can learn cobbling from Abraham the way I've wanted to. Aunt Polly won't like to see me idle." She was pleased to make Patsy laugh, but she was in earnest. Months ago Abraham had taught her to cut soft leather and use an awl at his bench in the tool house. She had made a pair of moccasins for a slave child.

All through the next twelve months a battle of women was in progress, with Benjamin not realizing it. He noted with satisfaction that his daughters were courteous to his wife, that his wife was considerate of his daughters. Lulled by the deceptive tranquillity of his house, he was not aware that Jane and her stepmother were contending for his vote in every decision, circling each other like cautious pugilists.

Mrs. Lampton had the edge, for Jane was vulnerable. Her grades at school were low, and she was preoccupied with dancing —a pastime Polly Hays had not indulged in. She had heard that Jane was cultivating every young person in the county whose family had a pianoforte or a violin and was inducing her friends to congregate at those places. Jane somehow knew all the steps, even the whirling twosomes, it was said, and was spreading her talents generously.

Her slippers were a minor indication. Mrs. Lampton sometimes commented on their condition in Benjamin's presence. "I never knew a girl so hard on shoe leather," she would say innocently. And one evening in the parlor: "What on earth do you do to your ankle laces, Jane? They look pulled to shreds."

"What do you suppose I do to them, Aunt Polly?" Jane fired back, causing her father to glance up from his newspaper and tell her to go upstairs to her room. "—without Patsy!" he added firmly, seeing Patsy about to follow. He would not, though, be drawn into a contention about dancing. At any rate, not then. Patsy reported that glad fact to Jane.

"It could happen any day, though," Jane said. "It could happen just before Julie Miller's party. Aunt Polly will keep gnawing away till Papa says no more dancing till my marks pick up at school. And I can't help my marks. Especially spelling."

They decided to take the matter to their grandmother at the plantation. Walking the distance one fresh April Saturday, they surprised the old lady at her hen-setting. Her pleasure at seeing them was touching, though she must have felt it in her bones that they had come for something. It soon came out. Jane began to remind her of the pleasure she had had in her girlhood, dancing to a fiddle at the forts "even with Indians around." In view of this, then, would she please speak to Aunt Polly? Jane explained Aunt Polly's attitude, and her hold on Papa. She even wept.

Mrs. Casey said she was sorry, but she could not interfere. "When your father married again—as I think he should have done, mind you—I lost my right to intrude in his house. Try to have patience, child. Another year's wait won't hurt you." Then she added thoughtfully, "How pretty you're both getting to be. Patsy, you're like your mother, but a sight more robust."

"And I, Grandmother?" Jane asked.

"Pure Lampton in looks. But don't be too much like them in other ways, Jane. I've noticed your father's brothers—Lewis at the Eagle House, Wharton and Joshua who drift in and out of here. There's not a taproot in the lot of them." Then, "Would you girls like to ride your horses now?"

They accepted gladly. Their mother's riding habits hung in an upstairs bedroom—the saffron yellow homespun made on the farm, the black broadcloth skirt and jacket made by Benjamin's tailor in Frankfort. Peggy had not worn the broadcloth much; its formality had deterred her, but the girls found it enchanting. Today they drew straws to see which should wear it, for it fitted both. Patsy, turning thirteen, was of a size with Jane who was still childishly slender. It was the year before Jane blossomed into beauty. Or whatever it was she had that took the place of beauty.

When Abraham carried them back to Columbia that evening in the farm wagon, the matter of Aunt Polly's attitude was still unresolved, but Jane had settled her most pressing problem—a way to get to the dance across the village a week hence. "Bed sheets tied together will do it," she told Patsy. "But you and Christina will have to help me."

Local history would attest to the success of that undertaking, for Mr. and Mrs. Ben Lampton were unaware for several weeks that Jane had slipped willfully out of her window that rainy night to join a young man sometimes called wild. The discovery may have had something to do with Christina's removal. Though not entirely, for Christina's clashes with the new Mrs. Lampton had become frequent and intense. When Benjamin traded her to the John Montgomerys for a calm young woman named Sarah, even Jane and Patsy were relieved. They could see Christina often at

53

Aunt Anne's, cured of her animosities, almost serene, no longer sticking pins in a dried gourd named Miss Polly.

That Jane Lampton had gone over the window sill to meet an undesirable young man surprised no one, for she attracted a good many of that sort. In her early teens she had not been romantically inclined. Growing boys had not contended to carry her school-books to and from the Reverend Samuel Robertson's Academy on the hill. None had sent her tender valentines. But now the young men were beginning to notice her, one here, one there, until she could be called popular. There was one beau from a Tuckahoe farm who was in debt from buying horses. Another from a Scottish family in town who took morphine for his insomnia. Another, of a prominent Glasgow family—she had met him when visiting Uncle Wharton—who had challenged his own cousin to a duel. That one read Sir Walter Scott's novels as they came off the press. Why Jane attracted so many erratic admirers may have baffled the unobservant. But the various young men had something in common besides a fundamental decency; they were quixotic and talkative. And Jane was a born listener.

She hung on their exorbitant words; and the theories they expounded, the dreams they confided, the boasts they made found reception in the fertile soil of her own imagination. Deprived of books because of her inadequate eyesight, and not aware of her lack because of an unscholarly mind, she read human beings instead and found them satisfying. She could never get enough of them if they were rare. And as surely as a wayward horse was more fascinating to her than a tame one, so was an original beau preferable to a predictable one.

Patsy's case was different. She liked jolly, uncomplicated boys who could be counted on for service and attention, and she had been attracting that kind ever since she had learned to roll her eyes.

Poor Mrs. Lampton became so engrossed in her husband's financial troubles that she could hardly keep watch on her enterprising stepdaughters. The store was failing. John Montgomery had pulled out of the partnership, paying Benjamin for that privi-

54

lege and removing his name from the store front. Augustus Cushing, the Philadelphia creditor, sued to collect the three-year-old note that Benjamin had pledged Lampton and Montgomery to pay, and a replevin was granted and deferred. Benjamin hastily disposed of the Pink Cottage and moved his family to the flat over his store. From his brother Lewis, whom he knew to be too tenderhearted to foreclose, he obtained some money by recording the following mortgage:

> To Lewis Lampton, to indemnify him . . . all of Lot 41 not conveyed to John Montgomery and William Quirey; a Negro woman Sarah, about 24; a Negro man Toby, about 45; one large road wagon, one bay horse, one gray horse, one Dearborn and harness; 4 featherbeds and furniture; one sideboard and furniture; one Secretary Bookcase and Books; one cupboard and furniture, one dozen Winser chairs all of which property I have now in my possession. And I also assign and this day transfer . . . Lot Eleven in the Town of Sparta, Tenn. Benjamin Lampton.

In the stark, high flat, Jane and Patsy disposed their belongings in the room assigned to them and complained normally. It had all been rather sudden. Their room had a rear-corner location, its side window looking sheerly down to the brick pavement, its back window overlooking a grass plot, some shrubbery and two vine-covered outhouses. Sarah had the other back room. Toby was quartered in the store, rather cozily. A parlor-dining room and the small bedroom of Mr. and Mrs. Ben Lampton occupied the front of the apartment. Midway was a cluttered kitchen and an entrance hall where the stairway emerged steeply from the street.

Benjamin assured his family that this humble domicile was temporary. And so Polly explained it to her brother, Dr. Charles Hays, a young physician reasonably concerned with her welfare. And so the girls explained it to their friends. Some of them regarded it as an enviable lark that Jane and Patsy had fallen into, though most of them expressed sympathy and dismay.

The cramped and uncomfortable way of living that the Benjamin Lamptons were reduced to was an indirect cause of Patsy's coming out into society before she was fourteen years old. One

55

evening she behaved pitifully while watching Jane dress for a party at Uncle Lewis's Eagle House—the Christmas Assembly, it was called. "Must you have all the fun?" she reproached. "I'm practically grown-up, myself."

"Yes, you are," Jane answered, turning to inspect her sister. "Your bosom's as big as mine. You're taller than I am. . . . Patsy, ask Sarah for a kettle of warm water! While you take your bath I'll find you something to wear."

It was not until Patsy was dressed in one of Jane's party frocks with her dark curls stunningly fixed on top of her head that they remembered Aunt Polly and their father.

"They'll never let me," Patsy moaned.

"They must," Jane answered.

They went hand in hand to the parlor-dining room where Benjamin sat studying his account books, with Mrs. Lampton at his elbow, knitting him a sock. The girls stopped in the doorway, making a pretty picture, a surprising tableau.

"What's this?" Polly asked sharply.

Benjamin laughed. "It's a sly trick, I'll be bound!" He studied them, and as he looked at Patsy his eyes misted. Mrs. Lampton's eyes merely narrowed. It was as if Peggy Casey Lampton stood there, young again, but vigorous and determined. She resumed her knitting, for the inevitable had happened. This comely, overgrown girl had kicked over the traces with the help and encouragement of her doting older sister.

Mrs. Lampton's unspoken blame was in her face and in every thrust of her knitting needle, and Jane accepted it as her due. She stood there meekly while her stepmother washed her hands of them in frigid silence, and then she addressed her father. "Patsy's going with me, Papa, if you don't mind."

"I've got no objections," Benjamin answered soberly. "It would be mighty dull for her here, with a party going on across the way. I'm aware she's young. Keep her in sight, Jane."

The door knocker sounded below, and Toby could be heard coming from somewhere to answer it. They all listened while Toby and a young man exchanged civilities down on the pavement.

Fortunately Jane's escort was beyond reproach. He was Allen

DeGraffenreid Pattison, a genial young man who was smitten with several girls at once. Jane took Patsy's hand and drew her after her down the long steep stairway to the street. "There are two of us, Graf'," she said to the surprised boy. "Do you mind?"

He said he was charmed and gave an arm to each. They half circled the public square, avoiding the depressions where the slush lay, and arrived at the Eagle House, alive with candlelight and music. It was merely a country hotel, frequented tonight by the beaux and belles of several rustic counties, but it seemed to all of them a very embassy of fashion. This dancing party was elevated to a ball by Uncle Lewis's aristocratic presence, his crystal chandelier, his polished floors, his three musicians brought on from Louisville.

They were a little late, and Jane arranged their entrance into the ballroom. She entered on her escort's arm, Patsy on Uncle Lewis's, just as the violins ended a waltz. There they stood, the pretty Lampton sisters, waiting for something to happen.

Uncle Lewis's wife, Aunt Jen', disengaged herself from the other chaperones and came to meet them. Uncle Lewis had ever found her to be an understanding helpmeet, poised in a pinch, setting a lavish table when the larder was full, substituting turnips for asparagus when it was lean, nodding nostalgically at the foot of the table when he told of Lambton Castle in County Durham.

She did not fail the Lambton-Lamptons now. If surprised to see Patsy, she concealed it. She took the hand of the blue-eyed, creamy-skinned, thirteen-year-old girl and presented her to the disapproving chaperones. She gave her a little hand-painted program and a pencil to write with. Then she summoned some stags, and Patsy was launched.

Jane, seeing all this, smiled happily. Nobody could understand it; contrary to custom and female behavior she was creating a rival for herself and setting the rival up in business. But, then, nobody was ever to understand Jane Lampton, quite. In after years brilliant minds and ordinary would try a little and fail, for her majestic simplicity would elude them. There was one facet of her nature that would shine as crudely and surely as a bull's-eye lantern on a foggy night. It would confuse the sophisticated and send them off on speculative tangents: she wanted every living creature to have fun.

8 ❖

Jane regarded age seventeen as high time to quit Robertson's Academy, and she met with no opposition. Benjamin could hardly have spared the tuition for both of his daughters now that his business was failing, and Jane's application to learning did not warrant a sacrifice. The Reverend Samuel B. Robertson, a beloved and lively divine, had valued Jane Lampton for her remarkable questions in the classroom and could rarely resist being led astray by them into telling, for instance, about the Black Hole of Calcutta or the Wailing Wall of Jerusalem when he had meant to take up American imports. But Mr. Robertson had recently retired from teaching to devote his time entirely to the ministry, and though the school retained his name in tribute to his founding it, a milder personality was in charge. This was Mr. F. F. T. G. Herald from Pennsylvania, a man who wrote a beautiful hand and stuck to his assignments. Jane's chief concern from the moment she laid eyes on Mr. Herald was to discover what his initials stood for; and when she had learned his full name she memorized it and often declaimed it effectively: Mr. Furney Fanton Thole Green Herald.

Patsy continued to attend school, off and on, until she was sixteen. She could add a column of figures more quickly than Jane, could read better, spell more accurately. But Jane would always care more about the Pleiades than Patsy would, and the strange customs of the Persians, not to mention the deadly habits of South American ants.

"Jane and Patsy are carried away with frivolity," remarked Aunt Polly sadly in her aerie above the store.

It was true. Frivolity was to run in their veins like a happy fever for several beautiful years while they ignored poverty and made-over clothes and became the lighthearted belles of three

58

counties. Patsy was a kind and agreeable girl in her unaware way and would not wittingly hurt anyone's feelings. Jane's graciousness was the more remarkable because it caused her a good deal of work. If she noticed a less-favored girl shrinking in dread at a party she would bolster her, include her, promote her until some suitable boy—possibly shy himself—was lured to take her over. She would see a wallflower unbecomingly dressed and do her best to remedy it in the dressing room, rearranging the girl's hair, loosening her neckline, lending her a brooch or a fan or a ribbon, linking arms with her for the dance floor. She was a born sponsor. Mystifying to contemplate, Jane was as sweet as the heroine of a book in a Sunday school library. It almost made no sense, Jane Lampton was so kind to people.

But when their balls or picnics were invaded by snobs or "hateful things" from the Bluegrass, as sometimes happened, the local girls could count on Jane to aggrandize backcountry society and squelch its detractors. In handling such visitors, Jane would be queenly, cunning, witty, or waspish—whatever she thought the pests deserved—and would send them back to their white-pillared houses at Danville or Lexington or Nashville, nursing their wounds.

"Do you ride?" was her favorite way of challenging a rival who looked down her nose at the "Pennyrile" counties. And then she would wait for an agreeable country boy to explain, "What Miss Lampton means is, how high a fence can you take?"

The weddings had begun among Jane's friends, and now she had mating on her mind. She must soon get herself betrothed as other girls did. She must become engaged to an up-and-coming boy with intentions, for Papa was broke, and things were going to get worse instead of better.

It looked as if none of her present beaux would do, not even the charmingly proper one in Greensburg, Richard Barret, whose father was so well off. Her heart pounded when she was with young Barret, and often when she merely thought of him, but she could see that he was wary of her wiles. He was mad to go to Transylvania College in Lexington and study medicine. A man needed a profession, he said. He talked of it even when holding her hand. Oh, if Richard were only inclined toward matrimony!

Jane's cousin Jesse Lampton had married Mildred Stone in November. And Betsy Lampton, Uncle Joshua's daughter, had recently wed one Joseph Palmer, coming up from Winchester to Uncle Lewis's house for the ceremony. (Uncle Lewis and Aunt Jen' and their three boys did not live in his tavern but in a tall brick dwelling wedged between the inn and John Anderson's counting house.) Jane was a bridesmaid. A distaff cousin, Polly Paxton, had just said yes to Dan Trabue; and Juliet Miller had captured Graf' Pattison and was wearing his picture in a locket. Nancy Cundiff, a dear friend, was marrying Daniel Suddeath, a successful young man in the chair-making business. . . . Among the Tuckahoes, Cupid was just as rampant. Emily Willis had wed William Garnett, one of the Huguenot descendants, with a big to-do at the Willis plantation. Her little sister Sallie, who caught the bouquet, was being courted by James Ewers.

A more sedate wedding was coming up among the Presbyterians at a farm on the edge of town. Mary Patterson, who had gone to the Shenandoah Valley to spend a year but had come home fancy-free, was going to marry her faithful squire William Stotts.

At that wedding reception Jane ran into Marshall Clemens, who bowed to her formally and picked up her handkerchief, absent-mindedly retaining it. She maneuvered him into a corner. "I saw you four or five years ago at my grandfather's funeral," she reminded him. "My grandfather was Colonel Casey."

"I know he was, Miss Lampton. And I've seen you now and then, since. Not to approach, though. You're never alone."

"I'm not hard to approach, I hope. Please call me Jane."

"Thank you, Jane. And I'm John."

"John?" she repeated in surprise. "But your own mother calls you Marshall. I thought everybody did."

"Yes, but I'd rather they didn't. I was named John Marshall after the Chief Justice and it's too big a name for me. I expect to be a lawyer. I read Blackstone with Cyrus Walker when Mr. Hancock can spare me at the farm. If I should call myself John Marshall in court," he said somberly, almost with a shudder, "I'd be laughed at by the prosecuting attorney."

Jane pondered this. She thought a good laugh might brighten up the courtroom before the lawyers got down to business but she kept the idea to herself. It was her custom to listen and sound the depths, so to speak. "When we met at Grandfather's," she said, "you were about to leave for Virginia with the Walker party, you and your sister. Didn't you like Lynchburg?"

"No, things didn't turn out right for me, Jane. Mr. Langhorne got me a clerkship in an iron foundry, as he'd promised, but I wasn't satisfied. There's no future in keeping books. I decided to come back to Adair County. My sister Betsy stayed in Virginia. She married Captain John Pollard and settled down in Bedford County."

"I'm surprised you and Mary Patterson didn't fall in love, too," Jane said, indicating the bride, who was offering her gloved fingers to a line of guests. "All that long horseback ride together, days and days of it, through the wild mountains, and Mary in her bottle-green riding habit."

Marshall Clemens laughed. He had nice teeth, and his narrow face lit up pleasantly. "Do you think people fall in love through propinquity?"

"Through what?" Jane asked blankly.

"It's a sort of Latin word," he said kindly. "It means a state of being thrown together."

"Well, it could happen that way," Jane insisted. "If you saw Mary Patterson every morning, say, drinking her breakfast coffee at a campfire or at an inn—wherever you stopped on the Wilderness Road—it might have come to your mind that you'd always want to have breakfast with her. You're both so serious, you know."

"A serious man doesn't need a serious woman," he protested. "Nor the other way around, I hope. Opposites should marry."

"Oh! So you hope a giddy girl will capture you!"

Jane was fascinated by this quirk, and she called to mind several lively girls who ought to meet him. One of the Pages, surely; and the Lincefield Grady orphans who charged so many things at the stores but had a guardian who paid; Susan and Peachy Grady were giddy all right and they would soon be looking for husbands. So would Patsy Lampton. Jane resolved to keep this clever young man in sight for them. Not for herself, though. Richard Barret's disturbing charms nullified him.

"Why don't you come to the dances?" she asked winsomely.

"I can't dance, Jane. Anyway, I'm too busy. In addition to studying law, I'm trying to settle my father's estate. He's been dead a long while, but we've just got around to settling. I'm the executor and the guardian."

"Is there very much to attend to?"

"There's a farm in western Virginia to be sold. It's at that famous place where the Kanawha River enters the Ohio. And there are ten slaves that had to be appraised. We four heirs, Betsy and Hannibal and Caroline and I—Pleasants is dead—had to divide the Negroes amongst us so that each would get the same value. It was a puzzle to work out, for we couldn't separate the slave children from their mothers."

"I should think not!" Jane flared. "That kind of thing is plain wicked."

He hardly noticed the interruption for he felt impelled to make a correction. Truth was in the very marrow of his bones, and he realized that he had overrated his properties. "The Mason County land is rather worn out," he confessed. "Then there's a small debt against my inheritance." He looked unhappy or resentful, Jane could not tell which, while he explained: "My stepfather has put in a claim for the years he supported me before I was old enough to work."

Jane's darting mind saw him for a moment as a sad-faced little boy being charged his board by honest but businesslike Mr. Simon Hancock. "Don't feel bitter," she said gently. Her sympathy was evident in her mobile face.

"No, I'm not bitter," and he smiled again, trying to prove it. "There's a handsome sideboard coming to me, I failed to mention that. Mother and Mr. Hancock are using it now, but I'll take it when I marry. It's a Sheraton piece my father bought in Richmond."

Jane exclaimed gratifyingly, and she made a mental note to

62

tell Patsy. Next to a roof that didn't leak and some hams in the smokehouse, the Lamptons valued a good sideboard.

Several young persons joined them, and Clemens went away, bowing formally and carrying off Jane's small lace-edged handkerchief. Like most persons, he had talked his head off to her.

If the flat over the store was a poor thing it was better than nothing, as the Lamptons soon realized. In the paying off of Mr. Cushing of Philadelphia, a more adamant creditor had been created at home in the person of William Caldwell, the county clerk of Adair since its founding and an expert on mortgages. He held a note against Benjamin and Lewis Lampton for two thousand dollars, and he was foreclosing. Jane and Patsy learned that Mr. Caldwell owned Papa, lock, stock, and barrel, and that Uncle Lewis was too hard up to redeem him. Caldwell's three eldest children, Maria and Matilda and Elizanne, were among the Lampton girls' dearest friends; they had deplored stepmothers together, had shared secrets from earliest childhood. But now they averted eyes when they met, for Mr. Caldwell was taking the very beds and chairs of the Lamptons. Not that he needed them. He owned a farm and several mill rights, and when he wished to have a stream dammed or a ferry established, he managed to achieve those things. When he took snuff, Adair County sneezed.

Benjamin, when the blow of eviction fell, asked no mercy of his creditor. And when he called his wife and daughters together for a conference he appeared to be as cool as a cucumber.

"Polly," he said to his wife, "you and I will go to Tennessee and see about my holdings in Sparta. Do you mind?" He meant ahorseback, for he had saved out two riding horses; they were eating away at Lewis's stable, very fit for travel.

Jane and Patsy watched Aunt Polly anxiously and were glad of her polite reply. "By no means, Ben," she said. "October is a good time to ride through the mountains. Let's see now. You'll leave the girls at the Caseys', I reckon?" (Her voice sounded almost merry, Jane noticed: *poor old thing! Has she hated us so?*)

"No," Benjamin answered. "Lamptons can still take care of

Lamptons. My brother Lewis has asked for them. He and Jen' want them to visit at their house, however long we're away."

Jane and Patsy exchanged relieved glances. The plantation had become deadly dull. Uncle Green's wife was mistress there, for Grandmother had turned over the reins to her. Young Mrs. Casey had come to frown on dancing and gallivanting. She was so strict with Uncle Green that he now did his circumspect drinking at a tavern.

"How long will you be away, Papa?" Patsy asked anxiously.

"I can't say, daughter," was Benjamin's honest reply.

Patsy went and stood close to Jane and held tight to her hand. She was the one with a sense of property. More than Jane, she was shocked to learn that they were penniless, frightened to learn that the provider had ceased to provide. Whoever wooed Patsy in the years ahead need not apply unless he could heal this wound by offering her security.

Mrs. Lampton asked her husband what was to become of Toby and Sarah.

"They'll go to the Eagle House," Benjamin told her. "Lewis already owns them. We've kept them through his courtesy."

He then suggested that they begin to pack, for he had no intention of lingering in Columbia as an object of sympathy. "That would be abominable," he said. "I want no commiseration."

Mrs. Lampton was told that she could carry only what clothing would go into her saddlebags. Jane and Patsy had better news; they could take every stitch they owned, for Aunt Jen' had an armoire in her spare room, and some storage boxes under the beds.

"Such things as pictures and silver and bric-a-brac, Lewis will store for us," Benjamin said. "But everything else here belongs to the great and mighty William Caldwell."

While his family looked at him in astonishment he began to sing in his pleasing baritone, and to take the pictures off the walls. He was somewhat ironic in regard to their plight, but not bitter. And if he felt depressed, he concealed the fact, instinctively conducting himself in adversity as an English country gentleman might do if deprived of his seat.

The departure took place next day after the trunks and boxes had been sent across the public square to Lewis's. Anne Casey Montgomery, seeing Benjamin and his wife ride off, said to her husband somberly, "My sister Peggy was spared all this, thank God. And I'm thankful we weren't asked to keep Jane and Patsy. I'd not want the responsibility—both of them so spoiled and flighty."

John Montgomery agreed. He had no bad conscience in regard to his unfortunate brother-in-law. He had bought out of the partnership fairly, as soon as he realized he was hitched to an eccentric.

In the late afternoon of Christmas Day, which fell on a Tuesday, Jane approached Uncle Lewis's house in a fluffy snowfall, feeling lighthearted. There was to be an assembly ball that night at the Eagle House. Richard Barret would come with the Greensburg set. Jane had been to borrow a pair of thread lace gloves from young Mrs. Charles Jones, the former Nancy Bridgewater, who had them to spare.

Up in Aunt Jen's guest chamber, now called "the girls' room," Patsy was waiting for her. "Guess what, Jane! A tall, dark boy that I never saw before has come to the tavern. I saw him dismount and go in. He gave Toby a coin to take his horse around to the stable but he carried his own saddlebags."

"What kind of a horse does he have?" Jane asked practically. She was in a hurry to show the gloves.

"A sleek sorrel, a pacer as sure as you live. He looked to be past twenty years old—the man, I mean. He was wearing a beaver hat and a broadcloth overcoat. Did you get the gloves?"

"Yes, here they are for you, Patsy. They'll reach to your elbows. Nancy was sweet about it."

"I do thank you, Jane, and I'll try not to get punch on them. I expect you dreaded to ask for them. It's hard to go begging."

"I couldn't bear for you not to have evening gloves, Patsy, after you lost yours. Try them on."

The fit was satisfactory, and Jane inspected her own gloves. They were white kid, several seasons old but successfully cleaned in corn meal. They tried on their dresses, discussed hair arrangements. They were very, very happy. The snow kept coming down.

The Eagle House had an entrance hall, so it was not necessary for guests to enter the public room to reach the dining, or assembly room. Indeed, Jane and Patsy had never set foot in the place. It had a bar where local men and travelers could take their drinks, neat and standing up: brass cuspidors abounded. Females were not expected there, not even Aunt Jen'. Traveling ladies might sit in Aunt Jen's little back parlor while waiting for their men folk, the parlor having a door connecting residence with tavern.

It was through this door that Jane and Patsy and their escorts passed en route to the Christmas dance, a little late, as was the girls' wont.

The dark young stranger was standing near the door with his host. "My nieces," Lewis Lampton told him. "I'll present you to them later. Do you see any one here you know, Mr. Hardin?"

"No, sir. But you've got some remarkably handsome people. It's equal to a Bardstown gathering."

"I'm glad to hear you say so!" The host continued to talk, but Parker C. Hardin (as he had signed himself on the register) was not heeding him. He was looking at the small and slight Jane Lampton, who reminded him of an undersized queen. She was all in white. Her neck and arms, as he frequently said afterward, were like alabaster. Her widely set eyes were a warm brown, her lips scarlet. The red hair that crowned her head and tumbled to her shoulders was like nothing he had ever seen before, unless a sugar maple in October. She was looking for someone, that was evident. While she talked to her escort she was searching the room for somebody she could not find, but had not yet given up.

"Come and meet Miss Mary Ann Waggoner, Mr. Hardin," Lewis invited. "She's considered our prettiest girl. The Waggoner name had only two syllables in Germany, of course. A good family. Numerous here. One of them was a general on Washington's staff—an uncle of the Adair men, I believe."

It was Lewis Lampton's concern to know the background of his every acquaintance, local or from afar, and when making introductions to pass on whatever items he had gleaned to their credit. Sometimes a man hardly recognized himself after one of Lewis's adroit summations. That he had learned a good deal about young Mr. Hardin while assigning him to a room goes without saying, and all this he was able to impart to Miss Waggoner, a lovely blonde girl in a beautiful gown.

"Mary Ann, please spare a dance for Mr. Parker C. Hardin—Mr. Parker Calhoun Hardin—if you can. He's a nephew of Congressman Ben Hardin of Bardstown. He's going south to choose a location to practice law. I'd not be surprised to see him end up in Nashville."

Later in the evening young Hardin stood near Jane Lampton, covertly watching her. He now saw that she was not really beautiful, once you got past the flaming hair. She had too much nose; her eyebrows were too close to her lovely eyes; and as for the eyes themselves under their curling lashes, they narrowed when she peered, as if trying to refocus. But her skin was even more exquisite at closer range, and her manner of speaking was a strange but musical drawl. She was with a boy named Robert Todd, and they had merged with two couples from Greensburg who had just arrived in a carriage, destined to spend the night with friends. The snow had delayed them, but all were in high spirits.

"Did Richard Barret's horse throw a shoe?" Jane Lampton asked them. "He's mighty late."

"He's not coming, Jane," one of the young men answered. "His family's having a Christmas supper, and he couldn't get out of it."

"Do the Barrets think this is New Year's Eve?" Jane mocked, somehow making them laugh. She was exactly taking off the elegant voice of Mrs. Barret, had Hardin only known it, for mimicry was a sinful art with her. She practiced it for her own amusement and for applause. With a pair of spectacles and thirty seconds to adjust her mind, she could become old Mrs. Ferguson disapproving of ankles. Given a fan and a lozenge, she was Mrs. Frazier late for church. With a quill pen and a clearing of the throat she became Mr. William Minter signing up an apprentice for the art and mystery of cabinetmaking; then, tousling her hair, she became that unwilling apprentice himself, one of the Dooley boys whom the court was forever involved with. She made you love young Dooley.

Parker Hardin knew nothing of this gift of Jane's, but he did know what a girl meant when she fluttered her eyelashes at him, and Jane Lampton was now deliberately doing that. "Come and join us," she called. "Uncle Lewis told me to look after you."

That was the way he met her—when she was disappointed and chagrined by the nonarrival of a boy named Barret. Hardin admitted to this afterward, but from the first he was too entrapped to care. Within a few days he was courting her headlong, and she was not saying no. Within a fortnight, at the first session of County Court, January 1822, he applied for permission to practice law in the court of Adair, proving himself qualified by showing his papers from Bardstown, "Athens of the West." He was granted a license.

In his bedazzlement he was consigning his talents to a rural area already overstocked with attorneys in search of clients, not to mention another one in the offing—John M. Clemens out at the Hancock farm, almost ready to hang out a shingle and watching him with a perturbed eye.

Parker Hardin tactfully removed himself from the Eagle House and went to board with Mr. and Mrs. Elsey Creel, Mrs. Creel being his distant cousin.

9 ❖

Young Mr. Hardin had several things in his favor as Jane Lampton's suitor, though one of them would have surprised him. Natural enough was her appreciation of his good birth and character, his polite manners, his success at passing the bar examination up in Nelson County before his twenty-first birthday. But what snagged her attention and won her admiration was something rash and impulsive he had done on Christmas Eve. It made him one of her lame ducks. In a rage at his uncle, Congressman Ben Hardin who had just made him his law partner, he had tossed his career away in a spate of words, packed his saddlebags and departed in a snowstorm without plan or destination. The cause of the quarrel was a slave boy whom Ben Hardin had had whipped. Unjustly, Parker thought. He had denounced his uncle before whites and blacks. He could never return to that place. The door was shut.

"Would you do it again?" Jane probed. They were riding, returning from a call on one of her friends. "Now that you've had time to think, would you throw so much away to stand by a Negro boy you don't even own?"

"You've got to do those things," he answered, not very articulate on the subject. "If you don't believe in the whip, you've got to try to abolish it."

"I know. Sometimes when I face up to men who're beating their horses I'm frightened. But I have to do it just the same. Will you own slaves?"

"I suppose so. My father lives on a plantation near Springfield, and he has a young Negro couple for me. They're legally married to each other of their own choice. They'd as soon come to live with me as not. Their names are Reuben and Mary. Reuben's grandfather was an African chieftan named Sambo—one of my forebears bought him from a ship's captain in Virginia when the Hardins lived near the coast. All his descendants have stayed in our family. Reuben is ebony and stately. He's got a temper like the famous Sambo. The other slaves fear him."

"Sometimes I wonder about slavery," Jane said. "Do you?"

"I think it ought to be ended by legislation, no matter what the cotton planters say. But of course those Africans captured and sold each other. That was the start of the thing, I've heard, but I wouldn't swear to the truth of it."

"People say the Bible teaches slavery," Jane offered. "I don't get the straight of it, but I think it hinges on interchanging the words slave and servant. 'Slaves, submit yourselves to your masters,' and all that."

"Negroes are more discerning than most people realize," Parker commented. "And on the whole, they're not cruel like Indians. I dislike Indians." He then proceeded to narrate the bloody Hardin

69

saga to illustrate his prejudice, the story of an old enmity between the Indians and his forebears that had taken many lives.

Jane then told about the Montgomery massacre, for she was not to be outdone. Her manner of telling the story, now in whispers, now in a rush of terrible detail, now with somber gestures for the aftermath—all this fascinated Parker. It was the nearest he had ever come to attending the theatre.

"I'd like very much to meet your Grandmother Casey who took part in that fracas," he requested.

"I'll try to take you there sometime," Jane demurred, suddenly reticent. She did not want to introduce this young man to her grandmother as if he were somebody special. For all that she liked him so much, she was only using him, she realized, trying to alarm Richard Barret. She would not do such a thing except that her infatuation for Barret had turned to love, and she was desperate for ways to prick him.

That summer she went to Green County to visit and attend a dance. Parker Hardin dutifully appeared at the festivity, as did her cousin Andrew Russell, whose devotion was more beau-like than cousinly. She flaunted their attentions, making herself conspicuous before Richard Barret and his two sisters, impeccable young ladies with suitable escorts. She saw that every one met Mr. Hardin, her eligible new conquest. She could not even fan herself or carry her own gloves.

Richard Barret followed her about, seeming perturbed and bewildered. Bewildered he truly was; by his yearning for this girl, by her flirtations, her threat to his ambitions, and his father's oft-hinted warnings in regard to her. All of his values were in conflict and he could not untangle or appraise them.

To do him justice, he was only eighteen years of age, a few months younger than Jane Lampton; but seemingly years older, for he was strikingly large and well-built, like a knight full-fledged for conquest. He was precocious too and was given to talking down to Jane; though gently and guardedly, for her flashing wit might trip him if he patronized. He was ready for marriage, but he must forego it, and that was his personal dilemma. These

70

conflicts attended him as he danced with the distracting creature and eyed her anxiously.

Jane returned to her native village somewhat encouraged. She had made Richard Barret miserable.

It was now time to release Parker Hardin from his bondage, especially as he was becoming importunate in his wooing, and fate served her well. A social mishap overtook him, a comedy of errors that disrupted his courtship.

Midway between the villages of Columbia and Greensburg there was a "meetinghouse" called Mount Gilead, used by several Protestant persuasions. The young people often journeyed to the little chapel, as much to see each other as to hear the gospel preached.

One Sunday afternoon such a group, well mounted and wearing their best clothes, was returning home to Columbia, Jane Lampton and Parker Hardin in the lead. Russell Creek was at low season, but Jane could not let well enough alone and ford it; she must find a clear water hole where the horses could drink. By chance her spirited horse stepped on a crooked stick on a sand bar, shied, reared, and threw her backward into the water. Parker, to pick her up, had to wade around his own horse and hers, and by the time he had reached her she had recovered from her fright and was surveying her ruined clothes—a bonnet unsuitably trimmed with flowers and white satin ribbons, a dress of lilac Canton silk, tricked out with ruffled petticoats.

Jane might have stormed and ranted over the rack of her finery, but the sight of her escort sent her into hysterics of a different sort. She burst into wild laughter and kept it up, begging one and all to "look at Parker!" It was not malice. She merely could not control herself. Indeed, Parker was worth looking at. While hastening to the aid of his submerged lady he had lost his tall silky beaver hat and was horrified to see it bobbing away downstream. Jane could wait, but the hat could not. He chased it, retrieved it and clapped it on his head, a desperate clown in painful pantomime. The hat was his joy, his pride. Jane had thought it funny from the first, especially when he wore it ahorseback, for no one in town or county had one like it except Mr. Goodrich

Lightfoot, the Tuckahoe attorney. And now, topping Parker like a leaking chimney, it was shedding rivulets of creek water and accenting his doleful appearance.

Jane expected him to lift her to her horse, but he stood still, shaken with anger. All of his new friends were swaying in their saddles from laughter, caring nothing for his wounded dignity. Especially hilarious over his plight was Patsy Lampton's escort James Trabue, a gay blade destined for the ministry but not yet heeding the call.

It was Jack Waggoner, arriving with another party, who waded into the creek and tossed Jane onto her saddle.

It was coming on to thunder and lightning and pour rain, and the horses were pushed to their limit. Conversation was impossible. When Jane told Parker good-by at her Uncle Lewis's door she saw that she had grievously offended him. She had not intended it, but so it had happened.

"He sees me now for what I am," she told Patsy when they had reached their room. "A flibbertigibbet flirt that's used him. I doubt if a girl could ridicule a man she loves. No, she never could."

"Well, now he knows," Patsy said.

Hardin did know, and he accepted it gallantly, even before he received a scented note telling him the cruelly kind truth: *Let us be friends only, for I can never care for you the other way.*

Jane was now guilt-free, aged eighteen years and several months, unencumbered by a conspicuous suitor. She served again as a wedding attendant. That meant nothing more than standing up with the bride in a made-over frock (for no money had been forwarded by Benjamin for a new one) but it caused her a unique uneasiness. It reminded her that the teasing phrase "Often a bridesmaid, never a bride" might cease to be funny as time went on. After one was twenty, say.

Her affair with Richard Barret began to flourish like a honeysuckle vine gone wild. All could see and speculate; all did. Would Adair County's unpredictable Miss Lampton, its near-hoyden darling, capture this prize? Perhaps she would, for he had eyes for nobody else. Some wagers were laid.

Aunt Anne Montgomery, when giving Jane new clothes to replace those spoiled in the creek, extracted a promise from her, the right hand lifted toward Heaven in a combination of legal and pious swearing, never to be alone with "that boy" until he proposed marriage.

Jane respected promises. In keeping this one to Aunt Anne she cast herself in a flashy role hardly foreseen by her anxious relatives. Though she kept to the open spaces, she encouraged endearments there. She was indeed careful not to be alone with Richard Barret, but they held hands in public as if nothing mattered except their touching one another. She was oblivious of criticism, or cleverly pretended to be. Once, during a day-long picnic at a charming retreat in Green County known as "The Drip," a fairy cove of a place with waterfall and pool and dell, she tucked her wading clothes well above her knees and displayed her beautifully tapered legs. And as if that were not enough for one day: where the waters of three springs fell over the projecting cliff, she and Richard Barret were seen kissing tenderly in the mists. . . . At other times they gave a new fillip to horseback riding, racing their horses at a challenge from Jane, taking fences and ditches that others avoided, and snatching eager kisses when he overtook her.

Afterward Jane was to claim that Richard was too shy to speak his love. If he failed, it was hardly shyness that restrained him, but caution. He was counting the weeks until he should enter Transylvania College—his fixed intent from boyhood.

10 ❖

On the first Monday in November, that autumn, the Clerk of Adair County recorded the fact that John M. Clemens was permitted to practice as an attorney in that court, he having produced a legal license and taken the necessary oath. To the young man himself it was a satisfying event. Touchingly so. It stamped him with gentility; it might send him to high places.

John Clemens was becoming more sociable; was learning to

dance and converse, was trying to be less stilted for the good of his career. Most of his associates had been friends and neighbors of the Hancocks, but now he wished to branch out. He looked about him. . . . Jane Lampton knew a good many people. He thought that was why he asked her for engagements. Jane found him rather appealing, and when she had nothing better to do she would entertain him in Aunt Jen's parlor with Patsy and some of their friends at games and singing. In return, he gave Uncle Lewis free legal advice.

John Clemens had gone to board with Mr. John Field, a useful citizen who had built too large a house a decade ago at Fortune Street and Pinckney Alley and must now rent rooms in it. Mrs. Field permitted the young lawyer to take his clients up her gracious cherry stairway to his big front bedroom, where he had a desk, his certificate hanging neatly above it.

During that winter of 1822–23 we can leave John Marshall Clemens to his orderly chores while he falls gropingly in love with disorderly Miss Lampton, hardly wishing to and not knowing why.

One day late in March, Patsy went to the store of Field and Creel to select a length of dress material, Aunt Anne having given her the price of it as a birthday gift. Jane had remained at home, writing a letter to some distaff cousins near Greensburg whom she hoped to visit, if she could wrest the invitation. They were the Allen Montgomerys, who had a calling acquaintance with the Barrets.

Jane was startled when Patsy burst wildly into the room, looking distraught. "What on earth, Patsy?" she called in alarm.

"Uncle Lewis is ruined," Patsy sobbed. "I've just heard it. Oh, what's to become of us, Jane? First Papa, now Uncle Lewis!"

"Tell me what you heard, Patsy! It's just a rumor, I expect. *Where* did you hear it?"

"At Field and Creel. I was behind a counter, looking at their dress goods. You know how I keep going there to look, because I can't decide between the green stripe and the pink sprig. A shawl that was hanging on a rack must have hid me. Some men were talking, but I paid no mind till I heard them say Uncle Lewis's name. Then I listened. 'Lewis Lampton is done for,' one of them said. It was Mr. John Grissom, who was a town trustee with Uncle Lewis. He went on to say how William Caldwell has foreclosed on the Eagle House, and this dwelling too. And the Bell brothers have foreclosed on the furniture. He said he had seen the furniture listings. Then he ran through the list, Jane, and as near as I can remember he said two sideboards, twenty beds, eighty chairs, some desks and commodes and cupboards. Tables, of course. And he even mentioned the big grandfather clock."

"Oh, no," Jane moaned. "There must be a mistake."

"It's all true, I tell you. Mr. William Hurt was in the group. And so was Mr. Winfrey who has the tobacco warehouse on Green River. Mr. Hurt said, 'Poor Lewis! he let his brothers bleed him white.' And Philip Winfrey said, 'Where's Benjamin and Wharton now, I wonder?' Then they must have seen me standing there. Everything got dead quiet, and they went out in a hurry. They looked to be sorry."

While Patsy wept dismally on the bed, Jane paced the floor. Presently she sat down, tore up the letter she had written, took a fresh sheet and wrote another. She got up and put on her coat.

"What are you going to do, Jane?" Patsy asked.

"I'm going to mail this letter to the Allen Montgomerys."

"I mean, what are you going to do in the long run, Jane?"

"I'm going to get married."

"Who to?"

"Richard Barret, of course. He's fixing to enter medical school at the spring term. I must go to Greensburg and see him before he packs to go to Lexington. I'll tell him what's happened. Then he'll have to ask me to marry him right away."

"What makes you think he'll do it, Jane?"

"Because he loves me. When a man loves a girl he'll give his very life to rescue her from trouble. Don't you know that, Patsy? Don't you know anything?" She went out and raced down the stairs with her letter, to catch the twice-a-week post.

Patsy wept on. She could not think of anybody she wanted to marry. Besides, she was still too young, not quite sixteen. She would have to go and live with Grandmother Casey. And how could she endure it, with Jane in Green County, married to Richard Barret?

When the invitation came from the Allen Montgomerys after what seemed an eternity to Jane but was only a fortnight, she packed a valise and caught the first stage. The Montgomerys seemed only moderately glad to see her, and this was humiliating, but circumstances forced her to use them. The following morning she donned her riding habit, borrowed their best horse, and went to town.

Stopping at the saddler's she dismounted and had a rip sewn in her glove. At one of the stores she bought a quarter-pound of tea, gallantly impoverishing herself but achieving two things: a little gift for her hostess and a discreet display of herself in the public square. She could reasonably expect to encounter Richard Barret, for though he lived at Rock Castle Farm, the family home, he usually rode to the village every morning for chores or sociability. He was vain of his horsemanship.

Jane was seen, hallooed, detained, chatted with by a number of persons, male and female. Sure enough, word quickly reached Richard Barret, and he came riding his big bay horse to the place where she was sitting her mount before the store and holding a little court. She was in the midst of telling a story about Sheriff Hugh French on a possum hunt, adding embellishments to the tale as she had heard it, when she saw Barret riding toward her, barehead, handsome, quizzical. She left a sentence hanging in the air while she smiled at him. The others went away, leaving them together. Afterward, Jane's friend Mary Brawner Carlile said of that meeting, "All at once none of us counted, and we knew it. Jane had come for something, and Richard Barret understood. 'Well?' we heard him say. And she said a funny thing in answer. 'The sun on your head,' she said, 'makes you look like your own ancestor that you told me about—master of the flagship *Jesus* with Sir Francis Drake.' Then they rode off together somewhere."

It was to the Allen Montgomery farm that they went. Jane had the situation well in hand, and she was keeping her promise to Aunt Anne. She was propriety itself as she told Richard he might accompany her the few miles.

76

They tied their horses and sat on the stile, within plain view of the front windows. "I wonder if you've heard what's happened to us, Richard?" Jane asked pell-mell. "To my family, I mean."

"My father told me yesterday. Because of his banking connections he hears a good deal. I'm mighty sorry, Jane."

He fell silent while he thought uncomfortably of his father's news: how "the crazy Lamptons," as Mr. Barret called them, had finally hung themselves with their own mortgages. Not even Elsey Creel, their lawyer, had been able to save them in this final crash, so Mr. Barret had pointed out; they were finished. And his next words had been, "Benjamin Lampton's elder daughter has been your chosen company for a year now. Your sisters tell me she's after you. They say she's attractive and unusual. Can you explain the term *unusual?*"

"Hardly, sir," Richard had answered, not caring to try. Nor in after years would he be any more able to define the essence of her attraction for him; he would know only that she was his first, his great love; and that when he had forsaken her for his ambitions, there would begin to visit him the occasional dark rages which he could not explain nor wholly control.

The senior Barret was not intentionally a tyrant in dealing with his children. He was merely a just and zealous man too richly endowed for comfort. He had more than his share of educated ancestors and had fallen into the error of supposing a good education to be the magic yeast that caused the Barret loaf to rise. In this he undervalued the family drive and rectitude; with the merest rudiments they would have succeeded. His father, the Reverend Robert Barret, educated at Oxford, had been a devout rector of the Established Church and a Virginia landowner, married to Anne Lee, cousin to Lighthorse Harry. William Barret himself, a William and Mary graduate before coming out to Kentucky, had married Dorothy Winston, a second cousin of Patrick Henry's, and had served in the Revolution as a captain of rangers under Francis Marion. The Barrets did their duty wherever duty lay, and they married their kind. It was unthinkable to Mr. William Barret of Green County that his children would not carry on in the tradition. His sense of duty had consigned Richard

Ferrell, his most promising son, to the medical profession with the boy's full co-operation. His worldly ambition had speculated on a good marriage for him. He regarded the Lampton girl as a menace. Certainly, he admitted to Richard, she inherited stout blood from the Scotch Montgomerys and from Colonel Casey, her homespun, incorruptible grandfather. But old Casey was dead and gone, his influence dissipated with the passing of the Kentucky frontier; and the Montgomerys spat among themselves for small holdings. As for the Lamptons, he was aware that they were as proud of their ancestry as the Barrets were of theirs, and they were gentlemen. But say that, Mr. Barret argued, and you had said all. They were uneducated, unbusinesslike, reckless with a dollar, given to frivolity, and downright eccentric. This redheaded girl was a Lampton in little. If she got Richard before he had his education, it would be over his father's dead body, so Mr. Barret had indicated.

"Well, Richard?" Jane said from the stile step, her head high, her heart pounding. It was the challenge, not evadable.

"There's never been any girl but you, Jane," he declared. Yet he stopped there, seeming to sign this beautiful declaration with a period.

Jane pushed on. "I know that's the truth, Richard. I'd not have come if it wasn't so. Pride would have stopped me."

"Just what have you come *for*, Jane? What do you expect of me?"

"Don't dare ask me that. You're the one to speak."

"I will then, though some things are better left unsaid. You expect me to propose marriage. But how can I when I've got four years of medicine ahead of me? We'd have to wait that out, to get married. That's the reason I've not proposed."

"Do you mean you'd put schooling before love, Richard?" A genuine, a profound wonder colored her voice, for she was puzzled to distraction. "You'd rather have college than me?"

"Yes," he answered firmly. "Yes, for now. I'll need three years at Transylvania with Dr. Daniel Drake. Think of it, Jane, I'm to live in the great man's house while I study! Then I'll go to a Philadelphia hospital for a year, to watch the surgeons work."

78

Brought back to earth by her nonplused silence, he asked, "Am I selfish to expect you to wait?"

"Yes," she answered angrily, "and cruel too. Or don't you understand my situation, Richard? In a few weeks I won't have a roof over my head."

"Come now, Jane. There's your grandmother's plantation."

"It's Uncle Green's now, and his wife's the mistress there. I tell you, I've got no home, Richard."

He stepped down from the stile and began to pace the roadway. "I'll talk to my father about it," he said agitatedly.

"And ask his permission? I can hardly keep from laughing, Richard. I'm the last girl in our set he'd choose for you. He's downright hostile to me. Are you scared to face life without his backing? Are you afraid to elope?"

"Afraid to elope? I've never thought of it!" He reached for her hand, and his face was quick and eager.

"I've thought of it, Richard. It would solve everything." She was asking him to take a ditch with her, and he was still following. "You'd find a way to make a plain living like other men. Or must you be rich and important?"

"I must be important, I think." He dropped her hand and made a gesture of futility. "A man needs a profession, Jane. Our family believes in getting the best education available. Take the Barrets in comparison with the—"

He supposed he had stopped in time, but he had not. "You take the Barrets," Jane said sweetly. "I'll take the Lamptons."

He failed to notice the edgy words or the suppressed storm in her voice and so he went on stupidly, "I'll talk to my father again. Maybe he'll give us something to live on while I'm in college. . . . But I doubt if he would, he's against early marriages. I must be out of my head to think of such a thing."

"I hate you," Jane said evenly. "And I hate your father. I hate the very name of Barret. No—don't try to touch me, just go. You're a wonderful milksop, and I should have known."

Furiously he untied his horse and mounted and rode away.

"Richard!" she called ringingly, already penitent. But he kept to his course. He used his spur, a thing which she hated.

She put her borrowed horse to pasture, went indoors, and smiled too brightly at her hostess.

Mrs. Montgomery looked at her curiously. "Wasn't that young Barret? I was just about to go out and invite him to come in."

"He had to be off," Jane replied in a measured way, and the words, like a line from a ballad, echoed curiously in the room. It was thus young men were spoken of when they went to war, or to the West, or to another state to claim an inheritance.

"We hear you've given up all your beaus for Richard Barret," Mrs. Montgomery said probingly. "You're engaged to him, naturally?"

"No," Jane answered.

"Everybody thinks you are. The courtship's been right showy, we've heard."

"Showy?" But Jane knew what she meant. Because she had discarded the rules, because she had loved Richard so dotingly, she had made a jilted woman of herself for two counties to pity. It hardly signified, though. The only thing that mattered was to get even, to wound him as deeply as he had wounded her. She would marry somebody at once.

In a trance she walked and talked and ate and slept in the house of her puzzled cousins until the next stage stopped, to take her back to Columbia.

11 ❖

When Jane boarded the stage wagon she shared her cross-bench with two men whom she knew. As was the custom, the lady sat between, giving the men the weather seats. Ordinarily Jane would have talked to those passengers, one of them being Mr. Morgan Morgan, as emphatic as his name, the other being elderly Mr. Flowers who owned Flowers' Ferry on Green River and always had an adventure to tell. But she spoke to them absently and hardly noticed when they conversed above her head. She was immersed in her own thoughts, wrestling with her consuming problem: whom to marry.

Her chances had been squandered, her eligibles diminished. Robert Todd, Scotch-wild but attractive to demure girls as well as bold, had fallen away as soon as he noticed her preference for Barret, and now he was courting Betsey Burk under the watchful eye of her father. Andrew Russell too was unavailable. He had protested her using him as a means of getting to Greensburg and had quit her last fall. Straightway he had succumbed to the wiles of a Miss Elizabeth Echols, whom he was going to marry next week. Next week! Never again, Jane realized, could she make a convenience of Andy.

Parker Hardin remained. Or did he? Lately he had begun to be attentive to Mary Ann Waggoner. Could he be reclaimed? . . . So ran Jane's thoughts in a treadmill.

The monstrosity of marrying for revenge eluded her. She had suffered a chill from Richard's rejection, a spiritual shock, and nothing warmed or revived her but the thought of repaying him. She was not herself. As the difficulties of accomplishing her purpose increased, so did her determination. She could not have been more dedicated if she had been planning Robertson's Academy's spring picnic.

When she alighted from the stage at the Eagle House and gave her valise to Toby, a girl came running across the square, calling to her. It was Mary Ann Waggoner. Jane summoned up a smile and waited for Mary Ann to talk.

"I came to town this morning with my father," Mary Ann said, "and I was hoping to see you, but Patsy said you'd gone to Greensburg. Did you have fun?"

"Well, no," Jane answered guardedly. "Maybe the moon wasn't right. What have you got in the hatbox?"

"A hat, silly. For Andy Russell's wedding."

"You look happy about it," Jane remarked.

"Oh, it's a sweet hat, Jane. I'd like for you to see it."

"Show it, then," Jane said, but she did not invite Mary Ann to come in. "Put the box on the step there, and open it."

Mary Ann did so, for she was a docile girl, devotedly subject to Jane's whims. She placed the little flowered conceit on her smooth blond hair and eyed Jane anxiously. "Is it becoming?"

"Yes, dear," Jane replied. "Who are you going with?"

"Parker Hardin. Oh, Jane, I'm so grateful to you for turning him down. I think he's beginning to like me a good deal. And it seems providential. I was the first girl he met, that Christmas night. Remember?"

"If I knew it, I'd forgotten it," Jane answered crisply. She hardened her heart against Mary Ann, a girl whose father owned a good plantation and doted on his children. She told herself that Mary Ann had more than her share of this world's luck—beauty and means. She would have to deprive her of Parker Hardin, because she, Jane Lampton, needed him worse. She needed him for the humbling of Richard Barret. "See here, Mary Ann," she said, "what makes you think I'm rid of Parker Hardin, or want to be?"

"Oh, Jane! Aren't you?"

Jane saw panic in Mary Ann's sweet and unguarded face. It was like a kitten begging not to be stepped on. She's fallen in love with Parker, Jane thought in wonder. Compassion touched her, and she knew she could not do what she had intended. It was too bad; the Hardin name would have impressed Mr. Barret: more Hardins than Barrets had died in the wars; and where was there a Barret County? "I was only teasing you, Mary Ann. Parker and I have been quits ever since the day I fell in Russell Creek. That broke us up, somehow."

Mary Ann laughed and seized her hand. "I'm glad, Jane! And I'm happy. I reckon you understand how it feels to be in love. Why else would you go to Greensburg, every chance?"

"Let me go, dear. I'm tired enough to drop. Here, let me help you tie up your hatbox." She felt leaden with defeat.

She watched Mary Ann cross the square, waved to her, and turned to enter Uncle Lewis's door. Out of that door came John M. Clemens, and his pleasure at seeing her was a wondrous thing.

"So you're back from your cousins'!" he said. "I've been indoors talking to your uncle. I'm his lawyer now. He said he didn't know what day to expect you home."

"No, I reckon he didn't, John. I got tired of Green County sooner than usual, and I caught the first stage." She looked at

John Marshall Clemens intently, and all at once she knew he would do if she could bring it about. Strange, she had thought of him for Patsy, but never for herself. He had not spoken a sentimental word to her in her life, yet he was looking at her ardently. Yes, he would do wonderfully. He was rather sweet, he was a gentleman, he had a profession. A man needs a profession, Richard had said.

"You look tired, Jane," Clemens observed tenderly.

"I worry so about poor Uncle Lewis losing everything."

"I'm sure you do. It's a sad havoc. But the Lamptons haven't done anything dishonorable, Jane. They've merely lacked shrewdness. Your Uncle Lewis is as fine a gentleman as I ever came across."

"Thank you, John." How good it was to hear a Lampton spoken of in praise, how comforting, how healing to the pride! She looked at the speaker gratefully, meltingly.

"Jane, I have your uncle's consent to address you. Is there any hope for me?"

"Of course," she said breathlessly. All her life she would remember the feeling of gratitude that his courtly proposal aroused in her. It was almost like love in its intensity.

They were both rather stunned, it had happened so quickly. But John saw nothing unwomanly in Jane's quick acceptance; from earliest memory he had been used to quick and forthright decisions from his Quaker mother. "Come and walk with me," he said to Jane, and he put her hand in the crook of his arm and led her away. Walking thus, oblivious of some surprised observers, they climbed High Street hill to the academy, descended to the village by way of Fortune Street, and came up short at Pinckney Alley. Here, in a semirustic setting, stood the good brick house of Mr. and Mrs. Field, where John boarded. He surveyed it with pride. "This is where I'll bring you to live," he said.

They stood in the lee of a large lilac tree, and so were private. "It's the handsomest house in town," Jane declared. She looked at it speculatively. Pinckney Alley was still a grassy path, and it would be some years before Mr. Field's mistake in facing his house upon it would be apparent. "The handsomest and the tallest

house in town; though maybe Dr. Gaither has a finer fanlight."
(She could hear someone saying to Richard Barret right soon,
*He's taken her to live at the big Field house. He must be doing
well.*) "But what will you do for a law office when I come to live
with you?" She blushed, but went on practically, "Can the Fields
let you have another room?"

"I think they can, Jane. By the way, your father's coming. At
least we expect him. Mr. Lewis needs to have him here for
County Court day, May fifth. I've written him a letter to that
effect."

"Then he could give me away Tuesday, May sixth," Jane said
thoughtfully. "Would that date suit you, John?"

"Yes, dear," he answered, dizzy with astonishment and delight.
He had expected a longer engagement.

"You can kiss me now," Jane said, and she went on tiptoe to
help him, for he was tall. He drew her to him and kissed her
tenderly, and lost himself in the happiest dream of his life.

Walking back to Lewis Lampton's house he confided, "The
Lampton failure is an unfortunate thing, and I regret it, but it
gives me the chance to serve you when you're in trouble. The way
I served my mother when my father was struck down. I was only a
little boy, but she leaned on me." His gray-green eyes narrowed
in poignant recollections he could not share. "I was only a little
boy but, young as I was, she needed me till she married Hancock."

Jane saw then that John Clemens valued her the more because
of her homeless, dowerless state, and this astonished and touched
her. Was there not an odd nobility in him, to count a woman's
lacks among her assets? She must remember that.

She parted from him at the Lampton door and went inside.
In the parlor she encountered her Uncle Lewis, resting in a chair
and looking pallid. She could not prevent him from rising.

"Why, Jane," he said, "I didn't know you'd returned home.
Did you come in the Barret carriage?"

"By the stage. I never expect to ride in the Barret carriage,
Uncle Lewis. Never, never, never."

"Oh. So that's the way it's turned out. I'm sorry, dear child."
He was trying to think what was expected of him, *in loco parentis,*

84

for he never shirked a family duty. "Do you want me to talk to young Barret or his father?"

"Heavens, no, Uncle Lewis! Richard and I agreed to part. He's going to be a doctor. That's all there is to it."

"I'm thankful to know your heart's not involved, Jane. While you were away, a very fine young man asked to propose to you."

"John Clemens. And I've just accepted him, Uncle Lewis. We've set the date for May sixth, if Papa gets here in time."

"Dear me!" Lewis Lampton was shocked and charmed.

"He proposed soon after I got off the stage, Uncle Lewis, and then we took a walk and settled things. He'll take me to live at the Fields' where he boards and has his law office."

Lewis Lampton's face lit up happily. Weary, ill, imposed upon, financially ruined though he was, he could envision a rainbow for another. "Ah, the law," he said. "That's where success lies, Jane. There's a fortune in it! And if Clemens chooses politics, let the Senate be his goal!"

One of his little boys—James, the middle one, especially loved by Jane—had come quietly into the room and was gazing at his father fondly. He was absorbing the philosophy that would emerge through Colonel Sellers.

Jane went to the John Montgomerys' next morning, and told her aunt of her plans to marry John Marshall Clemens. The news was received with chilly reserve. Anne Montgomery said little but looked volumes. Volumes of what? Jane could not tell. Aunt Anne had tried to keep abreast of her affair with Richard Barret; no doubt she was wondering now where she had lost the scent.

Mrs. Casey was yet to be informed, and Jane put off the chore from day to day. Others would have broken the news to her, but Jane knew a Lampton announcement was in order. She asked Patsy to be her emissary, and she begged Aunt Jen' Lampton to go with Patsy "for company." Aunt Jen' consented. She was very fond of young Mr. Clemens; and as for Jane's sudden switching of beaux, she was not a woman to question another woman's motives for choosing a mate. She was merely surprised that Jane had chosen such a practical young man.

Patsy and Aunt Jen' set out lightheartedly enough, riding the last two saddle horses in Lewis's stable and considering themselves to be the bearers of good news. But they returned crestfallen a few hours later.

"Your grandmother was very short with me," Mrs. Lampton reported. "She said Lewis and I showed bad judgment, to encourage such a hasty marriage. She said she withholds her consent."

"What else did she say, Aunt Jen'?" Jane asked nervously.

"She said 'Mercy on us!' and 'Tut, tut,' mostly. She wants to see you right away, Jane."

"My horse is still saddled," Patsy said. "You'd better go and get it over with."

Patsy felt a new and unexplainable uneasiness. Jane's sudden turn to John Clemens had surprised but hardly bewildered her, for Jane had not confided in her during the past year, and she herself had substituted other confidantes for Jane, such being the sisterly way of growing up. Jane's only divulgence to her had been brought on by Uncle Lewis's losses; she had declared that Richard Barret loved her madly, or something to that effect, and that she would go to Greensburg and wrest a proposal of marriage from him before he took off for college. But Richard had failed the test, apparently, and John M. Clemens had stepped in at the right time. It enabled Jane to save face. That Jane was going to marry attractive and promising Mr. Clemens in a big hurry had made sense to practical Patsy until Grandmother raised her eyebrows. What did Grandmother suspect? What did she fear?

Jane soon found out if Patsy did not.

When Jane arrived at the plantation she sought out Abraham and asked him to take care of her horse. "This makes twelve miles Brownie's traveled today," she said, "and there'll be four more on the return to town." She watched him rub down and water the horse, taking pleasure in the grateful fleck of the animal's ears. She loved horses too dearly, but what could she do about it?

Abraham, who had taught her to cobble, showed her some shoes he was making for a young Paxton, and she lingered to examine them. If only she might spend an hour or two here with Abraham instead of arguing with Grandmother! For argue they must, she had decided. She would not be dissuaded from marrying next week just because the old lady liked long engagements.

"Close the door, Jane," Mrs. Casey instructed her as she had done five years before when discussing another marriage. "Then come here and sit near me."

The Widow Montgomery-Casey inspected her eldest grandchild closely, scrutinized her slim figure from every angle. "I've never seen you look slenderer, Jane. If anything has happened, it has just happened. I'm thankful for that. Tongues are clacking. Let's not beat around the bush."

Jane sat staring at her, astonished, angry, tongue-tied.

"Your Uncle Green is capable of taking care of the Barrets, Jane! If it's young Barret you ought to wed, don't shield him. It would be wrong to let him off. It's not seemly for you to marry a trusting young man like Clemens if you've sinned with the Barret boy."

Jane was now bemused. So that's what people were saying. Not merely that she had been jilted, which she was prepared for; but that she had gotten into trouble and was marrying John Clemens as a way out. She thought of those cases of wronged girls that sometimes came up in court; a half dozen of them within her memory, perhaps more when the county was new. The bastardy charges were invariably brought by English fathers, she had heard said, "because the English think the law should settle everything." The girl's father brought the suit to make the boy acknowledge paternity and pay a pittance for the child's support; and the reason back of that was, the girl was thus legally proven to be not promiscuous, and in the larger sense was still a good girl; and so the law triumphed as a means of justice. But, strangely, there had never been a Scottish guardian in Adair County who took such a case to court. The indiscreet girl's father or brother or uncle, or a cousin of the blood, always "took care of things" and somehow brought the tardy lover to the altar. That was what Grandmother was offering in Uncle Green's name, in the manner of the Scottish pioneers.

When Jane thought this out, she was not angry any more, or

resentfully silent. "But I'm a virgin, Grandmother," she said patiently. "It's just that Richard has decided to do without me."

"Forgive me, child." The old lady folded her hands in her lap and lowered her lids, either in prayer or contemplation. Presently she opened her eyes and said, "Come and stay with me, Jane, while your hurt pride mends. You'll be welcome here. Don't enter into a loveless marriage to cover a jilting."

"You still don't understand, Grandmother. I'm not trying to cover the jilting. I'm getting revenge."

"To wed for spite! You'll pay for it, Jane."

"Oh, surely not. It's Richard's turn to pay. When he hears I've given myself to John Clemens he'll suffer as he deserves to. He loves me, but he let his father come between us. He's broken my heart, that's all. I'll not be able to make him suffer in the years ahead, he'll have forgotten me. It's only now I can do it. I've got no weapon but *the now*."

Mrs. Casey was startled by the girl's passion and bitterness. "What a fine mess of love gone to waste!" she marveled. After a silence she renewed her efforts. "The Bible has an answer for all this, Jane. Forgiveness." And she talked of forgiveness; she talked of God's grace that follows it. But she saw how her words fell on deaf ears.

"You're a willful creature," she said in defeat. "And you've never joined the church. Patsy has joined, but you've held off. Does it all tie up, I wonder?"

"I must start home now, Grandmother," Jane said cheerfully.

"Are you bound to marry John Clemens next Tuesday, as they say? Let me get it straight."

"Yes, I'm bound to, Grandmother. If my father comes, or not."

"Then promise me this, Jane, in the name of all the good women you descend from: as you make this bed, you will lie on it."

"I promise. I'll take John Clemens for better or worse."

"I must be satisfied with that, I suppose. Would you like to be married here in the plantation parlor? Your mother would want that. She used to say, 'My girls can be married here.'"

Jane accepted graciously. With her strange ability to extract

88

every drop of honey from any of life's bittersweet moments, she fell to planning her wedding. "I'll have Patsy as my maid," she said. "And Mary Brawner Carlile will be my matron."

"Ain't young Mrs. Carlile expecting a baby?" Mrs. Casey asked.

"It hardly shows, Grandmother. I want Mary Brawner, if you don't mind. She's a close friend of mine. And she'll represent Green County."

"Oh yes. Green County must hear about this wedding, by all means!" Mrs. Casey spoke acidly. "Oh yes, indeed!" But she added resignedly, "We'll find a scarf for the lady."

"And oughtn't I ask Mary Ann Waggoner and Cynthia Bowmer?"

"Two attendants are enough!" Mrs. Casey pronounced with a show of temper, for Jane had finally worn her out. "And keep your company to twenty-five or thirty people. Remember, I'm not the housekeeper here." She offered no wedding gown. Life must punish this girl for what she was about to do; it was inevitable. Let the punishment begin now with the simple lack of a wedding dress.

12 ❖

While Jane was at the plantation, her father and stepmother arrived in Columbia. They were installed at the Eagle House, but presently went to Lewis's house for a family conference. Patsy, overjoyed at seeing her father, sat beside him and clung to his hand. Lewis and Jen' completed the group, and Lewis announced Jane's impending marriage with appropriate formality.

"Young Clemens is an astute lawyer," he added, "or I'd not have asked him to represent the Lampton interests. His character is above reproach. His devotion to Jane is marked."

"I thought Jane was engaged to one of the Barret boys," Benjamin said, puzzled. "From a letter she wrote me last November, I judged she found him entirely to her liking. A letter from Anne Montgomery in February hinted at the same thing."

Polly Hays Lampton smelled a mouse. "Was there ever a betrothal?" she pounced, like a good cat. "Is there a broken engagement we've not heard of?"

"No," Lewis replied firmly. "The young man is simply not—" He made a sound like "available," quickly resorted to "eligible."

"Richard Barret is going to Transylvania College and study to be a doctor," Patsy explained, being frank as far as she went.

Aunt Jen' coughed delicately and began to talk of Lewis's disasters, a more vital issue to her. "We hardly know where to turn," she said, hoping Benjamin would help by repaying his loans.

Alas, Benjamin had come with empty pockets. But at least he was here, vulnerable to the arrow of censure.

Wharton had kept his distance. Nothing could have been helped by his coming; he would merely have filled another room in the hotel. He had winged in and out of Adair County too often: now raising a crop of tobacco on some land he had, now buying and selling town lots; and once, for an incredible half year, acting as jailer and convulsing the inmates with his British accent. Wharton was helpless without a few slaves to do his manual labor, and while he was the least demanding of masters, he often mortgaged his people to meet his debts, rendering himself temporarily useless for enterprise. At the moment, insolvent from a tavernkeeping venture in the neighboring town of Glasgow, he and his wife Diana and their ten children were sojourning with his irritated mother-in-law, old Mrs. Nancy Duncan, in Clark County.

Benjamin now broke the bad news that he had not been able to sell the property in Tennessee that had been their last hope. He referred to Lot Eleven in the town of Sparta, on which sat a good business house. The title's not clear," he confessed miserably. "The lawyers can't untangle it."

There was silence while this information was absorbed. Then, "Don't blame yourself too much for my plight," Lewis said to him. "I've been a lax innkeeper, giving credit, taking worthless notes. And Jen' and I have set too good a table."

Polly Lampton hastened to help Lewis condemn himself. "Yes, indeed, that's true. And you should have charged for the use of your assembly room, and for this parlor."

90

"That's true, Polly," poor Jen' sighed. "But Lewis is the soul of hospitality."

On a card table amidst them there lay, like a doom notice, the price placard that had hung in the public room since 1815. The justices had pegged prices that year; and though Lewis Lampton's inn was outstanding, he could charge no more than the poorest tavern on the highway. The sign stated:

A warm dinner with two or more courses, 25 cents
Cold do, 17 cents
Warm breakfast or supper with tea or coffee, 25 cents
Cold do, 17 cents
Lodging for night with clean sheets, 12½ cents
Stabelage and hay per night, 12½ cents
Corn or oats per gallon, 12½ cents
Wine, rum or French Brandy, per quart, 1.50 cents
Same per pint, 75 cents
Same per half pint, 50 cents
Whiskey, Peach or Apple Brandy per quart, 37½ cents
Same per pint, 25 cents
Same per half pint, 12½ cents
Cider oil per quart, 25 cents
Same per pint, 12½ cents
Beer or cider per quart, 12½ cents

Ordered that the several Tavern keepers sell agreeable
to the foregoing prices and do not exceed them.

"Even my livery stable has been mismanaged," Lewis said in a final burst of self-incrimination. "Too lavish with oats, by far!"

"What in the name of St. Jude will you do, Lewis?" Benjamin asked his harried brother. It was Jen' who answered him.

"Don't think we've got nowhere to go," she said with spirit. "The Gaithers want us to visit them for a month or two while Lewis looks around. We won't be on the street, I assure you." She glanced at Polly Hays Lampton when she spoke, reminding her that when her sister Martha Morrison had married Dr. Nathan Gaither she had done rather well. Dr. Gaither had a new house, ample and charming, enhanced by gardens and fruit trees. He had cheerfully offered to put his wife's sister and her family in the rooms over his kitchen wing, for he was fond of her and of Lewis.

"But we won't have to accept," Lewis declared. "Caldwell and the Bells are considering leasing me this house, with the furniture, so that I can take boarders. By crowding ourselves some, we could let two rooms and make expenses."

Jen' Lampton began to sob, an unusual exhibition in so cheerful a woman. "Now, now, Jen'!" Lewis said in distress, and he went and laid his face against hers.

"She's crying about their slaves," Patsy explained to her father. "She feels so sorry for them. For Sarah and Toby too."

"What's this?" Benjamin asked quickly. "My Sarah and Toby?"

For once Lewis spoke sharply. "If they are yours, Ben, then retrieve them for God's sake. I had to mortgage them to Milton Wheat soon after you signed them over to me. It's now or never."

"Then it's never," Benjamin said in abject humiliation.

"Our four people are of more concern to me than your two," Lewis stated. "They are now the property of William Caldwell. Dolly and her two older children, Delilah and Samuel, were Jen's dowry from her parents. She'd grown up with Dolly; she loves her like a friend. Jen' taught Dolly's Delilah to be a superior house-maid. The girl's not used to rough work—Jen's fears for her health. And you recall little Tom, born here? Your Toby's the father, it seems."

"I recall them all, of course," Benjamin said. "This is sad."

"And a living example of the evils of this traffic," said his wife, looking the Lampton men in the eye. Like her brother, Dr. Hays, Polly Lampton often spoke out against the institution of slavery.

Things were in a somber way when Jane burst into the room and ran to her father. "Papa!" she cried joyfully, for she loved him very much. "And Aunt Polly," she said, dutifully kissing her.

The atmosphere cleared, and Lewis clapped his hands and summoned a servant. It was ironic that though they had lost their own, they still had several Negroes belonging to others—persons behind in their board or bar bills. There was a young woman named Rachel, encumbered with an infant that Jen' had taught to toddle;

and two male slaves belonging to young Burdette Willis, who had inherited them and used them for currency because his notes were overdue, promising to redeem them. They looked to be happy here.

Lewis ordered some French brandy fetched for his brother and himself. Jen' had tea brought for the women, and they fell to chatting of the journey up from Tennessee which had called for five fordings. The brothers, grown cheerful, drank to "poor Wharton."

"Now about this wedding!" Benjamin said jovially. "It means I'll have only one daughter to take back to Tennessee with me."

It was Patsy's moment, after all. Jane sat quiet, grateful for a reprieve, while Patsy asked about social life over the border. Now and then Patsy exclaimed with pleasure at something her father related; especially about a Quarles family in White County with a number of handsome sons and daughters.

That hour, to Jane, merged into others leading to Tuesday, the sixth day of May. Her wedding itself she would never recall very vividly, except that it was in the late afternoon, and she wore a last summer's dress, freshly laundered. And the Reverend Robertson kissed her forehead gently after he had performed the ceremony, as if forgiving her for rejecting his weekly invitations to join Shiloh Church and become a called and elected Presbyterian. And she would recall Uncle Green giving her ten dollars, for her own. And Grandmother being especially kind to the groom, who was pathetically happy, almost above himself.

But there was an incident preceding the wedding that stayed in her memory, like a symbol of the day.

She and her father went with John Clemens and his best man, Tom Cheek, to get the license at the courthouse. And while the three men were busy with the clerk, Jane sat down on a bench beside a woman who was crying and dabbing at her eyes with a torn handkerchief. She was Mrs. Halloway, Jane discovered, by asking.

"See here, miss," the woman said, holding out a slip of paper with a seal on it. "I've got a summons. Hard-up widows get them. It tells me to come here next month, and I daren't not come. Jean Lucky didn't come when summoned, and they bound out her little children just the same, only harsher for her not being here."

Jane took the proffered paper and read it. *A summons against Sally Halloway to cause her appearance here at the next term of this court, to show cause, if any she can, why her infant children, Henry, Ann, Serene and Melvina, now in her custody, should not be bound out as apprentices as the law directs.*

"How old are they, Mrs. Halloway?" Jane asked.

"I can hardly state their ages at the moment, I'm that upset. But the least girl is too little to lift a skillet. And Henry has just learned to handle an ax. He splits our wood, God love him, but he puffs from it, being so little. When they're bound out, away from me, I mayn't see them except a little while on Sundays when they're allowed to come to me, if they can walk so far."

Jane wept with her. Oh, God, she thought, mystified, why are You so hard on mothers, white and black?

13 ❖

John Clemens entered into a time of love and wonderment. He could not understand how he had obtained this desirable creature for his own. She was tender, docile, considerate of his moods and feelings. Standing in her chemise with her flaming hair tumbling around her shoulders, she was almost too lovely. When he caught her so, coming into the room when she was unaware, he assumed a judicial coldness to hide his delight.

He waited for her to criticize or nag him—that being the prerogative of brides, he had heard—but she never did. Rather, she praised and encouraged all his efforts. It seemed to him that she was forever looking for new ways to honor and serve him.

And not merely in private; Jane was affectionate toward him in public. This startled and discomfited him. It was the fly in the ointment. Digging deep into his memories, he was reminded of things that had happened years ago. His mother, newly married to Simon Hancock, had kissed the happy, sweaty farmer too ardently when he came from the fields—in the grape arbor, on the long back porch, wherever they happened to meet. Only he, of her children, had cared. His resentment had been intense, though he did not know if the jealousy he suffered had been for himself or his dead father. But Permelia Hancock, noticing his shocked eyes looking at her one day, had caught on. Thereafter she had desisted from any show of affection toward Simon in the presence of her children. She conformed to the pattern of behavior the boy expected of her. Thus she sanctioned in him an admiration for marital reserve.

Jane, an uninhibited Lampton, did not know she was opening an old wound. The Lamptons kissed when and where they chose.

John Clemens tried to be tactful in correcting her breaches of taste. "It will be just as well if you don't take my arm, Jane, unless there's a bad place in the road. Don't cling to me without reason."

"Oh?" She almost flared in anger.

"That sort of thing is out of place in broad daylight on a good brick sidewalk."

"I hadn't thought of it that way, John."

Another day he requested earnestly, "Don't make a point of meeting me at the gate when I've been to the courthouse. The front gate is hardly the place to kiss a husband. It's too public, with people passing. Wait for me in our room."

In our room. Jane learned early. He could be ardent enough in their room.

In another matter she caused him consternation without being aware of it. Her clothes were often strewn about. She had a mania for airing the dresses that could not be laundered, spreading the bodices wrong-side out to ventilate the boned linings. Sometimes when John entered the room he could not find a chair to sit on until she swept one clear for him. She had a habit, too, of stepping out of her shifts and petticoats and leaving them where they fell, to be gathered up for the clothes hamper at her convenience. It was her mother-in-law who brought this to her attention. Mrs. Hancock came to call one day (she was somehow kin to the Fields) and found the handsome big room in a state.

"This won't do, Jane," she scolded. "You'll make Marshall sorry you said yes. He's mighty orderly. Do see how fast you can pick up this room for him. Remember, it used to be all his."

"Yes, Mrs. Hancock," Jane agreed. "It *is* a sight, ain't it?"

They liked each other. Permelia's criticisms of Jane were usually made to Jane herself. Rarely to others, though they baited her. And never to Marshall, as she still called her son. She was thankful he had won the girl he wanted, imperfect though she was.

Jane had brought three cats to live with her at the Field house without asking permission of John or their hosts. One was partially blind from a fight he had lost to a larger cat. One had a bent leg from an encounter long ago with Uncle Lewis's terrier. The other was a nondescript little tabby; not battle-scarred but *enceinte;* Jane hoped to save the kittens from the customary end.

There was another animal that had won her solicitation because of his condition in life and his personality. He was an albinic mule living in a field on the other side of town; aged, worn in soul, body, and tooth, but alert enough to know her and watch for her coming. One evening, late for supper, she explained that she had been to see "old white Jerry" and had found him in need of attention. "There was a thorn in his ear that he couldn't get to, and he let me take it out. I'm his only friend."

Her hearers supposed she was talking about an aged man, worse off than a slave. "I'll send him some food the next time you go," Mrs. Field offered. "What does he need?"

"He craves maple sugar," Jane told her. "He's mad for it."

When it came out that Jerry was merely a broken-down mule, the table rocked with laughter, but John Clemens sat silent and embarrassed. He saw that his wife was capable of looking on animals as human and becoming involved with them.

Mr. and Mrs. Field valued Jane for the lift she gave their boardinghouse. A small eater, she was an animated talker. It had been an inconvenience to let John M. Clemens' bride replace his desk, and to put the big desk and the clients in the hall; but now it was done, they would not have had it any other way.

Benjamin and Polly and Patsy had long since gone to Tennessee. Jane was forming her new life as best she could—a doubly strange new life because dear gay familiar Patsy was no longer

96

sharing her room, and a sedate young man whom she hardly knew, a reader of Blackstone, had taken her place.

She was doing very well until Uncle Lewis fell sick and sent for her. Mrs. Field brought the news up to her room while John was at the courthouse. "Mr. Lampton's colored boy Frank says please to come to see your uncle right away. He says Mr. Lewis has got to talk to you. Can I help you dress, Jane?"

"I've only to tuck up my hair and change my shoes, Mrs. Field. What can Uncle Lewis want, I wonder?"

"He's right sick, we've heard. Sicker than Jen' lets on. This town would miss Lewis Lampton. They're missing him already from the town board. He resigned when he couldn't pay his taxes last year—it was the suitable thing, he said."

"Was that why he quit?"

"Yes, dear. But not before he got things in order. It was Lewis who arranged to have the veins of the public spring cleaned out, and the well mortared. A lot of folks are still dependent on that well. His clean livery stable has been an example to the town, and he's kept down the smells in Columbia by urging quicklime for privies. He's bought and given away quicklime by the ton, I reckon. If our alleys are clear, it's largely due to Lewis. And he's urged men not to spit on the courthouse floor."

Jane, puzzled at being summoned, put on her new spring hat and left hastily. She was hardly stirred by the recital of Uncle Lewis's civic improvements, having taken them for granted. She had always known him for a clean man, changing his shirts often.

Aunt Jen' took her up to the sickroom and left them alone.

"Sit by the window," Lewis invited. "Good girl, to come."

"You've got something to say to me, Uncle Lewis?"

"Yes, Jane. Best to tell it now. . . . You weren't jilted, quite. I turned the tables."

"What can you mean, Uncle Lewis?"

"The Barret boy. He wrote me a letter before your wedding. Said he'd reconsidered. Asked to take you home from the Page party. Would propose, he said. Very condescending. I replied you were engaged to marry Mr. John Marshall Clemens, late of Virginia, at an early date. Used my best writing paper, Jane. The Lampton seal to close it. Always remember that."

Jane sat still and horrified. She was trying to scream, You terrible old man! You've ruined my life! but the sounds would not come. Uncle Lewis was looking at her pleadingly, his eyes large in his thin, yellowed face, a small bony hand extended in apology for the liberty he had taken with her life. In a slow and genteel way he was dying, and he longed to die assured. "I had to do it, you understand? The family honor—"

"Yes, dear." She went and kissed his forehead and forced herself to say, "I've been happy the way things are."

"Good girl," he whispered. He did not add, "But can you be happy after hearing this?" Shriven once, he gladly let it lie.

She could not go home. She walked for miles. Past the new cemetery; past the race course that Grandfather Casey had helped found; along Russell Creek, following its windings through farms and wood lots. She came to a rye field edged with pear trees in bloom, like tall brides in a procession. This was April, she remembered; like the April a year ago when her world had crashed.

She made her way to the pear trees and lay down among them, her face to the green sod. Grandmother had promised that she would pay for a spiteful marriage made in haste. She lay there making the first, the worst payment.

After an hour or so, her ever buoyant spirit stirred and lifted; John Clemens need not pay, she realized, for he was blameless. To spare the blameless is atonement. She got up and started home, hoping her new hat was on straight.

Uncle Lewis slipped away in a week or so, mourned by the wife and children who had had only tenderness and courtesy from him.

His funeral was well attended. The townspeople spoke of him kindly, even when attesting to his oddities. Some recalled his naïveté in backwoods fighting; how, when ejecting unruly patrons, he employed only his hands, disdaining the use of feet and elbows, and so was often floored. Others at the graveyard spoke of Lewis's fervor as a volunteer fireman; how he ascended to roof tops in his ruffled shirts and good vests with unrivaled zeal. That he should die without seeing the new three-story ladders, now on order, was considered ironic by the other volunteers, John M. Clemens among them.

But Clemens himself would not ascend those ladders.

A letter had come to him from Dr. Nathan Montgomery at Gainesboro, Tennessee, saying Jackson County needed another lawyer and asking if he would come and settle there. Quick at decisions, he replied that he would. And then he told Jane. Though she was surprised at not having been consulted, she was eager to go, for Papa and Patsy lived in an adjoining county.

John barely gave her time to say her farewells and to provide for old white Jerry's care. No one had time to give her a party. His own adieus were perfunctory; for he had learned, with pain and chagrin, that he stood last in popularity among the Green River lawyers. Only his mother and sisters and his brother Hannibal saw a regret of parting in his face. There was a twofold bond between John Marshall and Hannibal; both had loved Pleasants, the brother they had lost, the stairstep between them. Toward their stepfather, John was as reserved as ever. Right highhandedly he asked for the Clemens sideboard and had it transferred from Simon Hancock's dining room to his Dearborn wagon in the yard. Permelia and Simon made no protest; the heir had his rights.

Jane would ride her own horse to Tennessee, for Grandmother Casey had given her a young mare from the plantation, as she had given Patsy a mount the year before. Mrs. Casey had also endowed Jane and John with a slave called young Jenny, the daughter of an older Jenny, deceased.

Jenny had no desire to leave Kentucky, but her own unfortunate nature sent her to her destiny. Handsome and wild, unbiddable, selfish, and provoking, she was regarded uneasily by her own race and with antipathy by Mrs. Casey. Jane, in accepting her, was not elated but was reasonably grateful. The girl, still in her early teens, was large and strong. Because John was leaving his inherited slaves with the Hancocks, Jenny loomed importantly in their lives. Her chair in the wagon, upholstered with a bright quilt, had the look of a throne. Jane's cats, in a crate, were at her feet.

Thus Jane and John departed from the gracious house of their honeymoon, thus they left the village of Columbia. Jane, calling farewells, was so bothered by tears that she could hardly see to whom she waved, but hope and anticipation filled her heart. . . . "Good-by, Mrs. Atkins, youall go to see Granny!" . . . "Good-by, Mrs. Triplett, please write me a letter!" . . . "Mrs. Selby, don't forget us!" That elderly person was not apt to. Her late husband had spent his time trying to invent a perpetual motion machine, and young Marshall Clemens had been his sole disciple.

The ladies, waving and calling their replies, regretted to see the youthful couple go from them. Especially Jane Lampton, that was. How prettily she sat her horse, they said afterward.

14 ❖

Dr. Nathan Montgomery had found them a house that was to let and they were soon settled in it. John placed his desk in a downstairs room and hung out his shingle. Neighbors came to call and brought fresh vegetables and flowers. Colored folk made friendly advances to Jenny. A setter dog, indifferent to cats, took up residence with them and followed their horses when they rode. John was not too busy. Gainesboro drowsed in a crook of the Cumberland River, and most of its energy was seeping away to Nashville; perhaps that was where the budding lawyers had gone.

Jane was at peace. Peace is happiness to an uncertain heart.

Papa and Patsy came up from Sparta to visit in the fall—Aunt Polly regretted—and before the memories of that pleasure had abated, Jane learned that she was going to have a baby.

The importance of the coming event was reduced however by Polly Hays Lampton's performance. In February she gave Benjamin a son. As Polly was but thirty-seven years of age it was hardly miraculous, but to Benjamin's daughters it was highly inappropriate. "How smug of her!" Jane declared irritably.

Patsy, writing to Jane, said that Papa was not as overjoyed as you might expect and would just as soon have a grandson, at his age. He was being sued for three thousand dollars, Patsy confided, because of some transactions in Sparta, and the lawsuit took all of his attention. Aunt Polly had named the child James Andrew Hays after the two brothers she had lost, and she worried constantly about his health.

Jane vowed to John Clemens that she would never be able to love the child. "I can't place him, somehow. What *is* he to Patsy and me? A sort of nephew?"

"You know very well what he is, Jane. Your half brother."

"It makes no sense. I'll never so much as lift a finger for him!" She little dreamed how those words would be refuted; the mild and handsome James Andrew Hays Lampton, by his very vicissitudes, would commend himself to her.

Soon there came another letter from Patsy, announcing her intention to wed John Adams Quarles, aged twenty-three, "a catch, if there ever was one." He owned his own farm in the best part of Overton County and enough men slaves to cultivate it. His brothers and sisters, all born in Virginia but now Tennesseeans, had farms in three counties and often visited each other. Though they were "mighty jolly people," Patsy said, they had had a hair-raising tragedy about ten years ago. Their father, William Pennington Quarles, had been murdered by a highwayman one night on the Gainesboro road near White Plains. But the widow, Mrs. Ann Hawes Quarles, had stayed on at her plantation, and had raised John Adams, her youngest son, not to be afraid of anything. "You can hear him laugh half a mile away," Patsy said, "and he is very handsome. He declares I will never want or lack."

Jane could not go to the wedding because her confinement was too imminent. Her baby was born in the heat of July. The night of labor seemed to take her down into the shadows, for all that Dr. Montgomery and his wife could do to help.

When John Clemens viewed his son in the morning light, Jane told him, "His name is *O*rion out of the Bible. *O*rion is a star. I saw it lately." She mispronounced the constellation, putting the accent on the first syllable, but she correctly quoted some beautiful words out of a tangle of memory: "Seek him that maketh the seven stars and *O*rion, and turneth the shadow of death into the morning."

"*O*rion," John repeated suspiciously. He was not a reader of Scripture and he thought Jane had invented the name in a delirium of pain and laudanum. When its Biblical source was located for him in the Book of Amos by Mrs. Montgomery, he suggested that Amos be substituted for Orion. Would it not be better to honor the prophet-author himself, he asked, rather than one of his poetic allusions?

No, it would not, Jane assured him.

As the months passed she found no fault with her new village, for John was making a living there, and she had learned to love the gentle baby Orion as tenderly as she had ever loved a little animal. She rode her horse in good weather; gave tea parties; went to them; wore her best clothes with pleasure; wrote lengthy replies to the letters she had from home. When a carnival came to town, she and John attended. . . . There was one, showing wild animals (said the posters) that camped at the edge of the village; it was Cole and Quick's menagerie. Its assets were two tigers and a lion. All three baffled creatures paced restlessly, but the lion was the worst; perhaps because he had no companion, nothing of his own between himself and the far jungle. He looked Jane in the eye, and she looked deeply back, her heart overflowing with pity as she went closer, feeling the compulsion to stroke him; but John snatched her back. She believed the great mangy beast would have suffered her touch and would have sensed her love and her wish for his freedom. . . .

She got the first news of an impending move when she asked John for a carpet for the family room early in 1827. "I've saved enough woolen rags to have a good-sized carpet woven," she said.

"We'll not need anything further for this house," John surprised her by saying. "We'll be leaving Gainesboro as soon as the weather opens up. That new county to the east of us is about to boom. The time has come to tell you about this, Jane. I'm one of the commissioners. I've gotten in on the ground floor. I refer to Fentress in the Cumberland range. They're setting up a county seat at the settlement of Jamestown. It used to be called Sand Springs."

She said she had never heard of the place. What was it like?

"Very raw," he admitted. "But there's a chance to get rich there.

There's vast tracts available at ten cents an acre. Before long those mountains will be yielding coal and timber, even iron. I mean to buy up thousands and thousands of acres."

"How will we live in the meantime, John?"

"I'll practice law, of course, and the county clerkship's been promised me. I'll have a store, too. To finance all this I'm selling my slaves to the Hancocks. They've wanted them all along."

"I see." Jane turned and left the room, not trusting herself to say more. The worst of her shock was the realization of John's secretiveness. She thought back. He had written a good many letters lately, and he haunted the post office. But why had he kept her in the dark? Could he not trust her with his affairs? She knew she was not a betrayer of confidences or an inattentive wife; but what she was was unknown to her. Her compulsion to exchange news was not recognizable to her. She listened to others talk with unfeigned attention, drawing them out; but she ended by giving more than she got. In a benign way she was a gossip, making a good story out of a trifle, an epic out of folklore. Sometimes, in bringing a tale up to date, she would bypass a generation or two and festoon a man with the sins or honors of his grandfather. Her belief in human nature was resilient, bounding to ridiculous heights in defense of wrongdoers, but she was fascinated by sensational happenings, lurid or holy, romantic or desperate. In a musical drawl that drew attention she expressed her own opinions freely; speculated, guessed, reckoned, predicted. Reticent John M. Clemens had desired and married this highly effective feminine communication system against his better judgment, and now he was wary. Nor time nor tide could change her.

One blustering March day they departed from Gainesboro, facing their horses into the east wind. The confusion of the exodus, due to Jenny's sullen retardations and John's impatience to be off, caused the abandonment of Jane's hatboxes in an upstairs closet. Her several summer bonnets remained there until some children playing in the empty house found them and took them to the doctor's wife. "Dear little Jane," Mrs. Montgomery said sadly. "We'll get them to her when we can. I doubt if she needs them just now. The women at Sand Springs wear their men's old hats, I've heard."

They spent four days and three nights on the road in making the forty-mile journey. The second night's stop, as promised by John, occurred at the Quarles farm in Overton County's valley. Jane and Patsy were almost out of their minds with the joy of their reunion and the wonder of comparing little Orion and baby Benjamin Quarles. They began there the custom (to be resumed whenever they might be together) of calling their mates John M. and John Adams to avoid confusion. . . . While John Adams and John M. "walked over the place" in the farmers' ritual, and a magnificent meal was being prepared in the kitchen—Jenny enlivening the Quarles staff with peals of her famous laughter—Jane and Patsy reminisced and exchanged news. That both were *enceinte* again was an item.

Jenny's fraternizing brought on a crisis. The Quarles colored folk told her of the rough new country she was bound for, and the next morning when she was summoned to the wagon, she mutinied. She would not go a step farther, she told her master. "Here I'm stayin'. Beat me, it don't matter! Rip out my tongue, still I don't go!"

This savage suggestion met with a scream from Jane and a rebuke from John. "What kind of wild talk is that, Jenny? Stop it!"

Bears and wildcats would be coming to the door, Jenny accused. Owls would hoot the night through. Ghosts would ride the ridges to pester them.

"Is it like that, John?" Jane asked and she clutched little Orion until he wailed. She was almost as delicately triggered as Jenny. It complicated things for John to have her set off.

"Calm down, Jane," he implored. "Game is plentiful and pelts are easy got, but not near the settlement. As for ghosts riding the ridges, no sane man would comment on that." Meanwhile, Jenny had disappeared. He was for searching her out and thrashing her but Jane hindered.

"Leave her with the Quarleses a while," she urged. "She'd miss her own race where we're going. She'd be lonesome and scared."

"We'll pay you hire for her," John Quarles offered, generously making the matter feasible. Of necessity, it was settled.

The travelers set off then for Fentress County, Jane casting many a look backward as they quit one of Tennessee's mellowest vistas for one of its most forbidding.

Having no nurse now, little Orion had to be tethered. Sometimes he rode beside his father, tied to the wagon seat; at other times he slept in his trundle bed amidst the furniture. Jane, following on her horse, kept watch over him. The road was increasingly narrow and dangerous. After a climb, they must stop to rest the horses. Though John drove four now, it seemed at times as if they could not conquer the long hills.

Toward sunset the following day John called back, "We're pulling into Jamestown now!" and Jane rode forward to look. On a sandy plateau before them she saw a scattering of primitive cabins and a score of men sawing logs, burning brush, dragging surveyors' chains. That was all. Though John had called Jamestown raw, the warning had been diminished by Jane's optimism. Her imagination had built a more gracious settlement than this and had peopled it more numerously. The men came to meet them. Several were courteous. A few were mean-faced. The rest were nondescriptly earnest.

"What did you bring, storekeeper?" one of them called, and they hurried to see. To Jane's surprise, that was the chief concern of those town fathers, and they quickly unloaded the several barrels of merchandise that John had brought from Gainesboro. This they carried to a cabin spoken of as "the Store," previously stocked by proxy and protected by a great hasp lock.

They then unloaded the Clemens furniture and carried it to their temporary abode, an abandoned squatter's cabin down a steep hillside. It was near a brook, with a woods beyond it stretching away to infinity. There was a rail fence enclosing house and lot.

Jane had glimpsed women at some of the cabin doors but she disregarded them, gripped Orion, and walked cautiously down the hill to her home. A green wood fire was sputtering in the fireplace, and a hickory chair awaited her there. She sensed the loan to be somebody's treasure. A basket of fried rabbit and corn pones had been sent by one of the women and it rested on the hearth; another had sent eggs, others milk and butter. Jamestown had

105

done its best. Jane wept with gratitude, with fatigue and despair. How could she endure this place? She envisioned the seasons coming and going starkly while she and John became impassive mountaineers, indistinguishable from their neighbors, lost to the world.

Impassive, Jane was not to be. The next day while John was at the town site she killed a snake near the door with a hoe; a copperhead it proved to be when John examined it; he summoned aid and they removed rock piles to be sure the thing had left no mate. Anticipating bats—ever a torment to herself and Patsy— Jane armed herself with a suitable shingle; and hearing a lynx's wail across a glen she considered rifle practice, though guns frightened her. Soon, though, her fears receded and her surroundings lost their menace. A cheerful mountain girl came daily to help with the housework. Two lads from their own hillside came gladly to carry spring water and care for the cow and horses. It was a courtesy practiced by Jane and John to speak of the mother of those boys, and her progeny, as "the poor family." The woman was a light soul with no visible mate. She kept her cabin clean and seemed to cherish her children; but she was given to walking afield to gather berries and greens, and so to meet her current lover. Her husband had been killed in a feud, it was rumored; all of her children were wood's colts except the eldest. Jane often called a greeting to her, but John had forbidden her to do more.

John's stock was presently depleted and he must go to Livingston to replenish it. It was arranged that the hired girl should stay the nights as well as the days during his absence.

All went well and the time passed uneventfully. There was a new calf in the lot to divert Jane; the mother cow grazed beyond the fence. Some squirrels came often for food, charming Orion. Little children from the settlement came to play. One morning after the work was done Jane told her helper she might go home and see her own family, and the girl left hastily, for some mighty clouds were gathering. When the rain came it was like nothing Jane had ever experienced. She could not see a foot beyond the

106

cabin window, and when the sky had cleared somewhat she found that her brook had become a river. It had covered the lower hillside and the fenced lot; it was lapping against her house, muddy and swift.

She heard the calf bleating as it tried to get to the lowing cow beyond the enclosure. She might have taken her own child and fled to higher ground, for her door faced uphill, but it seemed to her of paramount importance to free the calf first. She put a chair across the doorway to keep Orion in, fearing to shut the heavy door lest she could not open it again. Then she waded into the knee-deep water at the lower side of the lot and let the calf out. The cow very sensibly took it off to a high patch of ground.

As she was making her way back to her door, dizzy from the swirling water, she saw the two chore boys running to her rescue. "Maw says come!" they called. "We'll carry your young'un!" A letter Jane wrote Patsy concludes the story simply.

> *The woman met me at the door and took me to the fire made for me. I sat down blue enough. I thought no odds about character, this woman is so good. I'll never forget her kindness. Her children took Orion off in another part of the room and he was delighted with his company. Soon a little child at the door called out there goes the store keeper. We went to the door. Then he saw me at that house, his child and I both as wet as water could make us. Patsy he said it was impossible to discribe his feelings when he saw us there in such a plight.*

As disturbed at finding his wife and son being cared for by a woman of ill repute as at finding them half drowned, John Clemens hastened to erect a dwelling in the village center. The hewn log house had several spacious rooms and a loft. Its windows were glass-paned, its walls plastered. By local standards it was an imposing house, fit for the Clemens sideboard. Jane was so taken with the smoothly planed chestnut floor boards, reminiscent of Adair County, that she declared they must have a party. Only another confinement prevented it.

The baby, a healthy little girl, was born without incident in mid-September and was named for John's mother. Sensitive to the way that name had been corrupted to Permelia, he warned that the correct English spelling was Pamela "now and always." But Jane, wanting a diminutive, was soon calling her Mela. The little one had red curls but in other ways resembled her father. She was so solemn of manner that Jane was rather in awe of her.

The courthouse and jail were going up under John's direction. His duties as county clerk had increased and he kept office in his store. He did no menial work, thought no menial thoughts. Wearing a well-fitted blue broadcloth coat, his hair brushed to a sheen, his face cleanly shaven, he was a credit to the legal profession and to the honorable name of Clemens.

His acquisition of land had begun. Five thousand acres at a time was the customary bite he took out of the ranges to the south, and whenever he had entered a tract in his name he would invite Jane to stand beside him and look away toward their domain. She caught his excitement. They were astute landholders, she agreed, with a growing kingdom, wild, scenic, promising. Nor was John's the only Clemens name registered among the grantees. Little Orion had a hundred perpendicular acres of his own. Hannibal had five thousand. And a Danville cousin known as James Clemens, Junior, at John's advice became the absentee owner of ten thousand acres.

The months sped. Little Pamela was followed too quickly by another child, a boy whom John asked to name for his two brothers, the deceased and the living: Pleasants Hannibal. He was never to sign his strange name. Frail, he went away with the summer. "Aged three months," intoned the traveling preacher at his little grave. Jane was deeply grieved. He was so small to be left alone there amid the limitless knobs. But a strange gain came to her in the bleakness of this sorrow. There was established between her and other women of the Cumberlands a peculiar bond: she had lost and buried a child. As opportunity came, many told her of their departed little ones with a pressed hand and a few faltering words; it was an inarticulate sorority.

Hannibal had married in Kentucky a suitable young woman named Jane Jones, and when the news reached Tennessee, Jane had exclaimed, "Drat it! that makes two Jane Clemenses! People will confuse us."

"Impossible," was John's dry reply. But they settled on calling her Janie for convenience. She had recently come to Jamestown with Hannibal who had moved his tannery there to be near his brother. It was a practical move, for cured pelts were still used for barter in the hills, and plain-dressed leather was sought by saddlers and harness makers throughout Tennessee. Hannibal had brought his three inherited slaves: Reason and Silas, experienced tanners; and Betty, Reason's mother, a capable house servant.

Janie had not wanted to leave Kentucky and come to the Fentress County mountains. But, as she complained to Jane, Marshall had a great hold over Hannibal. Jane agreed; she said she'd never seen a younger brother as loyal and admiring as Hannibal.

The two young women took comfort in each other's company. Jane borrowed Betty to watch her children (repaying her with John's best calicoes and trinkets) while she and Janie rode over the magnificent trails. She persuaded Janie to unpack her trousseau clothes and wear them, not dressing down to the settlers; for it was her belief that a pretty dress aroused more delight than envy in another woman's breast. It was their duty, she told Janie, to give parties and smarten up manners. At New Year's, they went from house to house with their husbands and a fiddler, setting up figures for reels and dancing the night away.

On the last day of May—it was 1830 now—a second girl was born to Jane. She was strikingly pretty from the first. Her eyes were Irish blue; her hair soon showed raven ringlets. Jane called her Margaret, for her mother, a fortnight before Patsy Quarles duplicated the name in Peggy Casey's memory.

Almost no legal work fell to John beyond his recording duties at the courthouse; the villagers and scattered farmers in the glens settled their contentions with fisticuffs or firearms, or merely by looking each other hard in the eye. His seventy thousand acres were unproductive; storekeeping caused him boredom. A great unrest assailed him. Learning of a productive little farm for sale

109

on Wolf River nine miles to the north, he bought it, telling no one but his brother what he planned to do with it.

"I'll have my own waterway now," he boasted to Hannibal. "When my crops are ready, I can float them to market. Another thing; with perfect seclusion and a swift little stream I can work on my invention. You may know I bought Mr. Lingan Selby's equipment from his widow. It's in those barrels at the back of the store."

Hannibal, questioning him, learned that there was a one-room cabin on the farm which John was having enlarged by adding an upper room, "safe from floods if the river rises."

"It will look a sight," Hannibal said, for once doubting his brother's common sense. "I wonder if your Jane Lampton will consent to go there? A glorified corncrib in a lonesome valley!"

"Jane is a dutiful wife," John replied. "She's never opposed me where the family welfare's at stake. The location is a beautiful spot—verdant, floral, fragrant. Jane loves nature."

He dreaded to approach his nature lover, however, and when he did so her response was even quicker than he had anticipated.

Jane claimed to Janie immediately afterward that she threw a book at him with all her might; though she later admitted that she only hurled it against a wall in his vicinity, wrecking the book but sparing his unflinching head.

"He asked me, Janie, if I was leaving his bed because I no longer liked its location. I said, 'Count that as the chief reason, John. But I'm also leaving you for a while because I'm tired of having babies. Four in less than five years; I reminded him. 'Go to your beautiful lonesome valley,' I told him. 'Work on your crazy invention till you've had enough of it,' I told him. 'I'll stay in this house with our children, my dear sir! At least there's help to be had here if they choke up with the croup!'"

"What did he say?" Janie asked, appalled.

"He agreed. But he looked at me like I was a panther."

He went to his bizarre cabin on the Wolf to carry out his intentions, retaining his county clerkship, arranging to return to Jamestown every court day to attend to public duties.

Hannibal and Janie and Betty moved into the house with Jane

and her children, and nobody called it strange. If lawyer Clemens felt the urge to raise some crops, he had bought the right farm; the soil was rich there. Nor did the women condemn Jane. Any woman would hold back from taking her young ones to Forks of Wolf, they said, if she had such a wondrous safe home for them in Jamestown.

15 ❖

John's nerves were frayed from hearing children romp at sunset and fret at dawn—times when a man needs to think—and Jane's ultimatum had given him a way out. Now, when not cultivating his small crops, he could concentrate beside his swift stream, tugging at the perpetual motion machine that had eluded old Mr. Selby. . . . A water wheel to operate a chain pump through a system of gearing; the pump to raise water to propel the wheel, and so on forever. The idea was ancient, and down through the years eager inventors had increased the number of wheels, all connected to a walking beam by crank and pitman. One wheel too many in Mr. Selby's case? It would seem so. One had come away like a comet, knocking Mr. Selby against a cliff and doing him in. But John was not dismayed by this grim joke. He respected good machines, and he would build the one that the world awaited—a contrivance that would lead mankind to cheap and effortless labor, making even African slavery unnecessary.

During a resolute autumn he harvested his small crops. (He had found them ready planted.) During a lonely winter he studied mathematics and walked the floor of his cabin in the throes of invention. But it was in the springtime that he went down in defeat. The sunpain of his boyhood returned, and on the moistly hot days that sent birds into an ecstasy of song and corn into a rapture of growth, it would strike—was it real or a morbid memory?—making the landscape shimmer and the earth rock.

When he acknowledged his illness and his failures to Jane, she declared she would go with him anywhere at all to help him get

111

his bearings if their children were not endangered. "Families should stay together," she acknowledged in turn. "I'll try harder."

He chose a settlement a few miles beyond his place located on the north bank of Wolf River and called, dismayingly, Pall Mall. The terrain opened toward Kentucky, Jane learned with delight. The little farms were numerous. There John bought and improved the general store and obtained a post office, himself to be postmaster. The year was 1832. And there, at last, they found a schoolhouse and teacher.

Mr. Renneau, a respected pedagogue, had established classes in a new cabin built on oaken piles. Children trudged for miles to attend, bringing whatever book was available to them. Orion proudly joined them. He went well equipped, carrying a primer and a spelling book that had been his father's. Little Pamela, though underage, also attended. A born student, she was as much diverted by Mr. Renneau's turning globe as by the grunting of hogs under the floor. Though the teacher lodged in his schoolhouse, having a cot and a cupboard and a trunk there, not to mention a washbasin, it was arranged that he should take his meals at the table of John Clemens in return for the children's tuition.

Mr. Renneau went on record as saying he enjoyed mealtime at the postmaster's roomy log house: Mrs. Clemens had taught her helper, young Abby York, to set a pretty table; and certainly there was conversation. But the meals were rather unpredictable, he said.

John became a trader. The valley farmers had no money to spend at his store but they paid in produce which he disposed of at the Louisville warehouses, enabling him to renew the stock on his conglomerate shelves. On his first trip to Louisville from Pall Mall his wagon carried the homely but profitable cargo of ginseng roots, turpentine, rosin, and kegs of much-sought lampblack. In November he added chestnuts for the groceries, goose feathers for the mattress factories. He hired extra wagons and drivers.

In Louisville that fall he bought for Jane a length of bronze silk to set off her hair; for his children some books and clothing; for Abby winter shoes. Jane took him aside (his aversion to dis-

112

plays of affection remaining unabated) and kissed him tenderly for his largess. He had bought nothing for himself.

More than gifts, John knew, Jane craved news from Adair County, where he had stopped a night going and returning. He reported in detail to gratify her, his courtroom voice relating progress, crime, and social minutiae with equal precision.

"There's been a wedding in Green County," he added as if in afterthought. "Your old beau Barret married his neighbor Miss Maria Lewis Buckner, daughter of Judge Aylett. They're just back from their honeymoon. They'll live at his farm, Clifflands. She's a collateral descendant of President Monroe, it seems, and her brother is in Congress. Last spring she visited him and was much admired in Washington. She's statuesque and sedate, they say."

"I don't remember her," Jane said, puzzled.

"That's understandable. She's ten years your junior, I hear. She's the age now you were—then." John Clemens left the room without looking at his wife, for he did not wish to see her face grow tender in memory of Barret. A man must wonder sometimes.

Jane had had news of Richard Barret in the letters of her friend Mary Brawner Carlile. Richard had graduated with honors at Transylvania College in Lexington and had become a resident physician in a Philadelphia hospital. He had returned home to practice, but he really didn't like sick people, Mary Brawner said. He mostly liked something called *materia medica*. She said she would never want him for a physician for herself or her family because when he was in medical school, they said, he experimented on dogs and cats and frogs; would cut them open to watch the workings of their hearts and nerves under opium and alcohol and the like. His thesis had to do with this and was called "Narcotics and Sedatives." All this was known as vivisection, young Mrs. Carlile explained without rancor, and was for the good of mankind, but it seemed just horrid; didn't Jane think so?

She did. She could not reconcile it with the Richard she had known. . . . And now she must focus her mind anew and picture him with a wife: Miss Maria Lewis Buckner—handsome, important, traveled, dignified, yet only eighteen. She lost herself in envious meditation; she could forgive him for marrying, but not for marrying so well.

Her helper came and shook her by the shoulder to arouse her. "Please, Mrs. Clemens, will you make your tea now? You know I brew it too bitter."

"Yes," Jane said, "yes indeed," and she began to talk frivolously, to the great pleasure of the girl, while they finished off supper. "An old sweetheart of mine has just taken a bride, Abby, so I've learned, and she couldn't be more different from me!"

"I don't know as I'd like her, then."

"Thank you, Abby York. That's as pretty a compliment as ever was passed me, but hark to this. She's got smooth gold hair and blue eyes, I think, and a drawer full of silk stockings inherited from Mrs. President Monroe. But she's never been known to show her ankles in public since she put on long skirts. He had to take her legs on faith. She's just the age I was then."

"Then, Mrs. Clemens?"

"Yes," Jane said, adjusting her sights for the confusion of herself and posterity, "the year I turned him down in favor of Mr. John Clemens. Hand me the baby now and I'll nurse him."

The baby was little Benjamin, predictable product of the reconciliation.

To the pleasures and problems of Pall Mall, Jane and John were preparing to say farewell. Two years had passed, and Pall Mall could now appraise them. Squire Clemens, the community called John, encompassing in that title his law certificate, his knob lands, his dignity, and the seal with which he stamped their letters. He was law and order. He was the United States mails. Mrs. Clemens had her own status. Though yoked to the impressive young squire, she was not his adjunct. When she went to the houses of those homespun people they sensed that she came as much for her own pleasure as theirs. She was more apt than not to take something away with her, and they were aglow with the pride of having dispensed. She might carry off a rare lily bulb whose bloom was praised, or a poke of dried herbs. Or she would leave singing one of their ballads—words they had taught her

114

that day to a dulcimer's chords. Once, having gone to take clothing to a needy young mother in the hills, she let the woman give her a dried-apple half-moon—a fried pie of remarkable density—and was forced to carry it along a rutted path, wrapped in dock leaves. She served it for supper, eating of it stoically and urging John to do the same, for soon she must reward the donor with praise.

Benjamin Lampton had gone to Missouri, and so had the adventuring Quarleses, and their letters had determined John and Jane to do likewise. Surely eastern Missouri must be the promised land. Come soon! they advised. The village of Florida in Monroe County was a town in embryo, Benjamin wrote. It was located on Salt River, a stream that needed only a bit of dredging here and there to make it navigable to the Mississippi. Government land was obtainable in the county. As for a lawyer's prospects, litigation was rife. John Quarles had leased a farm near the village to keep his slaves occupied and to serve the family as a temporary home. He had his eye on a farm to buy, out toward the prairie. Meantime he was keeping store for diversion and profit.

Jane shared John's enthusiasm. She might even see Grandmother again, she realized, for Mrs. Casey had chosen to emigrate with Green and his wife several years ago, albeit to free territory. It was slavery, after all, that was deciding the location of home sites: Illinois and Iowa for the emancipators, Missouri for the holders; though both elements were clustering up and down the big river almost within shouting distance of each other.

John was gratified when his brother Hannibal also declared for Missouri, saying he would set up a tannery there as soon as John could select a location for him. He would not travel light, as John planned to do, but would take several wagons, with his slaves to man them. In view of this, John sent the Clemens sideboard to him, along with some cherished chairs and trunks of clothing and the perpetual motion gear.

Jenny had come back to the Clemens fold. She was co-operative toward the move because the Quarles people had gone on ahead.

Only Patsy, ever frank, had sounded an ominous warning:

115

There is no society here at all, the people are too busy. But Jane did not care. She and Patsy would be together again.

Plans were speeded, for April is the year's best benison to travelers. Furniture and tools were given away to persons in need, gladdening hearts that would otherwise have been heavy at the parting. The Dearborn wagon was stocked with the last of John's ginseng and feathers, and a driver was hired, pledged to buy wagon and horses in Louisville. John had bought a barouche for their migration, a sprightly little equipage with a half top, two facing benches, and a driver's seat. It was an unsuitable vehicle and an extravagance. He had ordered it after gossip came from Green County that Dr. Richard Barret was about to transport his bride to Illinois in a carriage-and-four. Jane understood. If John's communications were wordless, they were nonetheless emphatic.

Barouche and wagon set off together, with Orion and Jenny on saddle horses. Among those who followed the cavalcade to a bend in the road was Mr. Renneau. He was not to lose these people, entirely, from his life. The letters they were to write him would be read aloud on request; and wherever Mrs. Clemens omitted punctuation he would put it in, making clear her sprightly meanings. As for the squire, they could expect him back. His Tennessee land would hold him hostage, though he went to the ends of the earth.

To Jane, their arrival in her home town of Columbia was a triumph. The flashy little carriage and span merited a second look even before John Marshall Clemens and his family were recognized. And certainly the manly boy and the handsome big slave girl made noticeable outriders. Dressed in her finest, Jane sat gracefully in the barouche with her three youngest children grouped around her: grave Pamela, going on eight; winsome Margaret, about to be five; sturdy little Benjamin, not quite three, looking about him solemnly. If Sir Henry Raeburn had been alive and in the public square of Columbia, he would have set up his easel on the spot.

Leaving the children with his gratified mother and half sisters Ann and Polly Hancock, John and Jane visited around the county. Some of their favorite memories had suffered change, but their

116

homecoming caused a round of entertainment. One night they slipped away alone and walked the uneven streets of the mellow village by moonlight, pausing at their first home and noting the lilac tree where they had kissed on becoming engaged.

They resumed the journey northward. When they had crossed Green River at Tebb's Ferry, leaving Adair County behind them and had made the long ascent of Muldrow's Hill, the achievement seemed notable. The mind moved ahead with the horses, straining for unseen places. Often Jane lightened the barouche by walking up a hill with the children. Birds sang and flashed to beguile them. Laurel and redbud and dogwood bloomed at the woods' edge, squirrels scolded, brooks offered gaudy pebbles, violets wanted picking.

At the pretty town of Lebanon, where they stayed at the best inn, some of the townspeople came to pay their respects, for it was a custom in that area to call on travelers making a genteel progress. At Bardstown the tavern was yet finer, the town more extensive; brick residences with charming doorways were prevalent. Here was the first Catholic cathedral west of the Alleghenies—St. Joseph's of the Ionic architecture, a sight for all pilgrims though its paintings donated by Louis Philippe had not yet been hung. John and Jane went to see it, taking Orion, an eager boy, sensitive and uncertain.

It was Jane's first contact with the civilization of Rome. She was soon genuflecting like the faithful—if anything, outdoing them in grace—when John caught her at it and requested her to leave off. Orion was curious. "Why, Pa?" he asked. Like most children of the region he called his parents Pa and Ma, rhyming the words with ah. "Why can't Ma bow in here?"

"Because it's not suitable for Protestants to do that."

"Are we Protestants?" Orion asked, wondering at the new word.

"We're not anything," Jane flared with reddened cheeks. She was as disturbed as when John had drawn her back from stroking the lion. "Now that I think of it, we're not anything."

"I am a deist, I hope," John said to her over their child's head. "You can hardly call that being nothing." Out of doors, he resumed his explanations to the boy, for he was a descendant of

117

that regicide Clemens who had helped deprive Charles I of his head, and he claimed an inherited aversion to the symbols of monarchy and church. "Those things smack of idolatry," he stated and became specific. Orion listened attentively, for he admired his father and was eager to please him, already aware, somehow, that he rarely did. He would remember this precise disposal of an enigmatic subject and one day would add to it the emotional reports of certain unfrocked priests roaming the West, sources his judicial father would not have credited.

Louisville was gained at dusk three days out of Bardstown. Not able to afford one of the new hotels, John took them to a respectable family tavern near the busy Ohio River. A week of rest here loomed brightly. Jane would see her first city. John hired a man from their livery stable to drive the barouche and take Jane and the older children sight-seeing. Sometimes he himself accompanied them; sometimes Jenny did, wearing a new tall turban in place of her bandanna. Jenny's headpiece was bought after Jane's encounter with fashionable Louisville. Until now she had never seen servants in uniform, nor had she known that it was chic for ladies to sit in their carriages before shops and have bolts of material brought out for their inspection. She had not dreamed the black coachmen could be as haughty as tribal kings, especially if their hair was turning gray. . . . John had his own bemusements. On passing the imposing home of George Keats he told Jane that Mr. Keats had only arrived from England a dozen years ago with a small inheritance which he invested in real estate. "Mind you, six thousand dollars was all he had! Before that, he was merely the amanuensis of his brother John Keats, the poet, and his literary agent. Now he's wealthy!"

"Could it be luck?" Jane asked, though she was less interested in how Mr. Keats had got his money than in how he spent it. Caterers were entering, and she sighed to attend the party.

It was disappointing that they could not take a swift packet for St. Louis, but the barouche and horses required that they travel by a more cumbersome boat. Bypassing the falls, they made their way slowly through the new canal, and John called Orion's attention to its construction. "Something like this, if smaller, is what I must promote for Salt River," he told the boy.

"Won't it cost a lot, Pa?" Orion asked.

"The State of Missouri will appropriate the money, son."

The pounding of the engines was already making Jane queasy. The next day, and thereafter, she had morning sickness. When they disembarked at St. Louis she was almost indifferent to the news that there was cholera in the town. She wanted only to get the journey over, to arrive at Patsy's house and go to bed and sleep the clock around.

And so, by barouche and ahorseback, they resumed the trek, crossing the Missouri River at St. Charles and following narrow roads that veered now west, now north. Right endlessly they passed tree stumps and rich farm lands where men persistently plowed the fields, and where assistance, when sought, was rendered with equal good will by Yankees, Kentuckians, and the gentle followers of Gottfried Duden, lately come from Germany.

The little carriage was threatening to break down, and only John's continual mending kept it going. At New London in Ralls County they lay over to have it mended. As they proceeded they were often in sight of Salt River whose dismaying curves were here and there evident. The problem was not lost on Orion. "Can you straighten it out, Pa?" he asked anxiously, riding alongside the barouche.

John's face had grown grim. His wife's relatives had misled him. If this stream's channel were dredged, large pirogues could navigate it, taking produce to market. But nothing more, surely.

Jane noticed that Orion was riding the larger horse, the big rough trotter. He seemed stiff and sore. "Son," she called out, "change horses with Jenny this minute! She's had the pacer all day. Jenny! You hear me, Jenny? Swap horses with Orion." The exchange was made, but Jane wished that Orion had accomplished it for himself. Would he ever stand up for his rights? This concerned her more than the navigation of Salt River.

They came upon the hamlet of Florida without recognizing it, but Benjamin Lampton, emerging from the Quarles store, saw them and set up a clamor. John Quarles too came shouting. Soon

119

they were at his farm beyond the village, being welcomed by a little colony of children and colored people. The journey that had seemed interminable had ended safely.

Jane and Patsy embraced and wept. Three years had passed since their meeting, though during much of that time they had lived but fifty miles apart. The demands of life had kept between them.

"Let me lie down, Patsy," Jane said. "I don't feel too well. Don't offer me any supper, please."

"Do you mean—?"

"Yes, I think so. It must have happened in Columbia."

"Poor dear!" Patsy mourned. She refrained from having her two youngest children brought by their nurses, though her sister had never seen them. They were her fifth and sixth: little Fred, a toddling native of Tennessee, and baby Tabitha, Missouri-born. It might seem unnatural not to display them, but Quarles babies had ceased to be a novelty; they were hardly worth trotting out, except in the opinion of John Quarles.

Patsy found a bed for Jane in the crowded house, at least half a bed, and brought her a pitcher of cold spring water. "Sleep now, Jane," she urged. "There're people aplenty to take care of the children."

Jane saw that Patsy, her darling Patsy, though still beautiful of face, had lost her figure. Childbearing and Jersey cream had finally had their way with her. She was now a big-bosomed Irish woman who moved majestically on aching feet.

16 ❖

"It's preposterous," John Quarles said to Patsy in a moment of privacy. "Clemens has showed up here without a stick of furniture."

"Hannibal will bring their sideboard and chairs in a few weeks," Patsy defended. "Trunks and winter clothes too."

"Beds are what's needed now. Didn't they consider that?"

"Jane brought bedticks anyway. Fortunately we've got some clean straw to fill them. Later, there'll be dry hay, sneezes or not."

120

"You've got some shortsighted relatives, Patsy. We'll make the best of it, though. You wanted your sister near you, and I wanted you to have her. We can put up with John Marshall, I reckon."

Awaiting the Clemens family was a temporary home in the village, a two-room clapboard house with good roofing and windows, rented from old settler William Nelson Penn. A lean-to was hastily built for Jenny. The interior was whitewashed, the well cleaned, furniture procured from a cabinetmaker at New London. The uncongenial brothers-in-law then entered into partnership as storekeepers, and John Clemens bought three tracts of government land recommended to him by Quarles.

Jane and Patsy and their father were much together. Orion found companionship with his ten-year-old uncle, James Andrew's mother approving. Polly Hays Lampton had not slackened her tenets: she was still hopeful of reforming the worldly Lamptons. When Benjamin took his two daughters on a jaunt to Paris to explore that easygoing little town and visit the race course, Polly watched the barouche take off right sadly. She protectively gripped one of James Andrew's arms, one of Orion's, while she spoke reasonably to them of the folly of horse racing. To raise horses for service, she said, was a noble calling. But to breed them with legs like broomsticks was a sin against nature, for they were fit for nothing but to run in circles with little Negro jocks on their backs.

A diversion was created in the early fall when Hannibal Clemens and his caravan reached the village of Florida en route to Scotland County, the destination John had chosen for him. Janie, who was several months along with her first baby, was bewildered by the vastness of Missouri, the outfit having come all the way on wheels, and she dreaded the idea of going yet farther. But a tannery was needed in that northernmost county, and Hannibal said they must push on, his young face firmly set to follow his brother's considered advice.

When October came, Jane noticed that the colors of the autumn foliage made her feel fairly intoxicated. "I can hardly stand it!" she declared literally. She had never before encountered such a profusion of hardwoods turning to gold and red and bruised purple. She would hurry through her chores in order to walk along the fringes of the woods, at times forgetting the children who were trailing.

Then, in the late autumn sky, they saw a comet—Halley's, John said it was called—a heavenly visitor which only the oldest Americans had ever beheld before. Night after night they watched its strange brilliance, and Jane's excitement was unduly great. The child she was carrying responded. A restlessness pervaded and possessed the little unborn creature, and she recognized it with alarm.

"I must settle myself," she told Patsy resolutely. "I must hold off till January's over."

But it was too late. The baby, a boy, was born on the last day of November, in this year of 1835, a seven-months child who seemed too frail to face the world. His clothes were not assembled. His cradle was not ready. Nothing agreed with him, nothing pleased him. He was a fury of a baby with red hair and wrinkled skin, and he seemed to be filling the little clapboard house and pushing them out of it. John Clemens was in no way drawn to him, but when called upon to furnish a name he dipped into early memories and bestowed generously: Samuel, for his father; Langhorne, for that distant relative who had befriended him in his youth in Virginia.

"A poor specimen," said Mrs. Penn and Mrs. Buchanan and chatty Mrs. Damrell, local women who were giving aid and advice.

"I'll try to raise him," Jane said fervently, "and it may be I can." He was not as mature of body as little Pleasants had been, and Pleasants had not been able to survive a salubrious mountain summer. But there was a determination about this one that seemed to defy the hardships of the winter ahead in a drafty cottage full of children. "Let's not stop up all the cracks," Jane implored. "We'll keep him warm, but let him breathe like people."

And so she brought him through that winter to the wonder of all.

With the coming of spring the Clemens family was able to move into a somewhat larger house, one obligingly vacated by Benjamin who was moving to the country. What a joy, Jane

122

enthused, to gain a room, and an attic you could reach by stair steps! As was customary with her, every improvement was seen in an exaggerated light. When her letter describing the new dwelling reached Granny Casey in Iowa, the old lady mistakenly envisioned two full stories connected by a graceful flight of stairs.

Thomas Jefferson Chowning, the young doctor who had delivered baby Samuel in the absence of the family physician, went one day that summer to examine the infant. Professional pride and curiosity prompted the visit.

"How do you find him, Dr. Chowning?" Jane askd.

"His little ticker and his bellows are excellent, Mrs. Clemens," he pronounced. "Dr. Meredith has brought him along finely."

Jane weighed the latter statement and found it wanting. "We can hardly say Dr. Meredith did it," she answered gently, "nor me either. The baby did it for himself. He had to, to live."

Dr. Chowning, but twenty-seven years of age, was shaken by this affront to the medical profession and lost no time in reporting it to the older doctor. "What do you make of her, sir?"

Dr. Meredith spoke out. "A good many people find that little woman fascinating, but I find her a trial. I put up with her for the sake of her husband. I'm an admirer of J. M. Clemens. He's a good lawyer. He's got talent as an engineer. But he married the wrong woman. I doubt if she'd understand a legal brief or the simple drawing of a river lock if he laid them down in front of her."

"She's keen in her way, though," Dr. Chowning protested. "And a polite listener. She's hardly a show-off. I notice she's even considerate of that hoity-toity slave girl."

"Granted, Tom. But try and pin her down to a routine. It can't be done. Several times I've left medicine for the children and found she's switched to some old Negro remedy. And once it was an Indian brew she'd heard about. Last week I called to see how Orion was coming on after a siege of sore lungs. I suspected she wasn't keeping to my powders. I found the boy alone, asked him how he was feeling. 'Ma said not to talk about it,' he evaded. 'She rubbed my chest with pepper-grease and told me to forget about it.' Fortunately John Clemens came into the room then and described the boy's symptoms in detail. Little Benjamin had gotten hold of my medicine, Clemens said, and thrown it to the chickens, so Orion had no benefit from it. I left another batch and instructed Clemens to administer it in person. I think we understood each other."

"Was Orion coughing and feverish when you looked him over?"

"He was on the mend, Tom, but that's neither here nor there. It's the woman's unorthodoxy I'm driving at. Jane Clemens herself is never ailing, though she's an erratic eater. For about a week this spring she almost subsisted on lemon pies, and so did her children. They'd gotten several dozen lemons from New Orleans, and Mrs. Clemens and the girl Jenny made them all up into pies. Clemens was worried about it, was chagrined too."

Dr. Chowning rubbed his chin, commented thoughtfully, "Well, lemon juice with the yellow rind grated in, fresh eggs . . . I expect her theory is, eat what you crave."

"Precisely. Eat what you crave. And she's got no schedules like other women. Do you know how she spent her time when they were shut in last winter? She cobbled."

"I'd think her too fragile for that."

"Not at all. She's got a bench on the hearth, and a number of shoe lasts. I don't know how stout her soles are, but she's made some original uppers for her children. Scalloped tops, fancy stitching, tassels. She cobbles the way she practices medicine, my young friend. For pleasure."

Dr. Meredith appeared so bitter that Chowning refrained from laughter. And he forebore telling that he had found Mrs. Clemens and her children tumbling the baby—that undersized, seven-months baby—on a quilt on the floor, teaching him some strenuous antics, as if he were a bear cub.

John paid slight attention to his children that year, for urgent duties were at hand: the project of making Salt River somewhat navigable, and the untimely scheme of building a railroad between the town of Paris and the village of Florida. He addressed citizens' meetings in the hamlets and became as well known in Pike and Ralls counties as in Monroe. Members of the Legis-

124

lature assembled at Jefferson City heard him out and were moved by his rudiments of engineering and his earnest statistics. The force of his misdirected energy transported them beyond their native common sense. As 1837 dawned, the year of the panic, a time when credit was collapsing and state bank notes had been nullified by Jackson's Specie Circular, when only gold and silver spoke with authority and few in the West had it, the Legislature of Missouri appointed John M. Clemens to head a board of commission to take subscriptions for the Salt River Navigation Company. A month later he was named leader of a commission to promote the short-line railway to his minute village. Nor was that all. With John Quarles and Dr. Meredith and others, he was encouraged by that same Legislature toward the founding of a school to be known as Florida Academy.

Truly, John was afloat with honors.

But Jane praised him absent-mindedly. Papa lay very ill with heart trouble at his farm home. She and Patsy and Uncle Wharton, now a Missouri farmer like his older brothers, went often to cheer him, invariably accompanied by some of their offspring. Of the children brought to see him, Benjamin had his favorites—Jane's toddler Sam with the red curls, and Wharton's two-year-old Eugene. One day he asked that they be lifted to his bed so that he could observe them at close range. This was done, but the little ones ignored the sick old man and fell to tumbling each other on the counterpane, yanking limbs and pulling hair. Benjamin Lampton laughed uncontrollably. When Wharton lifted the children down, Benjamin continued to chuckle and wheeze in mirth. And presently he died.

"Papa has passed away!" Jane called out to Patsy in awe.

It was a hard thing to explain to Aunt Polly and James Andrew, the widow and the orphan; that they had put young Gene Lampton and little Sam Clemens on Papa's bed, and Papa had laughed himself to death.

Benjamin was buried in the new cemetery at Florida village. Aunt Polly said he was laid to rest, but Jane hardly concurred. It was a gusty March day of scudding clouds and raw sunshine, like Papa's life; the grave would have a hard time confining him.

He had left his daughters nothing in worldly goods; indeed, he had never restored to them their mother's inheritance, long since spent. But the memory of his philosophy was a behest, exceeding a bequest: *be grateful for the gift of life.* Jane recalled how Benjamin had delighted in every small pleasure that befell him— in taking a horseback ride, in singing a ballad or hymn with a chance harmonizer, in drinking his evening toddy, in placing a backlog for a roaring fire—such boons he had celebrated and made much of.

Two more years, these weighty with events in that speck of a settlement. John M. Clemens built a dwelling on a forty-acre tract he owned at the village edge, a house hardly worth the mention, but his own. He ended his partnership with John Quarles, set up a sedate store across the road, half law office. Orion was taught to clerk.

John Quarles bought a larger farm out toward the prairies, sold his store to a pair of young Virginians named Moffett, and again became a country squire. He built a great log house and had a dining table constructed that would seat twenty persons. For his thirty-odd slaves he built adequate quarters. "Welcome all!" he shouted.

Jenny, deprived of close association with the Quarles people, became more unmanageable. One day in a high mood she added laughter to her defiance, and Jane Clemens picked up a whip reserved for the oxen and struck her about the bare legs. Jenny, with sinuous grace, seized the whip and held it over her opponent, undecided where to bring it down. Orion ran for his father. When John Clemens came on the run, he found the tableau intact and he took the whip and lashed Jenny angrily. The two women, left alone, looked at each other in disbelief. "A bad thing has happened to us, Jenny," Jane said. "I've struck a slave. You've dishonored your mistress." The statuesque Negro woman sauntered out to the barnyard and dealt gently with little Benjamin who had gathered a basket of eggs and dropped them.

John Clemens was appointed to a county judgeship and was paid in silver for the days he sat. It was the only money the Clemens family saw, for all was barter now, Monroe County re-

126

flecting the national panic. The Legislature of Missouri dropped its plans to develop backcountry waterways, and a light phrase was coined to illustrate the absurdity of such attempts: *Gone up Salt River.*

Jane helped John forget his humiliations by becoming pregnant again. The baby Henry was born July, 13, 1838—a well-endowed child who walked and talked early, destined to be as beautiful as a choirboy; reasonable, healthy, reliable, intelligent, obedient; a thorn in the flesh of his brother Sam. Soon after Jane had recovered from childbed, thirteen-year-old Orion, attempting to stable his father's two great oxen, was dragged by them along a picket fence and was saved from death by his mother and a wooden-legged man who was passing. That a small woman and a crippled man could restrain two mighty oxen headed for their evening oats was a miracle Jane would treasure.

When Henry was a year old he eluded the colored boy who was caring for him and toddled into the hot embers at a soap kettle. Jane laved the small feet in cold water to ease pain and prevent spasms, and Mrs. Penn came daily to apply her own concoction of "egg oil." The child healed without drawn tendons or scars.

While Henry was being tended, little Margaret of the dark curls and skipping feet came home from Miss Newcomb's school one day with her cheeks aglow and her eyes strangely bright. Dr. Meredith was sent for and he called it bilious fever. In a few days Margaret died. She was buried in the new cemetery beside her grandfather. *"Aged 9 yrs, 2 ms, 18 days,"* they wrote in the family Bible, numb with grief.

Presently Jane was racked with a new pity for John; word came from Scotland County that his beloved brother Hannibal was dead. He went at once to Janie to help her dispose of the tannery and prepare to return to Kentucky with the infant John Marshall.

Yet the changes were not quite finished. John hastily traded his Monroe County holdings for a quarter-block of property in the town of Hannibal, forty miles to the northeast. (Was it named for Uncle Hannibal? the children asked.) The mighty Mississippi would flow two blocks from their door. "The river will comfort us all," Jane said. "It's a feeling I've got."

"I dearly love this place!" Jane declared to her children.

She was setting the table at the close of their second day in Hannibal. The new residence was still in disorder because she had spent so much time at the river, marveling at it. The mighty stream was not muddy, for Indian summer had brought a season of dry weather. The neutral water took on tones of what it reflected—blue sky at a distance, bronze scrub oak and yellow-green willow along the bank. The wharf had a separate life; Jane had inspected that too. Tomorrow there was due the twice-a-week packet which plied between Keokuk and St. Louis. John expected to board it. About to become a storekeeper again, he must purchase merchandise in St. Louis.

The family ate supper amidst confusion, and afterward the children rummaged in barrels and boxes for their treasures.

John justifiably lost his temper. "Why can't we get our house straightened up, Jane?" he inquired sharply. He could not find the shears or his best cravat, though he had seen both go into a drawer when the packing was under way. Jane had also put the children's spare woolens into that drawer, along with the silver forks and spoons and her favorite cream crock. He had thought the assortment odd at the time but had said nothing. Since their recent sorrows, he and Jane had spoken no word of criticism to each other, but now he let fly.

"You very well know I'm going to St. Louis tomorrow," he reminded her. "I'll need my cravat. My good gloves and handkerchiefs too. *And where's my hat?* Will you, please, locate my necessities?"

Jane was contrite. She flew about to make amends, for she knew John must look his best; he would see businessmen of importance; he would visit his half sister and her husband, "that Englishman." She put the smoothing irons to heat and pressed all his shirts. Horrified that his formal hat was missing, she ransacked the house and found it in a corner where Benjamin had made the smallest cat a bed of it. "What luck!" she exclaimed, dusting it skillfully. "It's not hurt at all!"

Their new home was the Virginia House at the northwest corner of Main and Hill streets, a small frame hotel but three years old, the chief item in the parcel of property John had acquired from Ira Stout, the speculator. The Clemens furniture did not nearly fill the place, but they would close off the unused rooms, they had decided, and let the children play in them on rainy days. John's general store would occupy the public room, facing Main Street. Another room on the ground floor would serve him as a law office. Up Hill Street there was the inevitable stable and several pieces of rental property which had been included in the deal, mere shacks, suitable for a tin shop and the like. "Our buildings," Orion called them proudly.

John's departure for St. Louis next day was well attended by his family. Jane and the four other children accompanied him to the wharf, trooping like an honor guard, and Jenny soon followed with a clatter, drawing Henry after her in his little wagon. Jane suspected that Jenny had wakened the child in order to join the gathering, but she nowise blamed her; surely there could be few happenings around the globe today as stirring as this. More than half the town had come to meet the steamboat, some even to embark. A friendly din prevailed.

The saucy little packet, late out of Keokuk, blasted its whistle twice and came on. Water poured over its paddle wheels, smoke curled from its stacks; its gingerbread railings gleamed with white frosting. A bell clanged rather sweetly over the water.

Sam, aged four, held in check by Benjamin who was seven, lurched forward and reached out his hand. "Gimme!" he demanded.

"Ma!" Ben shrieked anxiously. "Sammy wants the steamboat!"

"I've no doubt," Jane called. "You're a good boy to hold on, Ben. Take him to Mela while I go to the plank with Pa."

John Clemens shook hands firmly with his wife and went aboard. From the deck he waved to them in a very grave way, for he was of the realistic opinion that no voyager could be assured of coming back from a steamboat trip intact. He watched the wharf of Hannibal village until a bend in the river shut it from sight.

Jane led Jenny and the children through the dispersing crowd, encountering a number of acquaintances. "We've been seeing Judge Clemens off," she explained repeatedly, whether asked or not. "He's gone to St. Louis to stock his store."

She had resolutely brought John's defunct title with them from Monroe County and had crowned him judge in perpetuum. When he would presently become a justice of the peace in Hannibal, the old title would add to his stature, would enhance him in the eyes of the townspeople and his children. Fortunately, he did not know how she built him up, or there would have been Ned to pay.

John planned to establish himself at a reputable hotel before dealing with the St. Louis wholesale houses, but first he would spend a night with his half sister Ann Hancock and her husband, William Saunders, who were expecting him.

The Saunders family lived at a good address, and John approached the brass door knocker with anticipation. He had never met his brother-in-law. Saunders had come from England to Kentucky and ultimately to Adair County for the purpose of founding a school and had accomplished that aim in the book-hungry community of gentry near the Hancock plantation. He had soon married Ann, one of Permelia's second crop of daughters. Now they were living in St. Louis where Saunders was the correspondent for a London newspaper, writing about the American frontier.

John was hospitably received in that house and soon expanded in the congeniality he found. An unexpected bonus was the presence of Polly Hancock, another of his half sisters, who had just arrived from Kentucky for a visit. She was a handsome young woman whose resemblance to their mother was remarked upon by all.

John perceived Mr. Saunders to be a man of charm and culture. Mr. Saunders perceived John Marshall Clemens to be literate and dignified beyond the average Western male, puzzlingly so. He discussed it with his wife at the first opportunity. "You failed to tell me what your half brother was like," he accused. "He's a type I've not described in my London letters."

130

"We Hancocks were children when Marshall left home," Mrs. Saunders explained. "We never felt close to him. But I think our mother has always loved him best of all her children. He's her oldest, the one she leaned on before her marriage to my father. I'm afraid Marshall always resented his stepfather."

"He appears to be well off," remarked Mr. Saunders, having the Englishman's usual preoccupation with money. "I recall the story of all that dormant land he owns in Tennessee. But he must have prospered otherwise. Did his wife bring him a dowry?"

"Jane Lampton? La, no! her highflying father was in debt to his ears. But Marshall got to be a lawyer and a landowner right young. I expect he's successful now. Yes, I'm sure he must be. You've noticed he's well-dressed. And he had a porter carry his bag."

John Marshall had no intention of disillusioning them. He talked optimistically yet honestly of the new town he was promoting up the Mississippi; his growth with the town's growth was implied.

Mr. Saunders, under the warmth of Madeira, spoke of his own prospects. He was about to go to England to claim an inheritance of four hundred pounds. On his return he would go into trade, "Perhaps start a candle factory. My sister-in-law Polly, here, has promised to stay in St. Louis with Ann and little Tip while I'm away," he said. "Tip is already devoted to her."

Tip, fetched down from the nursery, proved to be a clever little creature with a dismaying name, bestowed on her at birth by her romantic father: Mary Ann Pamela Xantippe Bryon Saunders.

Permelia Hancock's children talked finally of lovable Hannibal Clemens, so recently buried in that remote Missouri county that had had only the need of a tannery to recommend it.

"The fault was mine for sending him there," said the older brother bitterly. "I admitted as much in a letter to our mother. But what's done is done. May I go up to bed now, Mr. Saunders? Tomorrow I've a good deal of business to attend to."

"Of course!" said the host. "The girls will show you up if you are ready, and our colored boy will bank your fire. Breakfast's at

131

eight." He shook his guest's hand cordially and gave him a silver candlestick with a lighted taper to carry upstairs. "This is the last of my English candles," he said genially. "Good rest to you!"

John, before extinguishing that candle, consulted a memorandum. It bore the name *James Clemens, Jr.* and a business address. The man was the successful son of old Jeremiah Clemens of Danville in Kentucky, Jeremiah having been a cousin of John's father. It was a tenuous kinship, occasionally revived, rooted in old Virginia. In their youth, John Clemens and James had corresponded. And in 1832 John had advised James to buy ten thousand acres of Tennessee mountain land, acting as his agent. Would the shrewd financier now hold this against him? John nervously hoped not, for tomorrow he must ask him for a loan. Without token down payments at the warehouses, he could not secure his merchandise—a hazard of which Jane was blissfully unaware.

18 ❖

John's trip to St. Louis was in every way a success. He had renewed his ties with his half sisters, had met an English brother-in-law very much worth knowing, and had been well treated by wealthy James Clemens. Clemens had cheerfully granted the requested loan, and John, with that as down payment, had been able to purchase his stock at the warehouses on the usual terms of credit.

What with their many new acquaintances, some fine, some common, and with the novelty of the great Mississippi in its various phases, the winter passed divertingly for Jane and she failed to comprehend the occasional moodiness of her husband. He was often closeted with persons in his law office, but that seemed an encouraging sign. As for the store, she observed that customers came and went with regularity. Orion was clerk and manager. A handsome big boy of fifteen, he seemed adequate. She knew him to be courteous. She was not aware that he read behind the counter and never pressed for a sale. Not even his father suspected how often Orion gave credit to wheedling customers, though he had been warned to extract cash unless a man's credit had been approved or he was destitute.

In the late spring John Clemens was guilty of some strange behavior which should have given Jane pause. It hinged on her visit to Patsy Quarles, inspired by a season of beautiful weather.

Into the small spring wagon went Jane to drive. Went Jenny holding little Henry; went Orion and Pamela and Benjamin, and all the paraphernalia for the visit. Purposely omitted was four-and-a-half-year-old Sam, a child who could be counted on to make a vehicle intolerable to the other occupants. It was arranged that his father would bring him tomorrow, a Sunday, on horse-back. It was further arranged that Sam would play on Saturday with the Meredith children, and at eventide John would get his son, take him home, bathe and bed him.

All was accomplished as planned, but Sam was wakeful beyond his bedtime and used the well-known formulas to delay his retire-ment. John's patience was sorely tried, yet he kept his temper through every provocation which the shrewd and watchful child set for him. Father and son finally fell asleep in their separate rooms.

The next morning John wakened early with a blinding head-ache and the unhappy awareness that he was expected in Monroe County to join his family. He could not contemplate food, so he left the quiet house without breakfast, saddled his horse and rode away.

Habitually concerned with his health because of his dread of leaving his family in poverty, he magnified every illness that beset him. Especially headaches that manifested themselves after he had been in the sun. Might this present suffering be a return of his old sunpain? The idea distracted him, and so did the awareness of unpaid interest on his St. Louis debts. All his sources of income were failing because the villagers were not paying up. His clients, his customers, and his tenants owed him money. Those problems tormented him as he covered the miles, riding (with unconscious grace) his aging Tennessee horse. Unbelievably, he rode the twenty miles and arrived at Wharton Lampton's farm without giving Sam a thought.

"What's happened, John?" Wharton called out to him. Jane and Jenny and the children had spent last night at his house, breaking the trip, and he knew Clemens was supposed to have his red-headed little lad in the saddle with him. "Where's Sammy?" he shouted.

"What?" John asked blankly. Then: "God have mercy! I've forgotten him!"

"You can't mean it," Wharton said.

"Would I say so if I didn't? Would I joke about it? Give me a fresh horse, Wharton! I must go back!" He lurched dizzily in the saddle.

"Get down and go in the house," Wharton urged. "You're hardly fit. I'll go back for Sammy. Where am I apt to find him?"

"In the house," John Clemens said. "I left the place locked, the cookstove cold. He was asleep. Here's the key—"

But in the end, when he had drunk a dipper of water and eaten a corn pone, he borrowed a horse and accompanied Wharton, unable to bear the uncertainty of what might have happened in Hannibal. Arrived there, they unlocked the door and entered with dread. Sammy was in the kitchen. He had found a crock of clabber and had consumed it, spilling some. He had built weird settlements on the floor out of pots and pans. He had worked a hole in a meal sack and was letting the meal run out. His face was tear-stained, and he looked at his sick and shaking father resentfully.

"Carry him to his mother," John requested of Wharton. "Take my regrets to Quarles and Patsy. I'll go to bed now."

"Wouldn't you like to see a doctor?" Wharton asked.

"Yes. Stop at Dr. Meredith's, ask him to come here."

"You look pretty ill," Wharton said, reluctant to leave him.

"No, no! I need some of my pills, is all. Tell Jane to stay out her visit with Patsy." He did not look again at his child, feeling too weak to face that young hostility.

The visit to the Quarles farm (the first of several that would shine star-bright and gem-pure in literature) filled Jane and her

134

children with delight. If its perfection was marred by the peculiarity of Sam's arrival, Jane did not harp on it. John's sunpain, the familiar symptoms of which Uncle Wharton had described, made everything understandable, she said. Any man with a blinding headache might forget his child, was her theory. Didn't Patsy agree?

Patsy was not sure. "Does he have a lot of money worries now?" she asked thoughtfully. "Forgive me for bringing it up—"

"We're doing well," Jane assured her. "We own those good buildings in Hannibal, and John has some law cases."

"What about the store? Is it showing a profit?"

"I'm not sure, Patsy. We have the best stock of goods in town, but John has his other interests and he leaves the store to Orion. Sometimes I wonder if Orion's up to it. But a boy has got to learn, of course. When you doubt Orion the least bit he gets discouraged."

By the time his family returned home John Clemens had recovered from his illness and wore a cheerful countenance. By collecting some legal fees he had met the interest due on his most pressing debt, that to James Kerr, the wholesale merchant in St. Louis. He was not obliged to discuss finances with his wife and upset her serenity.

There followed a year of happy activity for Jane, a second summer as well, before she knew her husband had met with reverses. John made the dismaying revelation one evening in early October after returning from Palmyra, the county seat. He laid his hat and gloves on a table and said unemotionally, "We've lost this property, Jane."

Whenever she was startled her hands had a way of flying to her throat, like doves on a valentine. This happened now, and he quickly looked away, detaching himself from her emotion.

"Kerr wants the money I owe him. He has the right to repossess every dish and stove, every bolt of goods in my store, because, actually, it's still his."

"How humiliating!" Jane exclaimed sadly. She pictured the contents of their store being carted off to the dock while Orion wrung his poor boyish hands, and the rival storekeepers snickered.

135

"To prevent Kerr's taking the business away from me," John went on inexorably, "we must sign over this property to him."

"Is that all?" Jane's relief was profound. She recalled in a flash how, several times, Papa had signed over his real estate to Uncle John Montgomery or Uncle Lewis Lampton, and things had gone on as usual. Until, of course, William Caldwell had come on the scene. Mr. Caldwell had played for keeps, but perhaps Mr. Kerr of St. Louis was a less adamant man. They could hope.

"Next week you must go to Palmyra with me, Jane, and put your name beneath mine before a notary. On October thirteenth we must relinquish the Virginia House to James Kerr."

"I must mend that rip in my riding habit," was her reply.

"Great heavens," he muttered, confounded by the *non sequitur*. "Don't you comprehend what I've been telling you, Jane?"

"I do, John! Indeed, I do! I'll sign my name anywhere you say. But I want to look spruce when we go to Palmyra. It won't help you any, to have a dowdy wife. I could use a little curly plume for my hat. There's a green one in your showcase—"

"You can't have it," he said flintily. "It's not mine. Must you picnic through life?"

She stood desolate under the cloud of his misunderstanding. She had not thought of the trip to the Marion County courthouse as an outing. She had merely pictured herself as Lady Something-or-other in old England renouncing her titles, all her property forfeit; at such a time a woman needed to hold her head high and wear a plume. "It don't matter," she remarked, hastily returning to the nineteenth century.

"It *doesn't* matter," he said, more exquisitely pained than usual by her grammar.

"It doesn't matter," she repeated dutifully. "The feather for my hat, I mean."

After the formalities at the county seat John made some drastic changes in his affairs. Having no legal cases pending, he himself took over the running of the store and relieved Orion of his duties there.

"You've been a failure, son," he said, "both as a salesman and a

136

bookkeeper. You lack the firmness and sharpness a merchant needs. I can't use you in the store any longer."

"Where, then, Pa?" Orion asked.

Jane, who was present, saw how crestfallen the boy was, and how apprehensive. She could hardly bear it until John made a reassuring answer. "You are studious, Orion," he said. "There might be a future for you in the newspaper field. But you'll have to persevere and stop daydreaming. I've arranged to apprentice you to the *Hannibal Journal*. It's the best little weekly in this part of Missouri. You've heard me say more than once that I'd like to own it."

"You mean I'm going to be a printer's devil," Orion said unhappily. He looked at his handsome hands and his good store suit in a speculative way. Printing apprentices were necessarily ink-stained. And those in Hannibal, whether servants of the Democratic *Gazette* or the rival Whig *Journal*, were sent on such importunate errands that their ragged clothes flapped in the wind.

Jane sensed the trend of Orion's thoughts. "You needn't be as dirty as those boys you're thinking about," she told him gently. "Though you can't work in your best suit, of course. You'll keep that for Sundays and outings and calling on the girls."

"Will I live at home?"

In unison they assured him that he would, and he submissively accepted the future his father had chosen for him.

In late November, Judge Clemens brought an elderly Negro man to the kitchen and asked Jenny to prepare him a meal. He was a lean old man with pink gums and crinkled white hair. His name was Charley. He was very hungry, and he smiled at Jenny in an ingratiating way while she disdainfully served him.

"Do you know where Miss Jane is?" John asked the haughty Jenny.

"Yes, sir, I do. She's gone to Miz Horr's school for the speechifyin'. All three children are performin'. I don't look for her soon."

"Then you must help me fix up Charley, here. He's just come into my possession. He'll sleep at the store. Get me an old blanket and a washbasin. Some soap and towels too."

Jenny complied, making a good deal of noise and continuing to show her low regard for the old man who sat listening. "Did you buy him, Mr. John?" she asked incredulously at one point. "We need a new cookstove more'n we need a wore-out ole nigger."

"Of course I didn't buy him," John Clemens replied. "I took him on the settlement of a debt. A man out in the county pawned him off on me. Orion had let him run up a bill for staples and a plow."

Jenny gave a derisive laugh, establishing her status, and Charley kept smiling gently. Perhaps he was neither surprised nor offended. A spent slave without visible background or obvious future could not expect deference from the master race or his own.

"Don't speak of this to Miss Jane," Judge Clemens instructed Jenny as he led the old Negro off. "I prefer to tell her myself."

That evening after his children had gone to bed, John Clemens told his wife about Charley, but that did not conclude the news he had to impart. He was going south, he said. Going at once, while the river was still open. He had two urgent motives: he would attempt to sell part of the Tennessee land; and he would try to collect a debt of almost five hundred dollars which a man near Vicksburg owed him. He could, he hoped, sell Charley at one of the river towns for enough to finance the trip.

"Poor old darkey," Jane said mechanically. "Maybe he wants to go south and get warm. . . . Tell me, John, who owes you all that money in Mississippi? You've never spoken of it in my hearing."

"It's William Lester. He used to live in Kentucky, down about Monticello. He's been living in Mississippi for some years now. This debt was contracted in 1823 for something he bought of me."

"That was the year we married," she said, puzzled.

"Yes. It was a time when I needed money rather suddenly, if you'll remember. I sold one of my slaves to Lester."

"I thought you sold your people to the Hancocks, John?"

"Two of them, yes. But Lester offered me more for the boy Green than Simon Hancock was willing to pay. I saw no need to tell you about it. The sale was for two hundred and fifty dollars—high for that day. Unpaid interest for twenty years brings the debt

138

to four hundred and seventy dollars. The boy turned out badly and Lester repudiated the transaction, though he had no legal right to. I mean to collect."

"So you did separate a family! You once said you wouldn't."

"By the time I sold Green he was seventeen years old. A buck."

"All this slavery business—" Jane said. She got up from her chair and walked the floor. "And last year, that terrible thing you did at Palmyra!" She referred to his part, as a juror, in sending several abolitionists to the penitentiary for twelve years. The leader was a man named George Thompson, deeply religious, who kept quoting the Golden Rule. Thompson and his associates had helped five Negroes escape to free territory—"to head for the polar star," as the saying went—thereby converting valuable property; for each slave was worth five hundred dollars to his owner. John looked at the matter from a legal angle, Jane knew. And, though she was hardly aware of it, he was influenced by two elderly, upright aristocrats of the county, old Dr. Peake of Virginia and Judge Draper of South Carolina who valued property rights rather inordinately. Those old-school gentlemen admired "young Clemens," and he revered their conservative ways.

"What I did at Palmyra is beyond your comprehension, Jane. I've told you that subject is closed. You can help me now by getting all my clothes in order. The next boat going down is day after tomorrow."

"Yes, I know." She never missed a docking. "Can you go to see your mother before you come home?"

"I'll manage to, somehow. I want very much to visit her."

"It would make the trip worthwhile," she declared. "If I hadn't seen Orion for as many years as she's not seen you, I'd raise Cain. Do you want Orion put back in the store?"

"By no means, Jane. I've found a reliable clerk for the store. Orion's doing well at the *Journal*. He's applying himself. Who knows! If I can sell part of the land at a good figure, I can buy the Whig sheet for us, outright." Their talk ended on an optimistic note, the duration of John's absence being estimated as six weeks.

Two days later John and Jane went to the wharf, Charley following at a respectful distance. The old colored man was in good spirits. Jane had given him a warm scarf and a package of food. Snuff too, aplenty. "Good luck to you, Charley," she said fervently. "Maybe you will find your kinfolks down the river." Having learned that he formerly belonged in Nashville, she had urged John to try to dispose of him at one of the Tennessee ports.

In her farewell to John, Jane clung to his arm as much as he would permit, repressing her worries and uttering inanities. One such remark (when a river breeze raised skirts) was a delighted, "Look at Mrs. Holliday's striped stockings!"

The wearer of the diverting stockings was the full-blown, kind-hearted wife of Captain Richard Holliday, who had lately built a large house with turrets on the steep northerly hill. Mrs. Holliday invited Jane to go home with her from the wharf. "You'll be feeling lonesome after seeing Judge Clemens off," she said. "Do me the favor of having chocolate with me. You've not come to see me in a fortnight."

"If you'd not mind me bringing Henry this time?" Jane answered. "Jenny has the ironing to do and can't watch him."

Mrs. Holliday said to bring Henry, by all means. But how would Mrs. Clemens get him up the hill?

"He'll walk," Jane assured her. All of her children, encouraged at early ages to share her rambles, had developed a marked ability for negotiating rocky terrain and climbing hills. Little Henry, aged four, now demonstrated this gift as he and his mother accompanied their cookie-dispensing hostess to her impressive dwelling.

Mrs. Holliday kept a carriage and driver, but for short excursions it was more trouble to get the equipage up and down Holliday Hill than it was to go afoot. Besides, she was Scotch-born and a believer in exercise. Her father had been a British general in the Revolutionary War, and she wore his miniature, painted on ivory, suspended on a gold chain around her neck. In making the acquaintance of the Clemens family Mrs. Holliday had been entranced to learn that Jane's Grandfather Lampton of Virginia had had Tory leanings; that her great-grandfather had dwelt at the entailed family estate in Durhamshire before coming to America; that the present incumbent of Lambton Castle bore the title Earl

140

of Durham. Jane was not in the habit of boasting of her aristocratic origins; she would keep mouse-still on the subject in ordinary encounters. But Mrs. Holliday's own grandeur quite set her off, and their pleasure in each other's company waxed without waning.

As they trudged up the hill now they conversed in very good breath and enjoyed the fine scenery. "I was glad to notice," Mrs. Holliday said, "that Judge Clemens took his body servant with him. A man can attend to business better if he doesn't have to pull his own boots on and off."

Jane replied, "I agree with you." But being accurate where fundamentals were concerned, she added, "That old man with my husband is not his body servant. John has always waited on himself, in most ways." Still, she could not bring herself to say that old Charley was for sale. It seemed too horrid, as if John Marshall Clemens had become a slave trader. She diverted Mrs. Holliday and herself by exclaiming over a pair of late cardinal birds picking at dried berries. The male bird's plumage pleased them both and led Mrs. Holliday to tell of the wool dyes used in Scottish plaids. She was an interesting woman, or Jane would not have found time for her in the first place, turreted house or not.

19 ❖

Jane had never experienced as hard a winter. The river froze and sharp winds raked it. Firewood dwindled unbelievably, though she shut off room after room in the rambling house and drew her family together. Many essentials were blessedly available at the store—staples and shoes and boys' breeches, and yarn for the hose which she not too skillfully knit. But pork and beef from the slaughterhouse were high; root vegetables were scarce. The apples which the children craved were elusive, families with fathers somehow getting them first.

Though Orion had long hours at the *Journal* office, he manfully cut kindling at home, cleaned the stable, and milked the cow. The horses had been loaned to a farmer during John's absence; but the cow required attention, and Jane fed and watered the creature and gave it the run of the back yard, weather permitting. She had never acquired the art of milking. "If you don't learn to do certain things," she once told Pamela in confidence, "you'll not have to do them." Certainly she had never become familiar with a washboard, nor with such chores as cleaning poultry and making soap. At cooking, however, she was fairly adept. She could lay a good fire and keep it going. Her sewing and mending would bear scrutiny if studied for effect. At nursing she was as willing and dedicated as Grandmother Casey in her heyday.

There was a delight that winter. "Come quick and look!" Jane called to the children one morning, routing them from their beds. "It's an ice storm!" A misty rain had fallen and frozen—a more extensive sleet than Missouri had yet produced for them. Every shrub and tree wore glittering crystal, with frozen pendants swaying in the wind. As they watched, the sun came up rosily, making countless multicolored jewels. Sam clung to his mother's hand and trembled. "It's nothing to hurt you, Sammy," she assured him, supposing he found the spectacle frightening. "We've seen ice on the trees before, but never so fine and bright. Come eat your breakfast while it's hot. Jenny's cooked a big kettle of oatmeal for us."

During the bluster of March, Jane had a letter from Patsy telling that their father's widow, their "Aunt Polly," had died at her Monroe County farm and been laid to rest in the Florida cemetery. The funeral was well attended Patsy said. She expressed pity for bereaved James Andrew who seemed so boyish and lost. He was about to go over to Macomb, Illinois, she said, and "read medicine" with his Uncle Charles Hays. Jane and Patsy had long ago ceased to resent their stepmother, had even come to see her sterling traits; but Jane had never given up imitating her for the entertainment of her children. Abandoning her own musical drawl she would sometimes employ Polly Hays Lampton's twangy tones— hands lifted shoulder-high, eyes raised skyward—in such phrases as "Do tell!" and "Land sakes!" and "I never did see the beat of you children!" And at times she would admonish her boys, "Don't plague me! Don't get my dander up!" (Sam would one day borrow the vernacular for Tom Sawyer's grayheaded Aunt Polly,

142

effectively combining it with the gullibility of his younger and more tenderhearted mother.)

Writing to Patsy, Jane confessed that she was saddened by their stepmother's passing and regretted the way they had vexed and tormented her in their youth. She said she would like to atone now through James Andrew, poor Aunt Polly's ewe lamb. If James Andrew wasn't happy over there in Illinois, he must come to Hannibal and let her look after him as one of her own. It hardly occurred to her that Polly Lampton would have lifted her hands in horrified protest at such an arrangement. To Jane herself it seemed ideal. While the March winds howled and her temporarily fatherless children looked to her for guidance she was moved to include her orphaned half brother.

John wrote with regularity but brevity from the South. He made definite plans for returning; unmade them. Toward the end of March he arrived at Hannibal on the Keokuk packet.

His homecoming was not the conclusion of a successful mission. Only his visit to his mother had turned out well, and he might have accomplished that in weeks instead of months and at a fraction of what he had spent.

"That's the sum and substance of it," he told Jane after recounting his misadventures. He had gone by steamboat up and down the lower Mississippi offering Charley for sale and trying to dispose of his Tennessee lands to speculators from Memphis to New Orleans. No acceptable offer for the land was received. At Natchez he parted with Charley for forty dollars, the payment to be made in December in tar.

"In tar!" Jane repeated. It was like Oliver Goldsmith's spectacles, somehow.

As for the other undertaking, John had hired a horse, bought a used saddle and bridle at Vicksburg, and ridden forty miles inland to find his debtor William Lester. But he had not collected on the note because, as he explained to Jane, "It would have worked a hardship on the man to pay at that time." Indeed, though Mr. Lester was admittedly solvent, John Clemens had forgiven the interest on the debt, settling for the original two hundred and fifty dollars, to be paid in March. However a second trip to

Lester's inland farm a fortnight ago had not caused the payment to materialize.

"You were real hard on the black man," Jane said edgily. "You sold him at a Natchez dock, where he won't last long. He's too old for roustabouting in the sun. But you were mighty considerate of the white man. You were too easy on Lester, considering how your family needs money. You took your time, too! Building up your health, as you've admitted, by those long horseback trips. I could do with some horseback rides in a mild climate, myself!"

The older children were listening to this, her first tirade against the head of the house. Orion and Pamela would not forget their father's look of sad defeat when he replied to her, "I tried the only things I knew to do, Jane. I can't dig in the streets."

There was a coldness between them then, for each felt ill-used by the other. A reconciliation occurred in May, terribly accomplished. Benjamin fell sick with one of the river fevers and died with a suddenness that shocked even Dr. Meredith. He was not quite ten years old. Over the little boy's bed the stricken parents reached out for each other and kissed. It was an unprecedented sight to the children, made more strange by the circumstances.

Jane went down into the depths. Before the interment she knelt continually beside Benjamin's bier in the parlor, uttering low moans that came from a sorrow beyond her bearing. She had the children feel the face of the little boy, to make them realize with her that he was irrevocably distinct from them. "We must bury him in the ground tomorrow," she stated with a bleakness she could not soften. She did not mention God, seeing herself as not on speaking terms with Him. At the funeral, that sort of thing would be taken care of by the minister of the Methodist meeting-house where Ben, with the other Clemens children, had drifted into Sunday school.

To her husband, Jane Clemens said repeatedly in a very panic of surprise, "We hardly knew little Ben!" And she would elucidate that idea to the friends who came to console. "We know our other children well—Orion and Mela and Sam and Henry. We knew our Margaret who died when she was this very age and is buried beside my father over in that other county. I delighted in

144

Margaret. I remember every curl on her head. I made her the prettiest clothes! But Benjamin, we took for granted. We were always telling him, 'Watch Sammy.' I don't think I ever asked him, 'What are you thinking, dear?' And he was not the kind to tell you, like the others. It's odd. A boy so sweet and dear, and we hardly knew him."

As the weeks passed, her sorrow kept with her. She slept fitfully and approached her meals with aversion. Her face became bone-thin and pale. She could not swallow solid food, she declared, for it choked her. She subsisted on milk and the residue of cooked vegetables—pot liquor, it was called (Jenny ladled it out to her), a nutriment long used by slaves. She kept her strength and went often to the river to look out over the water, seeking the answers there. Like other mothers bereft, she was composing an acceptable Heaven where children would be themselves. And she was beating her wings toward predestination, solace of her Montgomery ancestors.

Her actions were observed in Hannibal with puzzlement and sympathy. It was thought "the decline" would be fatal to her. Persons who were well-intentioned tried to divert her when they met; and she would respond courteously, but as from a great distance. Toward animal life, especially anything young or small or imprisoned, she was becoming more painfully solicitous, giving rein to a bent already noticeable. She would walk any distance to avoid the sight of calves being driven to the slaughterhouse. She would not step on ant hills or permit her children to do so. She was seen to extricate a bee that had missed a dandelion and overshot into the mud.

"Yet Mrs. Clemens never goes near the burying ground," the townspeople commented. Furthermore, they said, the child's grave could do with some sodding. Mrs. Holliday sent flowers from her garden, thinking to improve the clay-dry little mound, but the stricken woman gave the bouquets away to anyone who admired them.

Jane had a dutiful conviction that she should not leave her husband at such a season of sorrow; but her wish to see her comprehending sister finally prevailed. Near summer's end she sug-

145

gested to John that she take Pamela and Sam and Henry and go to visit Patsy. When he consented she brightened visibly.

"I wish Orion could go, too," she said experimentally. "He had a hard winter for a boy his age." But John ruled that Orion must stick to his apprenticeship. He was no more inclined to spoil a son, he explained, than a slave he might own.

Jenny, it was agreed, would remain in Hannibal to keep house for the master and Orion. She received the news with elation. Steamboats had become her delight. The deck hands, the jolly big Negroes from St. Louis, vied for Jenny's saucy repartee as they unloaded the freight marked for Hannibal. "Miss Jenny," they called her, impressed by her arrogance and good looks. She could have taken her pick.

John Quarles sent for Jane and the children in his farm wagon, capably driven by a middle-aged colored man named Daniel. The young ones called him Uncle Dan'l, and even Sammy obeyed him.

When they were preparing to leave home, Jane permitted her children to choose some extra possessions that were important to their happiness: Pamela her new guitar brought from St. Louis by her father; Henry his story books; Sam his kittens in a basket, and his doorknobs. She was thankful Orion was not there to see them depart, for he loved a journey and was feeling put upon that he must set type while the more favored ones took off for Florida. Orion was not a boy to conceal his disappointments any more than his aspirations and triumphs. His great brown eyes would glint with tears as readily as with joy. But he would not be lonely. He "liked girls," and now, almost seventeen, he was invited to drink lemonade on the best porches.

The two little boys rode in the wagon seat with Daniel, watching the wonders of the road from a high vantage. Jane and Pamela occupied hickory chairs fastened to the wagon bed and were shaded from the August sun by large straw fishing hats. Pamela played her guitar, practicing snatches of ballads that appealed to her. Naturally musical, she would attempt to play by ear as well as note. The family was proud of her; and Jane was inclined to exclaim, "That's just too beautiful, Mela!" whether she strayed off key or not.

146

During a time of silence in the wagon Daniel said, "Mis' Jane, I was sick-sorry to hear youall lost Ben."

"Do you remember him, Daniel?" she asked eagerly. "Can you call him to mind very well?"

"Lord'a mercy, yes'm."

"Oh, I'm glad!" she exclaimed. "Tell me some things."

Daniel was silent, perhaps momentarily hard put to memorialize Benjamin, whose personality had emitted a soft glow but not a sparkle.

"Ben was so useful," Jane prompted hungrily. "He would do us any favor we asked. Sometimes we forgot to thank him. And I can't remember anything special we ever did just for him."

Daniel saw what was wanted of him and he delivered in spirit and in truth. His sympathy poured forth in a flood of little memories culled from Ben's visits to the farm. It was like a spring freshet. He repainted Benjamin for his mother, and in every scene the child was happy. There was nothing big to tell; only the trivialities, all good, and now become relevant and hoardable, that added to the boy's sum. His conclusion was a delicate masterpiece: "The *dee*light Ben took in helpin' folks was a caution. Now that I think on it, that little fellow had a lifetime of pleasure afore he was called!"

Jane wept. Presently she asked Pamela to play something lively.

Her reunion with Patsy was rich in talks and walks. For once, Patsy had no infant tugging at her breasts, her youngest, little Sara, having passed four years without a successor.

"I hope I'm through bearing children," Patsy said plaintively. "I've hardly been out of a wrapper since I married. Last year I had the best seamstress over in Paris—"

"Not the one in France?" Jane said in a burst of mirth. "You mean the county seat, I reckon?"

"Yes, the Paris where Papa took us to the races. It's good to hear you laugh that way again, Jane. Well, I had that seamstress make me several dresses. And John Adams took me to St. Louis and we stayed a week and saw all the sights. You remember my writing you about it."

Jane remembered, though the hard year had intervened. She had rejoiced that Patsy had at last gotten somewhere.

The sisters took long rambles through woods and pastures, now with a troop of children, now alone. They came back exhausted, to the benefit of both, Patsy having lost a pound or two, Jane having gained an appetite. Pamela's pale skin assumed a becoming color and her figure began to hint at the curves that Permelia Hancock's granddaughter had a right to expect. Sammy gained weight and ceased to be querulous. They forgot that he had been sickly. All this happened in the seven weeks John Clemens advised them to linger there.

He had his reasons; he had been trying desperately to rally his finances and keep a roof over their heads. But he had failed. When Jane and the children returned home she was told the news. Their creditors in St. Louis had ordered a sale of the Virginia House and the smaller buildings, the vacant lots and the contents of the store. All must be put at auction in a fortnight.

"Jenny may have to go up, too," John said, "unless you'll consent to an immediate private sale." He named the affluent man who had offered to buy their Jenny at a good price. "He can place her as a chambermaid on a steamboat, he says. A big boat making the St. Louis to New Orleans run."

"Let me talk to her," Jane said, shocked and bewildered. This news surmounted all the rest. She went to the kitchen.

The two women confronted each other, and Jenny took charge. "Don't take on, Miss Jane," she warned, "it won't do nary bit of good. Mr. John's failed in business all down the line. Mr. Robard's houseman told me so. He say everything's goin' to be auctioned off. Well now, *I* ain't aimin' to be."

"I won't let you be sold in any way, Jenny. I'll manage somehow. You're a part of our family."

"That's a white folks lie, Miss Jane. It's the way white folks lie to themselves and lie to us slaves. Come hard times, the chilluns stay on but the niggers have to go. It's just a question of how soon. Well, I've found my own buyer and he's been to see Mr. John. What I aim to be is a maid on a packet and I've got the qualities."

148

"The qualifications," Jane corrected, heavyhearted. She tried to think of Jenny's stubborn ways, her snobbishness toward her own race, her responses to correction that were on the brink of insolence. Instead, she recalled her sympathy in times of sorrow and her savage loyalty when the Clemens standing was belittled.

Jenny interrupted the reverie. "You know very well, Miss Jane, I can lace up a lady and fix her hair to a fare-you-well. Why else is Miz Holliday always borrowin' me? I spec' many a silver dollar will come to my hand for prettyfyin' the travelin' ladies on the steamboat."

"They won't all be ladies," Jane said quickly.

Jenny laughed. "Who's to know?"

"*You'*ll know," Jane answered. "Try to keep your feeling for what's good and what's bad, Jenny. Try hard." There was no more to be said, they both knew. In a slave, only the heart was accountable.

Parting with Jenny was the hardest of the ordeals. The rest of it seemed a routine to Jane, for such things had been happening to her since her girlhood. Nobody bid-in the property on auction day (out of respect for John Clemens, it was said), and they were permitted to remain in the Virginia House as tenants. John continued his law practice and storekeeping. In a local election he was made a justice of the peace, an office that permitted him to earn small fees in a variety of ways. Jane took to board their friend Miss Newcomb, the Virginian schoolteacher they had known in Monroe County, and a genteel Southern widow and daughter named Sexton with the pleasantest results.

Orion was doing well at the *Journal*, even selecting some of the space fillers which he set in type. He asserted his religious independence that autumn by leaving the Old Ship of Zion Methodists and aligning with the Presbyterians, who had no objection to his dancing and reading novels, as long as he did neither on Sunday. Pamela and the two younger boys attended Mrs. Horr's school, where Miss Newcomb was an effective teacher. Only Sammy resented and strove to evade the long hours of confinement. Pamela and little Henry found an almost intoxicating pleasure in the perusal of the printed page.

So passed a productive twelvemonth. But once again October brought its threat of calamity. This time Mr. Kerr took no chances. He divided the property into seven attractive packages, irresistible to Hannibal's businessmen. When the auctioneer's hammer had sounded its last thump, everything had been disposed of.

Wealthy James Clemens of St. Louis had sent an emissary to the auction—one of his clerks. To the agent's bid fell a narrow vacant lot, halfway up Hill Street (destined for a fame beyond their ken), and he informed John Clemens that he might use it to build a house on, if he so desired. Indeed, James Clemens strongly advised it. A yearly stipend could be paid as ground lease, the agent said, making the arrangement legal. Furthermore, the occupant must pay the taxes.

"I'm surprised and obliged," John Clemens said stiffly. The arrangement was rather complicated; he could not be sure of his cousin's motives. Pride of name, John suspected. The rich and prominent Mr. Clemens of St. Louis would not care to see another Clemens reduced to living in a shack just a hundred miles away on the same big river.

Yet there was more to it, and it soon came out. September-a-year-ago James Clemens, returning from a business trip to Burlington, had been attended at the Hannibal dock by Orion, sent there by John because he himself was unavoidably absent in Palmyra. Orion had delivered his father's apologies so courteously and had given such a good account of himself as an aspiring young newspaperman that Mr. Clemens was impressed. And now Orion was to have his reward: he could have, for the taking, immediate work, with pay, at Ustick's job printing house in St. Louis. If he but applied himself, he could look forward to a bright future in the city.

"Mr. Clemens has secured the place for him," said the agent, a brisk man, all business. "He recommends that your son be sent to the compliant firm as soon as possible, while the opening holds. A suitable place will be found for the young man to board. Something near to his work, with a homelike atmosphere."

"I accept the arrangement gratefully," John Clemens answered, for it seemed to him almost too good to be true. If he thought of talking it over with Jane and Orion, the impulse was fleeting. "Orion is already an accomplished compositor. I want him to have a newspaper career, if possible."

"And about the unimproved lot on Hill Street?" the efficient clerk inquired over his high collar. "What am I to tell Mr. James Clemens? Must he sell it? Or would you like to build your family a little dwelling on it?"

"I have to withhold my answer in regard to that generous offer. If there's enough money left to me after the creditors are paid, I'll gladly build the house. Ask my kinsman to give me a few months to get my bearings. But I'll send the boy to him on the next boat. That's to say, I'll let him accompany you to St. Louis tomorrow."

He broke the news to Jane and Orion with all speed. Jane's two doves flew to her throat, but she presently put them to work packing Orion's clothes. Her tears fell as she folded his things into their one good portmanteau. At intervals she smiled sunnily at Orion and reminded him of his good fortune. "So unexpected!" she kept saying.

John too encouraged the boy. "In another year you'll have graduated from typesetting," he predicted. "I know nothing of the Ustick people, but James Clemens knows them well. He apparently thinks an apprenticeship there will further your career. I'm gratified that Cousin James takes stock in you. It's like Langhorne's sponsorship of me when I was your age."

"Yes, Pa, I understand!" Orion exclaimed. "I'll make the most of my opportunities, count on that! I'll make you and Ma and Mela proud of me." Seeing Sam and Henry gazing at him as he jumped about, he added generously, "Some day I'll set my little brothers up in business. Any business they like."

And so next day in his best suit, become somewhat shabby and tight, Jane's bright and eager eldest son went out to meet the world.

As they left the corner of Main and Hill streets to go to the wharf Jane reminded him, "We'll not be living in this same house when you come back to visit us, Orion. You're absent-minded and you'll forget that. Don't let it upset you to find other people living

151

in this house." She could not tell him what door to knock on when he should come, but it was immaterial to Orion. His home would be where his family was, and he would find that place.

Taking their own furniture, they went to Pavey's Hotel; there was no other place to go. The move had to be made with doused pride, for it was not a first-rate tavern. Mr. Pavey, a huge, bearded man of European extraction, drank heavily and was brutish toward his wife and their three daughters. "A regular Corsican," people called him. Though he ate in the tavern's kitchen and kept out of sight, his un-American accents could often be heard roaring abuses. His womenfolk, patient and persevering and of refined bearing, saved the reputation of the place and gave it aspects of respectability.

Mrs. Sexton and her child Margaret went with the Clemens family to Pavey's, Mrs. Sexton being a rudderless woman who had become attached to Jane Clemens and objected to leaving her. The Clemenses were fond of the Sexton girl. To Sam and Henry she was enhanced by the wearing of the name Margaret, an appellation that had become beautiful to them through the legend of their lost sister. Even Jane had come to take pleasure in calling Mrs. Sexton's pretty child Margaret; though at first she had hesitated to take them to board, suitable though they were, because of it; she had thought she could not bear it.

The Clemens suite, a downstairs wing resting in the mud, became the salon for Pavey's best. Even the Pavey girls sought admittance to the circle, and Jane welcomed them warmly when they came timidly knocking. Because they were young and burdened and had no fun, she was drawn to them from the first. She made them each a "best dress" from some material their mother managed to procure for them.

"Don't let your father see you wearing your new dresses," she warned them, for she was aware of his insane rages and had no desire to stir him up. She instructed Sam and Henry to stay out of the man's way. "We'll not live here long," she frequently told them. "Before long, we're going to have a house of our own."

She often slipped off from the noisy tavern and took solitary

152

walks beyond the town, trying to understand the vicissitudes of her life. One bleak November day when walking through a barren pasture she resolved to become a declared Christian, to accept her infant baptism. It was partly through fear of the Almighty that she made the decision; for the theory had come to her ears that the deaths of her children seemed her special punishment for neglecting religion. If this were true, her other children also might be taken, one by one, until she was humbled. She must leave nothing untried. Already she was dosing them for every symptom of fever, cold, or rash. But perhaps she needed the Bible more than the medical book John had recently purchased. (It had come complete with an oak cabinet of remedies.) And if the Bible, then why not church membership? No doubt she had been wrong in supposing she could address God while admiring a sunset or a blossom; that was not the same as confessing Him before men. . . . There were three denominations in the town. The Presbyterian way would be the better. Granny Casey had told her that it offered a peculiar comfort through the doctrine of predestination, everything being a part of God's pattern somehow. Granny believed, as the poem says,

> *This great thing that befell you*
> *Is out there, now, in space;*
> *If you will observe it*
> *With a grave face.*
> *But it is there no more now*
> *Than always on the skies.*
> *God, ere it ever happened,*
> *Beheld it with grave eyes.*

She went home and told Pamela of her resolve. "I'm going to unite with the Presbyterian church," she said. "It's my choice because of predestination. But if you're fond of the Old Ship of Zion, Mela, stay on there. Let the little boys stay, too. There's no need for us all to do the same thing."

"But I'd rather go with you," Pamela answered. Already the Methodists were frowning on her guitar; she had a number of music pupils, but none was from the Old Ship of Zion. To that

153

dedicated parish in Hannibal, even the Scottish Highland fling was an invitation down the primrose path.

It was Pamela who broke the news to John. "Ma and I are joining the Presbyterian church next Sunday," she told him.

He was surprised. "I thought your mother might become a Methodist," he remarked. "She seemed to prefer that Sunday school for you children. Now and then she's attended services there."

"It's better this way, Pa," Mela said thoughtfully. "You've no idea how she's embarrassed me at Old Ship of Zion. When all the congregation says 'A-men'—which they do a good deal—Ma says 'Ah-men.' She drawls it out as if she were the only body in church. Even the preacher looks at her."

John favored his daughter with a rare smile. "There's this about it, Pamela, and you'll know it when you're older and wiser. She may embarrass you sometimes, but it won't be important." He made no effort to explain.

"What do you know about predestination?" Pamela prodded. "That's back of Ma's choice. She told me so."

"I know chiefly this, Pamela. It's a comfort to some people. To others, it's repellent. Will you feed the cats now and stop their meowing? If Pavey kicks them, there'll be trouble."

Jane, without delay, became an active churchwoman in good standing, attending service regularly, helping with suppers and other fund-raising enterprises as if her very life depended on it.

"Must you take your new religious life so hard?" John inquired.

"Whatever is worth doing is worth doing well," she told him as if he had never heard of the adage. The hardest chore for her was to sit through the long, doctrinal sermons; but she schooled herself to do it. The church had acquired the bell of the old steamboat *Chester* and its summons was pleasantly nautical, which helped a great deal. Soon the two little boys followed its peals to Sunday school. And now the Clemens family, all, excepting John, were "abandoned Presbyterians."

After the debts were settled, John saw that enough remained to meet his need, the building of a house on the lot proffered him by his cousin James Clemens. He drew plans, selected timbers and weatherboarding, set two carpenters to work. Jane and the children went every day to see the progress being made, taking apples or sandwiches for refreshment and making conversation with the carpenters. Sam collected curly shavings which he fashioned into a wig, and he negotiated the ladders very nimbly. Henry read through his entire primer while seated on a catwalk.

The new house seemed extraordinarily small as the timbers went up. Jane at first felt consternation but, quickly accepting the inevitable (Cousin James's lot being so narrow), she began to tell the family how cozy and convenient it was going to be. Though the mill work was shoddy and the tight little staircase lacked grace, the rooms were adequate in number. Tall windows gave an outlook wherever feasible and were to be equipped with shutters for reducing the glare of summer afternoons and the cold of winter nights. They would also protect a lamp-lit house, flush with the street, from stray pepper shots when the town rowdies led by the Hyde boys went on their sprees.

Jane ardently desired a spinet piano for the little parlor; Pamela needed it. By giving guitar lessons Mela had been able to pay for her own piano lessons. "She has a nice repertoire," Jane declared.

The dream piano was realized through a little legacy which arrived that year from Grandmother Casey. The stanch old lady had recently died in her eighty-third year, having weathered one more Iowa winter. In her last letter to her namesake and eldest granddaughter Mrs. Casey had written: *Now that you have joined the church my chief prayer for you is fulfilled. . . . If you and Patsy can come up the river to see me this summer I will be more than glad. We will talk of your grandf^r and Uncle Green and your mother. We will talk of K^y. I am not yet feeble nor failing in mind. Green's widow and children are my comfort. Write soon. Lovingly y^r Grandm^r.* Jane answered the letter, promising the visit.

She had not expected the legacy. "Should I divide it with Patsy, I wonder?" she asked John. "She got nothing, I hear."

"Patsy needs nothing," John answered shortly. "Mrs. Casey knew that. With you, it's a different story. Your lacks are infinite."

"I've lacked very little, John. Only some luxuries I wanted for us that we didn't hardly need."

155

"Don't double your negatives, Jane. Now that Jenny's not here to corrupt your grammar, try to improve it. . . . About the legacy. Spend the money on those luxuries you've wanted. It's your due."

"Very well, John. A piano for Mela. She gets tired of going up the hill to practice on Mrs. Holliday's."

He nodded. "Now think of something for yourself."

"I'd like to invest what's left in silkworm culture."

He was caught by surprise. "I can hardly encourage anything that freakish, Jane. Surely you remember those booms, ten or twelve years ago? Imported mulberry shoots changed hands a dozen times before planting. The money lost on them was deplorable."

Nothing daunted, Jane took a St. Louis newspaper clipping from her pocket and read from it animatedly. Missouri had the first requirement for local silkworm culture, said the piece; it was the native Osage orange tree, a species of mulberry which silkworm moths found attractive and the larvae found succulent. Some Frenchmen at Cape Girardeau who had engaged successfully in the industry in their native land were now backing an enterprise never before offered to Americans. "Silk cloth was first woven in 2600 B.C. for Si-ling-Chi, wife of the third Emperor of China," Jane read rhapsodically. "It was worth its weight in gold. In time, Japan, Syria, Persia, India, Italy, and France learned to make silk, to the delight of their women and the profit of their men."

"Great heavens, I know all that business," John said. "And I know you like the sight and feel of silk."

"Oh, I do! I even dote on the rustle of it. The bronze taffeta dress you bought for me in Louisville is now my best petticoat."

"I've heard of some fine stuff you once picked up without benefit of silkworms," John said with a laugh, for the joke was on Cyrus Walker, his former law teacher, now cool to him.

Most of Adair County had heard of the incident. Jane Lampton and her crowd had gathered at the home of her cousin Flora Montgomery Walker one summer night, and Jane had been persuaded to do her famous imitation of Cyrus Walker dancing the Virginia reel—the current version, which was formal. Every one was laughing at the mimicry when attorney Walker opened the door and walked in. He was just back from doing the circuit

156

courts on horseback and was carrying a roll of silk, two dress lengths in fact, which he had received as a fee for defending a client. "Jane Lampton's been imitating how you dance," his wife confessed. "Won't you do it again, Jane? For Cyrus?" Jane had declined with horror and was making a hasty retreat when Cyrus began to unroll the material, which was peacock blue. "Look, Jane," he said, "there's enough silk here for Flora and another person to cut a dress from. You can be the other person if you'll mock me the way you did the first time. I've wondered how I look, tripping it." Jane performed, not altering the caricature, and won the yardage.

"It was wicked the way I used to take people off," Jane Clemens said of Jane Lampton. "I must have wanted that silk goods awfully bad." Then, "Will you attend to this for me, John? When you go to St. Louis to get the spinet, will you buy into this company for us?"

"If that's your wish, Jane. If it's your determined choice. For all I know, it could be a reasonable venture."

That was the year, 1844, when the Grim Reaper laid about him promiscuously with his scythe. John had news of his mother's death in Kentucky and was troubled by her unfulfilled wish "to see Marshall once again," though he was comforted to learn from his sister Caroline's letter that "old Dr. Gaither" had attended her faithfully to the last. . . . In Hannibal, an epidemic of measles took away forty persons, many of them children. It seemed that Sam would be among them; but Dr. Cunningham and Jane promoted a dramatic healing of the child's body by packing him in bags of hot ashes. He had contracted the disease from choice, crawling into the unguarded bed of his sick playmate, little Will Bowen, in order to catch it.

Sam, no longer having Benjamin to restrain him, created a problem almost beyond Jane's ability to resolve. No doubt he missed Ben sorely and was baffled by the loss. Little Henry, immersed in his story books, was no comfort to him. He continually sought the company of the more active boys in his vicinity and sometimes followed them to the muddy little creek which drained the southern meadows. One hot summer day Jane missed him and searched with agitation. A colored man named Neal who worked at Pavey's was sent posthaste by her to Bear Creek, some clue having informed her of Sam's whereabouts. And Neal, arriving in the nick of time, pulled the child from a water hole and saved his life. Jane carried the news to John at the site of the new house.

John was disturbed as he faced the fact that Hannibal was dominated, so to speak, by Aquarius. "Sam must be taught to swim at once," he said. "It may be I can hire the older Blankenship boy to teach him. He's considered the best swimmer around here."

"I only know Tom, the younger one," Jane offered. "He's dirty but kind. Sometimes he condescends to eat an apple with us."

"We're going to live too close to that family, I'm afraid." John was looking distrustfully at the shabby, barnlike house that loomed back of them, the castle of Woodson Blankenship who worked, when the mood struck him or dire necessity impelled, at the sawmill. "On second thought, I'll teach Sam to swim, myself."

"We're to ignore the Blankenships, then?"

"We can accept them or ignore them, Jane—whichever way seems best. But either way, they'll give us trouble."

"I wouldn't be surprised," Jane conceded.

20 ❖

John loomed large in the little house on Hill Street and large in the town. His ambitions for the community seemed reasonable to his like-minded townsmen. He advocated the rebuilding of unfit roads (having studied the macadamizing principles of Scotland's Loudon McAdams), the promotion of a railroad from Hannibal to St. Joseph, a well-stocked library for the town and a cultural club in connection with it; even a little college, if some outside capital could be lured. Plans to detach Hannibal from politically torn Marion County and annex it to congenial Ralls County to the south, found him in accord. When committees met, he often drafted the resolutions, for none surpassed him in the writing of clear English.

Thus John was exaltedly engaged in 1845 and the following

158

year, though he made very little money. Jane was puzzled by his civic prominence and his flat purse. During the first months in the new little house they employed a woman servant at the rate of forty dollars a year from a master who offered her for hire. At year's end, John said they must descend the scale to something cheaper, so they obtained a little boy named Sandy, recently brought out from Maryland. Sandy lived with them but, being yet a child, could not meet the family's needs. A laundress must be hired once a week, and occasionally a handy man. Through such deals, cannily arranged, Jane managed her housework. A wash-woman might be had more cheaply on a Thursday than on a Monday; a carpetbeater was more readily obtained in July than at spring-cleaning time. "We're not choosy," Jane would say, knowing they could not afford to be.

One of the Clemens laundry days was memorable. John, finding himself with a legal client on his hands, a north Missourian farmer, invited the man to accompany him home and share "a plain wash day dinner." He sent a boy on the run to ask that an extra plate be put on. When host and guest reached the table they were astonished to see a large baked turkey gracing the board, hot, succulent, uncut. Jane could not understand John's frozen de-meanor as he carved. To ease the silences, she talked about farm-ing, a subject with which she was only superficially acquainted. She did not know until later that John was scandalized by the turkey.

"What will Wheeler think of me?" he demanded to know that evening. "'A plain wash day dinner,' I told him. Why didn't I get as much? Have you gone out of your mind?"

Jane was glad to explain. Tillie, the hired woman, had no more than arrived that morning when a boy came to the back yard dragging the poor turkey—a nice little hen, its head down, and gasping—and offered to sell it for fifty cents. "I wanted to get it out of its misery," Jane said. "I asked him if he could kill it neat and clean with an ax. He said yes, and did. Then Tillie scalded and picked and dressed it, and I cooked it. Tillie didn't get the ironing done, we ran late. But I never saw a prettier turkey on a platter, if I must say so, myself."

"I assume you gave it a good long drink of water before it was axed," John remarked.

"Yes, I did. I took the time. But how could you know that?"

Jane was becoming more occupied in brightening the Presbyterian socials and pouring at tea parties. She also attended whatever evening events the community afforded, accompanied by her austere husband and quiet daughter. Her delight in those things was unfeigned and the procuring of clothes for Mela and herself was a pleasant challenge. She was tireless in ripping up dresses, turning the cloth, changing necklines, adding furbelows.

John knew of her efforts but was only half grateful. He thought she got herself up too youthfully. By candlelight or lamp light she might be mistaken for Pamela's sister. Not that she painted. She did nothing to her skin except scrub it and protect it from the sun. In open daylight one might observe some crow's-feet and fine lines. But the texture was still good, and she was blessed with white teeth and red lips, not to mention her profusion of mahogany hair, fading a bit but curling as of yore. Her waist was small, her back straight. Her excellent ankles were too visible, John suspected as he guided her over the floor at dances in City Hall. (Balls, the newspapers labeled them when the Masons or Odd Fellows sponsored; cotillions when the young men of the area achieved something more select.) She had taught him to waltz while Pamela played the tempo. But in his own parlor or abroad, he held his partners more distantly than was the vogue.

Jane's social graces, like her unself-conscious camaraderie with Hannibal's poorest, were an asset to him. Encouraged toward politics by Judge Draper and old Dr. Peake, he expected to run for office. It was to his advantage that Jane's company was sought by Mrs. Garth, the tobacco manufacturer's wife; by Mrs. C. H. Bower whose husband was the Masonic bigwig; by Mrs. Thomas Miller whose husband was Bower's partner in the commission business. It surprised him agreeably that Jane was congenial with Mrs. Butler, a misplaced New Englander who was rearing her son formally, keeping him shoe-shod.

In the Clemens family now the young people seemed perpetually on the move; Jane packed and unpacked their well-worn

160

raiment. As soon as Mr. Cross's school released restless Sam for the summer, Pamela would take him to the Quarles farm. While there, she would give music lessons on Aunt Patsy's new pianoforte. Many persons rode a distance to be instructed by her. Some preferred the guitar, for that instrument was having a furor of favor and was more easily mastered. At other seasons, Pamela would hold classes in the prosperous town of Paris.

During such absences she was acutely missed. She and Jane were devoted in spite of the differences in their ways. Jane hoped Mela would capture a desirable beau during her peregrinations but, so far, she had not. John Clemens had several times warned his daughter, "Don't pick a callow youth without an education." That advice shaped her attitude toward the young men who clustered around her piano, for she rarely encountered one who was reading Shakespeare or could translate a line of Vergil; and if callow meant to caterwaul at the piano or strum a guitar, they were too often of that variety. To Pamela, her father's opinions were sacrosanct. She was aware of the touching sacrifices he made to buy books for her. She repaid him with gratitude.

Orion, the reluctant exile, spent all of his savings coming home for Sundays and holidays, the night boats making that possible. When in Hannibal he was usually courting unsuccessfully one or another of the local belles, their opinion of him being that he was "good company but a poor prospect." On one trip to Hannibal, Orion made a speech of a whimsical nature before the Library Institute. (He was studying oratory of an evening in St. Louis.) During another visit home he joined the Baptist church and was immersed in his best suit.

"Orion is looking for something," his mother said.

And now James Andrew Lampton accepted the invitation of two years ago and came to Hannibal to annex himself to "Sister Jane." But his new status was surprising. He was a bewildered widower at nineteen. Either with or without the consent of his uncle, Dr. Hays, he had become a bridegroom during the year following his mother's death. The young wife and her babe had died in childbed. This brief marriage to an orphan with an inheritance had left James Andrew with her dowry and her slave,

Lavinia. The woman had loved her little mistress possessively and had transferred her allegiance to the boyish, helpless widower.

James Andrew rented the dwelling next to the Clemens house and set up housekeeping.

Jane Clemens was put to very little trouble in regard to her half brother, had only to give him affection and advice. African Livy ran his house to perfection, while Hannibal's young set showered him with attention. He was handsome, gentle, agreeable. He had land from his mother in Monroe County and investments in Ralls County from his wife, not to mention the best servant ever seen in those parts. James Andrew was a catch, there was no denying it.

The months passed pleasantly. It seemed to Jane that her husband must surely succeed now, for he had allied himself with a town that was bent on becoming a city. The *Gazette* in advertising its own Job Printing revealed Hannibal's soaring aims: *We print Receipts, Business cards; Ball, Concert and School tickets; Labels, Circulars, Handbills as cheap as they can be done in St. Louis. We have on hand a supply of Flat Cap and Foolscap Paper. Cards of various colors for Balls and Concerts. Give us a call at the office of the Gazette over Owsley and Robards, Commercial Row.*

And there was the new barbering announcement, aimed first at the men, then at their womenfolk; it would have done credit to New Orleans: *Fashionable Barbers and Hair-Dressers; Ready to take you by the nose and with keen razors and practiced hands scrape your Phiz as clean as the nature of the case will admit. Your whiskers and goatees will be dressed and curled in the most fascinating manner. Your hair champooned and trimmed in the latest fashion and the ears never chipped. Wigs, Braids and Curls renovated and prepared. Ladies will be waited on at their residences, and their hair dressed in the most elegant manner for parties, balls, etc. at a moderate charge.*

Jane was considering one of those daring appointments for Pamela when John came home from the county seat with a deceptively simple announcement. "I've lost the lawsuit."

"Which one?" Jane asked, for he had several going. Mela ought

162

to have a piled-up coiffure, she was thinking, and a fringe of bangs, if they could afford anything so elaborate. She would ask John if he could possibly spare a dollar.

"I've lost to William Beebe. He's been suing me. We could do worse than accept Dr. Grant's offer, Jane. We can lease this house and move in with the Grants at once, rent free, taking them to board. It's the only way, as I see it."

"It is?" Jane asked blankly. Dr. Orville Grant was a druggist who lived at the southwest corner of Main and Hill Streets in the big frame house with the pilasters. His pharmacy occupied the ground floor; he and his wife dwelt in the apartment above. They were well-born Virginians. Mrs. Grant was patiently recovering from a fall. Dr. Grant was a friend of John's, a member of old Dr. Peake's clique.

"Orville Grant made the offer an hour ago," John said. "Mrs. Grant concurred."

"Mrs. Grant concurred," Jane repeated automatically.

Beneath the surface of her dismay her thoughts darted and retracted, minnows in a bucket. James Andrew was a fleeting regret, a haven no longer obtainable; he had given up his house and gone to St. Louis to study medicine, taking his furniture, his faithful Lavinia, his autograph album of farewell verses, his riding horse, and his boyish enthusiasms. He had forgiven a seven-hundred-dollar debt owed to him by John Clemens and had warmly invited them to stop with him whenever they came to St. Louis. So much for James Andrew. She groped for someone else to approach. . . . Wealthy James Clemens? Not again! John would die first.

It was evident to Jane that her husband expected some reply from her, but she could not fetch up anything worth communicating. They both knew that Dr. Grant's business was at low ebb (druggist Jerman in the City Hotel outflanking him with innovations), and his disposition was peppery. He had lately fought a sidewalk duel with another Virginian over politics, both of them using sword canes, and was still suffering the effects of it. He had been "punctured full of holes," gossip said. He needed a handy boy in the drugstore right badly. The youngest Clemens would fill the bill. Nine-year-old Henry was acclaimed to be the politest, the most reliable little boy in Hannibal. Dr. Grant often sent for him to make a quick delivery. And since the Grants were lately reduced to a life without house servants, it stood to reason they coveted Sandy for menial work. For cooking their meals—Jane Clemens, detester of kitchens, shuddered as she faced it—they wanted her, of course.

"One reason for our doing this," John stated, shocking her yet further, "we've got no furniture. We must offer up even Pamela's piano to meet the court ruling. I've been trying to sell the Tennessee land for twenty cents an acre. The deal has fallen through. Cheaper than that I'll not go. It's our children's birthright. . . . Can't you reply to me, Jane? Take your hands away from your throat and speak up! Shall we accept the Grants' offer, or shan't we?"

"By all means, John," she answered, looking gently into his desperate face. "I've always liked the Grants."

Scarcely a week elapsed before their furniture was discreetly carted off at William Beebe's direction. Jane held out the silver forks and spoons, which she realistically declared to belong to her children. She also held fast to her bedding, and concealed the books which she knew her husband valued more than his very shirts and breeches.

John watched, his face drained of color, as their bedsteads, their chairs and stoves, their tables and chests of drawers and the very clock that had stood on the mantel joined Pamela's new piano in the hateful wagons. He and Jane and the bewildered little boys (Sandy breaking into wild bursts of laughter at this, his latest insecurity) swept the empty house for the tenants who were coming in. Jane stifled her sobs and declared how lucky they were to have found good renters so quickly.

"We'll be coming back here," she assured dejected Sam and Henry. "Your father's going to be Clerk of the Circuit Court next August. Judge Draper says so. He'll travel from courtroom to courtroom, keeping everything straight for the lawyers and the judge . . . You, Sandy, do you hear me? We'll be coming back to this house then. Meantime, you mind Dr. Grant! All three of you boys mind Dr. Grant!"

To the house with the pilasters the Clemenses went then with their inherited knickknacks, their silver forks and spoons, their bedding, their books, their clothes. Sandy and the cats could be counted on to follow, Sandy bringing the broom and the cats' bowls. Jane felt strangely light. It was as if she were floating, though not in ecstasy.

It was time for supper when they arrived. Early that morning she had sent over a piece of beef and some potatoes and beets that she had. Mrs. Grant, a calm and cheerful woman, manipulating her canes, had managed to get them cooked.

"Welcome!" Dr. Grant exclaimed rather nervously. And this was sporting of him, for he must include Sam, almost eleven, a notoriously gregarious boy, addicted to using downspouts instead of stairways. "Try to feel at home during your stay. Please do try. And all come to supper now."

"Oh, we will!" Jane Clemens called out in her wonderful voice which some say suggested music but another has determinedly likened to firelight in winter. "We'll come to supper and we'll feel easy." John and the little boys, having deposited the family possessions in the two rooms allotted to them, were standing apart, each in his cell of homesickness and unreality. Right anxiously Jane strove to release them by her acceptance of the place, the time, and the persons assembled there.

She took off her hat and cape and dropped them carelessly onto a hall settle, to Mrs. Grant's wonder. Then the Grants and the Clemenses went in to supper, with John presiding in Dr. Grant's chair and carving the meat, as Jane had contrived it that morning in her head. A man needs to serve his own roast.

Early in March, when there was a break in the weather, Pamela came home from Paris to visit. She had not been with her family for a long time, not even at Christmas when Orion had somehow managed a stage trip home, and she was eager to see them. She thankfully slept on a narrow spool bed in the dining room, a sort

165

of couch, Mrs. Grant making her feel welcome and inviting her to hang her dresses on pegs in the back hall.

"I think your pa looks poorly," Mrs. Grant confided. "He's been electioneering in the worst weather against everybody's advice. I've never seen a man so determined to win office."

"Such a lot depends on it," Pamela answered in her thoughtful way. "There's a lawsuit pending, too. He's trying to get back at Beebe. There's been an injustice done us, Pa thinks. But I hardly understand the pros and cons."

The eleventh day of March produced bad weather—a cold, driving rain. Women and children gladly stayed indoors. John Clemens was in Palmyra attending to his lawsuit. Jane hoped he was keeping dry, for he had acquired a nagging cough that defied her elixirs.

It was cozy in her room, the coal fire blazing, her three children gathered there. They had a rather old newspaper which Orion had sent them, and Jane asked Pamela to read it aloud while she sewed the buttons on Henry's shirt.

The paper proved to be the *Daily Cincinnati Gazette* of January 1, 1847. Pamela began with something headed The Machine Type-Setter, which Orion had marked with red ink. The invention was opined to be of more trouble than it was worth; Jane said she was relieved to hear that, so it wouldn't be throwing Orion out of work.

"But Orion doesn't expect to stay a typesetter, Ma," Pamela reminded her. "He's studying law, every spare minute."

"Hm-m-m," Jane retorted. Orion's newspaper job was a bird-in-the-hand, paying regularly. She could not be expected to encourage his aspirations of law, a profession that had not supported his father, a more persistent man than Orion gave promise of being.

Henry, without being asked, went and got a scuttle of coal and replenished the fire. Sam was engrossed in making something out of a pair of empty spools; cord string lay on the floor beside him.

"What's that thing for, Sam?" Jane asked, point-blank. The contrivance hardly looked useful. She was uneasy about it, aware of Dr. Grant's suspicious attitude toward the boy.

"If you mean *who* it's for, Ma, I can answer you. It's for John Briggs. What he'll do with it remains to be seen."

Pamela had found the advertisements, began to read wistfully: "—rich lace robes for evening entertainments, of watered silk and illusion net—rich merinoes, double twilled, in crimson, gold, sky, jonquil, rose, straw, white." She sighed audibly. "Handsome Honiton lace for trimming scarves and bridal veils. Pocket handkerchiefs with rich embroidered edges. Paris kid gloves in white and colors, all sizes. Rich velvets for regalia—"

"—rich, rich, rich," repeated Sam absently, not concerned with his sister's futile longings. He was winding the notched spools with the cord string in a complicated way, and his task moved him to an outburst of mirth.

Henry told him to shut up. "Let Ma hear the newspaper, can't you?" Glares and unfriendly gestures were exchanged.

It was understood by Pamela that her mother "took no stock in the Mexican War." Indeed, Jane often said, "I just hate the whole mess!" And when letters came from her Kentucky friends, as many did, extolling sons and nephews for going off to glory in Mexico, she was inclined to raise her eyebrows and shrug. However if a casualty came to her knowledge she would weep and write a letter; for a dead youth touched her profoundly and stayed permanently in her memory. Fortunately the Clemens family was not divided on the war issue. John, as a Whig, disapproved on policy. There was more to be said against the war, he felt, than for it.

But Pamela knew that Jane relished heroes and she risked a battlefield intrusion now in order to present one. In her controlled voice that was neither flat nor vibrant, she launched forth:

"The Legislature of Louisiana has voted a sword to General Zachary Taylor. It was manufactured by Messrs. Ames and Company of Springfield, Massachusetts, and is as follows:

"The blade is of the finest tempered steel, and on its surface is the motto 'Bis vincit qui sa vinsit in victoria!' or Doubly does he triumph who restrains himself in the hour of victory. Very appropriate to the old hero. The scabbard is most beautiful, having on its sides etchings of the two battles, Palo Alto and Resaca de la

167

Palma, and the arms of the State of the Union. The handle is octagonal, formed of layers of chased gold and mother-of-pearl. The pommel represents the old cocked hat of the Revolution; in the crown a fine Cairngorm stone, such as is worn in the hilts of the daggers of Highland chiefs."

Jane alertly noticed the thoughtful, the entranced face of her son Sam who had dropped his ticktack to listen. She knew how General Taylor's sword must be almost too much for him, and she hoped it would not drive him outdoors in search of a Cairngorm stone. The weather was worsening, a mixture of snow and sleet coming down.

There was then a noise at the street door, and fumbling steps on the stairs to divert them. Hurrying into the hall they found John Clemens there, home from Palmyra, standing in a dazed way.

"I've taken my horse to the livery stable," he said in a rasping, peculiarly triumphant voice. "If they rub him down, he'll do. Another ten minutes, a sick horse." Then he coughed and held his side, apparently in pain.

Jane saw that he was very ill. "Come to bed, poor John," she urged. She guided him to the warm bright room where they had been reading the paper, his bedroom and hers, and helped him out of his icy clothes and into a fire-warmed nightshirt. His children reacted according to their several natures and hurried about, obedient to their mother's orders. Mrs. Grant summoned her husband, who summoned Dr. Meredith, and everybody commenced to come to grips with John Clemens' last illness, which was a virulent lung fever.

Orion, sent for by letter, came on the overland stage as quickly as possible, and he became his father's nurse, sleeping in a bedside chair. The illness fluctuated, the victim fought valiantly.

In the days and nights that followed, sometimes lucid, sometimes wandering, John Clemens gave voice to his problems. He said he would win the election; he said he would restore them to their own dwelling. At times he thought he was laboriously copying depositions, the task he had pursued as a justice to earn a few precious dollars; a blotted page (imagined) would raise his temperature. But most often he talked of the Tennessee land and its high promise. Once, feverish, he observed a cloud formation from the window and thought he was seeing mists over his vast acreage. "If I am called," he instructed Orion in a ringing voice, "cling to the land! If men seek to beguile it from you for a pittance, turn away!"

Jane expected him to recover until Dr. Meredith paused long beside the bed one morning and gravely shook his head. Pneumonia had set in, following the pleurisy. She sent Henry to find her pastor and bring him to the sick room. That day was the twenty-fourth of March, 1847. The Calvinist minister, having come quickly, bent down and addressed the sinking man.

"John, I am told your name was got through infant baptism. Do you now, of your own choice, witness the Lord Jesus Christ and believe that through His blood you can be saved?"

"I do," came the whisper. Then the pastor prayed over him and recommended him to God.

John Clemens noticed Pamela's yearning face among these gathered in the room and he beckoned to her. Rising a little and putting his arms around her young body, he kissed her cheek lingeringly. He fell back on his pillow then, spent with suffering, spent with the fight to live and succeed for his family's sake. "Now let me die," he pled. . . .

It was thus, soon after making his peace with God, and summoning Pamela as the representative of all his earthly loves, and relinquishing her, that John M. Clemens died.

Dr. Meredith closed his friends eyes and went to the window and looked out, lost in thought. Orion led his distraught sister from the room. Jane signaled for the minister to take Henry and follow. Sam was standing near her, watching.

She saw that the boy was suffering a private sorrow and knew he remembered how he had worried this steadfast man, and outwitted him, and had been indifferent to all the paternal hopes and ambitions. She wept in pity for his tardy remorse, and in pity for her widowhood. Her plight overwhelmed her, it being a sorrow encompassed by utter poverty. Not yet forty-four years of age, she had lost the familiar complement of her life, the provider, the

169

father of her children, the mate she had loved in every way except the customary one. She wept, but was not made homely by the weeping. It was some trait of hers, a gift in the cradle, that weeping, unless prolonged, did not redden her features; tears flowed and ceased, and that was the end of it.

She took her tense son's hand. "There, there, Sammy," she said. "It's all right. What's done is done, and it don't matter to him any more, not any more. But here by his side I ask you to promise me—"

He darted away from her and stood withdrawn and wary, his green eyes narrowing. "I'll promise anything," he offered, "if you won't make me go to school. Let me quit."

"A little more school, Sam, just a little more," she bargained. "But not on and on. Not the way he'd planned. Only promise to be a better boy, Sam, and not break my heart. Practice how to be honest and industrious so you'll grow up to be a man to trust, like your father, and never shame your family." In awe of her own next words and needing to measure them, she spoke in slower cadence. "It's not easy to be good, Sam, especially for you. But if you are willing to try, raise your right hand to Heaven and swear it." Her own slim hand went up instructively. She was wearing on her forefinger an antique family ring, a cumbrous amethyst; she had slipped it on that morning, along with her only lace collar, in rococo deference to whatever the day might bring. "Do you promise what I ask, Sam?"

He promised, lifting his right hand toward the heavens.

"By your good dead father, Sam?"

"By him, Ma!" (Later he told Tom Blankenship about it. "She did it right," he said. "She put a lot of style in it.")

He went into the hall, but the door remained ajar.

Dr. Meredith approached the widow and spoke without emotion. "The body can't stay here, of course."

"No. There's no parlor. The Grants sleep there now. And I've got no clock to stop for him. Poor John! No clock to stop for him, no parlor to lay him out in!"

"Yes, I know. Pull yourself together now." Hugh Meredith seemed impatient, urgent. "Listen to my offer, Mrs. Clemens. He

170

can lie in my surgery. I'll have him carried there without put-off. Grant and Cunningham and my eldest boy and I will carry the stretcher. You'll need to get this room fumigated, the mattress carried out and aired. I'll send a couple of porters to do all that— I've already told Grant as much. Have Pamela sleep here with you tonight so Orion can rest in a bed. He can use Pamela's couch in the dining room."

"You've thought of everything," Jane said, wondering. A vast relief descended on her, for she was exhausted. "Will you choose his coffin and see that he's dressed right?"

"Yes, I'll do that. Have Orion bring me his clothes in the morning. You'll want his best black suit, I expect."

"Yes. Tomorrow when he's in his coffin, Doctor, I want him carried to our church, to lie in state there till the funeral. And after the sermon I want the organizations he belonged to to follow the hearse to the cemetery, wearing mourning bands."

"I'll see to that, Mrs. Clemens. And now I'll ask this boon. While he's in my surgery, let me explore his chest. Dr. Cunningham would assist. If we could relate his cough to the looks of his lungs, it would benefit medical progress. When John Clemens was acting coroner he watched me do several postmortems. He had a scientific mind."

The request, when comprehended, stunned her. She gripped a table to keep from falling. But as usual, she came to terms with life and paid the piper. It was of no consideration any more that she did not like Hugh Meredith and his brusque ways. (He had been a sailor before the mast, he often boasted.) What mattered now was that he had never failed John in friendship, and that the Clemens family had received no bill from him in many years. The debt could hardly be leveled, unless in this strange way.

"If you'll not disfigure him—"

"I assure you." He left her alone then.

When she went to find her children, Mrs. Grant had assembled them in her room and was chafing Pamela's wrists. Orion was comforting Henry. "Where is Sam?" Jane asked anxiously. No one knew. Investigating, she found that his roundabout was gone, and

171

his best muffler. Even his overshoes. It was an indication that he was beginning to heed her wishes, and she took comfort.

Sam returned home before dusk. From a discreet distance he had watched the four pallbearers carry the sheet-covered litter around the corner of Bird Street and up the stairs toward Dr. Meredith's quarters. He had later trailed Dr. Meredith to Jacob Coffman, the undertaker, and watched him choose the coffin and engage Coffman's hearse. He had subsequently applied his eye to the keyhole of Dr. Meredith's inner office and had seen two men at work there. What they did, he could not see, for keyholes obstruct more than they reveal; but his imagination was fired almost to the point of mental hazard. That night he walked in his sleep and was not easily brought around.

The experiences of the day were to stay with him. The postmortem, which he had sketchily witnessed, must intensify in him a taste for the macabre, a preoccupation with body snatching and graveyards, extreme even for Hannibal. But a more useful stimulant had come through the impromptu session with his mother at his father's bedside. A boy almost insanely absorbed in seizing and maintaining privilege, he had been brought to see that his actions affected his family and others; he could never again, to his great annoyance and inconvenience, be entirely heedless. His mother, in accomplishing this, had not so much reformed him as snared him. Though unaware, she had used the vernacular of his gang: the uplifted hand, the hard-to-keep oath, in a somber setting.

Orion returned at once to his job in St. Louis, Jane accepting his offer to send home three dollars a week from his pay, which was ten dollars. Pamela went back to her music "scholars" at Paris. She could do no more than support herself, they all agreed.

Jane was quietly watchful of the Grants, wondering when they were going to ask her what plans she was making for herself and Sam and Henry. Mrs. Grant was walking now with only one cane, would soon be able to take care of her house. One day Jane overheard Dr. Grant (still suffering from his sword-pricks) become somewhat profane as he looked for a lost piece of wearing

172

apparel. "Dam'd if I can get used to being so crowded," he concluded.

"S-sh," Mrs. Grant warned, "you'll hurt their feelings."

Immediately afterward Jane suggested to Mrs. Grant that the Clemens family reduce its quarters. "I can move in with the little boys," she said, "if you'll let me put the spool bed in there to sleep on. That way, you and Dr. Grant can have your bedroom back."

"That's mighty thoughtful of you," Mrs. Grant agreed eagerly. "Are you sure you don't mind?"

"I'd rather do it than not," Jane answered in all honesty. She sensed that Mrs. Grant was waiting for her to say something else, but as far as she was concerned, everything had been said. She had come at last to one room. One room at the end of a road.

As often as she had thought of their taking refuge with the Quarles family, she had been forced to reject it. The log farmhouse, seemingly so massive, had but five rooms aside from its summer porch. It was full to overflowing. The planned ell had never been added, for John Quarles's whisky barrel had soothed him into what Jane sometimes referred to as "hillbilly ways." The older children slept upstairs in the two great rough rooms, dormitory style. The bedroom of Patsy and John had its extra confusions: a spinning wheel, a loom, a trundle bed for three-year-old John Polk. And now, as Patsy had plaintively written, her present nausea seemed to presage a ninth baby: in which case the well-worn cradle would be brought out again.

If Patsy had only needed her, Jane would right gladly have gone to the crowded farmhouse, taking her children and making the best of it. But with thirty slaves in the quarters, many of them women and children, Patsy had a surfeit of help. Jane wrote cheerfully to Patsy, more concerned for her childbearing sister than for her beleaguered self. She said they were well-situated at the Grants'; explained proudly that the undertaker had been paid, but she thanked John Adams just the same. As for the country produce which Patsy offered to send—a couple of hickory-smoked hams and some winter apples and potatoes—all would be welcome whenever Uncle Daniel could bring them.

One day in late April, not long after Jane had vacated her room and moved in with the boys, a fresh blow fell. Mrs. Grant received a letter from relatives in Virginia saying that her mother, Mrs. Crawford, would be coming out at once to stay with her.

"This has been threatening for some time," Mrs. Grant explained to Jane. "My sister-in-law is worn out with Mother's high ways. She says it's my turn to take her now, and she's right."

Jane could find no words. Mrs. Grant, seeing her fright, put out a kind hand. "My mother can sleep in the dining room the way Pamela did," she said. "She can hang her clothes in the back hall. We'll change the beds around again, only we must keep a parlor now. Mother's from Richmond. She couldn't stand a place without a parlor."

That was the day Jane saw Ira Stout's advertisement in the *Hannibal Gazette*, for she was an avid reader of both weekly newspapers. Mr. Stout, the man who had wrecked John Clemens' modest fortunes five years ago, was about to move to Illinois; was offering for sale forty acres of woodland, seven hundred lots adjacent to Hannibal (enough to double the town), seven choice building lots on Main Street, and "an elegant and commodious cottage, as good as any in the city for a residence." Jane put on her hat and went to find him at his place of business. He was engaged, he said frowningly. "I'll wait till you're alone," she told him and sat down to do so.

"Now, Mrs. Clemens," he said an hour later, making no apology, "to what do I owe this visit?"

Jane spoke calmly. "You're moving to Quincy, I hear. That's been rumored for some time. But I've only just realized how much property you hold. A stand of fine timber, all those building lots, and a good house besides the one you live in."

"I've been fortunate in my investments, Mrs. Clemens."

"Yes, you have been. And in your lawsuits. Not that my husband ever sued you. There's no law against the losses you caused him. You did it by word of mouth. By misrepresenting. You convinced him the property he took over from you was worth seven thousand dollars. A few years later, at forced sale, it brought less than four . . . Wait, Mr. Stout. That's not all. The land you got

174

away from John Clemens in Monroe County was worth twice what you allowed him in the exchange. How many thousand dollars, I wonder"—and she wondered it gently—"do you owe his widow and children?" Her eyes filled with tears, though not intentionally.

Big Ira Stout looked down at her. "Of course, Mrs. Clemens, if you've come for a little charity—"

"Don't dare say that word again!" She had not expected this turn. "If you offered me five thousand dollars, I'd not call it charity. I'd call it justice."

"And do you think I'm going to offer you five thousand dollars?"

"No," she said, remembering her manners and cooling down. "A good deal less. But something, I'm sure, for atonement. I'm living at the Grants' with my two little boys. The arrangement has got to end."

"You haven't lost your Hill Street house, have you?"

"Only because it's not ours, outright. A cousin of John's holds the title. It's leased till the new year. Then we'll go back to it if I can get some furniture to put in it."

"If you can get some furniture to put in it."

"Exactly. And until then, I could use that empty house you're advertising. I could take boarders and make us a living."

"So you want me to lend you a house and buy you some furniture."

"Yes. Good furniture, something that will last. I expect to be a widow for a long time."

"You're still a pretty woman, Mrs. Clemens—"

"Please don't act flirtatious with me, Mr. Stout. Don't change the subject. I'm hard pressed. Good furniture, I said. Enough to furnish a kitchen, a dining room, a parlor, three bedrooms. Then, a year's tuition for Sam and Henry at Mr. Dawson's new school. That will be forty dollars more. They're bright boys, especially Henry. They're worth a little education."

He walked the floor for a while, but in the end she was promised what she had come for, which was no more than the necessities for their decent existence. She spared him further criminations; he

175

spared her a second reference to charity and another attempt at gallantry. "Order the furniture through T. R. Selmes," he said. "I'll explain I owed John M. Clemens a little money. That way, your reputation won't suffer. Your husband cared a good deal about what people thought, Mrs. Clemens."

"Yes," she replied. "Thank you for reminding me, Mr. Stout."

She went back to the house of the pilasters and entered it almost lightheartedly. Now let Mrs. Crawford come. In confidence she told her glad news to the Grants. They had an especially good supper that night, generously portioned, tastily cooked, and the boys sensed that something had gone well with their mother.

When Dr. Grant had excused himself to go down to his shop, Jane brought up the subject of Mrs. Crawford. "I can hardly wait for her to get here," she said. "We'll give her a Virginia welcome, like the Tuckahoes back home."

"She knows Dr. Peake," Mrs. Grant said. "She remembers his old home near Richmond, with the British cannon ball in the wall. She'll enjoy reminiscing with him about that. And about the awful theatre fire in Richmond when she was young. She's a survivor of that fire."

Sam, quietly eating his second baked potato, resolved to be on hand when old Mrs. Crawford met old Dr. Peake in the Grants parlor.

21 ❖

In May, Jane's advertisement appeared in print: *Gentlemen wishing Boarding in a private family can obtain it in a business and pleasant part of the City, by enquiring at the "Gazette" office. Terms Reasonable.* There was no use for her to angle for "a small family to board." Some other Hannibal housewife had been doing that for weeks; if any small family craved board and lodging they apparently preferred the new City Hotel or the popular Brady House, or even Pavey's.

By the time the new furniture had arrived from St. Louis and had been set down in Mr. Stout's "commodious cottage," two

176

clerks had made application for board. They came recommended by Erasmus and William Moffett, the young merchants from Virginia who employed them. Jane accepted them; they were near Orion's age.

She wanted to be chaperoned by her little boys if she must take men to lodge. Besides, she could not have faced life that summer bereft of all her children. Sam, for the first summer within his memory, was not sent to the Quarles farm, nor was Henry, to whom it mattered less. Henry was content in Hannibal; he could get at books to read and could continue to earn a few quarters as Dr. Grant's handy boy. He was a solace to Jane because of his dependability. His fair curls and angelic blue eyes suggested a boyish sainthood, but he was saved from that condition by a necessity to engage unpredictable Sam with fists, clods, and even rocks when persecuted by him. Henry was also given to tattling on his brother, a form of revenge which was comforting to himself and almost indispensable to his mother.

Jane arranged to have Sam gainfully employed, carrying newspapers and running errands for the *Gazette's* editor, Mr. La Cossitt. The boy owed his employment to her *bête noire,* the Mexican War, for it was causing extras to be printed. Some of the reports came over the telegraph wire from the Illinois shore, some were reprints. Jane rejected them as reading matter, but sometimes a local item tripped her, as: *Horses for the Government wanted by James Bridgeford, who can be found at Brady House Livery Stable.* How relevant! How pitiful! How gory!

Orion from St. Louis was addressing Hannibal's readers on a gentler matter. Announcing himself to be the administrator of his father's estate, he was asking all persons indebted to make payment, and challenging those who held claims to exhibit them. *Every account belonging to John M. Clemens, dec'd, has been placed in the hands of L. W. Balthrope, Constable,* he finally warned. Nothing came of that except a few delinquent justice fees.

There was a southern custom, however, long ingrained, which served them better; it usually manifested itself at the death of a lawyer or physician in straitened circumstances. While legal debtors might turn away and default, friends of the deceased

177

would recall some professional advice had of him free of charge—perhaps pumped from the unwary one on the street or during a social hour—and they would step forward and pay. This conscience-money, so welcome to Jane as it dribbled in, enabled her to hire the uneasy Sandy for another year; to replace her old winter dress, a cherry-red cassimere, with something suitably dark; to buy lamps and crockery and dishes, including a china tea service at Margerem's specialty store. The tea service must all too soon be wrested from her by an odd quirk of fate, but just now it was her pride.

At the new year, when the narrow frame house on Hill Street was vacated, the Clemens menage moved into it—Jane, her boys, a gratified Sandy, and the two clerks.

One of the young men, a youth with helpful ways around the house and a yearning for "nice things," had become a favorite with Jane. He often complimented the new tea service, which she used regularly. She was pleased. "When you get married, Vincent," she impulsively told him at the supper table one evening, "I'll give you this tea set." He was making very little money at the time, could hardly meet his board bill, and there was no fiancée on the horizon. But springtime worked its magic. In June Vincent took a wife, a new girl in town, hastily courted, easily won, and moved to the house of his in-laws. Soon afterward, in telling his bride about his sojourn with the Clemens family, he described the china tea service which Mrs. Clemens intended to bestow upon him. The bride, presently meeting Vincent's Mrs. Clemens on the street, brashly reminded her of the pledged gift. Jane was too taken aback to reply, could only look at the hussy in consternation. Returning home, she wept tears of anger; and the little boys found her so, polishing her tea set and packing it in a splint basket. "Seventeen pieces, counting the two tops, and not a one chipped," was her mournful comment.

She instructed Sam and Henry as to its delivery. "Each of you take hold of the basket," she said, "and carry it like eggs. I never hated to part with anything so in my life."

"Then why are you about to do it, Ma?" Sam asked. "There's no law to make you."

"Yes, Ma," Henry prodded, "what's to make you, I'd like to know. Do you love the girl?"

"I purely detest her," Jane said. "She's grabby white trash, I'm afraid. But I promised Vincent, drat it! You both heard me promise him. I must keep my word."

The boys went somberly off, carrying the basket with exquisite care and pondering Ma's ways.

To replace the hastily married Vincent came twenty-year-old Jim Quarles from his farm home—Patsy's second son—committed to Jane's care and proudly handing out business cards that announced a tinning business near the river. *"Stovepiping, Guttering, Roofing Sold and Installed. Excellent Workmen."* Jim was no tinner, himself.

Young Quarles was dashing and attractive in a very Lampton way. He played the flute, exhibiting a fine ear, and his singing voice reminded Jane of her father's. She was proud to introduce her nephew to the town. Like James Andrew Lampton he was a feather in the family cap, and like James Andrew he was sought by the girls. His father had done well by him, had set him up in trade at a cost of three thousand dollars. Much might be expected from this promising young businessman, commented Mr. Ament, a new editor in town.

But the flaw in the youthful merchant soon appeared. He frequented the grog shops. The town knew it before Jane Clemens did, but soon it was apparent even to her. Over her pleas and protests he went to live at one of the hotels. Everything else followed. A slack store, run by the two fetched-on tinners; uncollected accounts and unpaid bills. A marriage carelessly entered—a neglected wife in a cottage with a weed-grown yard, like a picture from a *Godey's Lady's Book*. Leeching companions triumphed, and Hannibal had another town drunkard, this one conspicuous for his youth. Jim was threatening to go to the California gold fields, shucking his responsibilities.

"Poor Patsy!" Jane lamented to her friends. "Poor John Quarles! I ought to save the boy, somehow!"

Patsy, moved by her sister's letters of self-reproach, sent a sad and difficult confession by way of old Daniel, who was bringing

179

produce to her and to Jim's little wife. "Mis' Jane, Mis' Patsy beg you not to blame yourself. You done the best you could for the boy. Jim's been drinkin' since he was fifteen years ole. Got at his pa's whisky barrel right early. When the taste sets in 'em early, Mis' Jane, it 'pears like nothin' but the Lord Jesus can save 'em."

There was nothing Patsy Quarles could do for her black sheep except pray for him. She was involved with little Martha, her ninth child, and was trying to keep an eye on Margaret, her eldest daughter, now being courted by the swains of Monroe County. But Jane, converting impulse to action, joined a temperance crusade. The movement had come from the East and was sweeping the Valley. She had become a sincere if tardy supporter of the cause, pouring out all her homemade cordial and putting her little glasses on a high shelf. Though her abstention would not be permanent, it would last a decade with never a welch.

Orion had early espoused the cause and by this time had other enthusiasms, but on his next visit home his mother fired him anew. She recounted to him the downfall of his cousin, and she invited all three of her sons to gaze with her on the dilapidated house back of them, a monument to whatever alcoholic beverage Mr. Blankenship might be consuming. Orion thereafter gave temperance lectures on any platform that beckoned. He became his own stanch convert.

Jane, deprived of entertaining at tea because of her lost tea set, and unable to dispense cordial to afternoon callers, felt a lack and a letdown. The vacuum in her leisure caused her to become involved with the flowering Nicotiana. There was an old lady out in the county who paid her a visit whenever her husband came to town to buy staples. Jane was very fond of her—old Mrs. Utterback. (Sam Clemens, years hence, would borrow her fascinating name for use in a bawdy sketch for the *Golden Era*, affixing it to a ludicrous old woman downriver who sold wood to the steamboats. His mother would deplore the transfer.) Mrs. Utterback was a person who could heal pain by the laying on of hands and the simple command, "Believe!" She was a tidy woman, clear of eye, sunburned of face, somewhat withered in her clean starched clothes, but vitally healthy. Her conversation was innocent and ingenuous.

It was at about this time that Mrs. Utterback brought Jane Clemens a dear little clay pipe, newly made. She proffered it, and not apologetically, with some well-cured, crumpled tobacco leaves—"the light kind, from Virginny seed. I've always wished we might smoke together, Mrs. Clemens."

Jane looked at the gift thoughtfully. "Sam Clemens has been smoking behind my back for several years," she said. "It appears to mean a good deal to him. I just continually wonder why." She allowed Mrs. Utterback to fill the little pipe and hand it to her. She put it into her mouth, and Mrs. Utterback lighted it with a taper ignited from embers in the kitchen stove. "Now draw on it," the donor said.

"It seems real clean," Jane remarked judicially.

Recently she had given Sam a vigorous slap for chewing tobacco, having surprised him at it in the back yard. "Chewing's a nasty wet habit!" she had exclaimed. "It makes you smell bad and turns your teeth yellow, hear me?" She had looked hard at Tom Blankenship, similarly engaged. "And you, Tom! If you've got to chew, don't do it in our yard. Judge Clemens would of skinned you alive."

But now she smoked the little pipe with her caller, choking a little and experiencing heady flights of fancy which she found interesting. It was not her fault that the cigarette with the amber holder had not yet been invented. . . . "Don't speak of this to anybody, Mrs. Utterback. I'll only smoke now and then in private. It could be, just when you come to see me."

"I never speak of anything from house to house, Mrs. Clemens. Whatever is said to me goes in the garden of my soul. Seed, you might say. What sprouts up is, right often, helpful to others."

More than once Mrs. Utterback had cured Jane of the intense pain of neuralgia, the cures almost immediately following her firmly spoken exorcisms. There was the time, the preceding summer, when Jane and Sam, both suffering from toothache, had gone to the Utterback farm for treatment. Jane had borrowed a horse and sidesaddle from Mrs. Owsley, and Sam had ridden behind her, extremely uncomfortable. Jane was healed; nor did the ache return to plague her on the five-mile-ride home. But Sam's throbbing pain continued, unremitting, worsening, and he hated his mother for the triumph of faith and receptivity which she was enjoying, he being barred from it by his realism. His resentment would not go to waste, however. Later he would transfer it, wonderfully enlarged and articulated, to Mrs. Mary Baker Eddy.

Pamela, of her own accord, came home to live and share her mother's room. It was a comfort to Jane, awakening at night, to be able to reach over and touch the body of the softly breathing girl and realize youth and continuity. For real continuity, though, Pamela must get married, and Jane put her mind on it. She suspected why Mela had given up her music classes in Paris for the lesser prospects of Hannibal; it would be because she was in love with William Anderson Moffett, one of the town's more eligible bachelors. He was her senior by a dozen years. But no matter; she had never cared for boys her own age. Will Moffett and his brother Erasmus and their friend George Schroeter were commission merchants in Hannibal, doing well. Like John Clemens, they had kept store a while in Florida. Erasmus, the financially gifted one, had his sights set on Illinois, while Will—easygoing, wryly humorous, a Southerner to the core—was looking toward St. Louis. Could Mela, Jane wondered, capture this suitable young man before he took off? At times she doubted it, Mela being so reserved. Yet she was proud of her daughter for not showing her hand as some girls did. As one girl had done long ago.

Will Moffett came often to the little house on Hill Street but he expressed no wish to be alone with Pamela. Sometimes he accompanied her to gatherings at Mrs. Holliday's, where she played the piano graciously and well and was at her best. Jane, in her heart, blessed the sprightly hostess who was so useful to them. Mrs. Holliday, now a widow in reduced circumstances, was gallantly carrying on the formalities, still wearing her famous locket and providing ice cream and parlor singing for the younger set.

Jane herself could do no more than spare an occasional cup of molasses and a few cups of sugar for a candy-pull, for she was

182

again feeling the pinch of poverty. The taking of boarders had brought scanty profit. She had only one in the house now, shy young Jim Wolfe who had come from the country to learn the printing trade. Sometimes she could not see her way ahead. But "day by day" was her motto when firewood ran low and Patsy's last ham had been consumed; when Sam's appetite seemed prodigious and Henry had again outgrown his shoes. When she had patched her own soles until the uppers were weakened.

One of her pleasures was going to the post office three or four times a week when the mails came in. The acting postmaster, nervously awaiting his appointment, was a Mr. Nash, whose aristocratic old mother and saintly wife were her friends. Mr. Nash was a person embittered by bankruptcy and by misfortunes which had befallen his family, and one never knew what form his native wit would take; sometimes it was gall, sometimes it was persiflage.

One day he handed Jane a legal-looking letter addressed to her. "You are no doubt being informed of the death of a wealthy Kentucky relative," he said. "One to whom you were dear. It could hardly be otherwise, with your habitual good luck."

"That's right, Mr. Nash," Jane replied, examining the unfamiliar handwriting. But she did not relieve the postmaster's ironic curiosity by opening it. There was something uncasual about the letter, causing her to take it home for a private reading.

Standing by the parlor window she broke the wax seal and looked at the signature. She saw that it was from Parker Hardin of Adair County, whom she had once jilted. *Mrs. Jane Lampton Clemens, Hannibal, Missouri,* led to *My dear Jane,* thence to businesslike declarations:

> *Aware of your widowed state and oppressed by my own, I once again ask your hand in marriage. It is well known to you that your friend Mary Ann Waggoner was taken from me early, leaving me with little Bob, and that I gave him a mother by marrying Miss Caroline Watkins of Woodford County. Two years ago, when cholera came to Columbia, she too was taken, a matter possibly not known to you. I have, by Caroline, three little boys. Charles and Watkins and*

Ben. They are near the ages of your two youngest children, if I have been correctly informed regarding your family.

In addition to my affection and esteem, dear Jane, retained from our youth, I can offer you a life of comfort. I have just completed twelve years of service to my Commonwealth, eight as a member of the State Senate. I remind you that I am now forty-eight years of age, liberal to any religion, temperate in habit, a staunch Whig. I now aim to practice law in the Courts of Adair, Green, Casey, Russell, and Cumberland. Columbia is still a village, and may ever be. My home is not elegant but it is adequate. I have a farm in addition. My People are too numerous, yet a humane point of view forbids that I sell any of them and break their family ties. They are Reuben and Mary, gifted to me with several of their children when I married in 1824. Grandchildren have now accrued, crowding the Quarters and taxing my purse to keep them clothed. Such are the problems attending the institution of slavery.

You and your daughter, whom I would welcome, having none of my own, could each have a personal maid, trained in sewing. You would have your own carriage and pair, with Reuben, my coachman, at your disposal. There are several riding horses. Your son Orion could read Law with me, if so inclined. These material things I mention not so much to sway you as to inform you.

Your kind note written to me last year at the death of my son Bob, my first-born, in Mexico City, was received. I could not bring myself to answer at the time. Only his sword came home to me. He lies, like Henry Clay's son, in foreign soil among his comrades.

Asking your tolerance for this sad intrusion in a letter of such nature, and awaiting your considered reply, I beg to remain your faithful friend and admirer, Parker C. Hardin

When Jane had read the letter several times she went to Holliday Hill and sat on a ledge of rock and looked out over the broad Mississippi. She was tired and a little hungry, for she kept her intake of food to a minimum in order to stoke her three children and Jim Wolfe and Sandy. This morning, after her own breakfast, she had surreptitiously eaten the salt-rising bread crusts

184

left on Pamela's plate and had benefited, but now she felt rather empty again. She thought of Parker Hardin's smokehouse. Of his farm that supplied that smokehouse. Of his vegetable garden—cymlin's and sugar peas and Country Gentleman corn, and beans that climbed the corn with delicate tendrils. To one side, the strawberry patch, the asparagus bed. She proceeded then to his cows—he would have two or three—and to his butter and cream in the cool depths of the springhouse. She could hear the Negroes laughing in the kitchen as they fried the chickens and made spoon bread. . . . Less vividly but with sustained interest she pictured the carriage and pair, with Reuben on the box. She might say one week, "Parker, I'd like to take Mela to Bowling Green, if you don't mind." Another time it would be Glasgow where the young people danced so much; often Green County, and now and then as far as Lebanon, or Danville where the college was. Along roads winding through the lovely and interminable southern Kentucky hills the carriage would roll and creak. Through the enclosing hills, with never a glimpse of a great river carrying steamboats to the Gulf, and bringing steamboats back unless some act of God or error of man overtook them. Through valleys marked by plantations and cabins the carriage would roll, the occupants hearing the voices and laughter of people, the barks and lowings of animals, the crowing of fowls and the sweet songs of birds, but never the sound of a steamboat blowing for a landing. Never any of that sort of thing. Could she or her children feel wholly alive, having known the great river and been deprived of it? . . . And that other matter. Must she again marry without love while Richard Barret was still alive? She went serenely home, knowing she could not. Tonight she would write a letter to Parker—kind, formal, humorless Parker. Thanking him, she would again decline his hand.

Pamela was in the kitchen, wearing a large apron to cover her music-teaching dress. "The beef's been stewing an hour, Ma," she fretted, "but I'm afraid it's going to be tough. I've made dumplings to help. They've got an egg in them—that kind. When I didn't find you at home, I just lit in."

"That was smart of you, Mela. I went to the post office and

185

brought home a letter from an old friend. Then I went to Holliday Hill and sat there, watching the river. The *Lucy Bertram* for Keokuk went up, drawing deep. She's pretty."

"But there's another problem about supper, Ma. There are only five potatoes to cook for six people!"

"We'll save the baked skins for Sandy," Jane decreed. "He likes them. That way, everything comes out even. I hope you're not going to turn into a worrier, Mela? It could ruin your forehead."

The weeks that followed were rather exhilarating to Jane, for whenever she faced up to her forty-sixth birthday she remembered what a desirable suitor she had rejected. It more than balanced.

Her three children and Sandy seemed especially contented that summer, doing the work that fell to their lot and rarely complaining. Orion wrote every week, faithfully sending the pledged three dollars from his pay. Pamela's music pupils, though few, paid promptly. She had not yet had to spend her nest egg, the bit of money she had saved when teaching in Monroe County. When it seemed that the little hoard must surely go, the crisis would somehow be averted through Jane's manipulations.

Daniel regularly brought food from the farm, Patsy's concern for her widowed sister still taking that turn. The summer fruits and melons were happily welcomed by Jane and Pamela and Henry. If they were less interesting to Sam and his knight Sandy, it was because they had other ways of obtaining them. Sam Clemens and his friends were a refractory lot, finding adventure in play along the wharf, in borrowing skiffs and boarding barges, in exploring McDowell's Cave, in making midnight excursions to the cemetery, and raiding orchards and melon patches. During the spring of '49, just past, Sam had several times shaken the dust of Mr. Dawson's classroom from his feet and disappeared till nightfall. To try to school him further was futile, his mother admitted.

Jane's intrepid spirit kept her from being relegated to the role of poor Mrs. Clemens. Socially she kept in the swim, expertly towing quiet but talented Pamela. Though she was not such a civic entity as the Widow Fuqua, whose property was appraised at ten thousand dollars and who could alter the location of hitching posts, her opinions were considered. She expressed them pithily. "The woman thinks in epigrams," Mr. Nash said enviously.

No one was surprised when Simmons and Company, commission merchants, discharged their drayman. Mrs. Clemens, it was explained, had caught the man in crime. He was beating the horse when the cart, overloaded with kegs of nails, stalled on the river hill. . . . And no one expressed wonder that a Pavey girl, pursued by her brutish father—he was carrying a rawhide whip that could lay open a woman's face—bypassed a dozen stores and offices to take refuge in the Clemens doorway. It did seem, though, that Mrs. Clemens would have been wise to shut and lock the door, once she had drawn the girl inside. Instead, she had merely barred the doorway with her arms and had engaged old Pavey in conversation about the viciousness of his temper. She had shamed him for terrorizing a daughter so good and docile. "Her only pleasure is seeing the boats come in," she reminded the panting brute. "If there's harm in that, we're all guilty." The outcome was gratifying to the citizens of Hannibal: Pavey had said, "Ye're a brave woman, by God," and had gone peaceably away.

Jane's sympathy was becoming a public commodity, now that John was not there to quench her zeal. Disturbed friends and mere acquaintances sought her company as if she had some benison to bestow. Almira Owsley often poured out to her a double portion of sorrow. Three-year-old Ellen, her youngest, her darling (*the bud which earth had not corrupted,* said the child's elegy), had fallen to a fever that quickly took her off. It was soon after Almira's husband, proud and choleric William P. Owsley, had shot to death an old rustic who dared to heckle him on the street. Though acquitted through some vagary of the jury, Owsley became an unacceptable man, living in exile, occasionally slipping home to see his family and consult his business partner, Archibald Robards. (If the night was dark, his presence might yet be detected by the aroma of his fine Regalia cigars.) Though Almira Owsley had servants and a carriage and enough money to live on, and though her husband was a nephew of Kentucky's respected old Governor William Owsley, her shame was boundless, and Jane Clemens pitied her. For the playmates of Almira's children, when angered, would shout at them, "Your daddy kilt Uncle Sam Smarr, and now he's run away."

Another of Jane's sorrowing friends who counted on her for surcease was Mrs. Thomas Miller. She too had recently lost her youngest child. Little Laura had been scalded. Her obituary said: *She lingered day after day, until the Divine Redeemer who blessed little children when he journeyed on earth, claimed his purchased possession.*

To those friends Jane would say, out of an assured belief, "Your child was heaven-born. She couldn't stay. Like my Margaret. Like my Benjamin." There was no answer to that. There was nothing to do but have some sustaining tea (delicious green tea, amber pale) and talk hopefully of the children who were left. Mrs. Miller had a beautiful daughter in her teens named Mary. Sam Clemens, several years her junior, was smitten with her. "Go show off to the little Hawkins girl," Mary would tell him witheringly. "Can't you see I'm busy?" Jane and Mrs. Miller could laugh about that, for Jane would imitate Sam's bumptious behavior and Mary Miller's attempts to get rid of him; it was strange, how she could impersonate Sam. She seemed to get inside his skin.

One of Jane's dreads was that her house and yard would come to look like a widow's. She strove to keep the nails in the fence, the upright boards whitewashed. John Quarles, a generous purchaser of quicklime, usually sent her a keg of it when Daniel took the produce to Hannibal. Jane must now try to make the wash as John used to make it, following his formula on a piece of foxed paper: *Dissolve half a pound of salt in a gallon of water. Stir into it four pounds of caustic lime, making a smooth paste. Let stand several hours, stirring occasionally. When ready for use, thin the paste with water and add an ounce of powdered alum. Pour into it a pint of molasses to make the whitewash cling.* On a Saturday Jane would set Sam to coating the high board fence with a long-handled brush. Sometimes he shirked and loitered.

Mr. Dawson at school, Mr. Ament at the *Courier* worked him tediously; his leisure had become precious, worth scheming for.

Jane usually followed the job's progress and when she saw flaws in the coating—the blue look, indicative of thinly applied whitewash—she would order corrective measures. But there would be mornings when she would be sewing for Mela or cleaning the shelves or visiting friends on another street. Sam could then get the work done right pleasantly, after which he would inspect it with an uncritical eye and take off. In later years there would be no need for him to invent Tom Sawyer's methods, for they had been his own.

Jane spoke of Sandy as "my little darkey," not dreaming she was using a word of future disrepute. The word Negro was considered harsh by her; "nigger" was forbidden on her property. From the first, Sandy had substituted her for the mother he had been torn from in Maryland. On arrival three years before, he had sung his heart out in the Clemens kitchen, making himself so annoying with his piping voice that Sam complained: "Make him hush, Ma! He's driving me and Henry crazy."

"Poor thing!" Jane had answered in sorrow and vicarious guilt. "He's been sold away from his home. When he sings, it shows maybe he's not remembering. When he's still, I'm afraid he's thinking, and I can't bear it." So the family had come to regard Sandy's vocal flights as sounds to be encouraged. When he had committed a misdemeanor, Jane would rap him smartly on the head with her silver thimble, as she rapped Sam and Henry. But Sandy was touchingly pleased by the punitive attention, they discovered. It seemed to make him one of the family. Whenever his identity was questioned on Hannibal's streets he would proclaim with verve, "I'm one of Miz Clem's boys." He was not reproved.

It was hard for Jane to tell him that autumn that she could no longer keep him. "We're not tired of you, Sandy," she said gently, "don't think that. It's because we've run out of money. Your master wants more for you now because you're bigger and smarter. You'll be hired to people who can pay more than Mrs. Clemens can."

She spoke the family name plainly, needing to instruct him as to its final syllable. There might come times when he would be far from them and would want to ask their whereabouts. Now and again she had helped transplanted slaves recall their former white folks in Kentucky. Once a young girl could fetch up only "Missy Lou and Mas' Fred, three four miles from Horse Cave" as the owners who had been kind to her in her childhood before bankruptcy had taken her from them. Jane had ferreted them out, had written a letter, had received an answer that gladdened the girl.

"As long as you are around here, Sandy," she said, "try to slip away and come to see us. You'll always be welcome here."

She refrained from saying, "Stand up for yourself, boy!"—a bit of advice she often gave Orion and Henry. (Sam did not need the reminder.) For this one, the counsel would be unwise, perhaps perilous. Yet she would not bid him be spiritless to please a master. "We are going to miss you, Sandy. Especially Henry and I will. Sam must leave us, too, because he'll soon be fourteen. He'll quit school and earn his way—prenticed full time to Mr. Ament. He's going to live at Mr. Ament's place with the young men that set type. You and Sam must be brave, Sandy." She wept, but the boy looked at her with tearless, tragic eyes. Perhaps he had known all along that this happy interlude would end.

22 ❖

When Jane sent Sam from home to live under the authority of Joseph P. Ament, editor of the *Missouri Courier,* she did so out of stark necessity. He had outgrown his clothing and had no prospects for a winter suit. His erratic appetite sometimes enabled him to forget food from dawn till dusk, but in the end he might raid the cupboard and leave it bare. Pamela, about to assemble a meal, often uttered the plaint, "Sam has cleaned us out!" He was as acquisitive of raw food as of prepared, he and his peregrinating associates being the originators, it would seem, of the alfresco supper.

Mr. Ament was more than willing to arrange a bona-fide apprenticeship, having come to rely on Sam's quick-witted responses in emergency, his nose for news, and his ability to write readable prose. He offered to lodge him in his printing office with his other typesetters and to feed him in his own dwelling. Also, he would provide him with two suits of clothes a year.

Jane, striking while the iron was hot, selected a good winter suit for Sam and saw to it that the editor stood the bill. She rightly suspected it would be the last suit so acquired, Ament having the reputation of passing on his own worn clothing when his apprentices needed refurbishing.

Of these, he had two working for him, an inoffensive youth known as Ralph and a prankish young giant named Wales Mc-Cormick. Over them was one MacMurray, noticeable for his red goatee, an agreeable journeyman printer who had temporarily quenched his appetite for whisky by joining the Sons of Temperance. Sam had associated freely with them during his part-time employment at the *Courier,* but no harm had come of it. Jane Clemens, with her unaware instinct for judging character, had already accepted them.

It now fell to Sam's lot to sleep among his fellow workers in the printing office over Brittingham's drugstore—a cheerful, cluttered, stove-warmed room, sixty feet long. He took his meals at the Ament dwelling with the two younger men, though hardly in style. It was at a kitchen table in the basement where scanty fare was served. Only the good nature of the colored cook and her mulatto daughter made those occasions bearable for the hungry, boisterous boys. MacMurray, the compositor, dined above stairs with the editor and his bride and his managerial aunt, Miss Julia —an honor the apprentices might some day aspire to, declared Mr. Ament. However MacMurray too complained of short rations.

Those at the Hill Street house missed Sam's commotion at mealtimes and at night. But he sprinted home daily to see them and get apples or some leftover cornbread and meat to ease his hunger pangs. Though Jane doubted her son's outlandish tales of the Ament parsimony, she knew that his growing body craved more than the apprentice table offered. By saving for him a portion of her own food, she remained noticeably lithe and slim. It was com-

191

mented upon in wonder. "She likes to be shaped like a young girl," her more fleshy friends opined. They sighed enviously at the size of her waist.

Marion County had not recovered from the Mexican War when the California gold rush quickened. Captain Richard Holliday had joined a party going West in '49 and had soon died. So had a half dozen others of that county, emptyhanded. But 1850 dawned as a time of optimism, and Hannibal saw eighty of its sturdiest men equip themselves and depart. Among those were Dr. Meredith and his son Charles; Brittingham, the druggist; Mr. Briggs, John's father; Captain Arch Robards with a company of twelve, his golden-haired little son among them. The sight of the boy, outfitted for the plains and mounted on a spirited horse, filled his friends with an almost unbearable envy. Sam Clemens, smudged with printer's ink, brazenly smoked one of MacMurray's "Cuban Sixes" as he watched them ride away.

The departure which was to affect the Clemens family most lastingly was that of the Buchanans, "Old Bob" and "Big Joe," owners and editors of the *Hannibal Journal*. They advertised the *Journal* for sale at a bargain, yet in their haste to join the prospectors, paused not for a settlement. The office was left in the hands of their sons, "Young Bob" and "Little Joe," with a hastily acquired partner, a St. Louis dandy surnamed Raymond.

It was the sort of pie Jane Clemens could not keep her finger from. Who, she asked Pamela, had a better right to edit the *Journal* than Orion? It was the paper that had made a good typesetter of him, the one his father had dreamed of buying. Besides, Little Joe's mother had told Sam, point-blank, that they had rather have Orion for a partner than Raymond. She lost no time in recommending to Orion that he raise a loan in St. Louis and make an offer for the *Journal*.

Pamela too advised Orion to return to Hannibal, though she was less concerned than her mother with the outcome. She was engrossed in being in love with Will Moffett. Her chief interest in the Buchanan shake-up was that she had fallen heir to Mrs. Old Bob's excellent piano for the duration of the gold rush. She was

192

practicing love ballads and covered-wagon songs indiscriminately, and the Clemens parlor had become a salon.

In April, by prearrangement, came visitors to Hill Street—Dr. and Mrs. J. A. H. Lampton of Ralls County. This was James Andrew with a medical degree and a bride. Also with luggage and Lavinia, the faithful slave. They came in their own carriage. "Sister Jane," said James Andrew, handing out his wife, "I've brought my Ella to meet you. . . . Ella, this is my half sister, more like our father than I am."

Ella's greeting was effusive. Jane's was subdued in appraisal. Lavinia looked on inscrutably. The new Mrs. Lampton was a large, pretty woman, seemingly her husband's senior. She had been an impecunious widow, Mrs. Ella Hunter Plunkett of St. Louis, when James Andrew fell prey to her gay disposition and full-blown charms. She was of good western Virginia stock and was sharply class-conscious; she had not underrated the Lamptons. After embracing Jane she embraced Pamela and Henry with equal fervor, and they submitted courteously. It was evident to all that James Andrew believed he had found a jewel.

Livy was put up at the Robards quarters, a cabin there being empty because Captain Robards had taken some of his people on the trek, but she appeared at the Clemens kitchen in time to get the breakfasts and remained at the Hill Street place until she was no longer needed in the evenings. One of Livy's duties was to minister to the toilet of her new mistress, carrying kettles of warm water upstairs for the bath, carrying the used water down. Violets seemed to fill the air when Livy emptied the bath water into a weedy corner of the back yard, for Ella's soap and toilet water were of that scent, and so was the powder with which she dusted her body. She was careless about leaving her door ajar. Jane, passing one morning, saw Ella in the nude and stood stock-still, startled by the expanse of white bosom and shapely thigh displayed.

"Keep your door shut, Ella, when you're undressed," she said. "Henry and Jim Wolfe use the stairs."

Ella apologized. "I'm not accustomed to boys in the house," she said with a laugh. "I'll be more careful, Sister Jane." She was always good-tempered, agreeable to the wishes and plans of her hostess, kind to the cats and dogs, uncritical of the house's turbulence and the town's limitations. The concert of the Swiss Bell Ringers at the Presbyterian church filled her with enthusiasm, as did afternoon tea at Mrs. Richmond's and a trip to Ament's printing plant to see the presses work—Sam serving as their guide. She praised all of those things sincerely, intelligently, too loudly. She was especially at ease with men. Will Moffett declared her great fun and stood treat to a family boat ride so that Ella might glimpse their scenery; afterward he took them to supper at the City Hotel. Colonel Elgin, the tavern's host, bowed over Ella's hand. Mr. Nash, the acid postmaster, perked up whenever she dropped in for the mail.

Jane told Pamela about seeing Ella undressed "—without even her China silk robe on." She reticently described Ella's figure. "She reminds me of that woman in the Bible," she said gropingly.

"Oh, Ma! You surely don't mean Jezebel?"

"Certainly not, Mela. Ella's not vicious. I mean the one that Solomon spied from the housetop."

"That was Bath-sheba, Ma," Pamela explained, "She was taking a bath, as her name indicates. But it wasn't Solomon who saw her. It was King David, and he sent her husband, Uriah, to the battle front to be killed."

"That was the tale I had in mind, I reckon."

Later, in St. Louis in a confidential hour, they would bestow on Ella another Biblical title: "Potiphar's wife"—whispering it. And young Dr. McDowell, the homeless bachelor, would be Joseph, though hardly a reluctant Joseph.

The Lampton visit over, there was May Day to occupy them. Pamela drilled Miss Newcomb's schoolgirls in their singing and helped with the Maypole, conscious of her twenty-two years and a beau who loitered. At the noon picnic in the grove, attended by interested families, Sam Clemens engaged in fisticuffs with a larger boy and lost. This would not have been noteworthy except for the way he evened the score several weeks later, pretending to be hypnotized at a public assembly and chasing his enemy with firearms.

194

The itinerant mesmerizer who had hired the hall lingered in Hannibal two weeks, so successful did his meetings become. His genuine hypnotic powers were obvious, but his demonstrations were at first routine, due to his lack of imagination in directing his volunteers. Sam Clemens, at first a run-of-the-mill subject, presently became his own impresario and gave such stirring performances that he amazed the town's most skeptical citizens and the mesmerizer himself. His crowning effect came when he vividly described the Richmond theatre fire which Dr. Peake had witnessed early in the century and told of a cannon ball lodged in the old gentleman's ancestral home. Dr. Peake was enthralled. Jane Clemens, a devotee of the occult, was amazed.

"I've always known there's something different about Sam," she declared. Certainly no one contradicted her. Teachers, ministers, town fathers, and skiff owners had accorded him that accolade, usually with embellishment.

As the season advanced, a mixture of epidemics threatened, yellow fever and cholera among them. Many persons were alarmed, and Jane reacted dutifully to safeguard her family. After considering a number of highly publicized vapors and rubs and tonics, she settled on a fiery patent medicine known as Perry Davis's Pain-Killer. As regularly as morning dawned she caused Pamela and Henry and Jim Wolfe to take a teaspoonful of the elixir as a preventive. She would catch Sam as she could. One day he gave his dose to the family's veteran cat, and the stately creature bounded through the open window, shattering flowerpots as he went.

"What in the world is the matter with Peter?" Jane asked Henry. She sorted the broken crockery and her cherished geraniums and indulged in a rare moment of self-pity. "I can't have a flower garden because of boys and dogs. It's a shame now if the cats won't let me keep a few window plants. Where's Sam, by the way?"

"He lit out," Henry reported, "right after he gave Peter his own dose of that stuff."

"The idea! When it costs me a dollar a bottle!"

"Sometimes he pours it down the cracks in the floor," Henry said.

"Down the cracks in the floor!" A distant memory stayed the soaring wrath of Jane Clemens. The very place she had deposited embroidery needles.

Henry then asked a question long overdue from the Clemens children, though now and then bandied among them. "Why don't you take medicine yourself, Ma, the way Pa did? If stuff like this is so useful, why don't you give it a try?"

"My body doesn't need it," was her unassailable reply, cryptic even to herself. "But I do eat raw turnips, Henry. And I flex my fingers and toes and sleep with my window open and use cold water to bathe."

For her sons, she had gone further. Having read of the efficacy of cold sprays, she had devised a shower arrangement for them in the woodshed: a punctured lard can rigged over a washtub. The boys would pour for each other and their friends, having first lugged a block of ice from Mr. Davis's icehouse to chill the water. Their unrestrained shrieks of pleasure, as the cold shower hit them, often disturbed the Ladies' Aid in a neighboring church.

On the ninth of that July, 1850, President Zachary Taylor died, having been a year and a half in office. A fortnight later, Patsy Quarles died after giving birth to her tenth child and naming it Jane Clemens.

Daniel came for Jane when Patsy was sinking. She went with little hope, spending a despairing night at her Uncle Wharton's and being joined by him as the journey was resumed. She knew of her sister's hazards—the swollen tissues, the milk leg. Patsy had suffered those conditions in her previous confinement.

John Quarles met them at the gate. "She's gone!" he told them. "My beautiful Patsy's gone!" He laid his head on the fence's upper rail and wept in a terrible way. Jane went past him into the house, but the coffin had been closed, for it was July. She was spared the ordeal of viewing.

The funeral was held the following morning. The lamentations of the Negroes and the sobs of Patsy's multi-aged children at the grave caused Jane to remain stoically calm. This was a blow too shattering for response, a scene too davastating for the relief of tears. But once, losing reality for a moment, she asked, "Is that

196

my Patsy they are burying?" And a pitying neighbor woman answered firmly, "Yes, Mrs. Clemens. Her. Your only sister, Mrs. John Quarles." It was the therapy of the frontier.

The baby was puny, spitting up the cow's milk and barley water prepared for it, struggling for its little life. "I'll take it home with me," Jane said decisively to John Quarles. "I brought Sam through, and he was smaller than this. I'll find a wet nurse in Hannibal. There's a woman around the corner from us that's nursing a baby. She won't refuse me."

"Do you think I'd give up a child of mine?" Quarles thundered. "Do you think I'm going to let you have Patsy's baby to keep? That's what you're scheming for!"

The things they said to each other were past belief, so grief-stricken were they both, so torn. Jane dwelt on what a hard life Patsy had had, "—never getting to go any place, always bearing children, and killed by it at last!" She said Patsy wanted her to have this baby, or why had she named it for her when she was dying? She and Patsy had agreed long ago never to name a child for one another. "In breaking our pact," she argued, "Patsy left me a message: this baby was to be my charge. Look!" she said. "The little creature wants to lie quiet in a crib. It's being handled too much. Even a baby knows what it wants."

"You've let three of your own children die," Quarles said, and then he twisted the knife. "You don't notice a child is sick till it's got a hectic flush. Patsy once said so, herself."

Uncle Wharton led her out and helped her into the wagon. He was a tenderhearted man who loved his kin. Daniel, immersed in his own grief, picked up the reins and flicked the horse. From the quarters came the high voice of a slave woman in rhythmic chant, powerful and arresting. "Who is that, Daniel?" Jane demanded. "What is she saying?"

"That be Jozie, ole Hannah's girl, prophesyin' like Hannah use' to. She sayin' Mas' John goin' to sell his land and his people. She say chillun will be sold away from their mammies, Missy not bein' here to stop it. She askin' God to stay Mas' John's hand."

Uncle Wharton began to talk of the family of his late brother

197

Joshua, all living in Boone County, to the south, hoping to divert Jane. William Lampton had just joined the gold rush, he related.

But she laughed bitterly. "I hear one of Uncle Joshua's sons used to be county assessor. His chief duty was to auction off slaves on the courthouse steps. For all I know, he still does it. Buck Lampton, he's called."

Wharton flinched visibly at this unearthing of a family scandal he already knew. But Daniel remained calm. Mis' Jane in her misery was lashing at the white race, her own kin among them; her own kin most of all. She was flagellating herself, Daniel knew, though he did not know the word for it.

Orion came home in August to stay. He had not been able to raise the five hundred dollars asked for the *Journal,* but he had done very well with a tenth of that sum—fifty dollars paid to him for a fragment of the Tennessee land. With it he had bought a used printing press in St. Louis and had conveyed it by steamboat up-river, tenderly resting his hand on it much of the way, dreaming of the good Whig newspaper it would disgorge weekly; naming his newspaper; unnaming it; finally, under the stars, dubbing it *Western Union.*

His mother and sister embraced and wept over him. Businessmen dropped into his shop on Bird Street to watch his antiquated press being installed and to wish him well; for the gold rush had drained Hannibal of its young men, and they were pleased by the return of a native son—this cheery, handsome, bungling bachelor of twenty-five who had no enemies. Orion, accustomed to the anonymity and loneliness of his St. Louis decade, was touched. Even his brothers took part in the welcome; Henry by showing him reverence, Sam by refraining from rudeness. He was about to become a publisher and an editor.

It puzzled Orion to find his mother in a normal state, so soon after her sister's death.

"I was afraid it would kill her," he confided to Pamela.

"A strange thing happened," Pamela told him. "Right after Aunt Patsy was taken she acted a little strange and went for long walks, the way she did after we lost Benjamin. But one day she came bringing home the little Smith girl from over on North Street and made a tea party for her. The child is about ten years old, a quiet little thing named Edith. There're several boys in that family, but this is the only girl since her little sister died last winter in an accident. Ma kept bringing Edith here, and even made some clothes for her doll, and invited other children here to play with her. She stopped rambling by herself, she was so taken up with Edith. And she still is, you'll find. She's accumulated her; you know Ma. She never picks up people and drops them. She just keeps adding more."

"The little girl has lost a sister. It's that simple, Mela."

"Don't ever say 'it's that simple,' Orion, where Ma's concerned. She sees seven sides to a cube. Almost every day now she says to me, like a lesson she's studying, 'Just think! I had my precious sister for forty-three years! Edith had hers only five.'"

"Does she talk about Aunt Patsy?"

"Oh, yes, a lot. She keeps remembering funny things they did when they were girls. But whatever you do, Orion, don't ask her about Uncle John. Something's wrong there. Last week I read a letter she wrote to Meg and Puss, because she invited me to add a postscript. She hadn't mentioned their father's name in the entire letter! And she said to me, 'Don't make any reference to that brute John Quarles in your postscript, Mela.' So I didn't."

23 ❖

The *Western Union* was presently ready to issue. Orion hired Jim Wolfe as a typesetter and, with Jane's reluctant consent, twelve-year-old Henry as well. She had hoped Henry would be the family scholar, he so loved books; but when Orion announced to him that his school days must end, his gentle face showed sadness without reproach.

In vain Orion made overtures to Sam, who stubbornly remained attached to Ament's *Courier* and its congenial staff of pranksters. Only when it became evident to Sam that Ament was yet loath to put him on the payroll did he harken to Orion's call and his promise of three dollars and a half a week. The *Western Union* had acquired a bargain, for the boy was clever and skillful beyond his fifteen years. But Jane was anxious. The family eggs were all, now, in Orion's rather clumsy basket.

Pamela, diligent music teacher, dutiful daughter, was causing her mother concern. She moped pitifully for love of Will Moffett, who was transferring his business and his seemingly disengaged heart to St. Louis. Though he was regarded locally as Pamela's beau, this was as far as the affair had come. He had refrained from speaking of marriage. A large, handsome man in a square-jawed, level-eyed way, given to matter-of-fact pronouncements, he seemed never to have been a boy, always a reliable adult. Jane thought him lacking in allure, but he had a wry sense of humor that entertained her. Brevity was the mark of his wit. His comments were quoted. He had, too, a love of music. Pamela Clemens with her cherished guitar and borrowed piano, her singing brothers, a mother whom he considered droll, and a parlor immune to mud on the carpet—those things had enticed William Anderson Moffett persistently.

Jane attempted to advise Pamela. "If you would only laugh more, Mela! Will Moffett is a real witty man. Watch how Sam hangs around him."

"I've never been able to laugh at Will," Pamela said with quiet despair. "I can hardly think at such times as I'm with him."

Jane was grieved. It might be that Pamela was destined to forfeit love. In this they would resemble at last. In many ways the child was alien to the mother, her red hair being the only color she had got from the Lamptons. But Jane had never said as much; and she had not implied by word or look that she had lost a fairer daughter when she lost Margaret. Mela did not feel inferior. She was merely locked in by her own virtues.

The springtime of '51 seemed a bleak time to Pamela. Will, with two partners, had leased an office and display room in St. Louis at "Eleven Locust Street, Upstairs" and he could think of nothing else. When he returned to Hannibal in June to see his brother Erasmus he brought a sketch of their hanging sign that

read: W. A. Moffett—A. J. Stillwell—G. L. Green—
Commission Merchants.

Will went to call on the Clemenses and was being entertained
by Jane in the front room when Pamela came in from a music
lesson. Her greeting was calm but her mother suspected her inner
turmoil. The way she arranged herself in the chair farthest from
the caller showed it. Her hands gripped her music roll.

Will began to tell them of an intended visit to Virginia. "My
old parents are still living at the home place in Rockingham
County," he reminded them. "I want very much to see them. Between St. Louis and Louisville I'll travel by boat; the rest of the
way by stage. Coming back I'll be stopping in southern Kentucky,
Mrs. Clemens. In Green County. I'll visit my cousin Peter Anderson there."

They all knew that Peter Anderson, a Virginian, had married
Aunt Anne Montgomery's only child, Lucilla. They had discovered
the relationship when the Moffett brothers came to the hamlet of
Florida and they often talked of it, saying it's a small world. They
had declared it made them almost kin. Pamela, finding her voice,
asked for more details of Will's journey. How long would he be
gone? When would he get to Green County? "Just imagine!" she
kept saying between questions. She envisioned a collection of rural
Kentucky girls, somewhat bold and distractingly pretty, all angling
for a St. Louis husband.

Will recited his schedule. "I'll get to Green County the middle
of September," he stated. "I plan to do some hunting and fishing
with Peter Anderson. This is my first vacation in ten years."

Jane had been looking at him intently and she made an announcement which Pamela could not comprehend. "That's real
strange, Will. September is when Mela will be visiting her kin in
Green County. Some of the Keokuk Pattersons are going to Kentucky for a visit late this summer and they've urged Mela to go
along."

Pamela saw surprise take possession of Will's face, heard her
mother continue, "Mela has a nice little sum saved up from teaching music in Monroe County. She used to say she would keep it
for an emergency. But I think I've persuaded her there's no in-

201

vestment like a nice trip. Mela's got dozens of kinfolks in Adair County she's never met."

Pamela remained speechless, but her mother filled the gap. "Go and get the Patterson letter, Mela. It's somewhere in our room." There was indeed such a letter, and Pamela went and rummaged hastily, found it, delivered it in silence. Jane, nicely editing, read aloud some cordial passages suggesting that Jane Clemens and her daughter accompany the Iowa Pattersons on their homeward pilgrimage.

"It stands to reason I can't go," Jane said. "I must look after the boys. As I was telling you, Will, when Mela came in, Orion is dickering to buy the *Journal* to merge it with his *Western Union,* and things couldn't be busier with us. But Mela has agreed to spend her nest egg on the trip." Then she said imploringly, "Haven't you, dear?"

Mela met the challenge. "Without a single regret," she said. She described a traveling dress she would have made. She enumerated the relatives she would visit, locating their homes. And especially did she stress Aunt Anne Montgomery who was living with her daughter Lucilla Anderson in Green County.

Will Moffett looked at her thoughtfully. "It will be nice to find you there, Mela," he said. If he was aware that he was a trapped man it did not appear to disturb him. Perhaps he was ready for the halter. Why, else, had he come back to this shabby, red-carpeted room with the open windows and the open piano and a table crowded with newspapers and the inevitable vase of honeysuckle? When he bade Pamela good-by he was rather more solemn than usual. He told her explicitly that he would see her at Peter Anderson's in Kentucky at mid-September. It was an appointment, its *raison d'être* uncertain, but its keeping inviolable.

"Have a safe journey, Will!" Mela called from the doorway. She seemed to implore it. Jane, who had found cause to go and see about supper, was struck by the resonance in her daughter's voice, a released music. "I think I've made it happen," she reverently told the kitchen stove and God.

Outfitting Mela was pure pleasure for Jane. Her love of fine raiment was given full play. Mrs. Owsley's garret provided the

202

means. The murderer's wife, still living in Hannibal, still semi-widowed by circumstance, was gallantly rearing her children alone and stressing to them the importance of the Sixth Commandment, courtesy and a cheerful mien. Her trunks yielded muslins, moirés, merinos. Hat boxes gave up bonnets of Milan straw and velvet bought a decade ago in Louisville. Mela was all but exhausted by the enthusiasm of her outfitters. As *Godey's Lady's Book* was studied the dressmakers with glad cries fell upon whaleboned basques and contorted them to their model's lines. From a linen guimpe, convent-embroidered, they made small collars to encircle her firm throat. Skirts considered too skimpy were combined in striking ways, delighting their architects. A Swiss embroidery dress with dropped shoulders needed but slight alteration. Mrs. Owsley said to Jane quietly, "It would be lovely for an afternoon wedding, if she happened to attend one."

"Yes, it would be," Jane replied with equal discretion. They hardly dared look at the plain girl with the lovely figure as they made their suggestions. But Pamela was aware. She thanked them dutifully, brooding on the impractical journey ahead, a venture that could bring her heartache and embarrassment. It came to her mind that her mother was as reckless as a riverboat gambler, a parent her children should be wary of.

In the weeks that followed, Jane prayed for Mela's betrothal to Will. She found inspiration in the bells of the steamboat *Chester* when they summoned her to her stark little church; in the stars over the river; in the feel of the floorboards as she knelt beside her bed. If she had had a rosary, she would have petitioned the Blessed Mary.

One Saturday noon in the kitchen she opened a letter that Henry had brought from the post office. "What's this?" she exclaimed, reading. Henry and Jim Wolfe, washing up for dinner, came on the run and caught disjointed snatches. "Mela and Will Moffett are going to get married down there! Oh, to think of it! And a wedding trip to Niagara Falls! Dear Lord, how kind of You!"

She continued to divulge the letter's contents while the boys snatched their food from burning. Pamela asked her mother's and brothers' forgiveness for marrying away from home, and so impulsively. But Will had come to Kentucky a week early, to persuade her. They could return to Missouri by way of the Falls and Chicago, he said. Steam cars all the way! At first it had seemed too sudden, but Aunt Anne and the Andersons had urged her to accept Will's plans since it was plain to see she loved him. The wedding would be in their parlor, Saturday fortnight, the place filled with garden flowers and kin.

Henry took the letter, discovered it to have been written September sixth. "Saturday fortnight's today," he told his mother.

"You mean this very day? Oh, I must try to compose myself." She went to her room and closed the door. Henry and Jim greatly affected, ate their meal hastily, being more eager than usual to relieve Sam and Orion at the office. They would have the pleasure of giving them the romantic news and watching Sam set it up in type, if Orion approved of such a forward announcement. . . . The news would appear under the proud *Journal* masthead. Orion had borrowed five hundred dollars from an affluent farmer a few weeks previously and had secured the newspaper he so coveted— its good will, its name, its Whig tradition and its plant.

24 ❖

Orion delayed printing the tidings until the marriage had been confirmed by an appropriate letter from the groom. But Jane had already shared the news in a series of hushed confidences. Her spirits were afloat because of Mela's consummated romance. (Consummated indeed, for a baby was due at the eleventh month, had she but known it.) Letters from Pamela were reticent in regard to her personal life, but in describing her material blessings she spilled over gratifyingly. Like most St. Louis newlyweds, the Moffetts had gone to live in a boardinghouse pending the day when they could take a house and furnish it. Will Moffett had engaged bedroom and sitting room in a large brick house in a good street, where all the boarders were quiet and the meals tempting. The cook spoke both French and English, the landlady wore black silk.

204

Furnishings in their suite were of the best walnut; both of the rooms had fireplaces with hand-painted coal scuttles! These and other St. Louis refinements now enjoyed by Mela were a source of joy to Jane, but she refrained from boasting—that being her life's most practiced discipline—and she walked humbly before the Lord.

The community had the additional pleasure now of celebrating the marriage of Miss Mary Ann Newcomb, sometime Clemens boarder and long-time instructor at Mrs. Horr's Academy. Miss Newcomb, a self-contained spinster, had inadvertently won the heart of Mr. Davis, owner of Hannibal's new bookstore, her cultured mind and elegant Virginian accents somehow filling the bill for him. Jane gave a party for her, the refreshments paid for by a little gift from Pamela.

It was understood by Pamela Moffett that she must not reveal to her husband the dire financial condition of her family. Whatever money she sent to Hannibal was secretly extracted from her allowance. This seemed the best way. Her natural reticence aside, she would not have her adored husband wonder if she had accepted him to secure a provider. There was also her mother's pride and her eldest brother's self-esteem to protect. Orion, when he stopped with them during the ensuing year for a formal meal and a call, put up a brave front regarding his newspaper's health and growth. He did not reveal that whatever money came to him derived from advertisements; that most of his subscribers paid by barter—in produce and firewood, and even in clean cotton and linen rags, an accepted currency germane to the paper market.

Sam had received not a cent of his promised salary, Orion dramatizing his insolvency by turning his pockets inside out and extending empty palms. Nothing remained, he said, after the necessities were met. Heaven could attest, he reminded Sam, that he was the most frugal bachelor in town, declining shoe shines and inking his gloves. Had not Thackeray just said a gentleman wore out first at the extremities? But Sam was not amused by the drollery. Hope deferred had made his heart sick, and even the neighbors attested that "he let Orion have it."

Jane failed as a buffer in the tangled situation. "Sam's raising the roof again," she would say, shutting her bedroom door.

Orion's receipt of a hundred and fifty dollars for a parcel of the Tennessee land seemed to Jane and Sam and Henry to be a rectifier of their plight. But the hope was soon dashed. Orion laid out the new wealth in three parcels: fifty dollars in interest to Farmer Johnson, fifty for supplies to keep his newspaper going—all well and good; but the remainder, he decreed, must take him South to see about the land. Jane, fairly atremble to get her hands on the remaining fifty, reminded him that his father had taken the same journey ten years before to no avail. "All wasted money, Orion! Don't you remember?"

But Orion's great dark eyes were alight with determination to plat the tract and explore its potentials. He quoted their New York agent Arnold Buffum as he walked the floor and talked of their prospects. His step was firm, his new little beard became him well. He was overflowing with enterprise. His mother took comfort; perhaps he would triumph where his father had failed. Besides, he had been disappointed again in love; his adored Josephine Smith, a local belle who had encouraged him, was casting him aside for a well-to-do young man in Quincy; this journey might mend Orion's heart and pride. She ceased to oppose him. Getting out her cobbler's bench, she began to half-sole the family shoes, a thing she had vowed never to do again.

Orion, on his winter journey, wrote interesting letters home. In Adair and Green counties, where he paused, not to be outdone by Pamela, he sought out relatives of all ages. They made much of him. He was taken to see the peculiar grave of his mother's grandfather, Colonel William Casey, whose bones rested below in his great chair, as revered as a Cherokee relic in a mound. In Tennessee's Fentress County he marveled at the extent of the Clemens holdings but accomplished little in the way of mapping it. How could he, he reasonably asked later; he was not a surveyor. He returned to Hannibal early in the new year, his journey fruitless of anything but pleasure. In the spring, to atone, he betook himself to St. Louis. There he interviewed all the speculators recommended to him and glowingly described their dukedom.

Orion's absences, though hard on the family budget, wrought a benefit. Sam, as foreman, had to meet the responsibilities of getting out the paper. Dr. Hugh Meredith, back from a disillusioning trek to California, had been left in nominal charge. But between the young foreman and that man, a wary hostility persisted. Meredith received a cool welcome when he dropped in.

Sam was sustained faithfully by his two compositors, Jim Wolfe and Henry. Henry was, besides, a mine of unassorted information, deriving his jackdaw knowledge from every book and periodical he could lay hands on. It was Henry who recited to Sam the plot of *Bleak House* so that Sam might comment to subscribers on that serial run by Orion. It was Henry who knew the origin of Freemasonry, the mechanism of George Washington's false teeth, and the present strength of the United States Army. Henry, too, could explain why the Pope would not be transferring his headquarters to Baltimore or St. Louis; why the Hungarian patriot Lajos Kossuth was lecturing in America. And, most far-reachingly, Henry was able to outline Joan of Arc's career for Sam (when the latter chanced on her tribulations in a page lost from an old book), clearing up certain aspects that their mother had dismissed in a welter of confusion, delivered in her most moving tones:

"Oh, the poor Maid! She heard voices. She *had* to do what she did, though I've never got the straight of it."

Thus, by way of Henry, Sam contrived to satisfy many areas of his curiosity without applying himself to books. Most of his journalism was imitative, but now and again some opinion would flare with originality, some phrase would shine with style. Not all of his editorial work, his mother observed nervously, was of benefit to Orion. In well-set type Sam sneered at Mr. Ament of the *Courier*—his former employer—and twitted the editor of the *Tri-Weekly Messenger,* a Whig rival they all feared for the *Journal's* sake, accompanying his digs at the vulnerable Mr. Hinton with woodcuts of a rakish nature. Later, there were apologies in print.

However Orion saw that Sam had something to offer local journalism and he named the sixteen-year-old scribe subeditor and gave him a sounding board called "Our Assistant's Column." In his new capacities Sam reported town topics and made crude witticisms. He commented on river traffic, the foibles of women, the cult of Spiritualism (though guardedly in the latter case, for his mother was trying it out), and the pitiful ignorance of persons he disliked. Sometimes he signed himself W. Epaminondas Adrastus Blab. And once, in a romantic state, he wrote a conventional poem called "Love Concealed" and signed it Rambler. But the mood was considerably altered—whether accidentally or intentionally, one could not say—by its strange dedication: *"To Miss Katie of H————l."*

Jane read all three Hannibal papers and whatever others the boys brought home with them. To the *Journal's* office drifted worn papers from all the river-linked towns, and sometimes from distant New York or Boston or Philadelphia. To conquer the small print of the unwieldy pages, she used a magnifying glass, moving it across wide areas with dexterity. Newspapers were living things to her, every issue as fresh as a newborn babe and just as full of surprises. The *Tri-Weekly Messenger* alone that year carried such items as these to give her pause:

A Mr. Dickson of Kentucky, it is said, has discovered the principle of perpetual motion and has refused $500 for his plan. Had he got hold of some of John's unpatented ideas, she wondered. Maybe Orion should write a challenging letter.

A story in circulation in Middleboro, New York, is that some of the citizens in broad daylight saw what appeared to be an immense number of soldiers, some thousands, marching and countermarching through the air. This unique sight, it is said, was witnessed for the space of two hours. It seemed reasonable to Jane. They were the soldiers who had died in Mexico. But no horses? Strange!

Mr. Johnson Carter from Albemarle County, Virginia, arrived in St. Louis May eleventh with his family and one hundred and thirty Negroes. He designs settling permanently in the neighborhood of that city. The Negroes are said to be a likely, healthy, robust set, and will be quite an acquisition to the wealth of the county. Well, good Lord!

At Cincinnati a few nights ago a scoundrel was found in one

208

of the cemeteries in the act of robbing a grave. He was discovered and instantly shot dead by the keeper. How did my boys miss that one for the *Journal?*

THE LATE LADY BLESSINGTON QUOTED ON FAMILY AFFEC-TION: *As fathers love their daughters better than their sons, and mothers love their sons better than their daughters, so do sisters feel toward brothers a more constant attachment than toward each other. None of the vanities, heart-burnings and jealousies that—alas for poor human nature!—are but too apt to spring up in female hearts, can arise between brother and sister; each is proud of the other because it cannot interfere with self, is even flattering to self.* Part of that is nonsensical. It's true, though, that John Clemens doted on Pamela more than his boys.

PROGRESS OF THE AGE. *A Maine couple, Benjamin F. Shaw and Harriet N. Howard, have pledged to live together out of wedlock.* Those New Englanders. They could never do it in Missouri.

Horace Mann of Massachusetts is to become a citizen of Ohio, he having accepted the presidency of Antioch College. A to-do about it. Who is Horace Mann? I must ask Henry.

NEGROES FOR SALE. *A woman who is a fine cook, washer and ironer, having been raised to that business. . . . Also three boys from eight to ten years old, sound and likely.* Like Sandy when he came to us. Where are you now, Sandy? Are you still alive? Are you a grown man now?

And on October 16 when the low stage of the river threatened navigation: *The officers of the Steamer Nominee, at Galena, report a small rise in the upper Mississippi—a few inches only, but these days an inch on a sand bar is like an inch on one's nose, worthy of notice.* Sam will want to kill himself for not thinking of that one.

Jane longed to go down to St. Louis and see Mela and inspect baby Annie and the other Moffett acquisitions. To visit James Andrew and Ella too, for James Andrew had settled there after leaving McDowell Medical College. DR. J. A. H. LAMPTON said a brass name plate on his door, though his practice was said to be restricted; he could not bear the sight of blood! At medical school he had atoned for this very cleverly by substituting art for the

209

knife: his copy of *Gray's Anatomy* was the favorite volume of the dissecting room, for every artery was penciled in crimson, every vein in blue, every nerve in bright yellow. The elder Dr. McDowell, or Old Sawbones as he was called by his students, had given him a degree on the strength of his charts and his good recitations; but James Andrew was already moving into a new profession, that of politics. Both the Masons and City Hall were finding him valuable. Ella encouraged the mergence.

Pamela several times sent her mother money for a steamboat ticket to St. Louis, but Jane just as often was forced to spend it, some crisis at the *Journal* arising before she could secure passage.

But Hannibal had never been more interesting. The railroad to St. Joseph (John M. Clemens' dream) was now in operation, making the town a starting point for Iowa and Illinois parties bound for the West. Local merchants were outfitting them. River traffic was also causing prosperity. The booming little cities of Keokuk, Burlington, Des Moines, and St. Paul lay upriver, and speculators and investors continually stopped at one or another of Hannibal's hotels to get tips and warnings. Archibald Robards, back from California, now operated the Brady House; Toncray's had been modernized, the Monroe was flourishing, the City Hotel was holding its own. Nor were the taverns enough. The Oyster Saloon and Restaurant advertised: *Shell Oysters from Mobile Bay. Quail, teal duck, pheasants, plovers, fish, steaks, cutlets and hot coffee in a style to please the daintiest epicure. Confections, fruits, weddings cakes and party cakes supplied on order.*

In the midst of such mouth-watering viands the Clemens household dined on bacon and cornbread, potatoes and coffee. Winterstored cabbage was a luxury at three cents a pound. Jane lacked her tea. Molasses replaced sugar for sweetening. The only desserts they tasted were portions of wedding cake sent to the *Journal* in gratitude for the announcement of nuptials. (Sometimes the cake was accompanied by a gold dollar, making a plutocrat of Orion.)

There came the day, expanding frontiers or not, when Orion could not meet the rent for the rooms over Stover and Horr's Clothing Store which housed his business. His mother put her mind on it and acted. She emptied her parlor and made room for

210

Orion's press. Holding her head a little higher than necessary when questioned she said it would be "a lot more convenient for everybody."

Orion, to his mother's admiration and his assistants' dismay, nimbly covered the retreat by launching a daily news sheet in addition to his weekly. This was indeed flashy; the community had never had a daily newspaper. All the occupants of the crowded little house labored valiantly, the odors of cooking mingling with the smell of printer's ink, the clangor of the press shaking the pictures on the walls. It was nobody's fault, apparently, that a cow wandered through the open front door one warm spring night and consumed two of the *Journal's* composition rollers.

Sam had had enough of all this. He had raged boyishly at his brother's incompetence for several years. His revolt now at seventeen seemed a man's revolt. The menus which the Oyster Saloon used as advertisement hastened the climax.

"We could have teal duck and plover ourselves," he told his mother and Orion one evening, "if I had a gun. I know where to get a good secondhand piece cheap, one traded by a man going to California. I'd like you to fork up, Orion, and give me the money." He named a sum, aware that his brother had as much on hand.

Orion was humiliated by his inability to comply, knowing that the few hoarded dollars Sam referred to must go for ink and paper. He turned his refusal into a stern lecture on extravagance.

Jane wept. "Hush, Orion," she begged. "You know Sam's not extravagant!" Her next plea had a twofold purpose; it was a protest against hunting out of season and it was a red herring to divert the boy from his brother's rebuff. "The beautiful teals and the poor kildees are nesting now, Sam," she reminded him in a soft-spoken, dramatic way. "Squirrels and rabbits are feeding their young. Surely you wouldn't—"

"Wouldn't I!" Sam said. "I'm hungry. We're all hungry."

Orion left the room, slamming a door. There was a finality in the gesture, and the junior editor made his decision. He was going to St. Louis, he told his quietly listening mother. He would find work as a printer, then he could send a little money home. He would be going that very night. He was prepared to stow away, he said; there was nothing to it; he had done as much when he was nine years old.

"It's a thing I'd not want to happen now," Jane said, "your father's son leaving town like a vagrant! Wait till I get Mela's letter." She found it and extracted a bank note—money for a birthday present for herself, an open-and-above-board gift from both Moffetts. Her fiftieth birthday was looming, a thing Pamela knew, though Jane calculated the milestone to be a year away, having lied to the census taker ("a nosey man") in September 1850, listing herself as forty-six years old and thereafter sticking to her story.

Sam accepted the money gravely, promising to go straightway to Mela and stay until he had found work. Jane helped him collect his jumbled belongings, holding back her ever-ready tears until he should have quit the house. Then she got out the Bible and took his hand and laid it beside her own small work-worn hand. "I want you to repeat after me, Sam, these words," she said. "I do solemnly swear that I will not throw a card or drink a drop of liquor while I am gone."

He repeated the oath, and she kissed him; a rare caress.

"Remember that, Sam, and write to us," she said. She was not a delineator of character, but she knew he would go at life head-on. Whatever he did would be excessive. He might become the honored editor of a St. Louis newspaper—her highest dream for him; or, wandering, he might get the worst of a duel some sunrise and be buried in an unmarked grave in Natchez. "Keep in touch with us, Sam," she implored. "They say you write a real newsy letter."

It was twilight in late May, and she watched him go down the street toward the wharf to take the night boat, his red hair tousled, his step quick, carrying his possessions any which way. Her grief was as sharp for Orion as for herself. What would Orion do now without this brother's lively contributions, his gift for improvising in emergency? And how could she always remember that Henry was sweetly helpful beyond the call of duty, and Orion strangely in need of approval, without the stormy ways of Sam to measure them against?

As she passed the little mirror in the dining room—their sitting room now—she held the coal-oil lamp aloft and studied her sad face curiously, as she might have studied another woman's. She almost looked her age, her real age.

25 ❖

During June and July Jane had several cheerful letters from Sam, supplemented by communications from Mela. With Orion's reputation to back him, he had gotten work at Ustick's job printing house, and he gave satisfaction to Mr. Baird, the very particular foreman there. He was especially praised for the clean proofs he set for the *Anzeiger* and the *Watchman*, two periodicals which Ustick printed. The return of a regular compositor to Ustick's left him jobless, his family learned, but he quickly found work as a journeyman with the *Evening News*. As August came on, Sam's letters to his mother abruptly ceased. So did his modest remittances—hardly more, all told, than the money she had advanced to him. She supposed he was out of work again but reminded herself that he had a comfortable couch to sleep on in the Moffett sitting room and a place at their boardinghouse table. It seemed strange, though, that Pamela too had ceased to write.

Then came an amazing letter from New York in Sam's handwriting:

My dear Mother: You will doubtless be a little surprised and somewhat angry when you receive this and find me so far from home. . . . Well, I was out of work in St. Louis, and didn't fancy loafing in such a dry place, where there is no pleasure to be seen without paying well for it, and so I thought I might as well go to New York. I packed my 'duds' and left for this village, where I arrived, all right, this morning. . . . I shall wait a day or so for my insides to get settled, after the jolting they received, when I shall look out for a sit; for they say there is plenty of work to be had for sober compositors.

Then he mentioned seeing the Crystal Palace, and Jane realized why he had left St. Louis. It was to visit the World's Fair. Alarmed, she thrust the letter at Orion. She reminded him that his own newspaper had said *"the Crystal Palace is surrounded by throngs of drunk and debauched people."* Orion thoughtfully admitted this; it was an item he had picked up from a New Orleans paper. But he added by way of comfort, "Don't forget Robards' flour, Ma!"

He rummaged among stacked newspapers behind the press and came up with something in an April issue headed WORLDS FAIR; read to her: "Captain A. S. Robards, owner of the Arena Mills in this city, has shipped three barrels of flour aboard the Steamer *Jeannie Dean* and hopes to compete for the grand prize. The wheat was raised by Hiram Glascock of Ralls County last year. The barrels were made by O. G. Strong of this city—a fine example of coopering. The brands on the heads of the barrels were elegantly gilted by our artist and painter, J. R. Hardy, Esquire." They mused, and the distant city of New York seemed safer for a foot-loose boy because of the Arena Mills' three barrels of flour on display there.

Pamela sent word that she had not been able to deter Sam from leaving St. Louis. He had had it in his mind to go from the very first, she said, and as soon as he had saved enough money, he lit out. Aside from his transportation expenses, she divulged, he had saved a ten-dollar bill which he had asked her to sew in the lining of his coat.

A second letter from Sam conveyed comforting news. He had secured a situation with the John A. Gray printing firm at 97 Cliff Street, "—next to Harpers the most extensive in the city." He worked in a room with forty other compositors and lived at a printers' boardinghouse in Duane Street, a mile distant. He had just visited one of the finest fruit saloons in the world—the length of the glittering place filled with marble-topped tables covered with exotic fruits, the clustered gas lights representing grapes. *P.S. The printers have two libraries in town, entirely free to the craft; and in these I spend my evenings most pleasantly. If good books are not good company, where will I find it?*

Henry was envious at last: "I declare, Ma! He's finally doing his own reading!"

Sam's letters eventually conveyed homesickness and a complain-

214

ing spirit. Part of his peevishness derived from the hostile attitude of the Negroes he encountered. He thought they were haughty. He said they were better treated than white people in the East; he was considering blacking his face, he quipped. Actually, he was being repulsed by the colored people he hailed in camaraderie or kindly condescension, whichever, and he was resentful. It escaped his mind that the Fugitive Slave Law, but three years old, made a suspect of every white stranger who evinced an interest in the dark race; such a one might be an agent from the South, locating runaways. Sam Clemens with his drawl and his unexplainable cordiality could be nothing but anathema to such Negroes and their well-wishers. His puzzlement would take on a certain wistful humility as the months passed. From Philadelphia he would conclude a letter to Orion: *I would like amazingly to see a good old-fashioned Negro. My love to all. Truly your brother, Sam.* He meant a Negro who would look at him with friendly eyes.

The *Hannibal Journal* could not survive without Sam, either in its daily form or weekly. Its sparkle had died down. Not even his mother, Orion noticed, seemed in a hurry to peruse it; he caught her one day turning in ennui from his editorials. That night he sat alone in the printing office, their defaced little parlor, and thought it over. As he recounted that experience for Pamela: "The moonlight was glinting in at the open door. I threw my leg over the chair-arm and let my mind float. I decided to sell the office and leave Hannibal. I would take the five hundred dollars I'd been offered, pay off my mortgage and try anew, somewhere else."

The scene of his new endeavor was Muscatine, a hamlet in Iowa a hundred miles up the river, reputed to be in need of news service. An idle printing office was available for use, so Henry and Jim Wolfe and Jane followed dutifully as Orion prepared to issue the *Muscatine Journal.* It would be as Whig as Whig, he pledged; and he comforted himself by thinking he had brought with him the heart of his loved and lost *Hannibal Journal.*

The family, the furniture, and the cats fitted very well into a white frame cottage they had rented. There was a grape arbor beyond the latticed back porch; the grassy yard sloped to the river. Sunsets, reflected on the water, were notable. Henry, not continuously needed for so small a newspaper, found work at R. M. Burnett's bookstore and was contented. He could take his cultural problems to George Dennison, a young schoolteacher from the East.

Jane went everywhere there was to go and met everybody in the village. She found most of the women to be rather reserved, even when they came bringing gingerbread and Indian pudding. They were New Englanders, mostly, and they seemed to find her interesting. Sometimes she had the feeling they found her too interesting, a curiosity. Uneasily wondering why and not wanting to be a discredit to Orion, she removed some of the trimming from her hats and began to use the dust cloth oftener. There were incidents, however, not subject to reform, deriving from the warp and woof of her. . . . There came two callers whose ancestors had been sea captains who often sailed to India, and they told her of the long absences endured by such families. One of them had had a great-aunt who waited six years for her sweetheart to return before encouraging another suitor. The other woman told how her grandmother had looked out to sea in vain for twenty years before acknowledging herself a widow.

"How tragic!" Jane said, but she surprisingly changed the subject to trees. She described two beautiful ashes on a neighbor's property in Gainesboro, Tennessee; the owner of the property, over his wife's protests and her own, had ruthessly chopped down one of them because it shaded his currant bushes. "The other tree tried it alone for a while," Jane said. "It even put out leaves the next spring, like the other trees, then it died."

"Were the roots of the two trees mixed, Mrs. Clemens?" the listeners inquired, uncertain as to the point of this story. "Were they from the same roots, interlocked?"

"No," Jane answered. "I was just thinking of loneliness. Sometimes it kills, of course. The trees stood about thirty feet apart. They were just friends." The ladies could hardly wait to take their departure and talk it over.

Thus engaged with moving and getting acquainted, Jane forgot to write and tell Sam they had gone to Iowa. Pamela sent on a letter from him asking what on earth had become of the family.

216

"Ma," Orion said gravely, "how could you forget to tell your absent son anything so important? Are you like a cat that forgets its kittens as soon as they are out of sight?"

"No, Orion," she answered contritely, "I never forget anything I've ever loved. But sometimes I neglect them. Anyhow," she drawled, remembering Samuel Langhorne's treachery in going to New York without telling her, "it didn't hardly hurt Sam to wonder a little!"

Orion, editor and grammarian, let the double negative pass. He was not so tense a man as his father had been. And perhaps he was remembering that Jane Clemens had taken this latest upheaval "like a trooper"—one of his favorite expressions.

Winter came lashingly in early November and Jane responded with a cold that left her coughing. Orion mentioned it in a letter to Sam, then working in Philadelphia, and Sam sent a forthright opinion dated November 28. *My dear Brother,—I received your letter today. I think Ma ought to spend the winter in St. Louis. I don't believe in that climate—it's too cold for her.* Pamela too showed concern. She invited her mother to come to St. Louis before the river iced, offering the hospitality of the Moffett sitting room at their new boardinghouse, Mrs. Hunter's in Olive Street. Jane declined, being committed to taking care of her boys. As for Sam's anxiety, let him look after his own health. He had inherited her tendency to bronchitis, she reminded him. But she was canny in lessening her exertions. Several times in her life she had been on the brink of lung fever and had pulled back from it by extra bed rest, when she could snatch it, and a refusal to consider herself in jeopardy. That winter when a Muscatine woman, acclimated by New England winters, besought her to "look out for consumption," Jane's answer was, "Yes, I surely will. I don't aim to have it." A similar declaration had been made, the villagers recalled, when a cholera flare-up had threatened in September, soon after the Clemens arrival. Mrs. Clemens had said, almost carelessly, "We don't aim to catch it." Her preventive in that case had been stewed fruit and clabbered milk. She had grown tired of herbs and simples.

The winter had many bright spots for those in the editor's

217

cottage. There was coasting, a religious revival, bushels of hot popcorn in the evening, and some souvenirs from Sam. He sent Pamela a dollar to buy their mother a fine handkerchief. The money would have bought flannel for a new petticoat, rather needed at the time had Pamela known it, but she invested it as Sam had instructed. Jane flaunted the handkerchief shamelessly.

Orion's standing in the community was high. His *Muscatine Journal* was doing well, and the townspeople were impressed by his several trips to Keokuk on business; by his recent return to Hannibal to see about the family property and attend a meeting of the Scots' Club, of which he was secretary. Going down in March on the steamboat *McKee* he had written his impressions of the little voyage and the following week had published them in his newspaper:

On Tuesday night, pale-faced fog, that white robed messenger of Delay, stealthily crept around our boat like a winding sheet. It spread from shore to shore; it hid the river; it stole upon the deck; it hovered over the boat; it wreathed up between the chimneys; it was everywhere, gently whispering "Stop!" The Captain obeyed this noiseless but superior force. Thus the wide world over, firm gentleness is always powerful.

And so on.

While farmers and merchants may have been immune to this fine writing, feminine readers were calling him gifted. Why was this handsome man of twenty-eight, so talented and charming, not married? A certain absent-mindedness seemed to be his only flaw; and a quip from Hannibal that "Orion Clemens couldn't make money in a mint," was dismissed as spiteful. Several young ladies began to vie for his attentions. It seemed to his mother that one of the affairs was promising.

Then Orion surprised her with a confidence. A girl down the river, of whom she was unaware, had also engaged his affections; and he hers. She was Miss Mary Eleanor Stotts, daughter of Collector of Customs of the Port of Keokuk—a girl whose parents Jane had known in her youth. They were William Stotts and Mary Patterson, natives of Adair County, at whose wedding she

218

had followed Marshall Clemens with a cake plate, finally catching his eye. One of Miss Stotts' aunts, Janie Patterson, was the widow of Uncle Green Casey down at West Point; she had been a dutiful daughter-in-law to Grandmother Casey to the day of the old lady's death. Jane now mentioned those family connections to Orion, but he prodded her to recall Mary Eleanor herself.

"You must remember which Stotts girl I'm talking about, Ma? She's called Mollie. When you and Henry had the lay-over at Keokuk, coming up, you met her. She told me so."

"I wish I had paid more attention," Jane groped. "I can't seem to place her." This was no wonder, for Mollie Stotts was not a girl to lodge in one's memory. She was homely, yet not noticeably so, agreeable yet hardly gracious. Though ten years younger than Orion—almost of an age with Sam—her youth in no way rendered her shy. With tactical skill that summer she arranged for Orion to disentangle himself from the pretty miss he had courted in Muscatine and become firmly engaged to herself. Orion wrote a graceful note to her father, asking for her hand, and soon afterward they were officially betrothed.

That high point having been reached in the late summer of '54, an equally happy one climaxed it. Sam appeared unannounced one morning when they were having breakfast, back from his year's sojourn in New York and Philadelphia. He looked his eighteen years; and he was carrying a gun, reminiscent of the one he had been denied by Orion the night he left for St. Louis. Though he pointed only the butt of the weapon at them, Jane screamed for him to put it down. Then she went so far as to feel his cheek and lay her own against it. "Sam, Sam," she said, like a caress, "what a long time you stayed away."

Sam declined Orion's offer of partnership after investigating the *Muscatine Journal's* potentials, and he returned to St. Louis and a compositor's job on the *Evening News*. Though the Moffetts had leased a house with a spare room in Pine Street, Sam occupied it but fleetingly, having grown accustomed to his freedom. He went to board with Mrs. Pavey, late of Hannibal, now widowed by her "Corsican" and running a boardinghouse in St. Louis.

219

It was Jane who would occupy the spare room at the Moffetts'. Will was as urgent as Pamela in extending the invitation, and she accepted gratefully. Detecting certain managerial tendencies in Orion's wife-to-be whenever he quoted from her letters, Jane abdicated to her without a struggle. Actually, the nineteen-year-old Miss Stotts was rearranging the Clemens furniture before she arrived and was suggesting a good many rules of conduct for Orion to follow. Henry, docile and detached, would get along with her, Jane knew; he would be supervised and well fed. Orion assured her that Mollie was an excellent cook, and that when she mended her father's and brothers' clothes you'd think a tailor had done it.

The wedding was set for December 19, a date that might bring thick ice to the upper Mississippi. Jane could not chance it. If the steamboats should cease to run above St. Louis she might find herself an untitled person in the Muscatine cottage all winter, unable to depart. And so, late in November, when she found a reliable day servant to take care of Orion and Henry (Jim Wolfe had returned to Hannibal)—a woman pledged to shine up the house for the Christmas bride—she went aboard the *Golden Era* for St. Louis, her heart blessedly light. Thomas Miller, the family friend, the *Golden Era's* Hannibal agent, had secured her a commodious stateroom in which to deposit her amazing luggage. It was carpetbags and such, all held shut by straps and frayed ropes; but Sam would meet her at the wharf and convey her to Pine Street in style.

When the boat docked a while at bustling Burlington, the town Dr. Richard Ferrel Barret had promoted before moving on to St. Louis, Jane studied it with consuming curiosity from between the taller shoulders of fellow passengers. Was Mrs. Richard Barret in good health, she wondered. It was a conscious wonder, unashamedly faced, made plausible by an old romantic incident in the Montgomery family. Her grandmother's sister Anne, after the death of General Benjamin Logan, had married the dashing, erratic scout James Knox, her girlhood sweetheart. Both had been fiftyish. They became famous hosts at his house in Shelby County, running a carefree plantation for twenty years. And it was Knox,

220

went the rumor, that Anne Montgomery asked to be laid beside in the burying ground. Jane knew the story well.

She had brought some sandwiches in a paper poke to make a thrifty meal, but when Burlington was left beyond a bend in the river she impulsively gave it to a little boy who was eying it, and went to the dining cabin. There she ordered terrapin soup with French bread and Hyson green tea number one, all quite extra. "Hyson means blooming spring," she confided to a woman beside her who was having the *table d'hôte*. "I've just read that in my eldest son's newspaper. He's editor of the *Muscatine Journal.*"

St. Louis resembled Heaven as a place to attain, in that it exceeded expectations. Jane, accustomed to the boy-scarred furniture she had left, was hardly prepared for the room which Mela and Will had readied for her—so large an armoire, so comfortable a bed, so complete a sewing table, such crisp lace curtains and neat rugs.

The Moffetts employed a young German woman to cook and a youth to bring in the coal and lay the fires. As Will's business had to do with the distribution of food, his dining table was bountiful. Jane went to meals with carefully concealed wonder. For the first time in years she could help herself to food without restraint. And how fascinating it was to use a sterling silver bread knife whose handle was shaped like an ear of corn; one could slice the fresh loaves at table. She gained weight and was cured of her cough.

Sometimes she went to Mrs. Pavey's boardinghouse to see Sam and mend his clothes. And on Sundays Sam often came to the Moffetts' for dinner. They might find him entertaining little Annie when they got home from church, or skimming through a book. He nearly always carried one about with him now, for his roommate at the Paveys', a young man named Frank Burrough, had a fondness for Dickens and Disraeli and had passed on the contagion.

But with the Clemenses, nothing was permanent. There was a reshuffle when summer came. Mollie was expecting a baby. She hated the village of Muscatine, was homesick for Keokuk, her family and friends. At her instigation Orion sold his newspaper and purchased the Ben Franklin Book and Job Printing office in Keokuk. That town was booming; settlers were coming in from the eastern states and even from Europe, for it was now a railroad terminal as well as a river port.

Orion had plans for publishing a city directory, Keokuk being ready for one. It would carry, as introduction, a piece of regional history he had written, "Sketch of the Black Hawk War and History of the Half Breed Tract"—an ambitious undertaking. Though he had several local typesetters engaged as well as the faithful young Henry, he urged Sam to join him without delay. He would pay him five dollars a week, he said, and board him at a good hotel. Henry would continue to live with him and Mollie.

"I'd like to take Orion up on this," Sam told Pamela and Jane. "But ask Mr. Moffett what he thinks."

Will Moffett advised him to go. Perhaps Sam's aura of explosive vitality made him uneasy. The boy would not live with them and submit to regulations. He came and went without system, made unconventional friends, started arguments even in a man's parlor. Persons who met him socially found him hard to classify, especially when he had forgotten to scrub the ink from his hands and put on a cravat. Parents did not invite him to meet their daughters, a matter his mother and sister noticed with regret. Not even James Andrew Lampton and the sociable Ella were inclined to launch him at Verandah Hall, though they knew several girls who lacked cotillion partners. "He's too untidy," was Ella's honest comment.

One evening when Jane found Sam in the Moffett hallway, twanging Pamela's guitar, his hair uncombed and his collar awry, she flew into a temper. "I want to talk to you, Sam!" she exclaimed. "It's about your carelessness! My father used to say 'a man owes it to the world to look his best.'"

"Why, Ma?" Still strumming, he dropped to his knees and looked up imploringly. "Tell me why, Ma! Share this gem of wisdom with me and I'll put it in a song!"

Jane laughed helplessly. When she told Pamela about it the latter asked, "Why do you always let him get the best of you?"

"Because Sam Clemens is the funniest boy I ever talked to, Mela."

"A clown, you mean. You're diverted by a clown."

"No, no, Mela, it's more than his cutting up. It's the outlandish twist he gives to things. Right now I'm doubting if my own father's motto makes sense."

"Well, Mother," Pamela said, "accept the blame." (She had left off saying Ma since her marriage.) "All his life you've encouraged him by laughing. It's your way of applauding him."

They sent him up to Keokuk with a stout new comb and a leather toilet case, nicely stocked. They urged him to use the articles conscientiously, and they advised him to adapt himself to Orion and set a good example for Henry.

Those things he was presently doing. From his own letters and from Orion's they learned that he was lending himself to Orion's needs and was not trying to run the place. They also learned that he was rediscovering girls, a species once dear to him, then outgrown.

Mollie's relatives, the Pattersons and Stotts and Taylors, were among the town's leaders and those families had produced several pretty girls with bright minds and musical talents, much to Sam's taste. Soon he was studying the piano with Mr. O. C. Isbell who had a studio on the floor beneath the Ben Franklin shop, and was harmonizing with the girls and buying them the latest thing in sheet music. He had also joined a glee club. He lived at the Ivins House on the river front, where Orion paid his board with happy regularity. When an extra boy was needed for a social engagement, Sam would generously summon Henry, whose tall blond beauty might well have caused him jealousy.

Sam Clemens' conduct and status reached near perfection in Keokuk when he substituted for a speaker at the printers' banquet in honor of Benjamin Franklin's birthday and, according to Orion, drew enthusiastic applause.

Jane's mind being at ease about her boys, and her health restored, she went about the city and learned its ways. Sometimes she was accompanied by James Andrew and Ella, sometimes by

Hannibal friends come to town, often by the Daniel Trabues, junior, who had moved from Adair County to St. Louis years before—Daniel whose little brother had been murdered by the Harpes, Mary whose father, Captain Robert Paxton, had died at New Orleans. They shared letters from home and reminisced about their youth, their memories always including the episodes involving Patsy. At Jane's urging they turned every meeting into explorations of St. Louis, until Mary Trabue grew weary.

It was not until the Moffetts, needing a handsomer house to match Will's rising fortunes, moved to Locust at Eighth Street that Jane met her most congenial explorer, a scintillating young neighbor with restless feet. She was Mrs. George W. Berkeley, the former Mathilde Lagroue of St. James Parish, Louisiana, now bearing children but hardly hampered by it. They were enchanted with one another, and the enchantment included Mr. Berkeley, a former Virginian, connected with the St. Louis queensware house of Janney and Company. Usually they would be accompanied on their jaunts by little Annie Moffett, whom Jane took along as a matter of course to relieve Pamela of her care. Mr. Berkeley enjoyed taking his wife and Jane Clemens and little Annie and his own brood to see the steamboats at the docks; and frequently he would hire a hack and take them through the parks and suburbs. One of Mrs. Berkeley's favorite destinations was the market with its open stalls and French proprietors, especially on a fresh summer morning. Jane, in her wake, learned to appreciate such things as endive and scallions and long loaves of crusty bread.

The Berkeleys, being fond of card games, taught Jane to play whist, and she often made "a fourth" at their house next door. One memorable evening they took her to the theatre to see the family troupe of Field and St. Clair play *Shocking Events*, Mrs. Berkeley having chosen that over Mr. Kean Buchanan's *Macbeth* at another theatre. Though *Shocking Events* was a benefit performance, Pamela found its title dismaying and brought Jane to task. "Mother," she said earnestly, and she spoke with reluctance, "there's something you don't seem to realize. Mrs. Berkeley is every bit of fifteen years younger than you, and she's a giddy French Catholic."

"Of course I realize it," Jane answered her. "If we were all alike it would be pretty monotonous around here."

Mela repeated the remark to Will, who relished it. His mother-in-law brightened his household and seldom interfered with his habits and plans. All she asked, apparently, was that they not interfere with hers. He noticed that the Moffett house had more interesting callers than before her arrival, and they seemed to hang on her words. Not that her words were important; but they came new-minted, as it were, from her observations, spoken in her *grande dame* drawl with its still lingering broad a's and its occasional grammatical lapses.

He first noticed her social usefulness one evening when he and Pamela were entertaining a couple at dinner who were important to them. The conversation had reached a dreary calm from which they could not rescue it. Jane Clemens, who had been a listener, stepped into the breach. "You were talking a while ago," she said, "of the Gasconade disaster, and how some people didn't feel the shock of it till later. It reminded me of what happened to a friend of my mother's—or maybe it was my grandmother's—down in Kentucky." She then told of a hunting day in Green County, inserting colorful details to prolong it, for the dessert had not yet been brought on, and she somehow conveyed the feeling of tragedy to come. It did. The husband of the story's heroine, Jane related, was shot by his own rifle as he climbed over a rail fence "—shot dead through the heart, though he'd survived the Battle of the Raisin!" His friends contrived a stretcher of their hunting coats, Jane continued, while two others rode on ahead to prepare the newly made widow. "She listened to the tragic news with a still face, not uttering a sound. Then she unpinned the starched muslin cap she was wearing and laid it carefully on the table before she fainted dead away. She was unconscious for a long time—hours, I think."

There was another story she told about her native village—though not at the dining table—which stirred listeners to shocked conversation. It concerned some gossip passed on to her in a

225

letter from Columbia: "The Parker Hardins—Mr. Hardin is an old friend of mine—have a slave man named John who's been all his life in the family and has fathered seven or eight children. This might be an asset to some masters, but not to Mr. Hardin because he considers it his duty to keep the slave family together— John, his wife and all their children. Not long ago, John, a fine-looking big fellow, got notions of grandeur and declined even to split firewood. As coachman, it was his duty to keep the carriage clean, and presently he wouldn't do even that. One day Mr. Hardin yelled for him in a temper and told him he was tired of having the dirtiest carriage in Adair County. Told him things had to improve or he'd sell him to the traders. John knew it was a real threat. He went to the woodpile and cut off three fingers on his left hand with an ax—he didn't disturb his driving hand—and then presented himself to his master, dripping blood. 'Nobody's going to buy a chopped-up nigger,' he said. Mr. Hardin was just horrified at what had happened, and Mrs. Hardin took to her bed for a while. And now John's not even asked to wash the carriage. He just drives it in his new clothes after some of the younger ones clean it up."

Whereas Jane's darkey stories, as they were condescendingly called, had formerly illustrated the inertia, cunning, and delicious wit of the enslaved Negro, she was becoming prone to incorporate the race's sufferings in her anecdotes, her response to their plight being now an agitated pity. Pamela begged her for the sake of Will's business not to be controversial. "Will has never in his life bought or sold a slave," she reminded her, "but he has to do business with people who do." She also besought her mother not to risk life and limb by dashing into busy streets to stop draymen from beating their horses. That plea too was a waste of Pamela's breath, for she frequently got news of Jane's making a spectacle of herself down at the landings.

Pamela was beginning to regard her health as delicate, though she was still hopeful of producing a son for Will Moffett. She kept to a routine social life, returning her calls in a hired carriage and resting in the early afternoons. On Sundays she attended services at the fashionable First Presbyterian Church in Lucas Place, where

226

they had a pew. It was her regret that her mother rarely accompanied her, her husband never. The latter refrained because certain prominent members were considered by him to be hypocritical. "I can't stand to see men cheat at pork all week and sit in church on Sundays," Will stated. Pamela accepted this private decision without nagging. After all, her father had never attended church, nor had her Uncle John Quarles, they too having had their reasons.

Jane's religious life was so erratic that Pamela was unable to cope with it and soon left off trying. Having provided her mother with several costumes suitable to a woman with a successful son-in-law, Pamela had to let her go her way. And Annie with her, for the child found her grandmother congenial.

After dressing Annie to her taste, Jane would take her every Sabbath to a conveniently located Sunday school reached by a pleasant stroll. It was held in a small edifice occupied by the Congregationalists; but when that sect moved to larger quarters and the Episcopalians took over the building, Jane continued to lead Annie there and deposit her. "You can safely do whatever the others do," she assured alert little Annie. It was a while before Pamela, a sincere non-ritualist, noticed that her child was bobbing up and down when she prayed, and at times crossing herself.

Pamela was aware that her mother went often to the Jewish synagogue, then at its old location on Fifth Street. Though it had not attained to the grandeur of its new building, the music was sublime and the service impressive. There was one phrase heard often there which satisfied Jane Clemens more than a sermon. It was "the ever living God," and she sometimes quoted it. The Moffetts assumed she preferred to think of God as contemporary.

Pamela made no objection to her mother's going to the synagogue, unusual behavior though it was, for Judaism was the foundation of Calvinism. But perhaps Jane failed to tell her that she went also, at times, to the Roman Catholic Cathedral and waited alone in its vast depths while Mrs. Berkeley made her confession to one of the priests there. After she had knelt a while in the dimness, looking at the altar, the mystery of the Beyond came to her and became the believable. Once, as she and the Berkeleys were passing the cathedral, they saw Archbishop Peter Richard Kenrick walking about the grounds and they stopped and went to him and Jane was presented. His Grace, who had succeeded to the mitre of St. Louis a dozen years before, was an extraordinary person who spoke five languages and read Hebrew, Greek, and Latin for relaxation. He lived a simple, methodical life, depriving himself for his charities and entreating others to do the same. Jane had watched him several times at the cathedral performing his rites in scarlet wool and rose-point lace. It pleasured her now to meet him in simple black robes in his garden, making gentle Irish jokes and inspecting his hyacinths.

The Moffetts, established in their new Locust Street house, were discovered and visited by an out-of-town relative who wrote such elegant notes to announce his comings, and such graceful letters of thanks on departing that they began to call their spare room Cousin James's room. He was James Lampton, a son of Jane's Uncle Lewis who had been a factor in her early life. The town of Louisiana on the Mississippi bluffs of Ralls County was his home, and he had now and then got to Hannibal on business. Though Jane and her children had found him delightful (Sam especially was drawn to Cousin James and had known exactly where he was going when he became a stowaway in his tenth year and asked to be put ashore at the town of Louisiana), John M. Clemens had contrary reactions, some ebullience in Mr. Lampton's nature setting his teeth on edge. James Lampton's business in St. Louis was always of a promotional nature. He believed in his projects wholeheartedly, and sometimes he made money from them— enough at one time to build a white-pillared house in his home town. But when reverses overtook him he would temporarily become a "drummer," selling St. Louis products to the crossroads and making all manner of friends. He had the Lampton Tidewater accent and a kindly courtliness that extended to the humblest person he met. He rejoiced in the success of others. There was no envy in him. Whatever failures he himself underwent— and they were often catastrophic—were treated by him as mere inconveniences, certain to be rectified tomorrow.

The visits of this man, Jane's blood relative, remembered by her as lovable little James of the Eagle House, were among the delights of her life when fate threw them together in St. Louis. He seemed rather fabulous, so important were the names he dropped, so optimistic were his predictions for the world, for himself, for you.

Children, servants, and neighbors were always glad to note his arrival at Eighth and Locust. Unaware, the Moffett household was entertaining Colonel Mulberry Sellers of *The Gilded Age.*

26 ❖

Conditions in Keokuk, "the Gate City," changed. The town was too stimulated for health and it succumbed to its own inflation. Orion's city directory was issued, though many of the advertisers were already facing ruin. It was evident to Sam that his good quarters at the Ivins House must be relinquished, for Orion could no longer pay his board there and was urging him to come and share a bed with Henry and dine at Mollie's table.

Sam would have none of it. He had become fascinated with the possibility of making a fortune in cocoa along the upper Amazon. Lynch and Herndon's explorations there, described in Herndon's report of it, had set him off. With two friends, one of them a physician, he was attempting to organize a select expedition to South America, all the while keeping his plans from Orion who would surely frustrate them. But Henry and their mother and Pamela were taken into his confidence. He sent Herndon's report to St. Louis, replete with his own glowing notations, to catch his mother's fancy. Jane was allured and was presently studying ways and means of launching his expedition. Money for his travels would have to be found, but her innocence of geography made this seem a secondary matter; first she must pry him loose from Orion. Letters between herself and Sam probed the matter. Sam, writing to Henry who was visiting in Hannibal, revealed the depths of her irresponsible naughtiness:

Ma knows my determination, but even she counsels me to keep it from Orion. She says I can treat him as I did her when I started to St. Louis and went to New York—I can start for New York and go to South America.

On a bleak day in early November a gust of wind blew a fifty-dollar bill in Sam Clemens's path. If not sought by the owner, it would be his: money for travel, and a good omen besides. No one in disrupted Keokuk advertised the loss, and in due time Sam packed his clothes in the familiar valise and departed for St. Louis. There he bade his mother and the Moffetts good-by and renewed his promise to Jane to abstain from liquor and cards for the duration of his absence. Then, because of a suggestion from Pamela who admired the quality of his letters, he returned to Keokuk and made a deal with a weekly newspaper called the *Saturday Post,* George Rees its editor, to furnish them letters of his travels at five dollars each. They were to be burlesques, signed Snodgrass. That arranged, he departed by train for Cincinnati, where he would make the decision of whether to sail from New York or New Orleans.

In Cincinnati, his money consumed, he secured work at a printing firm and found inexpensive lodgings. The Snodgrass letters languished for lack of novelty, but his letters home were regular enough.

Jane, that winter, entered into a period of rare discouragement. Orion was failing again, which meant that Henry, brilliant, unschooled boy that he was, might soon be jobless. As for Sam, with her sanction he had wandered afield without benefit; he was a shabbily clad printer in a strange town, living in a cheap boardinghouse, rooming with an eccentric Scot named Macfarlane whom he quoted constantly because of his learning and who was teaching him to doubt that God made Adam and Eve.

Jane's depression was deepened by a great contrast which was brought to her attention. She had unfortunately made inquiries about the Barret family from Daniel Trabue, though it was a subject better left untouched and she knew it. What she learned was sensational, or so her searching curiosity deemed it. Richard Ferrel Barret had forsaken medicine, but his income from Burlington and St. Louis enterprises was said to be twenty thousand dollars a year. He had recently given his son Arthur Buckner (a handsome, competent, chivalrous young man, said Trabue) a large farm near Springfield in Illinois and had stocked it with fine cattle and thoroughbred horses. Another son, also promising and dutiful, had become his father's partner in real estate. As for the eldest son, Richard Aylett, that one had prepared for Harvard College at Phillips Exeter—it was an academy for especially bright boys in New England, Daniel explained—and was now at Heidelberg University in Germany, studying to become a doctor of physics.

Jane, though cheerful in company, was sometimes overcome by comparisons after hearing these things and she wept privately for her own uneducated, poverty-stricken sons.

Orion held on gamely in Keokuk and prepared to issue his second directory: *Business Mirror, 1857*. But he reduced his staff of typesetters, and he and Mollie and little Jennie went to live with Mollie's parents. Henry, homeless, came at the Moffetts' invitation to St. Louis and joined his mother at their house. There, in the spare room, he shared a bed with Cousin James when that blithe visitor dropped by.

The boy picked up odd jobs in the city, which was getting ready for the first of its fairs, and in his leisure time he made himself useful to the Moffetts and read books from the Mercantile Library. Jane, seeing his fair head bent studiously over a volume, sometimes thought of that academy in New England where he would have fitted like a hand in a glove. Perhaps Phillips Exeter was a name bringing her nearer to bitterness than any she would ever encounter.

The springtime of 1857 brought an announcement so bizarre that the Moffett household and its neighbors were thrown into a state of bewilderment and expectation. Sam, who had not been heard from in more than a month and was thought to be in Cincinnati, sent up a bulletin from New Orleans saying he was writing from that city and would presently be on his way to St. Louis. He would be on the little steamboat *Paul Jones*, he said,

Bixby master, and would be steering. Watch the wharves, he advised.

Jane, with first one neighbor and then another accompanying her, and with little Annie as well, haunted the waterfront. Also, at intervals, Henry would go to the levee and make inquiries. There was indeed such a riverman as Bixby, he learned, and such a boat as the *Paul Jones.* "When last heard from," reported Henry one evening, "she was near Vicksburg, coming up."

"Don't call the *Paul Jones* 'she'!" Jane exclaimed, her nerves a little frayed by this time. Her imagination endowed boats with the sex of their names, and the *Paul Jones* seemed historically masculine. She had been reading the steamboat items faithfully since coming to St. Louis. *Midas,* "badly damaged by a snag at Pawpaw Island," was male. So was *Ambassador,* "reported high and dry in a critical position below Mill Creek in the Ohio." Steamer *James Trabue,* "lost on Red River, cargo 738 bales of cotton," very masculine; named for Patsy's beau of long ago, Daniel's brother. But many of the steamboats wore feminine names, making their disasters seem especially touching: Steamer *Heroine,* "burst her boilers at Buckley's Landing, Mobile." . . . Lightning Line Louisville Packet *Diana,* "lying in Mulatto Bend above Baton Rouge with two feet of water in her hold." . . . *Forest Rose,* "badly damaged by collision with Steamer *Editor.*" . . . *Gazelle,* "collided with *Bridge City,* grain ruined." . . . *Gossamer,* "lost her chimneys in a gale," and right appropriately. . . . *Buckeye Belle,* "struck obstruction at Hat Island with 80 tons of lead and wheat." . . . *Silver Heels,* "sold to the bayou trade." Poor *Silver Heels,* who loved the open water!

None of the family saw the *Paul Jones* nose to a landing among the forest of smokestacks at the wharf. But Sam suddenly appeared at the door one April day, taller, more sedate than they had ever seen him, and he urged them to gather around and hear the news. He had persuaded Captain Horace Bixby to teach him piloting, he said, and had just clinched the bargain by paying Bixby a hundred dollars, advanced to him by Mr. Moffett.

"Oh, Sam!" Jane said, "what a lot to borrow!" And the young man replied, "Not at all, Ma, because I know I can pay it back."

232

This was no time to spread the news that Bixby was charging him five hundred dollars for the apprenticeship, the remaining four hundred to be deducted from his salary when he had obtained a license. "Where's Henry?"

They said Henry had a job downtown, something to do with "the Great Fair of the West," though nothing permanent. And Sam said he would remedy that. He could get Henry a clerkship with a steamship agent, he said; and in a year or so he, Sam, would be qualified to teach Henry piloting, free of charge.

There was rejoicing in the house that day, and congratulations from friends who dropped in. When Will Moffett came home from his office he added his calm approval, in no way seeming to regret his hastily advanced loan. Being a typical St. Louis businessman he regarded the river pilots as equals, in some cases his peers. And he judged Sam Clemens—persistent, keen, and brash—to have the makings of one.

Sam was on the river regularly that year, though not continuously. With his new assurance he obtained clerical work for Henry at the levee, as he had boasted he could do. The two young men boarded at the Moffetts, sharing a room when Sam was ashore more or less amicably, as in their boyhood. But they moved at the end of September to Mrs. Pavey's ever-welcoming boarding-house near the wharves because their room at Pamela's was needed for guests.

The guests were the Orion Clemenses, on their way to Tennessee. Orion had finally called the battle lost at Keokuk, a defeat less sad than his first, at Hannibal, and he was turning his attention again to "the Land." Mollie's eighteen-year-old sister, Belle, would accompany them as far as Adair County, so the house was full of trunks. Sedate little Jennie Clemens was quartered with lively little Annie Moffett for the visit, and Belle Stotts was graciously received in Jane's room. The family genius for enjoying the moment—Jane its lodestar—asserted itself. The Great Fair of the West was done in style; and when Sam left town with Bixby on the *Paul Jones* his admiring relatives waved him off. Henry substituted as Belle Stotts' escort right handily. They teamed with an adequately escorted girl of the Castle family, whose advanced age—she was past twenty-one—forbade that she be called anything but Miss Castle. She taught Henry and Belle the schottische in the Moffett parlor, her hand often lingering in Henry's as his remarkable blue eyes gazed at her for instruction.

Sam retained his room at the boardinghouse near the levee that winter. Henry too remained there, for he often did night work for the agent employing him. Captain Horace Bixby had taken on remunerative work on the Missouri River, but he did not release Sam Clemens from their contract; he hired him out as a cub to other Mississippi pilots. Thus it happened that Sam found himself acting steersman on the big steamboat *Pennsylvania* in the service of a pilot named Brown, a man he disliked and sometimes subtly taunted. They made the runs between St. Louis and New Orleans in a season of ice and thaw, but Sam seemed more stimulated than discouraged by the hazards.

In February, with the uneasy consent of his mother, he had Henry signed on as third clerk of the *Pennsylvania*. Jane had demurred that while steamboating was right for Sam it seemed wrong for Henry. Could he possibly be happy in any job but a bookish one? Sam explained that many a pilot read books between watches.

Henry, with his customary compliance, assumed his unattractive new duties. Uncomplaining in the foulest weather, he would go ashore when the boat came about for fuel, fully earning his title of mud clerk, to count the ricks of wood which the malarial natives turned over to the deck hands. On board, he carried orders from the captain to the pilot and performed other clerkly tasks. When he had an hour to spare he would read, or would watch Sam's skillful handling of the wheel.

That voyage down and back, Henry's initiation, ran a fortnight overtime. Above Cairo the crew frequently had to put out in yawls amidst the floating ice to find the current. The *Pennsylvania* docked at St. Louis on March 9 with tales to tell and weather records broken. Pamela and Jane thought the Clemens boys looked "done in" and persuaded them to give up their room on the levee and return to the comforts of Locust Street.

Sam wrote zestfully of the voyage to Orion and Mollie. . . .

234

His mother's interest in parades and stately funerals was shared by him, and he concluded his letter to them on that theme:

I got here too late to see the funeral of the 10 victims by the burning of the Pacific hotel in 7th street. Ma says there were 10 hearses, with the fire companies (their engines in mourning—firemen in uniform,) the various benevolent societies in uniform and mourning, and a multitude of citizens and strangers, forming, altogether, a procession of 30,000 persons! One steam fire engine was drawn by four white horses, with crape festoons on their heads.

Well, I am—just—about—asleep—Your brother Sam

Young Annie Moffett was to remember one peculiarity of the memorial parade which her grandmother explained to her. There was a break in the line, a lengthy space with just one carriage, and nothing following for a noticeable interval. Annie wanted to know if those mourners had the smallpox. No, something worse, Jane told her. The carriage belonged to a family who had "rented" a colored girl to work for them and had treated her so cruelly that she had tried to drown herself in the river. Though the court had declared it was unable to interfere, St. Louis, the good bad town, was sending that family to Coventry.

Henry had been on the river with Sam four months now.

One day in mid-June something occurred at home which Annie, aged six, was to recall visually. Her grandmother, her mother, and a young caller—a bride—were in her mother's room, which was used as an upstairs sitting room, and they were having a fine chat. The bride was carrying a card case of mother-of-pearl with a silver chain, and that was to become a lasting part of Annie's memory.

The maid came into the room and told Pamela Moffett that her husband was in the parlor and wanted to see her. Even Annie knew this to be remarkable, for her father never returned from his place of business at midmorning. Pamela went hurriedly downstairs, and Annie leaned over the banisters to watch. She observed that her mother was weeping and saying "No! No!" But her father held her gently by the elbows and repeated what he

235

had said. Then her mother, holding to the banisters, returned to her room and recited stiffly: "There's been an explosion on the *Pennsylvania* below Memphis. Henry is slightly wounded. Sam is missing. More than a hundred passengers are killed or injured."

The caller tiptoed from the room. Jane Clemens stood up, steadied herself, and led Pamela to bed. She poured water from the pitcher into the bowl, dipped a washcloth in it, wrung it out and laid it on Mela's forehead. "Go get me a little pan of ice, Annie," she said.

Several days of terrible suspense now, until there came word that Sam had not been on the boat at the time of the explosion, having left it at New Orleans. Jane was not at home when the news came. Restlessness had driven her out of the house to seek relief from Mela's distress and the smell of camphor. She had been to the docks. Annie ran to meet her and gave her the blessed news.

The mysterious circumstance of Sam's having left the *Pennsylvania* at New Orleans when he had been engaged to steer the round trip was confusing. They discussed it exhaustively while they sought further facts and wrapped parcels of books and comforts for Henry, who would be wanting them in the Memphis hospital. Even "slightly wounded," Henry would be wanting to read.

In the seemingly fatalistic way that things happened in the Clemens family, Orion was still in Tennessee, and he sent them a telegram saying he would proceed to Memphis at once. He had stayed in the South to finish his interrupted law course—Judge Goodall his interested teacher—and had just obtained a license to practice as an attorney at law. Mollie, with little Jennie, had returned to Keokuk six weeks previously, so Orion was unencumbered, free to go to the disaster. However, time was against him. When he reached Memphis he was useful, but in a tragic way. Henry had just died, and Sam, who had nursed him, lay in a stupor of exhaustion and grief.

Yet Sam, before this, had compulsively reached for a pen, as was his way. In the night watches of June 18, 1858, he poured out his anguish to the only person in the family who was composed enough to endure such a letter.

Dear Sister Mollie,—Long before this reaches you, my poor Henry—my darling, my pride, my glory, my all, will have finished his blameless career, and the light of my life will have gone out in utter darkness. O, God! this is hard to bear. Hardened, hopeless— aye, lost—lost and ruined sinner as I am—I, even I, have humbled myself to the ground and prayed as never a man prayed before, that the Great God might let this cup pass from me—that he would strike me to earth, but spare my brother—that he would pour out the fullness of his just wrath upon my wicked head, but have mercy, mercy, mercy upon that unoffending boy. The horrors of three days have swept over me—they have blasted my youth and left me an old man before my time. Mollie, there are gray hairs in my head tonight. For forty-eight hours I labored at the bedside of my poor burned and bruised, but uncomplaining brother, and then the star of my hope went out and left me in the gloom of despair. Men take me by the hand and congratulate me, and call me "lucky" because I was not on the Pennsylvania when she blew up! May God forgive them, for they know not what they say.

Mollie you do not understand why I was not on that boat—I will tell you. I left St. Louis on her, but on the way down, Mr. Brown, the pilot that was killed by the explosion (poor fellow,) quarreled with Henry without cause, while I was steering. Henry started out of the pilot-house—Brown jumped him and collared him—turned him half way around and struck him in the face!— and him nearly six feet high—struck my little brother. I was wild from that moment. I left the boat to steer herself, and avenged the insult—and the Captain said I was right—that he would discharge Brown in N. Orleans if he could get another pilot, and would do it in St. Louis, anyhow. Of course both of us could not return to St. Louis on the same boat—no pilot could be found, and the Captain sent me to the A. T. Lacey, with orders to her Captain to bring me to St. Louis. Had another pilot been found, poor Brown would have been the "lucky" man.

I was on the Pennsylvania five minutes before she left New Orleans, and I must tell you the truth, Mollie—three hundred human beings perished by that fearful disaster. Henry was asleep—was blown up—then fell back on the hot boilers, and I suppose that rubbish fell on him, for he is injured internally. He got into the water and swam to shore, and got into the flatboat

237

with the other survivors. He had nothing on but his wet shirt,
and he lay there burning up with a southern sun and freezing
in the wind till the Kate Frisbee came along. His wounds were
not dressed till he got to Memphis, 15 hours after the explosion.
He was senseless and motionless for 12 hours after that. But may
God bless Memphis, the noblest city on the face of the earth. She
has done her duty by these poor afflicted creatures—especially
Henry, for he has had five—aye, ten, fifteen, twenty times the
care and attention that any one else has had. Dr. Peyton, the best
physician in Memphis (he is exactly like the portraits of Webster,)
sat by him for 36 hours. There are 32 scalded men in that room,
and you would know Dr. Peyton better than I can describe him,
if you could follow him around and hear each man murmur as he
passes—"May the God of Heaven bless you, Doctor!" The ladies
have done well, too. Our second Mate, a handsome, noble hearted
young fellow, will die. Yesterday a beautiful girl of fifteen stooped
timidly down by his side and handed him a pretty bouquet. The
poor suffering boy's eyes kindled, and his lips quivered out a
gentle "God bless you, Miss," and he burst into tears. He made
them write her name on a card for him, that he might not forget
it.

> *Pray for me, Mollie, and pray for my poor sinless brother.*
> *Your unfortunate Brother,*
>
> *Saml. L. Clemens*

P.S. I got here two days after Henry.

Jane had not seen that letter, but she had other excesses to
bear. Sam was so distraught that he was thought to be losing his
mind. He came to them in St. Louis under the care of a man
chosen by some interested people of Memphis to guard him, while
Orion accompanied Henry's body on to Hannibal. There the family
gathered the following day with a host of persons who had loved
the quiet youth, and they gave him burial in his native town.

Jane stood proud and straight beside his grave, as befitted the
mother of a hero. For it was now known, through Orion, who
had got the story from survivors, that young Henry Clemens made
his escape after the explosion but had returned to the ship on a
raft to help rescue others. This he did voluntarily, though he had
inhaled steam and was internally injured. But for that terrible

exertion, he might have survived his ordeal. The family code, as undefined as a cloud but as firm as earth and stone, had impelled him. He had gone on the river a stripling; he had died a man.

There were persons who thought Jane Clemens behaved strangely, so great was her new composure. Her brother and Ella feared for her mind if she, to whom tears came easily at any story of pathos, failed to weep. She told them not to be concerned for her. "Go to Mela," she requested of them. "Help Will look after Mela. I must see to Sam."

Sam's belief that he was responsible for Henry's death through a series of circumstances seemed liable to destroy him. Jane fought to rid him of self-blame. It was all a part of God's wisdom, she told him and, telling him, believed it herself. There were two omens that seemed to have foretold Henry's being taken from them. On the wall of the boys' bedroom was a framed picture of the choirboys of the cathedral, a gift from Mrs. Berkeley who thought Henry should have been among them, "because Henry looks and sings like one of them." Henry was extremely fond of the picture. One day before the *Pennsylvania's* ordeal it had fallen from the wall, for no reason that Jane and Pamela could discover; seemingly it had been well hung.

The other omen was Sam's dream of a few weeks before, which at first they had tried to minimize to him, but which now, after Henry's death, had assumed a pattern of meaning. Sam had dreamed that Henry lay dead in a metallic casket, the casket resting on a bridge of chairs in the Moffett back parlor. On it lay a bouquet of fresh white flowers with one red bloom in the center. The dream was so vivid that Sam had thrown on his clothes and rushed from the house to walk the street in sorrow. Presently he realized that the scene he had quitted was not real and returned home thankfully and told his family the phantasy in detail. . . . The dream's fulfillment happened thus. Sam, coming to himself after Henry's death, went into the mortuary of the makeshift hospital, a warehouse outfitted to care for the *Pennsylvania's* victims, and there saw a metal casket resting on a bridge of two chairs; and this was strange, for the other victims who had died had been consigned to pine coffins. The casket held Henry's remains. The women of Memphis who had visited the sick and dying had become so attached to the beautiful, uncomplaining young man and were so grieved by his passing that they had contributed money to buy the metal casket. Sam stood beside his brother's body and remembered how he had seen this same picture in a dream. Only the flowers were lacking. Then a woman entered the room on her seemingly predestined errand. She was carrying a white sheaf of flowers, and in its center was one red blossom. Weeping, she laid it on the boy's casket and went away.

Being told of this by Sam, Jane laid hold of the oddity with a hope and cheer that derived from desperation. "It was all to be," she assured him and herself. "God has shown this by the fallen picture and the dream. He means us to take comfort."

She urged Sam to return to the river and resume his training. He did so, going as assistant to a pilot named George Ealer whom he and Henry had known and admired. The new boat was not noteworthy, it was a lesser vessel, but the pilot was a healing friend, musical, bookish, warmhearted, and entertaining. Sam responded in his mercurial way.

In September steersman Sam Clemens became pilot Samuel Clemens, licensed for the Mississippi River. Bixby took him as a working partner, and they divided the twenty-four hour watches between them. In only eighteen months, its latter phase tragically interrupted, he had learned "the River" and become one of its elite. The salary was princely, two hundred and fifty dollars a month. No longer need Mr. Moffett pay for Ma's clothes, he told Pamela proudly. As for himself, to quote Mr. Bixby, "he became dandified—given to patent leathers, blue serge, white duck, and fancy shirts." He wore muttonchop sideburns. When he entered the Association Rooms at New Orleans and made a payment he was careful to let a hundred-dollar bill show among the smaller notes. His family forgave him his boasting, remembering that he was but lately resurrected from a consuming grief.

Mollie, however, found one of his letters distractingly conceited when Orion read it aloud to her:

"Putting all things together, I begin to think I am rather lucky than otherwise—a notion which I was slow to take up. The other night I was about to "round to" for a storm, but concluded that I could find a smoother bank somewhere. I landed five miles below. The storm came, passed away and did not injure us. Coming up, day before yesterday, I looked at the spot I first chose, and half the trees on the banks were torn to shreds. We couldn't have lived five minutes in such a tornado. And I am also lucky in having a berth, while all the other young pilots are idle. This is the luckiest circumstance that ever befell me. Not on account of the wages—for that is a secondary consideration—"

"Indeed?" interrupted Mollie tartly, for they were again living with her parents, counting the pennies. "Let's hear more. Read on!"

Orion resumed, *"—but from the fact that the City of Memphis is the largest boat in the trade, and the hardest to pilot, and consequently I can get a reputation on her, which is a thing I could never accomplish on a transient boat. I can "bank" in the neighborhood of $100 a month on her, and that will satisfy me for the present (principally because the other youngsters are sucking their fingers). Bless me! What a pleasure there is in revenge!— and what vast respect Prosperity commands! Why, six months ago, I could enter the "Rooms" and receive only the customary fraternal greeting—now they say, "Why, how are you, old fellow— when did you get in?"*

Mollie found this bravado hard to forgive. "A year ago," she reminded Orion, "he was 'a lost and ruined sinner,' not worthy of the Lord's forgiveness. Now he's fortune's favorite, chosen among pilots, protected by Heaven from tornadoes. And rich, rich." Then she added, "But he lives in constant danger, that's a fact. You can't pick up a newspaper but you read of a steamboat accident. I wonder your mother encouraged him to go back on the river."

"I've wondered it myself," Orion confessed, "and Pamela argued against it. But Ma said it seemed the only way to save Sam's sanity. As for the danger Sam's in, at least he's relieved now of earning extra money. When he was a cub steersman and there were layovers at New Orleans, he used to guard the cargo on the docks at night, sometimes Henry with him. But Ma never knew that. Sam's always known just how much to keep from her. He says I'm a fool to tell her all my bad luck and get her stirred up."

"At least you're honest," Mollie commended. "That's more than you can say for Sam. I hope Ella Creel will never marry him. He exaggerates constantly, and he's always making enemies."

Ella Creel, whom Mollie hoped to save from Sam, was one of the prettiest girls in Keokuk, and musical; on her father's side she was Orion's and Sam's third cousin, on her mother's side she was Mollie's. Jane herself was against the match, though not for Mollie's reasons. She thought Ella was unsuited to Sam because she was a frivolous girl who disliked books and was not sympathetic—"all wrong for Sam."

Sometimes Jane wondered if the appealing Miss Castle of St. Louis might be suitable. She often mused on the matter while she was having her portrait painted. The sittings were an ordeal they all underwent that summer at the hands of a traveling artist named Brady. Pamela had decreed it, and Henry's daguerreotype would be transferred to canvas to join the family portraits on the parlor walls.

Jane put her theory concerning Miss Castle to the test early in the spring. Sam asked her to chaperone Ella Creel on his boat to New Orleans, and to invite any friend she wished to be company for herself. It was evident Sam thought she would invite Mrs. Betsey Smith of Hannibal, a confirmed traveler, a lover of steamboats. But she asked Miss Castle instead and she sprang her on Sam when the *Memphis* came down from Keokuk and docked at St. Louis. Sam looked at Miss Castle with surprise and interest—he had met her casually last year. Ella Creel looked at her with surprise and wariness. She had never met her at all, but she realized that Cousin Jane, in supplying Sam with a second girl, was up to no good.

Though Jane enjoyed the fine stateroom she shared with her charges, and though she relished the prestige of being the junior pilot's mother, there were times when she stood alone at the rail

242

in woe. Especially when they navigated those stretches of water associated with the *Pennsylvania's* disaster. To Sam, it was now history, for he had passed and repassed those scenes, and his very ship bore the name *City of Memphis*. His mother did not begrudge him his victory over sorrow.

She had been accustomed to watch the young people dancing in the main cabin, and now and then to take a turn herself when some polite young man or courtly planter bowed for permission. But one night, watching the Castle girl teach Sam the schottische and seeing the girl's hand linger overlong in Sam's, and then seeing Sam, as lithe as a cat, quickly embrace and kiss her, she flew into a secret rage and left the salon and sat alone on the Texas deck. Later she lectured Sam on the unsuitability of a pilot's dancing on his own boat, especially that boisterous fling, the schottische, and kissing and embracing young women—(Ella Creel too! I saw you!) in the presence of the passengers. What had pierced her heart was the sudden vivid memory of Miss Castle's teaching the schottische to another boy who had looked at her ardently, but had not dared to kiss her. And never would. And never would.

Sam, on his return to St. Louis, wrote all the latest news to Orion, including the New Orleans voyage, and he showed his mystification at their mother's hot and cold reactions. That the gay excursion had been, in some ways, a trial of endurance for her escaped him:

Ma was delighted with her trip, but she was disgusted with the girls for allowing me to embrace and kiss them—and she was horrified at the Schottische as performed by Miss Castle and myself. She was perfectly willing for me to dance until 12 o'clock at the imminent peril of my going to sleep on the after watch— but then she would top off with a very inconsistent sermon on dancing in general; ending with a terrific broadside at that heresy of heresies, the Schottische.

I took Ma and the girls in a carriage, round that portion of New Orleans where the finest gardens and residences are to be seen, and although it was a blazing hot dusty day, they seemed hugely delighted. To use an expression which is commonly ig-

243

nored in polite society, they were "hell-bent" on stealing some of the luscious-looking oranges from branches which overhung the fences, but I restrained them. They were not aware before that shrubbery could be made to take any queer shape which a skilful gardener might choose to twist it into, so they found not only beauty but novelty in their visit. We went out to Lake Pontchartran in the cars. Your Brother, Sam Clemens

That was Jane's only trip to New Orleans, but she frequently went upriver at Sam's invitation. She never declined when he sent for her but would take off, as Pamela complained, without stopping to pick up her room. She kept a bag packed, and if Sam sent word that he had docked and would be glad to carry her up to Hannibal, she would call a hansom cab and arrive before the plank was pulled up. She would visit in Hannibal a few days while Sam's boat made the upper ports, renewing her friendships, strengthening her old ties. Sometimes she would have Annie Moffett with her; and the child was to remember how the colored folk would run to her on the street with cries of "Mis' Jane!" as if they had rediscovered a lost treasure.

27 ❖

Will Moffett hastily decided to take Pamela and Annie to Virginia to visit his aged parents and other relatives. He said they must go before his native state became embroiled in conflict. The conflict might be averted if Stephen A. Douglas were elected President, he claimed, Douglas being one of your levelheaded Northern Democrats opposed to Secession, a man both parties might tolerate. But if a ruthless man like Lincoln got in, look out for war.

"Oh mercy!" Jane exclaimed without argument. "Anything but war!"

Up the river, Orion her eldest was campaigning for Lincoln, taking the stump for his election as vigorously as he had worked for the nomination. As the Whig party had given way to the Republican, Orion had merged painlessly; and in Missouri's Scotland County where he had recently hung his shingle (the county

244

seat was named Memphis, indicative of the Southern element which had settled it) he was extolling his candidate to the detriment of his law practice. Pamela asked her mother, "Why must Orion always swim against the current? If he had to choose a new location, wouldn't Illinois have been more friendly?"

"Orion puzzles me," Jane answered. "But let him be, Mela."

She helped with the hasty packing and saw the Moffetts off. She was looking forward to running the house and having a stream of company. The sociable German maid, Marget, lived in, and they liked one another, though their schemes and methods were divergent.

Sam was often ashore, and to him flocked young folk who admired him—the Conrads who were noisy, the Brooks girls and their brother Montgomery who was lame and musical, and young rivermen from other towns who made grateful house guests. Extra help had to be hired, and Marget was advised to leave off whitening the stone doorsteps. Sam was a willing marketgoer, carrying the baskets when his mother and Mrs. Berkeley raided the Broadway stalls for dewy fruits and vegetables.

Relatives showed up gratifyingly while the Moffetts were away. Any one who read the newspapers could see the advertisements of Will Moffett and George Schroeter—the new partner, a friend of Hannibal days—offering their stock as commission merchants. It was not unusual for Moffet and Schroeter to list several thousand hams on hand at one time, as well as kegs of mackerel and abundant dried staples. Certainly Cousin James Lampton saw those declarations of plenty and felt free to come and bring his family for a visit. Another to come at Jane's bidding was Tabitha "Puss" Quarles, her favorite niece, Sam's congenial cousin, with the financially ineffectual Mr. Greening, her husband. And some of Uncle Wharton's children from Monroe County arrived in orderly parade, gay and appreciative.

On the Moffetts' return from Virginia the Locust Street house was relinquished, and Will leased a larger one, located at 1312 Chestnut Street. Only a Washington Avenue address would have been more fashionable. While the place was being readied, the family stayed at the Planters Hotel, an experience Jane enjoyed.

She dressed for dinner and looked for celebrities in the lobby.

Pamela had made the arduous journey to Virginia and back without miscarrying the child she was expecting. A healthy little boy was born to her on November fifth in the house on Chestnut Street. His name was ready-chosen, Samuel Erasmus, for his mother's pilot brother and his father's financially successful one, a tribute to foot-loose adventure and cautious wealth in one child's name. The following day Will Moffett went to the polls and voted for Stephen A. Douglas.

South Carolina, before Christmas, carried out her threat to secede from the Union, but St. Louis took it in stride; South Carolina was not served by the inland waterways, so let her go Gallagher. That the ship of state could be breaking up seemed improbable to the citizens of St. Louis, for a handsome new steamboat was being launched every few weeks and easing up to her docks. The latest pride of the river was the *City of Hannibal*, recently completed at the Madison, Indiana, ship yards. If she was finer than her namesake the port, if fond local capital had secured her name, what of it? Her length was two hundred and fifty feet, her beam thirty-eight, and she would carry a thousand tons in deep water. She used four boilers with five flues each, her wheels were thirty feet in diameter. She contained sixty-two rooms and would berth a hundred and fifty passengers. To serve the boat's big dining salon there was a modern galley, a pantry with iceboxes, a dishwashing room. Further to bless the passengers were maids' quarters and a nursery. Taken for granted were the landscapes on the stateroom doors and the easy flights of stairs.

Sam Clemens was honing to pilot the *City of Hannibal*, but time was running out. As he and a pilot friend, Zeb Leavenworth, came up the river from New Orleans one April day on a steamboat named the *Uncle Sam* a volley of artillery crossed their bow at Fort Jefferson, carrying a message they could not ignore. They came about and were boarded for inspection, questioned, allowed to proceed—the last boat that would pass without a government mission for some time to come. Mr. Lincoln had just replied to the seceding cotton states with a blockade of southern waters, including the lower Mississippi.

The Union sent out a call to the loyal states for seventy-five thousand volunteers and issued a warning that river pilots would be drafted. Sam, undecided in his loyalties, went into hiding. Jane said she would not subscribe to the lie that he was not at home if "they" came looking for him, so he took sanctuary in the house of George Schroeter. Her own loyalties were fluctuating.

After a few days someone did come looking for Sam, but it was not a government agent. Jane was relieved to recognize him as a young man named Smith whom they had known in Marion County. He said Sam Bowen and a couple of other retired pilots up at Hannibal wanted to see Sam right away. Otherwise he was uncommunicative, though Jane questioned him as craftily as she could before sending him to Sam at the Schroeter house.

The following day Sam was a passenger on the boat that had so interested him and was writing his brother Orion one of the strangest notes ever to come from his pen:

Steamer Hannibal City
Under Way, April 26
My dear Brother: I am on the wing for Hannibal to collect money due me. I shall return to St. Louis tomorrow. Orion bring down "Armageddon" with you if you have it. If not, buy it. Yr. Brother, Sam Clemens.

Orion was no doubt astounded by the communication. Here was no praise for the new steamboat, no statement of plans; just an urgent request for a book written by a Baptist preacher in Nashville. The book, as Orion knew, predicted the world's end between 1860 and 1875, prophesying the site of Armageddon to be the Mississippi Valley, with the United States defeating Russia and other European powers, after which Republicanism and the Millennium would hold sway.

Evidently Orion did not get the book to Sam on time, for he threw in his lot with his persuasive Rebel friends in Hannibal and was presently a member of a Confederate company of soldiers, about fifteen youths all told, organized to repel Yankee invaders from Illinois. They marched toward New London and were well treated at several farmhouses belonging to sympathizers. One Colonel Ralls of Ralls County, a Mexican War veteran and a politician, administered the Confederate oath after providing a good breakfast. Other farmers contributed horses, mules, firearms, and paraphernalia. Sam's mount was a small mule named Paint Brush. Sam himself was a second lieutenant. When the town of New London heard of the youthful cavalry unit, interested persons rode out to their camp to wish them well. Among those was Ella Lampton, who had taken refuge at New London with faithful Lavinia because of the St. Louis invasion scare. Ella sent an amusing description of the outfit to her husband, and James Andrew hastened to take the letter to his half sister Jane at the Moffetts'. Jane and Pamela saw no humor in the situation. The young men had firearms, they were undisciplined, and Sam was committed to the Confederate cause without conviction.

The campaign was a military farce of three weeks duration, a little show of bivouacking, of dodging, of quarreling, of enduring boils and boredom. When the outfit disbanded, most of its members joined a recognized unit of the Confederate forces, but Sam refrained. He told his mother he had had time to think it over, and he now saw the Rebels as a bunch of hotheads who had rather fight a war than stay in the Union. And how about it if they should win that war and put a chain across the Mississippi River? Two countries declaring, "This is my half of the river, that's yours!"

It would be downright absurd, Jane agreed. And she made no effort to persuade him to legalize his status with the Confederate Army. It was a relief to her when St. Louis presently came under United States martial law, and the local Confederate general, Sterling Price, with his volunteers retreated to the Ozark Mountains.

Will Moffett, however, regarded the retreat of Price as a calamity. He and other Southern sympathizers felt that the Confederate Minute Men, as they were called, would have insured neutrality for the city and delayed conscription. He himself would never take up arms against the American flag, he told Pamela and Jane; yet he would go to prison before he would be drafted by Lincoln's government and be forced to attack his native Virginia and his

248

relatives wearing the gray. "Not if the United States confiscates my business!" he swore.

Jane felt as if she were witnessing a contest in a bad dream—Orion pulling for the Union, Will for States Rights, Sam sitting on the fence, calling himself a Know-Nothing and viewing it all with a cynical eye. Though the United States agents continued to press for river pilots—even Bixby had offered his services—Sam continued to evade. He had no intention, he told the family, of standing on a steamboat deck and being rattled with crazy Rebel artillery; he would think of some less showy way to be useful.

And what of Orion? His adherence to Mr. Lincoln through the debates and his struggle toward the presidency gave Jane a peculiar satisfaction, though the satisfaction had nothing to do with politics. (When Abraham Lincoln first loomed on the horizon she had got his Kentucky beginnings from Daniel Trabue, and she still thought of him as "a poor boy," six years younger than herself, born over in Hardin County the year the Lamptons moved to town.) Her pleasure had to do with her son's new stability. It was the first time Orion had stuck to a cause without "seeing the other side" and switching. Sam had scoffingly predicted that Orion would stump for every candidate in the field before the election was over, if the candidates were sufficiently persuasive. But Orion had held his ground even when things looked darkest for Lincoln, and when the compromisers were at their zenith.

And now he had an unexpected reward, first hinted to him by his friend Edward Bates a few weeks after Lincoln's victory. Its confirmation came in the mail out of Washington, where Bates had been sworn in as the new administration's attorney general. Orion Clemens of Scotland County, Missouri, had been named Secretary of the Territory of Nevada!

As usual, Orion was caught without funds. He and Mollie, with their child, returned to her parents' home in Keokuk and discussed ways and means. It was imperative that Orion get himself to Nevada before summer's end and take up his territorial duties in style. But money was tight now; everyone was hoarding. There was nobody in Mollie's family, Unionists though they were, willing to back Orion. But there might be someone down in St. Louis:

Sam was very much at loose ends and he used to have a bank account! When Orion got around to this prospect, Mollie concurred wholeheartedly. "And take him with you, if he'll go! It would relieve the family."

Orion went to St. Louis and closeted himself with his brother. Did Sam have a few hundred dollars saved from his piloting? Sam cautiously admitted that he did have. Then would he, Orion implored, accept the position of the Secretary's secretary and stake them both to an overland journey? Sam whooped with pleasure and accepted. Orion returned upriver, and both young men began to organize for their trip.

"Don't talk about it," Pamela warned her mother and Sam, for the family position was too confusing to clarify. Especially her own position. Her husband was a Confederate merchant with a pro-Union partner in a pro-Southern city occupied by United States troops. A scatterbrained younger brother had "resigned" from a Rebel outfit and was going to accompany a conspicuously Republican brother on a mission to a Territory firmly held by the United States and destined for Unionist representation in Congress.

But the word got out, through the exuberance of Sam and Jane; and Annie was presently informed by a playmate: "One of your uncles is a Black Republican, like Colonel March across the street." Annie thought that meant he was one of the Devil's angels, but Jane explained it only meant that Uncle Orion wanted to see the slaves freed "the way most of us do. Your Uncle Orion is a very smart man, Annie, and don't you forget it!"

Such a refurbishing of male wardrobes had never been undertaken by the Clemens family. Up in Keokuk, Mollie was sewing frantically, making Orion shirts and nightshirts and handkerchiefs that would look well on a government clothesline. In St. Louis, Pamela called in her seamstress to help mend Sam's old linens and turn out new, while he himself explored the outfitting stores for colorful top clothes.

Jane was carried away by an advertisement she saw in the *Missouri Democrat*. *Acetous Extract of Lemons—This most highly concentrated extract, while it affords at any moment a pleasant lemonade and an antidote to the foul water so often met with on*

250

the plains, is at the same time an approved prevention of scurvy to which California emigrants are exceedingly liable. Put up in small cases with sliding tops, containing one doz phials. Collet and Johnson.

She invested generously in this luxury, sensibly expecting that it would have priority in her sons' baggage. She pictured them now and then adding the lemon extract to their canteens of water, and to the canteens of the driver and the scurvy-menaced passengers as the stage rolled over the great plains. But alas, only a token box of the brave extract was accepted by the Messrs. Clemens; for in addition to their clothes and writing materials, great quantities of tobacco must be carried by Sam, or he would not budge from St. Louis; and Orion must have his huge unabridged dictionary.

Thus they departed one sultry morning on the muddy Missouri River for the first lap of their journey, a stream so shallow and devious that Sam would afterward declare their steamboat needed stilts. But the entire adventure was accomplished safely, and in September, when Mollie had received her first letter, she would record in her notebook:

They left St. Louis on the 18 of July on the Sioux City for St. Joe. There they took passage in the overland coach, a mail conveyance which has begun to run daily between St. Joe Missiouri and Sacramento, California.

They left St. Joe on the 26 of July, arrived in Carson City, Nevada Territory on the 14 of Aug. 1700 miles from St. Joe, and 580 miles west of the Great Salt Lake City. M. E. Clemens.

Jane, ever one to fill the gaps left by departures, now found a situation to engross her, though not a happy one. The family faced a scandal. Ella Lampton had a lover, or so went the rumors, and her husband seemed blind to it.

The man was young Dr. John McDowell, a handsome, morose bachelor, who was both family friend and physician. Just how the entanglement started, no one could say; but when Dr. John's dominating father, "old Dr. McDowell," departed for the deep South to become a Confederate Army surgeon, his repressed son leaped to freedom, as it were, and went to reside with the J. A. H.

Lamptons. They took him to board, an arrangement common enough in households where there was a room to spare, a reliable servant or two, and the need of extra income. Lavinia was the servant in this case. James Andrew and Ella, a few years before, had provided her with a trousseau and a sedate wedding in the parlor when she announced her intention to take a husband. And then, as an ultra wedding present, had offered her freedom papers. But Lavinia declined the gift, preferring, she explained, to stay on in her accustomed state and visit her husband at intervals. What lay back of Lavinia's decision to remain a slave until freed by Mr. Lincoln's proclamation was merely a deep attachment to her master. She had inherited him from his little bride, the girl that she, Lavinia, had helped raise, and she would never willingly renounce her charge. With the intuition of her race, she had known the second Mrs. Lampton's potentials on sight and had fatalistically waited for them to develop; Lavinia wanted only to shield her master from the knowledge that this woman, his affectionate and attentive wife, was something more.

Ella, for her part, knew that Lavinia knew. The secret lay between them, unspoken but strangely safe.

One might wonder how young Dr. John happened to betray the Scottish McDowell code of honor and make love to his friend's wife. The truth was, he had been blighted in childhood by his father. Jane and Pamela and many others in St. Louis knew the story. Joseph Nash McDowell, Dr. John's father, had studied medicine in Danville, Kentucky, with his uncle, Dr. Ephraim McDowell, the Edinburg-trained physician who had performed the world's first ovariotomy—a man all but worshiped for his skill, kindness, and piety. The apprentice doctor had fallen in love with his first cousin, Dr. Ephraim's daughter. Being rejected by the father and the girl herself, he betook himself to Lexington's Transylvania College to study under Dr. Daniel Drake, the West's authority on general medicine, and presently he married Dr. Drake's sister. Going to St. Louis in 1840, he founded the McDowell Medical College which later, because of its excellent courses and its impressive architecture, became the Medical Department of the University of Missouri. . . . The erratic Dr. McDowell was a skill-

252

ful surgeon, as attentive to the poor as to the rich, and a compelling lecturer. But his students, his children, his wife (early to die), and his patients found his changing moods terrifying. Before taking off a maimed limb he made it a point so to berate the victim for the accident that had befallen him that the poor man submitted to chloroform and amputation with relief. It was said too that Dr. McDowell encouraged his students to steal cadavers for dissection. But to many persons his most repellent act had to do with the cave he owned in Hannibal and which he had at one time stocked with ammunition in anticipation of a Mexican invasion. In that cave (later frequented by small boys, including Sam Clemens) he had placed the body of his little dead daughter in a glass coffin, suspended in clear alcohol. Though he presently removed the casket and buried it on an island which he owned near St. Louis, the story of the glass coffin and its little corpse was so distressing to Jane Clemens that she would never enter the cave, even when picnic parties went there freely, and when its bats were said to be at a minimum.

With such a macabre father, with such a childhood to remember, young Dr. John groped toward normalcy and, in a manner of speaking, he found it in hedonistic Ella.

After he took up residence with the gad-about Lamptons, he shed some of his Byronic gloom and became socially acceptable. He was invited out to dinner; he became a potential catch for girls approaching spinsterhood. Jane Clemens, with intent and purpose, introduced him to an attractive young widow of their acquaintance. She accomplished the meeting as if by accident, right under Ella's eyes. For a time it seemed as if something might come of it. Jane watched the progress of the affair hopefully. "If we can only get the man married!" she would say to Pamela in private.

It was a matter of great relief to Jane and Pamela (for if Ella had this lover, she might have had another) that little Kate, Ella's child born in St. Louis in 1856, had the Lampton red curls and James Andrew's features. Those tokens made her conclusively their own.

Young Dr. John was still the family physician when Mollie

Clemens brought her sick child to St. Louis in November. Mollie came for the purpose of having him treat Jennie's ague, for he was an authority on the river fevers. Like his distinguished uncle, the late Dr. Drake (who had absorbed the best of Benjamin Rush and discarded the worst), he was continually studying the inland scourges and fighting them.

During Mollie's visit she wrote Orion a letter which succinctly disposed of Dr. John socially while accepting him medically:

Uncle James and Aunt Ella are coming round to spend the evening. Of course the Dr. will come too. The occasion of the call was to hear the reading of a letter from Sam, telling of his and Orion's investments in gold mine footage. It irked Mollie that Dr. McDowell should share the family bulletins.

Much of her letter to Orion dealt with Jennie's illness and it fluctuated with hope and gloom, like the child's own chills and fever.

I cannot tell what is to become of Jennie. . . . I have been up with her three nights till after midnight. . . . She appears tolerably well during the day. I think she has "dumb ague" and slight chills. Dr. McDowell is treating her just as Dr. Hughes did. I am giving her quinine today, he gave her calomel last night and Oil and Turpentine this morning. She appears quite weak today. . . . I think she will be better soon. Everything will be done that can be—and remember to ask God to be the great physician. He and He alone knows the end from the beginning and He will do what is best for her.

Jane embroidered some challis frocks for Jennie, like the ones she had done for Annie, the patterns copied from *Godey's Lady's Book* and applied to the material with chalk. Fine sewing had been denied to her through lack of patience and a damaged eye, but the gaudy new school of floss embroidery was something she could cope with right dashingly. Flowers and fruits of every hue burgeoned under her large embroidery needles, and scalloped edges abounded. The more her heart was wrung by the sufferings of Jennie, her namesake, the more lavish became the floral paths around Jennie's skirts. Mollie had to request her not to use so much red in her designs.

254

"But red will make her happy," Jane explained.

Pamela, who had heard, said, "Not necessarily, Mother." Jane had persuaded her to carpet the double parlors in red, and it was rather overpowering in certain lights. She had also managed to secure red hangings for her own bedroom, and had purchased red merino for a robe last winter. "Red makes you and Sam happy," Mela said, "but there are other people it makes nervous."

"Like bulls," Jane said, choosing a strand of floss. It was burlap brown, in atonement for advancing her own preferences over the more sedate tastes of others. She often wore sackcloth but rarely applied the ashes; a little contrition went a long way.

Mollie's brother John Stotts had brought her and little Jennie to St. Louis, but his politics forbade his entering Will Moffett's house. One day, however, he stopped in a hack at the door to get Mollie and the child and escort them to Benton Barracks, the new show place. The government, with West Point efficiency, had transformed Price's old encampment into a square mile of orderly tents, white-washed officers' quarters, parade grounds, and bugle calls. That evening at supper, after Mollie had visited the post and witnessed a cavalry drill, she talked so effusively of "our troops"—though Jane was kicking her warningly under the table—that Will Moffett asked to be excused and left the room. The next day she and Jennie returned to Keokuk to wait out the weeks until Orion could send for them.

Orion was performing his duties well. He stood in for the territorial governor, James W. Nye, a New York Republican politician, when the latter was absent; and he was respected by all elements. But his salary was not large, and Sam was constantly drawing on it for the furtherance of gold mining schemes that might enrich the family. Sam's letters home caused Will and Pamela to become infected with the rapacious gold fever, for he wrote with utter assurance:

This is just the country for Cousin Jim [Lampton] to live in. I don't believe it would take him six months to make $100,000 here, if he had $3,000 to commence with. I suppose he can't leave his family, though. Cousin James appreciated the compliment.

255

James Andrew Lampton also was beguiled by Sam's invitation to come to Nevada and make a fortune, but Ella declined for them. She was just as averse to the idea of James Andrew's becoming clerk to the surgeon general of the Territory, a position available to him because of his medical background.

"I find St. Louis more to my liking," Ella decided amiably.

Jane too was immune to Sam's gold field raptures, and very early sent this admonitory response:

We are all delighted to receive your letters saying you have such good prospects of making you both independent in this world's goods and a prospect of me getting out there before long. I hope you will lay up treasures in heaven two. She knew there were three ways of spelling the final word but early in life had adopted the numerical one, thereby saving herself a good deal of head-scratching.

Her desire to get to the West was a response to sheer beauty when Sam began to write of Lake Bigler (soon, to Sams disgust, to be called Tahoe): *It throws Como in the shade. . . . And whenever I think of it I want to go there and die, the place is so beautiful. I'll build a country seat there one of these days that will make the Devil's mouth water if he ever visits the earth.* After exploring a portion of the lake with a boy from Cincinnati named John D. Kinney, he informed his family, he had entered a timber claim two miles in length, one in width, on "Sam Clemens Bay" in the names of Sam L. Clemens, William A. Moffett, Thomas Nye, and three others. But soon, by way of a careless campfire, he destroyed much of his timber. His description of the great crackling trees reflected in the clear waters of the lake filled his mother with sad horror.

The war was on now, in earnest. To Will Moffett's satisfaction, Virginian troops had repelled Yankee invaders at Bull Run. He began to contribute to Southern families in distress whose men were at the battle front, straining his finances to do so. And though he remained taciturn, not airing his views in public, Pamela knew that the crackdown, as it was called, might come to them at any time. The Robins family, their neighbors, through an indiscreet letter which United States government agents opened,

256

had all their worldly goods confiscated; Pamela, Jane, and Annie, watching in consternation, saw the Robins furniture, pictures, stair carpets, and window shades carried off in government wagons. Their own landlord, wealthy Mr. Small, an articulate Southern sympathizer, suffered a similar fate. Jane began to use initials instead of names when writing to Nevada—a habit that would linger for years, causing Sam, a lover of gossip, a good deal of frustration.

Jane's correspondence with Kentucky friends and relatives became strained and guarded. Most of them had a man fighting on one side or the other. Mary Brawner Carlile, her girlhood confidante, her bridesmaid, wrote one day from Green County to say: *Both of my sons are now Union officers. Tell me, Jane, how is it with your two surviving boys?*

Jane handed the letter to Mela without comment. Orion's position could be explained with a certain pride. He had campaigned for Lincoln; now he was advancing the frontier at a rugged outpost, with small pay. But Sam's absence from the States had little to recommend it. He was merely digging for gold and silver out there as if his very life depended on it. His claims in two Esmeralda mines, the Monitor and the Flyaway, seemed to surpass in importance to him the fact that his country was splitting asunder. Yet his exertions were arduous and dangerous. Any day might be his last. Was he driving himself in order to forget the war? He had a way of brushing aside the unhappy reports they sent him. When they wrote him that Dick Higham, one of Orion's Keokuk compositors, had been killed in February, charging the works at Fort Donelson in Tennessee, his reply seemed casual:

I was sorry to hear that Dick was killed. I gave him his first lesson in the musket drill. We had half a dozen muskets in our office when it was over Isbell's Music Rooms.

Perhaps Jane could have brought him home to serve the Mississippi fleet if she had written the right kind of letter. The government had its gunboats now for reducing the Southern ports, and its packets for transporting troops to the battle sites, navigating even the tributaries. But she never wrote such a letter. Let Mollie make the most of it, she never did. War was still the world's grim-

257

mest error to her, a useless horror that magnified hate and spawned dead men, widows, and orphans.

She was thankful when Fort Donelson on the Cumberland fell to the Union forces, and Brigadier Simon Bolivar Buckner, disappointed in reinforcements, surrendered to General Grant and, by so doing, prevented the deaths of thousands of soldiers on both sides. It seemed as if the war might end then, and council tables replace carnage. It was a time of hope.

It was but a lull. The mid-South quickened. Kentucky, seeming to repudiate Buckner, her thoughtful native son, produced John Hunt Morgan the dashing cavalryman, and his brother "the other Morgan"; and young men who loved merely horses and sabers and the romantic code of the South thought they loved war and joined the Morgans on forays across Kentucky and Tennessee, burning railroad bridges, seizing supplies, charging breastworks. Raw volunteer infantrymen from Illinois and Ohio and Indiana, absorbed into Kentucky's Federal regiments to help hold Kentucky in the Union, beheld the mad calvarymen in wonder and fell back.

The engagements at Tennessee's Shiloh and Kentucky's Perryville were, in Jane's estimation, too obscenely terrible to discuss, pitting brother against brother, as they did, more than any other battles. They were noted for their repeated anguished charges against raking artillery, the maddened, defleshed pack animals, and wounded men inaccessibly dying of thirst. Those things happened in areas familiar to her and they were her Civil War. . . .

Sometimes there would come flashes of gentle humor in letters from Adair and Green counties. A good many colored men in that area, expecting to become soldiers, had gone off with troops from north of the Ohio River. But usually they were denied firearms and were put to work as cooks and body servants, working as hard as they had worked in slavery and forced to sleep on the ground besides. Sometimes they ran off and came back, from sheer homesickness. One said he couldn't stand it because the Yankee men called him Dick when his name was Dexter.

Usually, said the letters, the uniforms of both Federals and Rebels were so muddy and nondescript that passing outfits were not readily recognized. But it made little difference; both sides stripped your smokehouse and took your horses. Courtesy often came when least expected. While the Nashville General, Felix Zollicoffer, and his officers were very brusque in their demands, the Minnesota troops were charmingly polite. It would always be remembered, too, that after the battle of Green River Bridge a Michigan regiment lingered to bury the Confederate dead and bring help to the wounded.

St. Louis's hostile factions had settled down to surface fellowship under the watchful eyes of Benton Barracks. The churches kept to the gospel, the theatres kept to schedule. Passenger steamboats resumed limited service under masters and pilots who had taken the oath of allegiance, stopping short only of Vicksburg and its Confederate cannons. Business in St. Louis was somewhat hampered, but reasonable profits accrued to wholesalers who supplied the needs of the United States Army. Moffett and Schroeter were among those.

Will became a director in several banks and insurance firms. He was one of the founders of the new Merchants' Exchange.

It was but natural that Annie be sent to Miss Long's select school where she was taught French by Madame Gilbert. Baby Sammy had a uniformed nurse, an expensive rocking horse, handsome clothes. The children's shoes interested Jane in a peculiar way. Once, examining a pair of Annie's pretty slippers, she said to Pamela, "This is a far cry from our Florida and Hannibal days, Mela. Do you remember those little square-toed things I used to make for you?"

"Don't!" Pamela cried out, putting her hand over her eyes. "Can't you let us forget Pa's failures?"

Jane accepted the rebuke with surprise. She had not thought of her cobbling as deriving from John Clemens' failures; it was just something she had done because it needed to be done. "I think you're oversensitive about your father," she said. But always afterward she refrained from alluding to their former poverty in Mela's presence.

The greater the Moffett prosperity, the more persistent were the

259

attentions of poor friends and relations, and none was rebuffed. Among the more trying was Mrs. Holliday of Hannibal, now quite eccentric and wonderfully restless. Once when Pamela in a talk with Sam remarked that "Ma is an aristocrat to her finger tips," Sam had asked her what she based that conclusion on. "On the way she makes us treat old Mrs. Holliday who's a social liability," Pamela said. "We used to need Mrs. Holliday, you'll recall. She had her 'castle' and she was kind and generous. Now she's broke and a little zany. So when we find her in the vestibule with her old valise Ma cries out. 'How good of you to remember us, Mrs. Holliday! Come right upstairs to my room and make yourself comfortable!'"

It was true that Jane had incurably imbued her children with the obligation to remember past benefits; and although Will Moffett and Sam Clemens often conspired to shorten Mrs. Holliday's visits and shift her about, they did it with kindness and tact.

Orion had finally put by enough to send for his yearning wife and child, and September '62 found Mollie and little Jennie leaving for New York to take ship for California. Right willingly would Jane have accompanied them, and she had hinted as much, but had received no encouragement at either end of the line. She was indispensable to the Moffets, would be useless to Sam, superfluous to Orion. Mollie and Jennie would not be alone on the voyage. They had the company of Mary E. Clagett of Keokuk who was bound for Nevada to join her husband, a lawyer turned prospector.

Jane and Pamela were vicariously affected by the journey. Jane felt impelled to discuss "Mollie's opportunity" with every friend she had. In a welter of maps and borrowed travel books, new horizons took on a satisfying familiarity.

Pamela, on the other hand, thought shrinkingly of little Jennie's being conveyed halfway across the continent to New York with four train changes en route, then down the eastern coast, across the Isthmus of Panama and up the West Coast to San Francisco, thence by stagecoach to Nevada. The contemplation of all this sent her to bed for frequent rests, and she could only wonder weakly what her overly stimulated mother might be up to.

Jane customarily reported her activities at tea, as they called supper. Will Moffett shed some of his wartime gloom at such times and was diverted by his mother-in-law's direct quotations from Mrs. Sexton and Margaret (now living in St. Louis), Ella Lampton, Cousin James the plunger, and "the other Mrs. Berkeley," who was the wife of the rector of nearby St. George's and the alert daughter of oceanographer Matthew Fontaine Maury.

A brisk exchange of letters and newspapers kept the scattered family together. Mollie was in her glory. Orion had got a house for them, and it was the cultural center of Carson City. In the absences of Territorial Governor Nye, Orion was the acting executive and was addressed as Governor Clemens. Mollie, whether Nye was present or absent was the Territory's first lady. Jennie was none the worse for the multifold journey. She had withstood the Isthmus crossing very well, and the salt air of the two oceans had strengthened her.

The news from Sam was also good. He had given up prospecting to become a reporter for the *Territorial Enterprise* at Virginia City, one of the more important papers of the West. On the strength of some letters he had written from the gold fields, he had been hired and put to work at a hundred dollars a month. Of this, he was budgeting twenty dollars a month for his mother. Jane resolved to enjoy that serenity while it lasted.

Mollie, several months after her arrival in Nevada, reported to the family in St. Louis that Sam was now signing himself Mark Twain, a steersman's term he had picked up on the Mississippi. Be glad the Clemens name was not being used, Mollie advised, for Sam's stories were rather rough—almost as crude as the two letters he had signed "Josh" for Keokuk's *Gate City*. That was unwelcome news to Jane; she had deplored those contributions, had told Sam she was ashamed of them—a strong statement. Well, let him use a nom de plume!

Jane and the Moffetts, piecing together Mollie's version of the ensuing months, Orion's version, Sam's version, learned that Sam was surrounded by political and journalistic friends who called him Mark and thought him immensely clever; that dressed in high fashion he came often to Carson City to cover sessions of the Legislature, making himself a popular and conspicuous visitor at the home of his brother. Did Mollie imply too conspicuous a visitor? Jane and Pamela read it so between the lines. None knew better than they how Sam took over. When he stood in a room and began to talk, narrowing his eyes and teetering on his toes, now and then rumpling his red mop as if surprised to find it still on his head, everybody in sight came in close to listen. . . . And he was aware of his cleverness, that was the worst of it. There was the letter he wrote them that summer from San Francisco, where he had gone for a fling:

Ma, you have given my vanity a deadly thrust. . . . You gravely come forward and tell me if I work hard and attend closely to my business, I may aspire to a place on a big San Francisco daily, some day. . . . Why, blast it, I was under the impression that I could get such a situation as that any time I asked for it. . . . Everybody knows me, and I fare like a prince wherever I go, be it on this side of the mountains or the other. And I am proud to say I am the most conceited ass in the Territory.

"Without the shadow of a doubt," Jane commented to Pamela.

Yet Mollie's jealousy of Sam at the time was not warranted, for he was keenly anxious to promote Orion's future. The Territory would soon become a state, positions would be elective, influence would solidify, and he was prepared to back Orion with all the flamboyance at his command. He had no wish to usurp his brother as The Clemens, head of the clan. He merely wished to be chief gillie, and free.

Mollie, for her Christmas gift that year, asked Orion to give her a family Bible. He did so. It was a sturdy volume, just issued by the American Bible Society, "Translated out of the Original Tongues." Before he presented the gift to his wife, Orion recorded their births and their marriage under Family Records. His own birthplace was listed as Gainesboro, Tennessee. Mollie's as Sangamon County, Illinois—a prairie region she was once indifferent to, but now claimed proudly.

Following an old Scottish superstition, Mollie opened the Holy Book at random, and each "took" the verse their eyes lit on. Mollie's verse, recorded by her on the flyleaf, was Joshua 4, verse 1.

It was not applicable and must have been disappointing to her. But Orion's—Joshua 3, verse 7—had great significance for them: *And the Lord said unto Joshua, This day will I begin to magnify thee in the sight of all Israel, that they may know that, as I was with Moses, so I will be with thee.* It was a verse that bolstered them, for at that time they were organizing a Presbyterian congregation (Mollie the motive force), and Orion must soon declare his candidacy for Secretary of the Union's thirty-sixth state.

Yet the next entry under Family Records was a quick and pitiful one, having nothing to do with ambitions:

Jennie Clemens, daughter of Orion and Mary E. Clemens, was taken sick on Thursday morning, January 28th, 1864, at Carson City, Territory of Nevada, with Spotted Fever, and on Monday, February 1, 1864, at Sundown, she died. Buried at Carson.

The brothers were fated to share that family crisis as they had shared all others. Sam was at Orion's at the time, reporting politics and preparing to give his first speech with charged admission. The proceeds were promised to the new church. He delivered his humorous talk on schedule in the territorial hall the evening Jennie developed her fatal illness. It was a burlesque of the two legislative houses and was called The Third House Message. It netted the church a gratifying sum. Mollie, whose concern for Jennie kept her from attending, expressed appreciation. Sam turned quickly from levity and gave himself to the household sorrow. It was he who wrote the news to St. Louis.

Jane replied with a letter the bereaved parents would keep. She used her best penmanship and suitable writing paper (usually she wrote on any unmatched sheets that came to hand), and she spoke her heart:

To my dear children.
A few days ago we received a letter from Orion one or two days after one from Sam. Sam's was written first. . . . Mollie, you have the sympathy of all your friends as much as any person I ever saw. Jennie was an uncommon smart child, she was a very handsome child, but I never thought you would raise her, she was a heaven-born child. She was two good for this world.

Orion must have found comfort here. Mollie at times subscribed to the theory, extracted from the darker reaches of Calvinism, that Jennie's frailty was sent to punish them for their sins, either of omission or commission, such being one of the teachings of the Presbyterian Old School sect which the Stotts family adhered to.

Among the sins Mollie felt herself and Orion to be burdened with was the countenance of drinking in their home. Though they did not serve liquor, Governor Nye and the legislators carried their own bottles and, especially if Sam was present, felt free to uncork them in the kitchen.

At the adjournment of the Legislature, Sam departed for Virginia City and did not return to Carson. His niece's death depressed him, Mollie had become more rigid, and Orion no longer listened to his advice. Troubled with bronchitis, he went now and then to Lake Tahoe to benefit by the climate, and to Steamboat Springs to take the baths. In May, having come to the verge of a duel, he hastily left his berth on the *Enterprise* and went to San Francisco, a city which had lured him. There he went to work on the *Morning Call* and contributed literary articles to the *Golden Era* and the *Californian*. He continued to send twenty dollars a month to his mother. Once, when he doubled that amount, she anxiously wrote and asked: *Where are you getting all this money?* He had made no effort to hide from her the fact that he was associating with free souls who liked to explore the city after the paper was put to bed, and that he imbibed strong drink whenever he took a notion.

"Even champagne!" Jane said to Mela after one of his letters. She was making one of her continual adjustments.

Orion, at Carson City, was being carried away with Mollie's temperance drive. To take a stand against saloons in a mining region was like trying to hold back a flood with a broom. Yet Orion so declared his intentions, aware that he would be deprived of the nomination to continue in office. He also declined to accept a good offer for the Tennessee land—obtained by Sam with great difficulty in San Francisco—because the purchasers intended to use the mountain slopes in the European manner to cultivate wine-producing grapes. Hoping that virtue would be rewarded, or in any case would not be penalized, he dusted off his ATTORNEY AT LAW shingle, hung it on his dwelling house and settled down to wait for clients.

Jane was nowise absorbed by her sons' financial problems. Greater matters were at stake. In the new April of '65 General Lee surrendered to Grant, and the war ended. The long war, the cruel war was over. But reconstruction in the Southern and border states was yet to be faced. No sympathizer of the defeated Confederate cause knew what might be exacted of him; for Lincoln, the compassionate man shot dead, had been replaced by the avengers.

At the Moffetts', the head of the family was not relieved of his tensions. During the war his devotion to his native Virginia had not wavered, and he had regularly sent money to destitute relatives there. Yet he had early come to hope for a Federal victory. Quantrill's bushwhackers and other Missouri guerrillas had offended his sense of decency from their beginnings; and Lincoln's Emancipation Proclamation in '63 had defined the war for him as something deeper than States Rights.

His business firm was "very shaky," so his mother-in-law confided to James Andrew and Ella; the partners had taken some chancy steps. Anticipating the return of free trade, they had ordered a first-class steamboat built, and in an unexplainable accident it had burned to the waterline. Other efforts miscarried where formerly all had prospered. One August day in that confused year Will Moffett's torn emotions gripped him in a flash of pain and he died.

Jane had her moment of defiance to God. "Why do You keep at us?" she asked, striking the wall with clenched hands. Receiving no answer, she quieted down.

Pamela collapsed after the funeral, and even her mother thought it suitable. She was inclined toward severe headaches much like her father's. Without ever offering herself to the sun she suffered from something resembling his sunpain. And now grief and shock were added, producing the fashionable nervous prostration. When George Schroeter tried to explain to her the affairs of Moffett and Schroeter, she scarcely heeded. Jane begged her to listen and try to understand.

The most pressing matter was the steamboat. It had been built jointly by Andy Fuqua of Hannibal, Will Moffett, and George Schroeter. When lost to fire it was yet new; but it had been christened, unfortunately, the *William A. Moffett,* a name not pleasing to reconstructionists on the insurance board. George Schroeter reported that insurance compensation was denied them "because of some technicality." The steamboat was by no means paid for, he further explained, pacing the floor in a sweat of regret; and since the fire insurance claim was not honored, Pamela Moffett must use Will's life insurance to meet her share of the shipbuilding bills.

"What's to become of us?" Pamela moaned. Mr. Schroeter had no ready answer to that. The firm itself was endangered.

The following day Jane donned Mela's black silk dress with the hoop skirt—she had no black dress of her own—her best hat and gloves, and went forth to do battle. She took no joy in it, for she had always preferred the oblique approach when dealing with men. But she had two former victories to encourage her. After John Clemens' death she had gotten the desperately needed furniture and the little boys' tuition out of Ira Stout; and last year she had extracted a hundred dollars and interest from Captain Horace Bixby for Sam, a sum Bixby had borrowed of him and later repudiated.

Today she went directly to the head of the insurance firm, a man active in the Lucas Place Presbyterian Church, and laid before him the plight of Pamela Moffett and her children. "We've not met before," she confessed, "because I rarely attend church at Lucas Place, but the widow Moffett is my daughter. You know her faith in God and her devotion to that church."

He said that he did. "Then maybe it will cause you to review the insurance claim on the steamboat *William A. Moffett.* Your company, one that Will Moffett himself was a director in, has disallowed it, though the claim is written up fair and square."

"Did the co-owners send you to me, Mrs. Clemens?" he asked.

"No," she said, "they're too proud to send a woman begging. I came under my own steam." She was fond of using the latest slang, and she brought an incongruous dignity to it. "Whatever you decide in this case, kindly don't tell Mr. Schroeter or Mr.

Fuqua that I've been here. It's sad that Will Moffett lies under the sod, no longer able to vote as a director, and there's only me to fight for his burnt-up boat."

As usual, she knew when to leave off talking; it was a gift she had, like Boone's feeling for east and west on a dark night. Curtsying deeply, she showed her erect little back and departed. Somehow she had conveyed drama and had personified Eternal Woman in distress. Perhaps the embattled man thought of Harriet Beecher Stowe, or Mary Todd Lincoln (those dresses, how similar!), or Florence Nightingale, or merely his own Aunt Sarah who had seen a lot of trouble in her time.

The insurance claim was paid in full rather soon.

Mr. Schroeter told Pamela Moffett and Jane Clemens that he and Fuqua felt like reprieved men when they were informed of the decision in their favor. He said he had no idea what had caused the reversal.

Behind his back, Jane winked at Pamela, who smiled wanly.

28 ❖

In November the New York *Saturday Press,* an unimportant little sheet, got hold of a sketch Sam had written called *Jim Smiley and His Jumping Frog,* signed by his now accustomed nom de plume of Mark Twain. Writing to Jane and Pamela from San Francisco at the new year of 1866 he complained: *To think that . . . those New York people should single out a villainous backwoods sketch to compliment me on!* In a few weeks' time, though, he changed his tune. *The Jumping Frog of Calaveras County* was becoming folklore and had earned him an enviable assignment: the *Sacramento Union* sent him on the windjammer *Ajax* to the Sandwich Islands to report on the life there and the prospects of American trade. As the *Ajax* was also steam-driven, the voyage was made in eleven days.

But all haste was abandoned thereafter. A pleasant languor possessed him, and the month's stay he had planned lengthened. Remembering that Orion and Mollie were expecting him in Carson

City that summer to help them break up housekeeping and return to the Mississippi Valley, he wrote concisely to Mollie in May from one of the islands:

My dear Sister,—I have just got back from a sea voyage from the beautiful island of Maui. . . . It has been a perfect jubilee to me in the way of pleasure. . . . I set sail again, a week hence, for the island of Hawaii, to see the great active volcano of Kilauea. I shall not get back here for four or five weeks, and shall not reach San Francisco before the latter part of July.

So it is no use to wait for me to go home. Go on yourselves.

If I were in the east now, I could stop the publication of a piratical book which has stolen some of my sketches.

It is late—good-bye, Mollie. Yr Bro Sam

Though his letters to his newspaper were long and hand-tiring, he was dutiful in writing to Jane and Pamela, knowing how his exotic reports would relieve the tedium of Pamela's new widowhood. As:

I have ridden on horseback all over this island (Oahu). . . . I went with the American Minister and took dinner this evening with the King's Grand Chamberlain, who is related to the royal family, and although darker than a mulatto, he has an excellent English education and in manners is an accomplished gentleman. The dinner was as ceremonious as any I ever attended in California—five regular courses, and five kinds of wine and one of brandy. . . .

The Crown Princess is dead and thousands of natives cry and wail and dance for the dead, around the King's Palace all night and every night. . . . Hon. Anson Burlingame, U. S. Minister to China, and Gen. Van Valkenburgh, Minister to Japan, with their families and suites, have just arrived here en route. . . . I climbed out of bed and dressed and shaved pretty quick and went up to the residence of the American minister and called on them. . . . At his request I have loaned Mr. Burlingame pretty much everything I ever wrote.

Pamela said she hoped the ambassador would advise Sam to polish up his journalism.

"Then he could sign his own name with pride," Jane said wistfully. Though she was aware that "Mark Twain" meant safe soundings in steamboat parlance, it bothered her that Sam was losing his family identity. Once he had ended a letter to her, *Yrs aftly, Mark*. But he never did it twice. As she told Pamela, she laid him out for it. "I've got no son named Mark," she reminded him by return mail. "Your father and I raised four boys named Orion and Benjamin and Samuel Langhorne and Henry."

But what she wanted most achingly was for her sons to come home; she had not laid eyes on them in five years.

Orion fulfilled the wish. He and Mollie returned to the Mississippi Valley that summer, the hard way, the cheap way, by overland stage and Missouri River steamboat. Their more cherished possessions followed by freight. One crate contained the unabridged dictionary and Jennie's little rocking chair.

At 1312 Chestnut Street there were tears at first as the family referred to the child who had not returned from the West and to Will Moffett's absence in the house. But after the healing weeping came the jollification that Jane invariably arranged at a homecoming. Friends and relatives were summoned, and there was company at almost every tea, company that lingered on into the gas-lit evening. Orion was treated as a distinguished person, and no one pressed to know why he would not be returning to Nevada.

They went up to Keokuk presently, so he could "look around."

All that winter he looked around, and he barely missed several good connections. More than one *Gate City* man considered making him a member of his firm because he had been the acting Governor of the Territory of Nevada; but second consideration seemed ever to bring the thought: after all, this man is only Orion Clemens in a frock coat, and the arrangements never materialized. They made their home with Mollie's parents.

The family in St. Louis and Keokuk awaited Sam. But they need not have. Arriving at San Francisco in August, he was taken with the idea of delivering a lecture on the Sandwich Islands, its natives and its sights. He hired the new Academy of Music, no less, for his debut. Successful, he obtained an agent and toured the area as far as Carson City. From the newspaper accounts received by his family, he was as blithe and expansive in the mining camps

269

of Red Dog and Grass Valley as he had been in San Francisco's opera house. He might easily have come home then, but he sailed from San Francisco in December, crossed the Nicaraguan Isthmus and took ship on New Year's Day for New York. On the voyage he was becalmed in a vessel infested with Asiatic cholera, an experience his family thought he deserved.

It was March when he reached St. Louis. Jane observed that he looked older than he should; she regretted, almost bitterly, the young years of his life she had lost. Could he not have done as well by staying at home? Already thirty-one years of age, he had not much to his credit. Only some travel letters about the Islands, and a book of humorous sketches, hardly off the press— that *Frog* again. Yet he was full of plans, determined to travel. And he had annexed a good many people (as she herself had done in her more limited sphere), and they had become important to him. He must keep on doing that, she suspected, until his time and spirit were saturated with them—hundreds of intimates, countless acquaintances. When he was a boy she had relinquished him to the village and the river. Now she must relinquish him to anybody crossing his path who struck sparks, and their name was legion.

But there was Orion who still needed her.

She asked Sam to let Orion manage his lectures in Keokuk and Hannibal, for he was going to give his seriocomic talk in those places.

"It will make Orion happy," she said. "Orion will throw himself into it, heart and soul!" And so would Mollie, she added ruefully. Her daughter-in-law's propensity for management sometimes inconvenienced her, but she accepted it as uncritically as she accepted her elongated Scottish face, her competitive housekeeping, and her harmless little vanities. She admired Mollie's stanchness and grit, valued her for her devotion to Orion.

Orion proudly offered his office as headquarters for Sam. The room had been spruced for the visit; the desk was stocked with pens and foolscap paper in case Sam should care to dash off a sketch for the *Gate City*. A shelf contained their father's law

270

library. The unabridged dictionary was in evidence to set them reminiscing about Nevada, and chairs had been borrowed to accommodate visitors. Those were never empty, friendship and curiosity prompting half the town to drop in.

For all Sam knew, some of the callers were Orion's clients. When he returned to St. Louis he told Jane and Pamela he was glad Orion was doing so well at law, and there was no contradiction. That satisfied him well enough. He wanted to leave the Valley without having to lend Orion any money. A great project awaited him in New York if he could but get himself backed by the press. The ship *Quaker City* was scheduled to sail for Europe and "a Holy Land Excursion" early in June, and he had instigated plans for joining the tour as a correspondent. He wrote urgent letters to several important editors; two were fruitful. Presently it was good-by, Ma and Pamela. Good-by, Annie and little Sammy. Fare ye well, relatives all!

Ella remarked practically (they had settled down in the parlor one evening, breathing his dust), "But all those serious people aboard—preachers and teachers! He'll not fit in!"

"Oh, I expect he will," his mother said, and she went and got a letter he had written last year from California—a letter that shouted Sam's awareness of his family's sense of humor. She read it aloud, drawling it suitably.

"San Francisco, Dec. 4, 1866.
"My Dear Folks,—I have written to Annie and Sammy and Katie some time ago—also to the balance of you.
"I called on Rev. Dr. Wadsworth last night with the City College man, but he wasn't at home. I was sorry, because I wanted to make his acquaintance. I am thick as thieves with the Rev. Stebbings, and I am laying for the Rev. Scudder and the Rev. Dr. Stone. I am running on preachers, now, altogether. I find them gay. Stebbings is a regular brick. I am taking letters of introduction to Henry Ward Beecher, Rev. Dr. Tyng, and other eminent persons in the east. Whenever anybody offers me a letter to a preacher now, I snaffle it on the spot. I shall make Rev. Dr. Bellows trot out the fast nags of the cloth for me when I get to New York."

Laughter closed in on the reading, and James Andrew requested a second rendition while Annie and Katie made lemonade.

Orion, as always when in desperation, put his mind on the Tennessee land. Mollie again abetted him. She persuaded her brothers John and Joseph Montgomery Stotts to go down to Fentress County with him and help him investigate the market, taking their pay in acreage. There was a grandeur which she and Orion enjoyed in offering the Messrs. Stotts five thousand acres each, or, on a bright day, twice that, for a little financial assistance. Some of the claims had lapsed and were in need of renewal at Nashville. A penalty must be paid to redeem them, and here the Stotts brothers soon proved useful.

No purchasers were found however, though Orion wrote hopefully to Mollie of "Kingston's man at Clinton." He softened the news of his failures by telling her he had started a Sunday school in Jamestown. It was indicative of Orion's and Mollie's peculiar integrity that they did not regret the lost wine growers, though they knew they were considered eccentric to have rejected the offer, and Sam swore he would never forgive their stupidity.

The family must now operate without Sam's occasional financial help and his ever-ready advice. Having given a successful lecture at Cooper Institute in New York on May 6, 1867, to a papered house, he had departed on the *Quaker City* on June 8 for fabulous adventures almost beyond their comprehension. They read of all this in the newspapers he had ordered sent to them, the *Alta California* and the *New York Tribune*, both of which were receiving his travel letters. Jane and Pamela were enthralled with their wanderer's brilliant and impudent reports.

Orion stopped in St. Louis after his Tennessee efforts. His plight reached dismaying depths while he looked for work. Jane gave him the Lampton spoons to sell, declining a last look at them and making light of the sacrifice. Pamela had her own silver, she reminded him; and Sam had no wish for any. "The spoons are yours because you need them, Orion." He took them gratefully and disposed of them. A few years hence Sam's wife would express a wish for the Lampton spoons, and Orion and Mollie would humbly try to trace them; but Jane would never revert to the matter; when she had done her best, she considered a day ended.

The Moffett share in the earnings of Moffett and Schroeter was but a fraction of what it had been in Will's lifetime, and Pamela was having to adjust. In order to keep the comfortable big house in Chestnut Street and her excellent German house-keeper, Marget, she was resorting to a few congenial boarders. Her mother encouraged and aided her. The boarders need never feel cheated when "Mrs. Moffett won't be coming down to break-fast this morning," nor would Annie and Sammy notice their mother's absence, for Jane would preside, serving lavishly and quoting the conversation of such neighbors as had been loqua-cious, the early edition of the *Democrat,* and the Negro iceman of the wonderful chant.

Jane was an early riser who had no fear of the dew. Their neighborhood was one of handsome three-story brick houses with white stone doorsteps and narrow lawns, tree-shaded. She was acquainted with every family in the block, their children and their pets. Her rating of those persons was high, on the whole. But her rejections, few in number and usually secret as to reasons, were inflexible.

Orion at first had a bedroom at Pamela's, but as his poverty increased, he went elsewhere to lodge out of consideration for his sister's status. His clothing was shabby beyond his mother's ability to mend, and he was further embarrassed by questions concerning his occupation. Having been addressed as "Governor" but two years ago, his complete comedown unnerved him. He had the added trial of being unable to send for Mollie, who was living at her father's and suffering depression because of their separation. On September 6 he wrote her in regard to some repair work needed on his clothing, and other urgencies:

My dear Wife:

Yours of Tuesday received last night. I went to see my maker [tailor] this morning. He asked 50 cents. It was ten cents more money than I have. The same as to the worsted. I asked McKee for a situation anywhere about his office—job office, newspaper, or reporter. He said he would let me know if there was a vacancy, but job printing was very dull. He had discharged half a dozen hands last week. I went to the Republican office, but there were only a few men in the job office, and half of them seemed to be idle. I went to Levisons. Two men were at work but seemed to have little to do. I asked Ustick for work in his job office. He said they were full. Business may pick up in ten days but there is little prospect sooner.

Two men came yesterday from Philadelphia who saw John [Stotts] *and Goddin Tuesday* [in Tennessee]. *They had sold a large portion of our land and Goddin was in high spirits. They were waiting for papers. Goddin is not expected home till the 20th. I do not know what papers they could have been waiting for, unless they had sent to Sparta for certified copies of the grants. I did not see the men.*

I am sorry you are not well and have been so unhappy. It is my intention to have you with me as soon as I can. As soon as I get some money I will send you those things.

Pamela has all teachers and provides two meals a day. She has bought a pretty carpet for the second story front room. Two young men and one young lady besides these are talking of coming.

I sent you a Democrat last Tuesday with a telegraphic dispatch relating to the reception of the Quaker City excursionists by the Emperor and Empress of Russia. . . .

Annie has commenced going to the High School.

Jennie Lampton is in town for a few days. Bettie is going to teach in Illinois. (Two of Cousin James's girls, he means, Julia, the family beauty, had lately gone insane from brooding over the Civil War. Cousin James was bearing it with fortitude, reminding one and all that most aristocratic English families had a touch of madness, and the Lamptons could not expect to be immune.)

James and Ella (Orion resumed) *are going to board at the Everett house. Dr. McDowell also.*

In recounting that item, Orion's handwriting waxed large, but he abruptly dropped the subject. The family permitted themselves no written opinions concerning the triangle, only statements of facts. But later, behind closed doors, they would thrash it out.

With the land's sale so promising, Jane and Pamela urged

274

Orion to return to Tennessee and attend to it, Pamela supplying enough money for his expenses. He stopped in Louisville to see his relatives: Aunt Polly Hancock Saunders, whom Mr. Saunders had married after Ann's death, the lively Tip, now a portrait painter, and Dr. John Marshall Clemens, a rising young physician. The latter had more than a cousinly interest in Orion's visits; he was entitled to ten thousand acres of the land, which his father, Hannibal, had bought before he was born.

Hastening southward, Orion forced himself to investigate the Clemens claims, but he had more interesting fish to fry. He began to collect lurid stories of the recent war and its aftermath. If Sam could write travel letters, so could he. As fast as he had penned his hair-raising reports, signed "Cumberland," he sent them off to an obscure partisan newspaper which had contracted for them.

At Gainesboro, his birthplace, he was so offensively critical of the defeated Confederates, and so in favor of disfranchising them, that he became an object of suspicion, a mysterious menace. He was as heedless of danger as Sam, in spite of his maturity, and there is no doubt that he owed his life to a kindly landlady who urged him to leave town without delay and not to proceed toward Nashville as he had planned. She had overheard a lawless group of vigilantes in her tavern plotting to dispose of him without gunfire, relying on the favorite reconstruction retaliation, a well-aimed rock at the back of the head.

Orion quickly decided to put away his pen and forego Nashville. Hiring a horse and an escort he left Gainesboro before sundown, proceeded in cautious stages through Overton County and reached the mountain fastness of Fentress County where his land lay. Here he proved agreeable to the natives, who were Unionists. Remembering the urgency that had brought him to Tennessee, and having lost the buyers he had come to meet, he turned his talents to a prospectus for mailing, picturing the Clemens land as an Eden of opportunity. There were no lasting results except for a resolve he made: he would never come again to Tennessee.

In St. Louis, good fortune awaited him when he resumed his rounds of job hunting. The *Missouri Democrat* engaged him as a full time proofreader; his pay, small at first, would increase as he gave satisfaction. In hiring himself to the *Democrat*, he had no scruples to overcome. The paper had never advocated secession, and it had not accepted advertisements from the slave traders. Its owner and its editor, William McKee and B. Gratz Brown, had been friends of Will Moffett's.

Jane and Pamela were elated at Orion's having found such employment, aware that he was well qualified. Yet how utterly fundless he was, they could not know. He concealed the matter from them cunningly and declined his mother's offer of a small loan. Small remunerations came to him from Keokuk. Mollie, for all her little vanities and acute pride, had not scorned to become a bill collector for Keokuk's merchants, using Orion's legal letterheads when writing her duns or, those failing, trudging on foot to accomplish her unpopular missions. Presently she received a letter from Orion which might have reduced many wives of like social pretensions to tears, but which she found acceptable, even sweet:

St. Louis, March 5, 1868
My Dear Wife:—
Last night I rented 3 nice rooms in the 3rd story over Lynch's grocery store, West side 12th, between Chestnut and Pine, for $20 a month. I am to pay in advance next Monday, when the rent begins. Of course it will take every cent of this week's wages. I mean to go over and keep batchelor's hall, for a few weeks, so as to save enough to get a start toward furnishings, before you come. Therefore, please send bed clothes, sheets, pillows, slips, and towels. I wish you would send at the same time, the oil stove old Boyd gave me in Carson City, if we brought it with us. You may have room in the box for the big dictionary. If so, send it, unless you want to use it yourself, till you come down. Have the box directed to No 113 North 12th street, between Chestnut and Pine. If I am not there, Lynch will pay the freight and drayage and send the box up to our rooms, and of course I will refund to him. Two of the rooms are large, and connected together. One and a small room front on 12th. The two large ones have grates and also a flue for cooking stove. There is besides a wash room on the 3rd floor, to be used for washing by all on that floor, there

276

being four other rooms, now empty. An inside porch runs along in front of these rooms and the wash room, and at the end of this is the [watercloset]. Water is brought in by pipes. The rooms we are to occupy look clean and neat, and Mrs. Lynch says they have been lately cleaned.

Mollie was happy at the prospect of being again with Orion. If his income was dismayingly small, at least it would be regular. And a grocery store so handy, and wilted vegetables at nightfall so redeemable by a good cook!

Jane shortened their separation by buying the furniture they needed. She was again receiving money from Sam, who had returned from the *Quaker City* cruise and was living at the Willard Hotel in Washington, serving as secretary to Senator William Stewart of Nevada. Her wealth weighed heavily on her until she was permitted to spend it so.

Mollie's dignity and her excellence as a housekeeper converted the flat high over Lynch's grocery into an acceptable home, and a place their relatives need not dread to frequent. Except for the stair steps. Those were breath-taking. Mollie's one luxury was the colored washerwoman who came one day a week.

Once when Jane was making a call at the flat, Mollie asked her to interview that young woman out in the washroom and pass judgment on her character. "Sometimes I wonder about her morals," Mollie said piously. "She's got a couple of children, but no husband that I've been able to discover. Orion said, 'Get Ma's opinion.'"

Jane went to the washroom and was soon engaged in conversation with the laundress while she manipulated the hissing flatirons between stove and ironing board. Mollie could hear a good deal of laughter and chatter. At Jane's return she inquired anxiously, "Well, Ma, what do you make of her?"

"I think she's real entertaining," Jane said. "Real smart."

"But her morals! I asked you to form an opinion."

"Oh yes. Her morals." Jane had forgotten the purpose of her interview, but she quickly recovered, and right practically. "Her morals are fine. Just fine. If a good-looking young woman like that is willing to climb these two long flights of stairs and wash

277

and iron all day for a dollar and a little lagnappe, she's of saintly character. A marriage certificate won't alter the case, either way."

Mollie was appeased. But such flippant judgments as this on the part of Jane Clemens sometimes caused her to lie awake and wonder why the family ever accepted them. On what were they based? Not on the Bible, certainly: the reasoning was too worldly.

Pamela too considered her mother too volant, and she longed to alter her to a more conservative pattern. There was the matter of Jane's conspicuous rejection of veal, at table. She had never served it in Hannibal, but that was not questioned, as veal was expensive. Later, at the Moffett table, her aversion had come to light, and her panic in declining it was noticeable. "It would kill me if I tried to eat it!" she several times declared dramatically, but always without explanation. Her reasons were simple. She had had a pet calf when the Lamptons lived with the Caseys and was accustomed to caress it and weave it clover chains. Missing it from the lot one morning, she learned what had happened from Jenny—the mother of the younger Jenny, a woman of like disposition. "We ate little calf last night," big Jenny said with a raucous laugh, "leastwise part of 'im. You ate some of 'im yourself!" Jane Lampton, the child, became ill, and all of Grandmother's reasoning could not reconcile her to what had happened.

Pamela, believing her mother's distaste for veal to be an affectation of some sort, set a trap in the presence of the boarders. She served veal and called it lamb, and Jane partook. The following day, noticing that her mother was in good health and spirits, Pamela triumphantly divulged her duplicity. Jane went upstairs and went trembling to bed, and there followed all the symptoms of ptomaine poisoning. She kept to her bed several days, and forced Pamela and Annie and Marget, the conspirators, to wait on her, hand and foot. She was not merely ill, she was also angry and told them why. Ella came one day while the commotion was going on, and when she asked for "Sister Jane," Pamela recounted the matter.

"You see, Ella," she concluded, "it only proves how right I was. My mother's inability to digest veal was altogether in her mind. She was healthy until I told her what she'd eaten."

278

"It's all the same thing, Pamela," Ella said sharply. "It's stupid of you not to see that!"

Ella's ability to understand neuroticism was rather profound for one who seemed entirely physical. It was this comprehension, no doubt, that made her indispensable to her husband and her lover.

Dr. McDowell was no longer the Clemens family physician. Will Moffett had terminated that connection during the war, and perhaps McDowell was as relieved to be rid of the relationship as were his patients. But he continued to come to the house socially with James Andrew and Ella and was courteously received. Now and then Jane would introduce him to an eligible woman, though no longer very hopefully. Saddened by the strange situation, she accepted it for reasons she regarded as important: James Andrew needed Ella; and Ella, in her way, loved James Andrew.

Dr. John's father was so shocking a character at this time in St. Louis that his son's following his friends to the cheerful Everett House did not seem unnatural. Old Dr. McDowell's medical college had been restored to him by the Federal government, though hardly intact, for it had been used as both hospital and prison. His bitterness over the shambles he found it in, added to the greater bitterness he had built up while nursing the Confederate wounded and dying in the South, gave him a maniacal hatred of his enemies. Somewhere in the depths of his medical school there was a room he had equipped with flora, fauna, and live snakes surrounding the figure of the late Abraham Lincoln hanging in effigy. The room was prominently marked HELL. Soon now, forsaken by his children and friends, his mad hatreds would burn themselves out. He would turn to Roman Catholicism and die among the gentle nuns.

The only member of the Clemens family who had ever upbraided Ella in regard to her sins was Sam. While he was a riverman and knew all the gossip of the pilothouses, he had heard rumors of her out-of-town meetings with her lover, and he had somehow, somewhere, taken her to task. She had evidently looked at him levelly and innocently, giving him *honi soit qui mal y pense*. He retreated, but she was never to forgive him. Later, from the West, he sent the Moffetts a picture of himself, *"and one for*

279

Aunt Ella,—that is, if she will have it." Ella both repelled and fascinated him. And when, after James Andrew's death, she cheekily asked financial help for her daughter Kate, an accomplished secretary, he responded. Finally, as the great Mark Twain, he would jot down a bitter memorandum, looking backward:

Young Dr. John McDowell boarded with them, followed them from house to house; an errant scandal to everybody with eyes— but Jim hadn't any, and believed in the loyalty of both of them. God took him at last, the only good luck he ever had after he met Ella. . . . Dr. John and Ella continued together.

This appraisal of the affair did not probe its depths, of course. It was James Andrew's knowledge, not his blindness, that merited the pity. Jane could have enlightened Sam.

29 ❖

Orion would have remained contented at his job if it had not been for Sam's rocketing prospects. Hearing of it was almost too much for him; for his wife and sister too. As Mark Twain, Sam was invited to speak at the most important banquets in Washington, and a half dozen newspapers across the country were requesting his letters. He had been offered a consulship. The postmastership of San Francisco was his for the taking. Could he not secure a government appointment for his brother? came a duet from Pamela and Mollie. Surely Orion had his share of the family brains and deserved to wear a good suit to work?

Sam agreed. Indeed he had been the first to think of it and had already investigated a clerkship in the Patent Office. But aware that the administration would soon change, he advised Orion to settle down and wait a while. Orion tried to do so. Heretofore his flightiness had been self-motivated, but now it was deriving from the backwash of Sam's success. Adding to his confusion was his wife's overestimation of his talents, his sister's nervous counseling, and his mother's pity.

Jane, taking serious thought, warned Mollie, "I think you and

280

Mela are stirring up Orion too much. He now speaks of his proof-reading as something picayune. He's lost interest in the whole blessed *Missouri Democrat* that feeds him. He's trying to invent a machine of some sort back there in your washroom."

"It's a little drilling machine," Mollie defended. "Munn and Company are interested in it."

"Don't encourage it!" Jane begged. "Inventions nearly drove his father crazy. Orion's eyes are red. He looks worn out. If he's not more settled, he can't be a good proofreader."

"Why should Orion be a mere plodder, Ma, when Sam has such distinctions?"

"Let Orion forget Sam's hurrahs, Mollie. Sam admits he's in debt, and he can't make up his mind what he wants to work at."

Sam's mind was presently made up for him. A publisher in Hartford named Elisha Bliss, Jr., snared by the *Quaker City* Letters to the *New York Tribune,* asked the privilege of publishing the series in book form by subscription plan, and Sam accepted eagerly.

During the following months, and into '69, Sam was all but lost to his family in St. Louis. He must go to San Francisco, where most of his travel sketches had been sent, and retrieve them from the *Alta California.* He must lecture there by popular demand. He must go East again and lecture continuously, too engrossed to stop at St. Louis, ever, though once he sent his trunks there as a token of his coming, and his mother watched every carriage and omnibus that traversed Chestnut Street.

The facts were, he was in love. He was courting Miss Olivia Langdon, a young lady of prominence and means who dwelt in Elmira, New York, and sweetened the very airs of heaven with her virtues. He must prepare his Letters for publication, refining them under his true love's supervision. He must lecture for Mr. Redpath in order to buy an interest in a newspaper called the *Buffalo Express,* to enable him to support his true love, who had finally accepted him. And he must write effusive letters of appreciation to a Cleveland woman who had been an excursionist on the *Quaker City* as correspondent for her husband's newspaper—Mrs. Mary Mason Fairbanks. She had censored Sam's travel letters on shipboard, culling their first vulgarities. She had sewed on buttons for him and for several other young men in the party; had given them sage advice, corralled them for prayers with the "pilgrims" in the ship's cabin after supper, encouraged them playfully to call her "Mother," though she was but forty-two years old—Pamela Moffett's age.

When Pamela heard of it, she felt, somehow, outraged. Nor did it sit well with Jane. It was all very well for Sam to be engaged to wed the beautiful and saintly Miss Langdon; but for him to be also bedazzled by a portly literary lady in Cleveland who advised him how to write and was referred to as "Mother" was something of a stinger.

"Maybe I'm getting hard to please," Jane said to Pamela when Sam's book came out. The title was *The Innocents Abroad;* its subtitle, *The Modern Pilgrims Progress;* a copy had come to them from the American Publishing Company. The book was dedicated to Jane, they observed, but in a strange and stilted way, as if Sam had picked up the words somewhere and used them absentmindedly. Such was the case. He had plagiarized Dr. Oliver Wendell Holmes, it turned out, from having read Dr. Holmes's *Songs in Many Keys* several times while lying ill with a fever in the Hawaiian Islands. The dedication of Sam's book said meaninglessly: *To my most patient reader and most charitable critic, my aged mother.*

"What next!" Jane marveled, laying the book on the parlor table. "I've not been his patient reader, ever, nor an easy critic, either. Sometimes I've roasted him. And I'm a far piece from aged. I'm just sixty-five years old."

"Sixty-six, Mother," Pamela corrected patiently.

"Yes," Jane Clemens conceded, "I'm sixty-six." Now that she thought of it, there was no need for her to be sixty-five. . . . Richard Ferrel Barret was dead now. She need never bother, more, to try to be his age. He had not died at his St. Louis estate but up at Burlington, the town he had promoted. The St. Louis newspapers had reported it, listing his accomplishments, naming his prominent children. Well, he would never know now that her wandering younger son, the steamboat pilot, was a dashing wit named Mark Twain—more famous than any of *his* sons—who had written a travel book that had gone five thousand copies the first month and was selling at three dollars and fifty cents in its cheapest edition. Such was the height of Sam's fame, as Jane visualized it, and Richard Barret would never know! He had eluded her again.

"Mela," she said, "I was born for something, but not for luck. Never mind what I mean." She resignedly accepted her fate. She was entirely aware that though humankind, by its very nature, childishly aims to get even, few accomplish it. And she had never asked to be the exception; therein she differed from Sam.

Before the year ended, *The Innocents Abroad* had reached a sale's crescendo of thirty thousand copies. Mark Twain was a name said oftener than U. S. Grant, and with more pleasure. He lectured several times a week while his books rolled off the presses; packed houses found him adorable. He was quoted from coast to coast, and an ordinary family could hardly eat breakfast without buttering the muffins with his witticisms. Nor was that the only sort of acclaim. William Dean Howells, a young writer-critic of a more mature genius than his own, himself on a spectacular rise, noticed him favorably in the *Atlantic Monthly*, America's literary magazine.

Sam's doting father-in-law to be, Jervis Langdon, presented him with the twelve thousand dollars needed to buy a partnership in the *Buffalo Express*. A house in Buffalo, expensively furnished, also awaited him when he should have conducted his bride thither. The wedding was set for February second in the bright new year of 1870.

News of the bride's trousseau, being assembled in New York City, filtered through to the family in St. Louis. Jane, whose own wedding gown had been a freshly laundered swiss from the previous summer, and Pamela and Mollie who had fared better, thanks respectively to Mrs. Owsley's trunks and the up-to-date stores of Keokuk, drank in the details thirstily. Olivia's father had given her free rein, Sam wrote them—indeed, had urged her to buy lavishly, for she was a quiet, delicate girl of serious mind, more given to charity than to self-adornment. The New York modistes were turning out for her a velvet suit, a cloth suit, a gray silk suit, a purple silk suit, and a modestly décolleté wedding gown of white satin and illusion with which she was to wear French kid gloves that reached to her shoulders. The length of the gloves was discounted by Jane and Pamela and Mollie as a sample of Sam's exaggerations, but it was confirmed by the Reverend Thomas K. Beecher after he had officiated at the ceremony; the bride, remarked the unworldly man in wonder, was wearing the longest kid gloves he had ever beheld. Sam's reporting was accurate.

In a practical dash to prepare for his new responsibilities, Sam first took care of the old. He bought a life insurance policy worth ten thousand dollars; he assured his mother that she would be the beneficiary, though he admitted he had not bothered to specify her; the angelic Livy would see that she got it in the event of his death. Jane kept a dignified silence in regard to the life insurance (did Sam suppose she would advance a claim over his rightful heirs?) but she right joyously accepted a draft for five hundred dollars from his royalties. After banking some of it, as Will Moffett had taught her to do during the war, she summoned Mollie from her lofty flat, and they went forth to shop at the more expensive stores. And Orion was measured for a suit and topcoat by the best tailor in Olive Street.

The Landgons were warmly urging the groom's mother and sister and niece to attend the wedding, and Sam had sent a hundred dollars for railway fare. But in the St. Louis household there was a flurry of indecision. Jane was holding back. "Since I didn't see you married, Mela, nor Orion, I'd not feel right to see Sam married." Besides, she went on, she was needed to look after Sammy; Marget could hardly keep house and manage a nine-year-old boy with an excess of curiosity. The latter argument carried no weight, for Marget was more inclined to "hold Sammy down" than was his grandmother. But it was evident to Pamela that Jane did not want to attend the Clemens-Langdon wedding. Did she, for the first time in her life, perhaps, feel socially inadequate? Did she shrink from meeting these people who had scooped Sam to their elegant bosoms and were so sure of themselves and had never known poverty?

Whatever Jane's reasons, she had her way, and she sat out the wedding with equanimity, pretending to Orion and Mollie, who had not been invited, that the whole thing was small potatoes.

Pamela and Annie returned from the wedding as they had gone, by way of Cleveland and Chicago. In Cleveland the redoubtable Mrs. Fairbanks had entertained them, and they had also shared pleasantries and caterer's food with her at the wedding supper.

They were somewhat altered by their experiences, Jane thought, seventeen-year-old Annie seeming more effervescent than before, her mother more primly formal. Reports of the goings-on were recited while Jane listened attentively. Annie had helped Livy address wedding announcements; had heard her give the day's orders to her cook and coachman—a white man who wore livery; had sat beside Livy as she received callers in her beautiful parlor—it was called a drawing room and had delicate blue satin walls; had watched her arrange hothouse flowers for the little reception room with the scarlet brocade upholstery.

"Does Sam Clemens sit in those rooms?" Jane asked, puzzled.

"Yes, he does," Annie said, "and even brings in mud on his shoes. But Aunt Livy won't let him smoke in those places. She's firm about that. And she has him asking the blessing at meals. Another thing—Uncle Sam has stopped swearing. And if he drinks now, I never saw a sign of it. Aunt Livy has simply made him over, and he appears to like it. They kiss and laugh a lot."

"So she's made him over," Jane said. "A real feat!"

Pamela's revelations were equally arresting. "The Langdons are richer than I supposed," she confided importantly. "Coal. The son Charlie whom Sam knew on the *Quaker City* cruise is to be sent around the world soon, with a tutor."

"You can't mean it!"

"Yes, Mother, that's the fashionable way now. But being fashionable is just secondary with the Langdons. They're very kind to people. Livy's older sister, Mrs. Crane, has provided a milk route for the poor. I believe you'd call Mr. and Mrs. Langdon freethinkers. They attend a Congregational church without a creed, and sometimes they entertain Frederick Douglass, the Negro abolitionist, at dinner."

"You can't mean it!" Jane said again, but the item was soon

deleted from her mind by Pamela's next pronouncement. Sam was moving them, Pamela revealed in a nervous rush of words, from St. Louis to Fredonia, a town forty miles southwest of Buffalo, as soon as they could pack up. She said she had gone to Fredonia at Sam's request and had rented a house there. "It's a very attractive town," she added imploringly.

Jane's hands had flown to her throat in a gesture John Clemens would have recognized. She looked at her daughter in stunned silence.

"Won't you say something, Mother?"

"Yes. I'll say I shan't leave St. Louis. My friends are here. The river's here. Orion's here."

"Orion *won't* be here, Ma," Pamela explained, reverting to the old name. "You know the job Sam had in mind for him—well, it has worked out. Orion is to be editor of a little magazine Mr. Bliss is starting in Hartford. Sam says Mr. Bliss will be ready for Orion the first of next year, though Orion won't know it till he gets Sam's letter."

"Where is Hartford?" Jane asked.

"It's in Connecticut. It's between Boston and New York City. Sam is providing for us rather well, Mother. He's doubling your allowance. He can look after us better, he says, if we're living closer to him."

"Do you think for a minute, Mela, that Sam will stay in Buffalo? Do you give him longer than a year or two there? Then where will we be? Abandoned in a strange town—a Yankee town, without kinfolks, lonesome for home."

She saw that Mela looked startled and distressed, and she knew, suddenly, that it was Mela herself who had suggested their move from St. Louis. She sensed something of which she had been unaware; Mela wanted to flee from the scene of her widowhood. Since this was so, she must not make it hard for her.

"Must you walk the floor, Mother? Are you so upset?"

"A cramp in my foot is all," Jane answered. She was subject to that annoyance. She made a circuit of the room and looked at the family portraits on the wall, especially Henry's, portraits that would go with them, wherever. "Now that I think of it, Mela, a change of climate might benefit us all. St. Louis weather gets

286

very sticky. But tell me how Sam happened to pitch on Fredonia for us."

"Because it has such superior people in it. That's what decided him when we were discussing which town would be best." She refrained from telling Jane that Sam had seen Fredonia only once—if it could be said that he saw it then. He had arrived there one evening after dark to lecture and had left the next morning on the early train. But a well-dressed, responsive audience had filled the assembly hall. They had laughed at the right places. Such pleasant, intelligent, well-educated people he had rarely encountered. Then Pamela pronounced the supreme accolade: "Fredonia is a little Boston, Sam says."

"A little Boston!" Jane was aghast. She had heard about Boston.

Well, earth-rocking moves had happened to her before, and only once had she ever instigated the move—that was the migration to join Patsy. A half-dozen times, otherwise, some male creature had catapulted her into a place of his choosing. She had acquiesced each time. Yet always within the framework of that other's choice, she had managed to live her own life. Let Fredonia beware.

Mr. Small, owner of the Chestnut Street house, quickly found a new tenant to take over the Moffett boarders, and so much confusion prevailed that there was little opportunity for lamentations.

Jane was thankful. She had come to know that people did not part from her resignedly but took her removal to a new location as an unwarranted catastrophe that might be overcome by argument or persuasion. She had no idea why this was so, for she was not aware of the warmth of sympathy she generated in her contacts. She only knew their loss of her was an ordeal she must add to her own sufferings, at partings. She eased the St. Louis exodus by imploring friends and relatives to visit them in Fredonia, and by assuring them she would return to St. Louis, though the skies fell.

Marget was to go with them. That severance was spared them.

The furniture, including the piano and portraits, well crated, went off by Railway Express; and Pamela and Annie and Marget followed directly. Jane, entrusted with Sammy, set out circuitously by steamboat for Louisville, for it had been decided that she must have her long-wished-for visit to Kentucky at this time.

Jane was wearing a full-skirted dress of rich silk poplin, brown in color, made in fashion's height except that it escaped the ground by six inches. "To avoid the dirty pavements and steamcar floors," she explained sincerely, for she detested to change "dust braid" that had become soiled. But Pamela knew her mother's other reason for rejecting floor-length dresses; she wanted to show her ankles. (Puss Quarles, on one of her visits, seeing Jane in a brief petticoat, had exclaimed in wonder, "Aunt Jane, you've got the prettiest feet and legs in St. Louis!" and Pamela had moaned, "Must you tell her?")

The wrap to accompany the traveling dress was a cape of Bismarck brown wool, fitted at the waist. Bronze beads trimmed it, a band of sable at the neck gave warmth. She thought it heartless to wear more fur than necessary—and never squirrel, preferring animals she knew nothing pleasant about. A sable collar was acceptable; the species were bad-tempered little beasts, she had heard, entirely carnivorous.

The steamboat journey to Louisville, though made in the inclement weather of early March, was rousing fun for Jane and Sammy—a boy of extraordinary intelligence and good will. He was permitted by his grandmother to handle the tickets and baggage checks. The arrangement was considered strange by purser and passengers alike, but no harm came of it. At Louisville they went with their luggage to the home of Dr. Clemens, where they were expected. They would also spend a few days with Jane's sister-in-law Polly Hancock Saunders and her family—her English husband and his daughter Tip, the portrait painter.

At the Saunders home Jane displayed some family photographs she was carrying with her, including a tintype of Sam and a daguerreotype of his bride. Livy was pronounced beautiful and ethereal. "And Sam has a fascinating face," Tip mused. "I'd like to do a portrait of him."

288

"You would?" Jane asked in surprise. "That's nice of you, Tip. I'll tell him. But Orion's much the handsomer. You've seen Orion, you should know that." She was beginning to suspect that Sam's notoriety would win him all the family favors.

Presently she noticed that everyone invited to meet her questioned her about her son, the platform wit and writer, for they had either bought or borrowed his book, and read it. As who had not? It was pushing every other book in sales, almost equaling *Uncle Tom's Cabin* in the race. Thirty tons of paper had already gone into *The Innocents Abroad,* it was reported; and salesmen were knocking on doors in every sizable town in America with order blanks in hand. "Is all this actually true?" the practical Mr. Saunders asked Jane. He had become one of Louisville's most highly paid auditors. "Is it possible?"

"Sam says so, Mr. Saunders," Jane proudly admitted, "so do the newspapers. I reckon it's all true." Then she saw that he was looking at her in a new way; he was looking *through* her, at something bigger. Near panic assailed her. Was she about to become Mark Twain's Mother?

Leaving their trunks and taking only their new valises, she and Sammy went down to Adair County by stagecoach. There she was herself again, and the famous book was rarely mentioned. It warmed her heart to notice that Henry's daguerreotype was handling most lingeringly of all her pictures. "He was as brave as he was beautiful," she assured them, unable to refrain.

With her polite little grandson in tow, she made the rounds. Many dear friends were missing, but in such cases their children knew of her and were attentive. Of her old beaux, there was Parker Hardin. With his shy wife he entertained her at dinner. Caroline Lewis Hardin knew she owed her title to the Widow Clemens' rejection of Parker twenty years before, yet she said a gracious thing to her:

"When Mr. Hardin sees a redheaded woman on the street, Mrs. Clemens, he follows her! I think it will be so till he dies."

Out in the country a novelty occurred that captivated Jane and Sammy Moffett, a show embodying fortitude and theatrics. They were visiting Mrs. Lucy Hancock Browning, near whose home the event took place. It was a baptizing, conducted by the "Christians," or Campbellites, in a creek pool on a sunny March day. But the springlike weather was superficial. There was a topping of ice on the water from a previous freeze, and this crackled as the brave candidates entered the pool to be immersed. A Hancock granddaughter was among the number. Beneath her angelic robe she was wearing snug flannel underwear, Jane was told. But what fervor had kept these converts from waiting till June? Was it the lingering magnetism of the Reverend Alexander Campbell?

A slight but unusual honor was accorded the visitor before her departure, and she made the most of it. She was asked to name a baby in the town—the little grand-nephew of Andrew Russell, dear Andy, her friend of long ago. She said she must consider it overnight in order to do right by the child. This was thought fit and proper by the babe's family, in whose house she was quartered, and all retired early. The next morning Jane admitted, "I must have thought of a hundred names last night! I mulled them over and discarded them, one by one. I've now concluded to name the baby for my own son, if you'll forgive me. It will honor the man and the child too."

Expectancy had become fulfillment, almost. The Russells wanted the distinction of a boy named Samuel Clemens, yet had hesitated to bestow the name; this maneuver had seemed more tactful.

"The name I've chosen," Jane Clemens informed them, "is Orion. A dearer man never lived, and he hasn't a child to his name."

"Orion?" the Russells repeated, and young Mrs. Russell had tears in her eyes. They knew Orion Clemens. He had passed that way frequently, trying to get rid of his Tennessee land. *"Just Orion, Cousin Jane?"* someone asked, pleading now for a middle name.

"Just Orion," Jane said firmly. "Orion is a star. You wouldn't hitch it to something earthly. And always pronounce it *O*rion."

Her relationship with Orion, and his with her, can best be seen in a letter he would write to his brother Samuel on November 1, 1890, soon after her death:

290

My Dear Brother:—

I am very sorry you were delayed; but it could not be foreseen.

You have nothing to regret toward Ma. You did all you could, and nobly and generously; but I feel that your praises are not deserved. I am stung with remorse. If I had her back I would recall and abolish every harsh and over-loud modulation of voice; I would talk and listen to her more; I would cheer her oftener with hopes of the impossible.

This was the son Jane had provided with a namesake in Columbia, her native village, just before taking off from there to resume the journey to New York State with young Sammy Moffett.

30 ❖

Jane made her most famous blunder in Fredonia before she could remove her chic little hat. People said she was a careless guardian of her grandson, young Samuel Moffett, sending him to Buffalo alone to get the baggage when he was not yet ten years old. The story would grow, enlarged by Annie and her Uncle Sam, who liked to exaggerate the episode, and they would say she set off for Lake Chautauqua to join Pamela without ever leaving the Dunkirk station. The actual facts were less incriminating, though they were unusual enough to raise eyebrows.

Fredonia was not on the railroad line but was served by Dunkirk, four miles away on the shore of Lake Erie. Horsecars ran between the two towns; and Fredonia did not begrudge Dunkirk its rail tracks, its cinders and whistles as the trains labored from Cleveland to Buffalo, and on to Albany.

The first mistake was made in Louisville when Dr. Clemens' handy man took Jane and Sammy to the depot and checked their trunks through to Buffalo. His impression was, the lady was going to visit her son in Buffalo, and he acted accordingly. When Dunkirk was reached at early morn two days later, Jane and Sammy with their hand luggage alighted from the train; and there, on the platform, equipped with a valise of her own, was Annie Moffett. She was amazed to see them. Jane had failed to keep them posted in Kentucky; had even neglected to send a telegram stating when she and Sammy might be expected; train schedules were beyond her and she did not bother with them.

Annie hastily explained that her mother had gone to Lake Chautauqua to take some treatments recommended for nervous exhaustion, the move from St. Louis having disabled her. Annie was going there now, to see about her; the local train would be coming through in a few minutes. "You and Sammy come with me," she urged her grandmother. "It would cheer Mother up. Nobody's at home but Marget."

Jane, though travel-tired, agreed, but a call of distress from Sammy up at the fore of the train divested her of the plan. "They won't put our trunks off!" Sammy was shouting. "They say our trunks have to go to the Buffalo station!" He had climbed into the baggage car and was addressing them from the open door; being but nine and a half years old, he had lost his argument with the baggagemaster. "I'm going on to Buffalo with our trunks and bring 'em back!" The choice treasures of his St. Louis boyhood were in his own trunk and he had no idea of separating himself from them.

"Do that, Sammy!" Jane called to him, "but come straight back on the next train! If you have any trouble, go to your Uncle Sam at his newspaper office! It's the *Buffalo Express!*"

The "all aboards" were being shouted, the engine was accelerating its hisses, and Sammy rode away beside their trunks in the baggage car, waving cheerily.

Annie was surprised, but long association with her grandmother had given her a confidence in her that was almost unshakable. Jane's next words, however, spoken in awed contrition, were startling: "Sammy has our trunk checks, Annie, and all our ticket stubs, but he's not got a cent in his pocket! He's spent all his money with the train butchers. I should have thought of that!"

Annie's alarm made her noisily reproachful. "What have you done, Grandma!" she wailed. "Uncle Sam and Aunt Livy are not in Buffalo now! They're down in Elmira with her people because her father's sick!"

That was a blow to Jane, but she rallied. "Sammy's wearing his

292

watch," she said. "He'll put it up for ticket fare. He'll be back here on the first train returning, mark my words." The train for Chautauqua came in, but they both knew Annie must not get on it. If she should see her mother, she would have to divulge Sammy's plight, and poor Pamela would go to pieces. It was pointless to wait at the Dunkirk station; Sammy could not possibly be expected before the next westbound train. They took their valises and went home to make the best of it.

Marget gave them a good deal of trouble, as Jane knew she would, but they felt they must tell her all the circumstances, even Sammy's moneyless state. Though she refrained from reproaching Jane, she was free in expressing her opinion to Annie. "I had my doubts Mrs. Clemens would get here with the boy alive!" she pronounced in carrying tones. "The freedom she allows him! In Germany they would call her crazy and lock her up!" She passed on the news to neighbors and tradespeople, for she was genuinely distressed and could not contain her anxiety. Soon the story was all over town. Editor McKinstry called to offer his aid. The Presbyterian minister came to express condolence. Jane bore it all with humility and a chastened spirit. "I should have gone with the boy," she acknowledged. "I see that now. I often see things too late. But I'd rather keep the Buffalo police out of it. My grandson is resourceful. I'm sure he'll be back on the evenin' train."

He was. They awaited the train prayerfully, and it was a beautiful sight to see Sammy Moffett jump from the baggage car and wave the trunks to the platform. A conductor stepped from a passenger coach and he was swinging Sammy's watch on its chain. He genially named the sum that would redeem it, and Jane paid it to him and took the watch.

"That's a smart boy you've got there," was all he said.

"You've been more than kind," Jane told him with brimming eyes. "You're a regular Yankee!" Strangely, she had used the word in tribute.

After seeing the trunks loaded onto a dray, they boarded the horsecar in high spirits. The following day Jane and Annie went to the lake to fetch Pamela, leaving Sammy with Marget to learn the town.

293

"With *me*, he is safe," Marget assured the many Fredonians who showed an interest. They could draw their own conclusions as to his previous condition. And did.

The house Pamela had rented was downtown at the edge of the commons. It was the Episcopal rectory, that year lacking a resident rector. Jane thought the location choice. It was close to the custom shops and the stores. The commons was a natural little park, frequented by boys with whom Sammy merged inconspicuously but effectively. Jane noticed that his methods were different from those of the cocky Sam Clemens of long ago. Sammy Moffett bored from within.

There was no use denying that Jane was keenly homesick for St. Louis. Often she would find herself saying to Pamela, "I wonder what the Berkeleys are doing tonight." Or she might wonder if Chestnut Street had got its new lamp posts, or if James Andrew liked his new political job, or if Cousin James would rent a furnished house in St. Louis, as he had planned, "to cheer up Julia." And one nostalgic September Sabbath she said to Pamela while the tears rolled down her cheeks, "Orion and Mollie will go to both services today, wearing their new clothes. I hope Mollie won't scold Lucas Place for not being Old School." She had to laugh at the possibility.

Sammy was observing her and he asked curiously, "Why are you crying and laughing at the same time, Grandma?"

"Because I want to," she snapped, letting the tears course.

Pamela offered a humorous thought. "There's one advantage to being so far from St. Louis, Mother, and we ought to appreciate it. Mrs. Holliday won't be dropping in."

"I wonder where she is now," Jane answered, diverted. Mrs. Holliday had spent the previous winter in New Orleans and had not been on hand at the time of the Moffett breaking-up. She could be less frugal now, for she had gotten some returns from a little investment she had made in a gold mine—a matter of chagrin to wiser heads whose stock had not panned out. It enabled her to live in better boardinghouses than formerly and to ride oftener on the steamboats.

Very soon after their conversation, as if by magic, Mrs. Holliday arrived in Buffalo with her valise and rang the doorbell at 472 Delaware Avenue. The master of the house answered, as he often did, and he took in the situation at a glance. The cabman, who was turning his vehicle, was ordered to halt, and Sam Clemens led Mrs. Holliday in a mesmerizing way down the walk, holding firmly to her elbow and her valise. He put her into the cab, and all the while he was explaining the situation, one which he did not need to exaggerate: there was a guest in his house very sick with typhoid fever, doctors came and went, the house was rife with nurses.

"But Ma and Pamela are dying to see you, Mrs. Holliday," he told her and explained that they lived in the town of Fredonia forty miles distant, accessible by an afternoon train that stopped at Dunkirk; that at Dunkirk she had the choice of an omnibus or a horse-drawn rail car to Fredonia; that the Moffett abode in Fredonia was the Episcopal rectory. He extracted fifty dollars from various pockets on his person and placed it in her purse, patting her protesting hand. Then he handed the cab driver some additional bills and instructed him to buy his passenger a ticket to Dunkirk and put her on the westbound train.

"Leave my vehicle and put her on the train myself, in person?"

"Yes, yourself, in person. And if you fail in this assignment," said the gentleman on the curb, beetling his brows and lowering his voice to a dangerous purr, "S. L. Clemens, otherwise known as Mark Twain, will crush you to a pulp."

Mrs. Holliday arrived in Fredonia without mishap, for she was very sharp at getting about. At her own request she was set down at the Episcopal church, then dark and in disuse. Sammy Moffett saw her there and heard her pounding on the door and exclaiming, "Has it come to this? Pamela Clemens living in an old church?"

"Why, Mrs. Holliday!" Sammy called out, and he ran to her and they embraced. He led the way to the rectory and there, like an echo from his earlier childhood, he heard his grandmother greet Mrs. Holliday warmly and tell her to come right in.

Thus Mrs. Holliday became their first out-of-town visitor and, as such, commanded a good deal of attention. "This is our good friend Mrs. Holliday of Hannibal, Missouri," Jane would say on introducing her. The dear old soul was fantastically overdressed, and was addicted to rouge, a habit she had acquired in New Orleans. Pamela was hard put to locate her rouge jar and confiscate it, but with Jane's help, that was accomplished. The old lady stayed with them a fortnight, and nobody tried to explain her to the Fredonians except Marget.

Perhaps Mrs. Holliday's visit was the crowning cause of Marget's homesickness. She felt an overpowering longing for St. Louis and she said she must return there. This prim town where all the people were so alike, where one never heard the German tongue, or the French; where one never smelled coffee roasting at the levee or saw families drinking beer in little back gardens—it was more than she could endure. Sam, hearing of her intentions and considering his house to be understaffed, prevailed upon her to stop with him and Livy a while, luring her with a fine trunk and some new clothes. But her pause was brief. Soon she was back in St. Louis, telling her relatives strange tales of a people who put molasses in the beans and sugar in the cornbread.

After Marget had gone, Jane made the observation that she felt cut loose from St. Louis. The adjustment would have been easier if Sam could have run down to see them often, as he had predicted he would do. But his honeymoon year, which had begun in such an Arabian Nights fashion, was changing into a cycle of tribulation. Livy's adored father had become mortally ill in March, and as his condition worsened, Livy and Sam went to Elmira to help Mrs. Langdon and Mrs. Crane nurse him; Jervis Langdon was not a man who chose to depart life under professional care. In August he died, and Livy and Sam resumed residence in Buffalo. To relieve Livy's depression, her former schoolmate Emma Nye, then living in South Carolina, was summoned to visit her. Miss Nye immediately fell ill with typhoid fever (it was thought she had arrived with it) and at the end of September she died in the Clemens house. Nurses and doctors had attended her, as Sam indicated to Mrs. Holliday. There came another friend to cheer Livy. On her departure, Livy accompanied this one in the Clemens carriage to the railroad station. But neither the luxury of the little carriage nor the careful driving of Patrick McAleer, the young coachman who would grow old in their service, could prevent the cobbled streets of Buffalo from shaking the fragile, pregnant Livy in an alarming way; and in early November, baby Langdon Clemens was prematurely born. Though his father called him the prince and wrote charming letters announcing his arrival, his frailty was evident from the start—four and a half pounds was his weight when clothed, and his skin was marble white. Livy herself was marble white; and her invalidism, which had begun in her girlhood with a fall on the ice, had resumed. She could not endure the city of Buffalo where so much trouble had beset her. At her request Sam put their house and his interest in the newspaper on the market, and they left Buffalo, not to return. The summer of 1871 found them at Elmira—at Livy's old home and the summer residence on the hilltop, "Quarry Farm." They were deciding on a place of future residence. Hartford, in every way suitable, was chosen, and in the autumn they went there to live.

Jane's prediction that they could give Sam but a year or two in Buffalo had been accurate. Even without Livy's urging he would have weighed that place against the literary atmosphere and cultural excitement of Hartford and have found it wanting. . . . Good-by, Ma and Pamela! Good-by, Annie and Sammy! I wish we might have been together more. Indeed I do.

It is said that persons shipwrecked on a distant shore are gripped by restlessness as long as there is the possibility of rescue, but once they have abandoned hope of outside assistance, they become energetic and contented. So it was with Jane Clemens. What did Fredonia have to offer an undemanding, well-disposed woman who liked novelty?

There were the people themselves, only two generations away from pioneerhood, their grandparents having come here from New England, mostly, when the lake shore was still raw and dangerous. But they had brought an excessive respect for education with them. Even the tinsmiths and coopers and saddlers and such in Fredonia talked "like schoolteachers," Jane remarked to Mela. She said she would be ashamed to say "no how" in their presence.

"I hope so," Pamela murmured fervently.

The women who came to call were kind and interesting, if often prim. Jane and Pamela had the assurance of being accepted, though whether for being themselves or for being the near kin of Mark Twain, it was impossible to know. Once when they discussed it, out of the children's hearing, Jane said with a laugh, "Let it pass." It was an expression she had picked up from Sam.

Though happy to adjust and be a credit to her family, she had no intention of making herself over. She continued to offer cordial to afternoon callers, though they almost invariably declined it and accepted the alternative, tea. Sam and Livy had sent her a set of grape-etched cordial glasses with lovely stems, and Sam had also supplied the cordial. With serene detachment Jane would take her cordial while the callers and Pamela took tea. And she continued to say "this evenin'" when referring to the interval between noon and sunset, because the word afternoon was not in a rural Southerner's vocabulary unless employed by lawyers in a legal trial. She continued to call an affectionate "Howdy!" when encountering children, and a genial "Howdy do" when greeting adults. And if annoyed she was apt to exclaim "Hang it!" or "Drat it!" like the Western women. She refused to lengthen her skirts though Pamela advised it, and she stayed away from church services as often as she attended. All of those things were commented upon, as Annie was to learn, for Annie would marry into that town.

It was vastly interesting to Jane that silk had been woven in Chautauqua County; for her love of the stuff remained intense in spite of that reckless plunge into the silkworm market long ago. The Pettit family in Fredonia still had its cocoonery, built a quarter-century before, though now in disuse. A daughter of the family showed Jane how more than a hundred thousand silkworms had been nurtured there on Chinese mulberry leaves that were locally grown, and then supplied with branches of the shrubs on which to affix their cocoons. Later, Miss Pettit explained, the silk threads were unreeled on power reels that were manufactured in Fredonia. Miss Pettit had assisted in all this—had even woven cloth for family use—and Jane was filled with admiration. She

298

would have told Miss Pettit about her former cobbling, thus establishing a sort of trades sisterhood, if Pamela had not been so sensitive about it.

There was a well-kept trotting track at the edge of Fredonia known as the Driving Park. Jane attended the events there whenever Annie could be persuaded to accompany her. Annie now had beaux, and those young men made useful escorts for such outings. They were interested in the records of the horses and the purses offered. Jane was interested in the horses.

And there was always Lake Erie, less appealing, by far, than the Mississippi, but awesome in its flat extent. After a storm one could take a conveyance and ride to Dunkirk harbor and see Lake Erie lashing away there. Or, for a different view, to Van Buren Point where a breakwater had been made of immense timbers long ago. Sammy Moffett always accompanied his grandmother to the scene of action, and it was his pleasure to shed scientific light on the uniqueness of Lake Erie. Because it was so shallow, he said, it was dangerous; it kicked up the biggest waves in a storm of all the Great Lakes. Sammy, ever dependable and fact-hungry, collected such items and stored them permanently, as became a future editor of *Collier's Weekly*. Except for the Lampton curiosity about life, he bore little resemblance to the other Sam whom Jane had raised. He was less intense, less belligerent, less grasping, less egotistical, and less fun. But sensibly planned adventures appealed to him mightily, and he could expect more of such outings in his grandmother's company than in his conventional mother's. Physically, Sammy was rather delicate, and it was Jane's scheme to help him "grow out of it" by dedicating him to tree-climbing and other open-air ventures. In Fredonia's Canadaway Creek he became an excellent swimmer, always aware of the limits of his strength and of where he had left his clothes.

"He's named for the wrong uncle," Jane told Pamela after observing these manifestations. "It's Henry he takes after, bless his heart."

A serious adversity hampered Sammy when an attack of measles left him with weakened vision. Their physician said he must rest his eyes and not open a book during the coming year or he might lose his sight. With winter coming on, the reading ban seemed a catastrophe to the family. Fredonia had opened its new school—the Normal School of the Eighth Judicial District was its official name and it had absorbed the proud old Fredonia Academy. Sammy was enrolled there, and the doctor's verdict left him white-faced and stunned. Jane said there was a simple way out; let Sammy attend his classes and *listen*. The results were gratifying. When examinations were held, Samuel Erasmus Moffett led all the rest, his own tests being oral but otherwise similar. His promotions, thanks to an interested faculty, came rapidly, and Sammy's determination to compensate soon threatened to make a prig of him. His grandmother then had his smugness to deal with; but she had her ways.

Though it was Pamela who read to him from his textbooks and always coached him after school, it was Jane who made his winter evenings bearable. When asked by Pamela, who had been reading Emerson, "What in the world are you forever holding forth about, Mother?" Jane replied: "Why, I'm just telling Sammy all the living I've seen." Certainly she told him about some of the dying too, the outcome of those wars she regarded as avertible and bloodily expensive. When he said he would like to go to college at West Point she disapprovingly asked him why. Because it was free, he replied, and a very handsome place, not too far from Chautauqua County. "Soldiers are to keep the peace," he reminded her, "like the sheriffs."

"That's so. You've got a point there."

She had run out of heroes and heroines, had actually worn to a shred her stories of General Benjamin Logan's adopted Indian son. When Sammy's eyes strayed longingly to the bookcases she was forced to cut her anecdotes from any mundane cloth that came to mind; and she told him of persons, black and white, who had no drama in their lives except a strength to endure and a will to overcome. She talked of the poors' kindness to the poor, and of a rich man's opportunities to share, in case he, Sammy, should ever be rich. They discussed that a good deal, how he might bring aid to widows with empty coal bins and to moneyless heads of families stricken with rheumatism. She held forth chattily on the

300

pleasures of travel, the intelligence of animals, the probability of certain old houses being haunted, the advisability of walking ten miles a day, the presence of guardian angels (however you can't count on them continually), and the several manly ways of avoiding a fight (though once is enough to turn the other cheek). They spoke together feelingly of orphans left without guardians and watertight boots. They touched on the pitiful plight of slum folk who had never picked a wild flower.

Who would deny that such dialogues in the boy's formative years bore fruit? For Samuel E. Moffett, who would drown in 1909 at forty-eight when joyously swimming by moonlight in a high surf, would have this eulogy written of him by a fellow editor, though the century was young: *Anyone who discussed with him* [Moffett] *the things he advocated stood a little awed to discover that here was a man who had carefully thought out what would be best for all the people in the world two or three generations hence, and guided his work according to that standard. This was the one broad subject that covered all his interests; in detail they included the movement for universal peace about which he wrote repeatedly; so small a thing as a plan to place flowers on the window sills and fire escapes of New York tenement houses enlisted not only the advocacy of his pen, but his direct personal presence and co-operation; again and again, in his department in this paper, he gave endorsement and aid to similar movements, whether broad or narrow in their scope—the saving of the American forests, fighting tuberculosis, providing free meals for poor school children in New York, old-age pensions, safety appliances for protecting factory employees, the beautifying of American cities, the creation of inland waterways, industrial peace.*

The world, in asking what effect Jane Clemens had on the writings of the great Mark Twain, might also ask what impression she made on the thinking of this unsung grandson who left such practical ripples of human faith and progress.

In the early spring of 1873 Jane and Annie went to Hartford to visit, for Livy had graciously invited them to come "two at a time," and Pamela had thus paired them off. Jane was especially eager to see Orion and Mollie who were, as Livy had written at

301

Christmas, "very cozily situated." Annie left her best beau, young Charles Webster, reluctantly; yet where but at Uncle Sam's and Aunt Livy's could she hope to wear so effectively the ermine tippet and the silver hair ornament they had given her for Christmas? Was Fredonia ready for such refinements? Muddy streets and galoshes had delayed the test.

Jane divided her time between the two contrasting homes. After a whirl at Sam's where luxury and confusion were dismayingly blended and famous persons interrupted you at breakfast, she went for a quiet visit to Orion and Mollie. Orion—gentle, sedate, whimsical—was unchanged by his lofty association with Sam's publisher. Mollie too was unaltered except that she was temporarily calling herself Mary; the prevalence in Hartford of housemaids named Mollie had decided her, she said. Jane strove to follow her daughter-in-law's wishes, though usually she came through with "Mollie Mary" and was forgiven. The three of them talked contentedly about things not mentioned in the presence of the smart folk at Sam's: Hannibal and Keokuk and St. Louis and the old triumphs and disasters. Jane was happy that Orion spoke of "Pa" without bitterness, even praised his erudition. It eased her heart that this son in looking back beheld his father without Pamela's pity and without Sam's censure. After their talks, when the coals had burned low, she would sleep comfortably on the couch beside the fireplace in the sitting room. She wished things might always stay this good.

The trip home necessitated a change at New York's central railway station, and Sam had asked Charlie Langdon, Livy's brother, to find them and put them on the right train for Buffalo. "How will he know us?" Jane asked Annie, somewhat worried. "He's never laid eyes on us, and I doubt if Sam could tell him what we're wearing. Sam doesn't even notice what Livy's wearing."

"If you'll just keep talking," Annie said, "Mr. Langdon will recognize us. He's probably heard about the way you drawl."

"Nonsense! I talk just like anybody else." But, sure enough, she was talking away, marveling at the crowd and exclaiming over the wonders of modern travel, when Charlie Langdon passed by them, searching. He stopped short and said with relief, "Mrs.

302

Clemens, I'd have known you in Timbuktu! You sound exactly like Mark."

But things did not remain as they were. A half year later when Ella Lampton wrote Jane from St. Louis, *Everybody is happy for you that your family is doing so well,* Jane hardly knew how to reply. It was true that Sam's success was increasing. He had brought out another popular book, this one called *Roughing It,* and was even then in London being applauded and toasted. But Orion, alas, had been "let go" by Mr. Bliss in Hartford, and he was adrift in New York City, a compositor for the *Evening Post,* barely able to shelter and feed Mollie and himself on what he earned there. They lived in a two-room flat at 97 Varick Street, where Jane sometimes sent Mollie a bank note.

But soon even that retreat was beyond them. In October, Mollie wrote that she was returning to Keokuk, her father having sent the money for railroad fare. Orion's job with the newspaper was terminating. Perhaps it was his own fault, Mollie said, for his mind was on an invention—something to do with a flying machine—and he was like a man in a dream. She had begged him, she said, to take notes on the novelties of New York, the foreigners and all, and sell the series to a newspaper back home. But he was not able to concentrate. His notebook was blank except for drawings of a flying machine.

"A flying machine!" Jane said to Pamela. Words failed them. There had been the wood-sawing machine in Keokuk, which worked splendidly but had already been patented, and the little drill in St. Louis which had just missed promotion; then, in a national competition, the mechanics of a steam canal boat—not without merit, the experts said. . . . "But a flying machine! Have I read it right, Mela?"

She quickly conveyed her concern and agitation to Orion, staying away from church to write the letter, though a misplaced calendar kept her from dating it:

On the Lord's Day
Fredonia Nov the
My dear son You remember days gone by that Sam took an oath before his mother, that oath saved him. Now my dear son

I wish with my whole heart you will take a solemn oath and write it on paper and send it to your mother. I will keep it as long as I live and leave it in my will to Mary. This oath is that you will not let a single word come from your mouth nor even one thought come in your mind about an invention of any kind. My dear son promise this. . . . When you have made a good living a regular income make that over to your wife and you have nothing to do with it. Then work at your invention. I will be perfectly willing. My dear son you say you cannot get work. Go out in the streets Wall street and all and make acquaintances. Orion you know a man without acquaintances is without friends. . . . Now my dear son you and Sam are my own children one is just as near to me as the other. One is just as well fitted for making a living as the other but not alike. Sam gives his whole attention to his book writing and management. But the secret with you is Orion you work with your pen but your mind is not on it. Management is a very important matter in this fast day. Now my dear son you know all this but your mind for years has been on nothing but inventions. . . . When you are in Wall street and every other street making acquaintances and friends keep both eyes and both ears open take notes all day at night write them out and send the letter to Mary, in some future day they may be of value to you. When a nervous person is worried they cannot sleep at night. Next day they feel miserable all day. My dear son this is a long letter two much for my head but I write with the hope it will do us all good.

She concluded with a postscript that was typical of her: *Orion this letter is badly put together but you make it read the way I intended*. It was ever her custom to invite her children to alter her hastily written letters until they made sense, for she preferred that to perusing and rewriting them; let the recipients supply their own commas.

She next wrote a beseeching letter to Sam, telling him of his brother's plight and giving him the address of Orion's lonely New York room, 40 West 9th Street—a letter Sam failed to receive until February. It is true that the brothers' paths had just crossed. But they had not actually communicated, so great was the razzle dazzle. Orion had met Sam and his family at the boat on November second and had derived great pleasure from being in the distinguished company of Mark Twain, not to mention sharing several fine hotel meals with him and sitting beside him in a theatre box to see Edwin Booth play Hamlet. But as Sam was returning to England on the same boat that had brought him— he had only come over to bring his family—Orion did not break in on his preoccupations to tell him of his lost job.

When Sam received his mother's letter on returning from London he responded quickly. No doubt he felt contrite because he had not, himself, unearthed Orion's misfortunes, had not questioned him as to the cause of Mollie's return home. If Orion had had enough of New York, Sam wrote his mother, he would send him the money to return to Keokuk and buy the little farm Mollie craved. He also promised to refrain from scolding and belittling. Sam knew, even better than his mother, that he had precipitated Orion's failure with Bliss; for in July 1870 he had plainly instructed Orion by letter:

He [Bliss] is going to issue a monthly gratuitous paper, say about 100,000 copies, to advertise his books in, & will get all his authors to contribute occasional articles. . . . Well, you see he offers you the editorship of it at $100 a month till he can do better by you. . . . I desire that you throw up that cursed night work & take this editorship & conduct it so well that editorships will assail you at the end of a year. . . . He is shrewdly counting on two things, now—one is, by creating a position for you, he will keep me from "whoring after strange gods," which is Scripture for deserting to other publishers; &, 2ᵈ, get an occasional article out of me for the paper. . . .

Sam financed Orion's and Mollie's move to Hartford and found pleasant quarters for them. They were radiantly happy in their new environment, their new importance. Orion plunged into his assignments and produced editorials and articles that even his brother praised. But when he kept importuning Sam for contributions, as he had been hired to do, the ax fell. Sam wrote him angrily:

Dear Bro:

*I do not wish to write on the subject of articles any more.—
Leave me out of the paper except once in 6 months, & don't write
me anything more about it—either you or Bliss. I know that you
both mean the very best for me, but you are wrong.*

*You both wrote me discouraging letters.—Yours stopped my
pen for two days—Bliss's stopped it for three. Hereafter my wife
will read my Hartford letters & if they are of the same nature,
keep them out of my hands. The idea of a newspaper editor & a
publisher plying with dismal letters a man who is under contract
to write humorous books for them. . . .*

Poor Orion. The magazine and his job dissolved together. He
had failed to deliver. Sam was able to make amends—rather
cheaply, after all—at nine hundred dollars. That was the price of
the little Iowa farm, two miles up the river from Keokuk, which
Mollie wished Orion to purchase from her father. They were
resolved to raise chickens.

Orion received Sam's offer of rescue eagerly, for he had reached
rope's end. He had lately tried, as "Mark Twain's brother," for the
assistant editorship of a small paper in Vermont, but even that had
eluded him. Right gladly he returned to Iowa and made arrangements to buy Mr. Stotts' *de trop* little farm. All that he asked,
further, of Sam was a light spring wagon to convey Mollie to
church. He himself could easily walk to services, he explained,
but the Iowa mud was too lush for a lady's shoes in wet weather.
Sam complied. It seemed a small thing to do for his brother's
wife when his own wife rode in a carriage driven by a coachman
who tucked her in with a fur-lined robe. He accepted Orion's IOUs,
elaborately itemized, politely, though he berated him in letters to
his literary friend, William Dean Howells. He even suggested,
"Let's put him in a play!" but Jane never knew.

Soon Orion was writing enthusiastically to Jane and Pamela
about his "excellent new property." By shipping fowls and eggs
to St. Louis, he said, they could not fail to make a comfortable
living. And the rusticity would provide him leisure for writing
the book he had in mind, a travesty on Jules Verne.

"Chickens!" Jane said resignedly to Pamela. "Dirty hen houses, and wet feathers on rainy days, and roosters that crow before sunup!" But she wrote no discouraging word to Orion. His New York experiences had been humiliating and disturbing. Let him look to the country skies for healing.

Jane enjoyed a relaxed springtime and summer because of Orion and Mollie being so well settled, and because Pamela was well, and Sammy's eyes were improving, and she herself was making her first and only civic contribution to Fredonia. Surprisingly, the coup was in the field of literature, where she knew she was considered mighty deficient—"a woman who read nothing but newspapers." She secured the first volumes for the town's new reading room, named by some Dickens-lover "Holly Tree Inn." She did it by letter to Sam and Livy as soon as the idea had popped into her head.

She explained to them about the recreation room which the women of the town had fitted up with games and newspapers and magazines *to draw the young ones from the saloons. I don't mean the young ladies from the saloons, only gentleman. The reading room was opened by giving a supper. There was a large crowd there. The book case was open but not one thing on the shelves. Livy it ocured to me that you and Sam would like to do good. You have many books that perhaps you can spare to give to them. Please tell Mr. and Mrs. Warner that if they have any books to give away send them here particularly Mr. Warner's and Sam's. The ladies will be pleased to get them and they will pay the Express charges. Sam if you and Mr. Warner write your names in every book the name will recommend its self.* Then she added a bit of sugar, knowing that Sam admired broadminded clergymen, especially if, like his intimate friend in Hartford, the Reverend Joseph Twichell, they admired him in return. *At the supper last night I was introduced to a minister who told me he was proud to shake the hand of Mark Twain's mother. . . . Love to all, particularly Mr and Mrs Warner when I ask a favor of them. Your Mother.*

The books came to her promptly, sixteen volumes of the works of Mark Twain and Charles Dudley Warner, and she and Sammy proudly carried them to Holly Tree Inn where a committee received them. She was formally thanked.

Into this agreeable atmosphere that August of '74 came Samuel L. Clemens and his family for a visit. Sam was tearing himself away from his new study on a hill top at Quarry Farm, and from the nostalgic book he was writing there, *The Adventures of Tom Sawyer*.

Ample notice had been given, and Pamela knew what preparations she must make. There would be Sam and Livy, little Susie aged three, baby Clara, and the nurse. (The frail little boy who had been the first born had died two years before, and one was careful never to speak of him.) Livy was very delicate now but was courageously determined to travel. There were times during the recent trip to England and Scotland when she had collapsed for days at a time after a series of entertainments or a round of public appearances. In coming to Fredonia, and in stopping at Buffalo to visit her husband's friends the David Grays, she was making a supreme effort to do the gracious thing; but she begged Pamela not to entertain for her, asked her even to spare her the ordeal of callers.

Thus it happened that when the ladies of Fredonia leaped at the interesting social bait in their midst, Pamela had to withhold it; Mark Twain's wife could not receive. She hesitated to say, "My sister-in-law is an invalid and sometimes travels on a mattress." She merely said that Mrs. Clemens had not regained her strength since her last accouchement and was sorry she must keep to her room.

A likely story, was the general opinion. Everybody knew about the Mark Twain dinner parties at Hartford and how much they gadded, said the frustrated ones to each other. Fredonia, they concluded, was unimportant to Mrs. Clemens; it was merely a place to rest between engagements.

But Mark Twain himself was available, Pamela assured all inquirers, and she arranged to hold open house for him one evening. She had prepared cake and fruit punch, purely fruit punch, and hoped for the best. Sam beetled his famous eyebrows when he tasted it. That Fredonia was on a temperance tangent which had just resulted in the formation of America's first WCTU chapter had been explained to him; certainly he could not have expected his widowed sister to serve hard liquor or even the native wines in the face of it. Nevertheless he was annoyed that "those women" could dictate a town's punch recipe, for he was accustomed to relaxing the frenzied pace of his activities with something alcoholic. He seethed and smoldered as the evening wore on. The person who finally, because of some opinions he expressed, became the target of his bad temper was the local banker. He was a man who had been especially kind to Jane Clemens and Pamela Moffett. It was an agonizing situation. Jane went upstairs and wept. The banker found his hat and departed; his friends soon followed him.

Sam's letter, after the visit, was in his best vein of self-denunciation:

My Dear Mother and Sister,—I came away from Fredonia ashamed of myself;—almost too humiliated to hold up my head and say good-bye. For I began to comprehend how much harm my conduct might do you socially in your village. I would have gone to that detestable oysterbrained bore and apologized for my inexcusable rudeness to him, but that I was satisfied he was of too small a calibre to know how to receive an apology with magnanimity.

Pamela appalled me by saying people had hinted that they wished to visit Livy when she came, but that she had given them no encouragement. I feared that those people would merely comprehend that their courtesies were not wanted, and yet not know exactly why they were not wanted.

I came away feeling that in return for your constant and tireless efforts to secure our bodily comfort and make our visit enjoyable, I had basely repaid you by making you sad and sore-hearted and leaving you so. And the natural result has fallen to me likewise—for a guilty conscience has harassed me ever since, and I have not had one short quarter of an hour of peace to this moment. . . .

The baby is fat and strong, and Susie the same. Susie was charmed with the donkey and the doll.

Ys affectionately
Saml.

P.S. Dear Ma and Pamela—I am mainly grieved because I have been rude to a man who has been kind to you—and if you ever feel a desire to apologize to him for me, you may be sure that I will endorse the apology, no matter how strong it may be. I went to his bank to apologize to him, but my conviction was strong that he was not man enough to know how to take an apology and so I did not make it.

"And now am I expected to apologize for him, Mother?" Pamela exclaimed. "This is the last straw! I'm too nervous to undertake it. Suppose the apology is rejected? It would humiliate me."

"I'm the one to do it, Mela, because I won't expect to be rebuffed. What Sam means, and he knows it, and he knows I know it, is that he was not man enough at the time to *make* the apology. He's twisted his thinking to lay it on the other fellow. Sam never has grown up. I'll go now and get it over with. Find me those Paris gloves Livy brought me. If I must wring my hands I want to do it in style."

Annie, sensitive to all the winds that blew in her adopted town, was soon reporting to her mother and grandmother that she noticed "a coolness" here and there. "Even Charley's mother and father," she moaned. Charley was Charles Luther Webster, her devoted beau, not yet an announced fiancé. One could hardly object to him. He was an upright young man who lived in a charming house with a large lawn and had impressive New England ancestors, Governors Winthrop and Bradford and Endicott among them. (Those names meant nothing to Jane, but Pamela found them alluring.) Charley was educated to be a civil engineer and was just getting started in his profession. Annie thought him perfect. His parents were gentle, friendly people who valued good manners; Mr. Clemens' Fredonia caper had not amused them. Annie continued to bemoan this. "They used always to ask about Uncle Sam, but since his visit here, they never mention him."

"Then your Uncle Sam's punishment has begun," Pamela said. "He had rather be beat with thongs than not mentioned."

After the banker's feelings had been appeased—not healed, for

310

that was more than they could hope for—Jane suggested that they ignore the whole thing when writing to Sam. Otherwise, Livy would find out and worry. Livy was fidgety about Sam's manners, she pointed out; Livy suffered when he was rude.

Pamela and Annie agreed. They knew, as all the intimate Clemens correspondents knew, that Livy often read Sam's letters before he could get at them; he had made her free to open his mail. She pleasured in it; and unless he acted with speed, she read his outgoing letters too and added spontaneous messages, some of them very witty.

Perhaps Sam made his own confession to Livy; for though she made no reference to the late unpleasantness, her several letters that fall conveyed a tinge of sadness. Her Christmas gift to Pamela was quite lugubrious: a handsome gold-edged edition of *Forest Scenes, Drawn by John A. Hows. Merry Christmas to Mrs. Pamela A. Moffett, 1874, Livy* the flyleaf was inscribed rather inappropriately, for one could not examine the book after a hearty Christmas dinner and stay merrily awake. Mr. Hows had illustrated with hoary vales and stark trees and wild waterfalls the most dismal poems of William Cullen Bryant, Henry Wadsworth Longfellow, Fitz-Greene Halleck, and Alfred B. Street. Beginning with *The groves were God's first temples,* it advanced through *The melancholy days are come, the saddest of the year,* to conclude with:

Tameless in his stately pride, along the lake of islands,
Tireless speeds the lonely loon upon his diving track;—

Pamela devoted herself to the poems and engravings most of Christmas Day, for she was as tireless in pursuing culture as was the loon in seeking sustenance. But Jane, after a fleeting look at the book, dropped it like a hot cake and devoted herself to altering Annie's dress for a holiday party. Annie and Charley were officially engaged; the Christmas season, to Jane, seemed to sparkle with sleigh bells and romance. There was no wealth, no art, no attainment in life, she felt, that could equal the simple wonder of love fulfilled. Only one who had experienced love unfulfilled could know that.

311

From the Fredonia *Censor,* September 29, 1875: *Married in this village, Sept. 28 at the residence of the bride's mother by the Rev. A. L. Benton, Charles L. Webster to Annie Moffett, all of Fredonia. St. Louis papers please copy. The parties started on a bridal tour to Rhode Island and to visit the bride's uncle, Mark Twain, at Hartford, Connecticut.*

After the wedding journey the young couple made practical arrangements, for Charley's income as a civil engineer would be intermittent, and he would often be traveling far from home. Soon he was due at a railroad camp to use his surveyor's compass and engineer's chain in the mud of southwestern Missouri. He had previously been employed there and knew it was not a place to take a wife.

The young Websters, with the approval of his parents and of Mark Twain and Livy, rented the charming house at 36 Central Avenue with six bedrooms, double parlors, a circular staircase, a tree-shaded lawn and a stable, and took to board the bride's mother and grandmother and brother Sammy (now fourteen and "going into Greek").

Fredonia, where almost every house had its three generations, thought it an excellent arrangement. And so it would prove to be. It would endure until Mark Twain lured Charles Webster to New York City to work for him; and even after, for Charley would commute for a year before Annie permanently joined him there.

Jane spent one of these years, almost ecstatically, in St. Louis and Keokuk. Orion had disposed of his chicken farm and resumed the practice of law in Keokuk. If clients were few, he and Mollie managed well enough. Though they had consumed, in frugal living, the thousand dollar bonus Sam had paid Orion for his notebook on which *Roughing It* was based, they now received from him a small pension which they could count on—sixty blessed dollars every month. Jane's board added to their decent security.

She might have lingered with Orion and Mollie another year—or always—except that Sam ordered her back to Fredonia. He wished to tell her good-by, he said. He and Livy and their two little girls and their German-speaking nurse and Livy's friend Miss Clara Spaulding were going to Europe to live a while. Perhaps two years, so he could write another book—write it in peace. They would sail early in April.

Right wearily Jane packed her trunk and set forth in raw March weather for Fredonia. It was one of the few times in her life she had traveled without the pleasure of a companion, and she was almost seventy-five years old. Before departing she confided to Mollie, "I've begun to resent being ordered around. I mean I'm sick'n tired of it! But I don't dare reject a good-by. There was a woman in Green County who did that, and her brother was killed by a steer in Kansas before they met again, and she went stark raving mad and lost all her hair."

Mollie said to Orion, "Does Ma mean to be funny when she talks that way?"

"We've never known," Orion answered honestly. "Sometimes we've thought her innocent. At other times we've suspected our mother is a practicing wit."

She settled again in Fredonia without complaint. She was glad to see her loved ones again, especially her grandson Sammy Moffett who was planning an economical trip to Europe and the British Isles. West Point and Annapolis, both, had rejected him because of his impaired eyesight, and now he was trying to be a self-educated journalist. He would visit the *New York Herald* reading rooms in Paris and see how the overseas journalists did their work, he said, and he would explore England on foot, like the German students.

"Try to visit the Lambton place in Durhamshire," his grandmother implored. "You might catch sight of the monster in Wear River, or anyway learn if the castle's haunted." Sammy courteously made a note of it, much as young Henry Clemens would have done: *Lambton Castle at Chester. Inquire for Worm, Ghost. Ascertain Ghost's age, sex.*

Jane tried to pick up the New Englandish life of the town where

313

she had left it, but changes were becoming harder (she saw that), and her heart was back at the Mississippi. Yet she put on a brave show for Sam Clemens when he came; and when he talked of the year in Germany he had planned for himself and his family, and the leisurely months of travel to follow, she strove to hide her consternation. The letter he wrote after his Fredonia visit showed that she had succeeded.

My Dear Mother,—I have told Livy all about Annie's beautiful house, and about Sam and Charley, and about Charley's ingenious manufactures and his strong manhood and good promise, and how glad I am that he and Annie married. And I have told her about Annie's excellent house-keeping, also about the Bacon conflict; (Sammy Moffett had championed Bacon or Shakespeare, one or the other, and the debate had rocked Chautauqua County.) . . .

And I have told her how beautiful you are in your age and how bright your mind is with its old-time brightness, and how she and the children would enjoy you. And I have told her how singularly young Pamela is looking, and what a fine large fellow Sam is, and how ill the lingering syllable "my" to his name fits his port and figure.

Well, Pamela, after thinking it over for a day or so, I came near inquiring about a state-room in our ship for Sam, to please you, but my former resolution came back to me. It is not for his good that he have friends in the ship. His conduct in the Bacon business shows that he will develop rapidly into a manly man as soon as he is cast loose from your apron strings.

You don't teach him to push ahead and do and dare things for himself, but you do just the reverse. You are assisted in your damaging work by the tyrannous ways of a village—villagers watch each other and so make cowards of each other. . . .

I find here a letter from Orion, submitting some new matter in his story for criticism. When you write him, please tell him to do the best he can and bang away. I can do nothing further in this matter, for I have but 3 days left in which to settle a deal of important business and answer a bushel and a half of letters. I am very nearly tired to death.

Affly yrs.
Sam

The stay of the Mark Twains in Europe was shortened to sixteen months, to Jane's joy, and on their return they went immediately to Elmira, their summer home, and still the home of Livy's mother.

A dutiful visit to Fredonia followed at once, and everything was harmonious. It was as if Sam Clemens had become circumspect and was determined to atone for the social disasters of five years ago. Livy "received," and Sam himself was as pleasant to the townsfolk as if he were running for office. He had brought his own beverages and his little measuring glass, as he called it, and considerately consumed his drinks in his bedroom in order not to offend callers. He was concluding a book—his publishers were waiting for its final chapters—and he would sit in the bow window of Annie Webster's back parlor to scrawl at a littered table. The neighbors could see him there, off and on, all week and were gratified. As word got around, many strollers appeared and glanced discreetly at the open sun-drenched window and its engrossed occupant. From his mother, interested persons learned the title of his labors: *A Tramp Abroad;* and they were informed that he was finding it hard going. "He can't keep his mind on his work," Jane Clemens explained, puzzled. "We've given him the most comfortable chair in the house."

But the neighbors were not puzzled. In the house with the harried scribe were young Mr. and Mrs. Webster, the hosts; Mrs. Moffett, rather nervous; Mrs. Clemens, too vital at seventy-six; Sammy Moffett, nineteen and jobless; Alice Jean Webster, aged three, an avid collector of pens, as if already plotting *Daddy-Long-Legs;* Willie Webster, aged one, a very disrupting baby; Livy Clemens, correct and delicate, accustomed to luxury; the Clemens children: Susie aged seven, Clara aged five, both precocious; their German-born nurse, much traveled and used to giving orders; Hannah, the hearty Webster servant (called "Hanner" in the Fredonia way), and such extra help as could be summoned at random. The senior Websters might also be listed, for they dropped by daily to see Charley's children.

The weather was pleasant—hot and dry—and at times the whole shebang (or so it seemed) would set out for Van Buren

Point to spend the day at the beach. Mark Twain and his wife, so the town learned, said the young Websters must build a cottage there—a shore house was almost a necessity, they said, where there were little ones—and they purchased a choice lot on the lake front and told Charley and Annie Webster to consider it their own.

To Jane, the visit was a time of unalloyed pleasure. She was especially drawn to Susie Clemens, a child as beautiful and tactful as her mother, who shared her room and often spoke dismayingly but musically in German.

Sam's bread-and-butter letter from Elmira on September 15 was addressed to his sister Pamela. Its first paragraph concerned finances: he had instructed that a draft of $175 be sent them, part to pay for the Van Buren lot, *and $25 for Ma, to repay the money I borrowed of her.*

We arrived all right, & less than an hour late. We had a perfectly delightful supper, hot & juicy, in the hotel car.

Have received a letter from Orion, proposing to send me some heterodox MS. for my judgment. I suppose he is going to try to make hell unpopular, now. . . .

We had a charming visit with you all, & achieved a higher opinion than ever of Charley, & his energy, capacity & industry. But mind I tell you, in all affection, SAM had better look out or he'll be another Orion. This may be a false alarm & I hope it is— but isn't it really time Sam was getting at something?—He has got a mighty good head—he ought by all means to go into the law with that young Woodford. They would make a success of it, sure.

I was going to write a few lines to Ma, but this is the sixteenth letter I have written since I sat down, & I am getting tired. . . .

We had a charming visit with you—Susie wants to go back & "stay forever."

> *With love to all.*
> *Sam*

Jane was glad to have the memories of this successful house party to bask in, for the news from Keokuk was all bad. Orion had been expelled from the Presbyterian church for heresy. As if

316

both shocked and exhilarated, he was flying off in a half-dozen directions. At one point he rashly pawned his furniture to secure some expensive books for research, and his mother had to send money to redeem it. He was writing a treatise on religion, which Sam, unfortunately, was encouraging. The title was *Man the Architect of Our Religion.* He had delivered the framework of the treatise in a lecture at Red Ribbon Hall in Keokuk—indeed, it was this that had caused the Presbyterian Session to examine and expel him—but now he was enlarging it ambitiously. Mollie was in great distress; her husband seemed to be attacking the very divinity that had sustained them. She had first noticed Orion's digressions three years before and had implored Jane, as his mother, to reason with him. Jane tried to do so. Looking at the crisis through Mollie's eyes, she had begged Orion to shun blasphemy, or whatever it was he was doing, and return to the fold. His reply had a certain compelling sincerity. It was a sort of Unitarianism that he advocated, apparently, setting forth his disbeliefs in the vengeful God of Moses, and thereby disavowing the Old Testament as Holy Writ. He also questioned the New Testament's claims of Christ's divine birth. Yet he wrote reverently:

Barbarism was at its end when Christ came to lead the van of a civilization founded on love and self-sacrifice for others, for which I sincerely love and adore him.

There was nothing flippant in those reflections, Jane noted. Orion, being so flexible, might sometime accept the Trinity again, she told Mollie. . . . But now Mollie's hopes for his return to orthodoxy were dashed, for Sam himself was applauding him, was egging him to more daring self-arguments by praising Ingersoll the atheist.

"Did a woman ever have two such terrible sons as I've got?" Jane asked Pamela.

"Not outside of prison," Pamela replied grimly. She was angry with Sam for likening Samuel Moffett to Orion. She knew them to be utterly different, except that both had a diversity of interests and were unemployed. "Sam often says very hard things to me. I wonder if he ever remembers that my husband launched him with a hundred-dollar loan?"

In the spring of 1881 a change entered their lives in a roundabout way. Charles Webster, dissatisfied with the engineering profession which kept him from home and family, had gone to work for the Howard Watch Company of Fredonia as a promoter. The firm thought it would be a feather in its cap if Mark Twain would buy stock, so young Webster was sent to beard the lion in his den. But the lion took him over, as Pamela revealed in a letter to Orion and Mollie:

The Howard brothers sent Charley to Hartford to try to get Sam to take stock in the watch co. He took $5000. He kept Charley there three weeks looking into some of his affairs, and finally persuaded him to come and take charge of his Kaolatype business. It is a company, but Sam owns a controlling interest. She went on to say that Charley had to give up important business at home, to do this; *it involves considerable loss. He will leave the family here and he will come home every few weeks and spend a few days.*

It was a hardship for everybody concerned, Pamela continued. She herself had been suffering from "nervous prostration," Willie had fallen down the stairs and cut a great gash in his head, Alice Jean had had an indefinable children's disease, and Annie was down with a severe cold at the time her children were at their worst. *All this in Charley's absence,* she confided to Orion and Mollie.

Aside from the maid Hannah, only Jane seemed to be upright that spring, nursing the sick and caring for the great-grandchildren as she had nursed the sick and cared for the grandchildren in St. Louis emergencies. She functioned especially well when Annie went to New York to spend a week with Charley, and her only registered complaint during that period was that she had been seen "looking a sight" by some family friends. It had been her lifelong custom, even in days of poverty, to be as clean and neat indoors as when appearing on the street. But now it was impossible to remain presentable at all times; for Willie (a difficult child, even when not suffering from head wounds) had driven off the nurse Annie had left in charge by throwing a fork at her. It left Jane with a great deal to do. Called from a menial task one morning by Willie, who had decided to wander, she was forced to accompany him, disheveled though she was, to a neighbor's yard, and was seen by the Babcocks and Haywards in "a dress that was ragged and dirty." It was like being caught undressed in a nightmare.

But a postscript she added to one of Pamela's letters that summer was blithe enough: *Orion hurry and finish the book. Osgood and Co. are printing Sams. a Boston co. Mother.*

No one could say she was not interested in her sons' literary careers, though the title of Sam's new book, *The Prince and the Pauper*, eluded her. She had heard it was on the dainty side—something Livy liked very much and even Susie listened to.

Concerning Orion's book, Jane was better informed, or thought she was. It was his autobiography, and Sam had induced him to undertake it. Often last year she had responded to Orion's request for her recollections for his book. She had begun them vigorously enough with stories of her forebears, and John Clemens', and her own happy youth. But as the sterner incidents of her past were offered up at Orion's insistence—the accidents, illnesses, and deaths of her children—she suffered intensely, and her hand shook as she wrote of them. She urged Orion to come to them at Van Buren Point where Pamela had rented a cottage, *"and we will remember together."* When Orion replied that he had no money to make the trip, she appealed to Sam by letter, including Livy in the saluation: *Dear children*

Sam I don't know that you will approve of the advice I gave Orion. Orion is at work now. I told him to give his undivided attention to his work until July or August. Then come to Van Buren. We will be there. Mela will give him a room upstairs in her cottage. We can all three sit up there and talk and he write. In that way many things will come to us that we have forgotten. . . . In my opinion his book can be made a great deal better by coming to Van Buren. Than any other way. You kindly sujested I would take a little pleasure trip to Keokuk but I think Mela ought to help Orion and me. It will cost less for Orion to come than for [us] to go. I could not go alone.

Livy, I hope you are well. and the children and Sam. Love to all. Old Mother. (She had had an attack of rheumatism in her shoulder. At such times she was apt to allude to herself as "an old citizen" or such.)

Pamela added her endorsement to Jane's letter and said, *We are all very much gratified with the high opinion you express of Orion's book. . . . Van Buren would be a good place for him to write. . . . If he is ever to unearth what is hidden away in ma's memory, the sooner it is done, the better.*

But Sam, though doubly bombarded, realistically vetoed the plan, for the situation Orion had just obtained was that of local and news editor of Keokuk's *Gate City.* What if the pay was only thirteen dollars a week? It was regular.

The biography faded away. One could not say what became of the bulky manuscript, but it was a blessing that his mother never laid eyes on it. Sam had advised him to write it in the style of the French diarists, though anonymously, and to hold back nothing. Orion, lacking deep sins to conceal, had magnified the lesser; had brought forward every wrongdoing from childhood on, had accented every emotion, laid bare every pitiful failure. When Sam showed the finished portions to William Dean Howells, that civilized man was shaken to his foundations. The *Atlantic Monthly* could not use it, he said. It was too stark, too intimate. He advised that it be retired to oblivion. Sam's interest in the effort then ceased, and he conveyed the news to Orion.

Presently Mollie notified Jane by letter that Orion was losing his mind from shock and disappointment. He was more unconsolable now, Mollie said, than when his travesty on Verne and his thesis on religion had been rejected by Sam. He was keeping to himself, silent and hurt. He seemed half crazed.

Jane became deeply involved. Among her pleas to Sam (for some reason including Livy) were these distraught ramblings:

My dear children.
I have grieved until I am sick and all the medicine will not help me. my trouble is my only two sons are not like brothers. . . . O my dear Sam I fear you have more to answer for than you think. When you banished your brother I consented but when I saw him [referring to 1877] *my heart sank it is no better*

320

now. . . . Now his mind is not right. We have been very par-
ticular not to let it be known there is anything between the broth-
ers but brotherly love. It is so mortifying to a mother. But I have
reason to think it is known here in some families. . . . My dear
Sam don't say light things about your brother it grieves your
mother. I have to stop. [She did so, to put cold cloths on her
head.] *. . . If I remember right or understood you right you*
told me about writing something to keep him from troubling you.
My dear son I never was so happy as when I could write some-
thing to make my sister happy. Now my dear son write to him and
tell him to finish his book and send it to you and you will take it
to Boston and have it published. don't send It. take it your-
self. . . . I don't say anything about his mind any where but to
Mela. I don't wish you or Livy to say any thing about it to any
one. Neither Annie nor Charley. Love to the children. . . .
When my children were small I was fretting over them, an old
uncle [Wharton Lampton] *came in, he called me Jean. Never*
mind Jean he said they are tramping on your toes now. by and by
they will be on your heart. O how true. Love to all.

Poor old mother

The discredited manuscript was not carried to Boston for
Osgood's consideration, and it is doubtful that Orion ever set pen
to it again. He knew now that what he had been creating was
not the masterpiece he had come to consider it. But he had his
mother's genius for healing his own spirit. And Sam's natural pity,
which was always just below the surface in dealing with Orion,
came to the fore. That Christmas Day—it was 1881—Jane, in a
greeting to Sam, acknowledged herself at peace.

A Happy Christmas to all. little Jean two.
Saturday morning we were starting to the stores when a letter
was handed to me. . . . It was your letter. Today Christmas I
am alone. no one in the house but one little cat. All gone to
church. No one in the kitchen. You see my hand trembles. My
dear son I have read your letter over and over. I feel better than
I did before. I excuse you. And if you have done wrong I forgive
you. But you have not.

She meant, apparently, that he had atoned, had somehow tried
to lift Orion's spirit and burdens. It was a letter she feared might

be seen by Annie and Charley who were spending Christmas with Sam and Livy and so Orion's name was mentioned only once, and then in a cryptic way. It was evident that Sam had charged her with being too sensitive about Orion, for she wrote guardedly: *If I could place you where I was for a few years your eyes would be opened.* The conclusion of the letter held no secrets: *Dear son, Mela and I am watching for that new book. We will be very thankful to receive it.* She acknowledged also the check which had come with his Christmas letter, but not effusively. She took his gifts of money as a matter of course; it was only his kindness to his brother that seemed to stir her deeply. She concluded: *I told Mela she could go and stay with Annie as long as she feels like it. I can stay with this family. I am much better now than I was but not able to travel. Livy love to you and all of the children. Mother*

Nothing now, after Sam's letter, could sadden her Yuletide. Not Christmas morning alone in an empty house; not Sammy Moffett's departure for California nor the absence of Annie and the little ones in New York, where they had gone to live; not the prospect of Pamela's going to visit them and leaving her in the care of a strange family,—for her sons had reconciled.

Pamela delayed her visit to New York until March and took Jane with her. The young Websters were living in a furnished town house at 418 West 57th Street. The visit would last several months, part of it spent at Hartford with Livy and Sam. Pamela had come to make her farewells, for she had decided to join Sammy in California and keep house for him. He had won his spurs as a journalist with an Oakland newspaper. Jane, of her own choice, was going to live with Orion and Mollie at Keokuk. She was determined not to be sidetracked, though Orion and Mollie were, themselves, trying to get to California. Orion thought San Francisco offered rare business opportunities, or perhaps journalistic chances such as Sammy Moffett had seized; Mollie thought its climate might remedy her health. Mollie was convinced she had "an internal cancer," for her doctor had told her so; though he had not, she said, speculated on her life limit.

322

Jane, in a ladylike way, hooted the idea. "Mollie was afflicted that way ten or twelve years ago," she reminded Pamela. "They consulted John Clemens in Louisville, and he said it was nothing of the sort—just female trouble. When I get to Keokuk, I can talk Mollie out of that nonsense. I once talked her out of the galloping consumption."

Jane's decision to spend her remaining days with Orion and Mollie was not due to a lack of alternative. Sam Moffett, perhaps the only youth on record to do such a thing, had urged his grand-mother to come and make her home with him. Possibly he was dismayed at the prospect of living with his overly serious, hypo-chondriac mother without his easygoing grandmother to mitigate her. Pamela Moffett's principles were noble, her reaches were all toward enlightenment, and for this her son honored her; but it was evident to him that she would wish to dictate his editorials and the spending of his income. She would consider it her privilege, for she had financed his year abroad and had advanced him money (his own father's money) to live on while he estab-lished himself on the West Coast. Young Moffett, following an elaborately whimsical plan devised by his uncle, Samuel Clemens, had worked on an Oakland newspaper without pay, concealing his connection with the great Mark Twain. But it had been Sammy's own idea to lease a little fruit ranch and work it on the side. And then, finding this to be exhausting and impractical, to locate himself at Berkeley so that he might attend classes at the University in his free hours. And now, aged twenty-one, perhaps to his Uncle Sam's astonishment, Sam Moffett was a valued writer for the *Oakland Herald,* a matriculated student at the Uni-versity of California, and an editor of the campus newspaper. Pamela's letters to him from Hartford probed all this.

My dear son: . . . I received the Berkeleyan in its new dress in N.Y. It is much improved in appearance. I liked your editorials, but I rather think the freshmen had sufficient reason for taking offense. I hope you rec'd the Draft for $200 I sent you March 8th.

We had as comfortable and pleasant a trip as possible from Fredonia to N.Y., & Charlie to relieve us of all care; but we were quite exhausted with the journey & had to take several days to rest with Annie before proceeding on our way. We reached here about noon yesterday. Ma seems bright & well today, & I am myself again. Ma's mind is so much affected by fatigue, for several days she could not remember anything. It was pitiful to see her bewilderment.

Pamela was prone to exaggerate her mother's memory lapses. Jane was coming down with a cold at this time and had been rapidly shuttled from train to train and from house to house. No doubt she had been given a sleeping potion the night of her arrival, such as the doses often administered to Livy. She might easily have wondered whose bed she was in, where had she lost her lavender shawl, and why they had ever left Fredonia. A subsequent paragraph of Pamela's attests to her mother's return to *mens sana: Ma desires me to say she rec'd your letter and the pressed flowers, & she would be delighted to be out there & help you raise flowers, or help you do anything else you are doing, but she is afraid to undertake the long journey. . . . Sam and Livy both have severe colds. I wish I could describe their beautiful home to you:—it is much improved since you saw it. You may address us here until the last of this month. I do not think it would be wise for O. & M. to go to California. I can explain some other time. Affectionately, P. A. Moffett*

Ten days later Pamela revealed that the handsome Hartford house was more of a hospital than an Eden: *March 24, 1882.*

> *My dear son:*
> *It is strange I do not hear from you. . . . We have all been sick with colds. The doctor has been coming every day for the last week, & sometimes had five or six patients at once. . . . Livy's distressing catarrh & pain in her head still continue. . . . Miss Clara Spaulding arrived yesterday from the south, where she has been travelling for some time. . . . She said she enjoyed the little visit you made her [in Europe] so much.*
> *Sam likes your editorials. Livy hasn't read them, & papers all go into the waste basket here. Livy is so overburdened with care, household cares, & the children & company, that she doesn't find time to read much of anything. She and Sam both seem to be*

324

*very fond of you but Livy says she was very much worried at the
way you wasted splendid opportunities in Europe. You did not
read and talk with Baroness, nor write the language as much as
you ought to have done. If you had done this, & in Paris had
confined yourself to French speaking people, studying the language all the while, you might have learned to speak both languages correctly, & with a pure accent. Then she was worried
about your spending your time in the Herald office, instead of
seeing Paris & its wonders. Surely it was a waste of time and
money. I had given you credit for more wisdom, else I should
have kept you at home. . . . I hope you will give time enough
to your essay & thesis to make them creditable productions. . . .
Will I have any use for thick dresses in California?*

*Lovingly
P. A. Moffett*

Pamela's letter of April 6 was equally full of admonitions;
Sammy must not buy them a house with a half story, she instructed:

*Half story rooms are unhealthy & uncomfortable. Don't forget
this. Make a note of it & treasure it up in your memory. . . . I
hope you will have a home in a beautiful spot, where pleasant
scenery will be always grateful to the eye & heart. I think in such
a place I would not be lonely. Yet I cannot bear the idea of living
on a fruit ranch where the fruit is a show;—beautiful to look at,
but tasteless. . . . Your grandma asks me to tell you that she
wishes she could go to Cal. but she can't:—it is impossible. She
wishes you would come east & get editorial work to do in some
city.*

*You accuse the "preps" in the gymnasium of being conceited.
I hope you will never be conceited yourself:—it makes anybody
very disagreeable. Livy dislikes it very much in Charley.*

*They all here consider the anti-Chinese bill very disgraceful to
the country & are glad the president vetoed it. . . . Lovingly,
P.A.M.*

It was a relief to Jane when she and Pamela packed their trunks
to depart. Poor Livy had become a little waspish, she noticed,
criticizing Pamela's son and son-in-law to her face. And Pamela
was waxing politically contentious. Mela wanted the Chinese im-

migrants admitted, but she insisted they be scattered throughout the United States. Some even in Connecticut! This was more than Livy and other Hartfordites had bargained for. Often Sam too would get into the arguments, walking the floor and tearing his hair when Pamela had goaded him too far. At such times Jane fled to her room and kept there. Why were all her children so taken up with setting the world aright, she wondered innocently, taking none of the blame. That their abstract theories had been kindled by her concrete humanity did not occur to her.

After an Easter spent with the young Websters in New York City, Pamela and Jane went to a water cure for several weeks, a spa in the Catskills recommended by Miss Clara Spaulding. The place made little impression on Jane except for the exquisite greens of springtime in a lush mountain valley, and some pleasant peripatetics she encountered exercising their pets. At the first of June they returned to the bustle of West 57th Street, and to the problems of the young family residing there. Often above the rumble of traffic from without and the noise of children confined within, young Mr. Webster, outraged, could be heard reading to his wife such a letter as this from her uncle: *"'Dear Charley—Yes, I received & banked both of those checks—and then forgot it. Damn that Bliss statement. I forgot to return it to you—I wish you had sent me a copy. I have left the blamed thing in my portfolio of business letters under the table of the billiard room at home.'*—And yet I'm supposed to investigate Bliss's sales of his books, Annie!" said the harassed Charley. "He suspects Bliss!"

On Jane's birthday a four-generations picture was made of the distaff line: Jane, Pamela, Annie, and little Jean Webster. Jane was wearing a handsome arrangement of lavender flowers and ribbon on her head. She was smiling vacantly, as at a command from the photographer. Another picture of her, taken alone at the same appointment, showed her looking rather cross. It revealed that a button was missing from her basque and that her brooch was pinned on sideways. As it held a miniature of Orion's face, it laid him on his ear. She said she didn't care; she was worn out with New York—the poor dogs on leashes and the horses so overloaded.

326

They presently returned to Fredonia in a private railway car supplied by Sam Clemens. Annie and the children accompanied them to escape the heat of New York. Besides, Annie must relinquish the house at 36 Central Avenue and arrange for the shipment of the furniture to New York; Charley could not be spared to do it. But Orion and Mollie would soon be coming from Keokuk at Sam's expense to help Pamela wind up her affairs and to take Jane home with them. Every one was satisfied.

As Jane packed her trunks, entirely without system (John Clemens had lived in vain in that respect), she often sang contentedly at her task, eager to be off and away. She had nothing against Fredonia, and there were some valued friends here she would regret to leave. But she had never shared Pamela's sense of belonging, nor did she have Pamela's expectation of returning when Sammy should have taken a wife. Indeed, Fredonia had irked her after her year's vacation away from it, and she had combed it restlessly for benign aberrations.

Recently she had made a little drama for herself by putting away her beautiful cordial glasses and pinning on a white ribbon. That occurred after two drunken drivers on the road to Dunkirk, racing with each other, had crowded Pamela's buggy off the road. But as no harm ensued, she was as delighted with Mela's prowess in meeting the situation as she was indignant with the drunkards. Mela's little grandchildren had been with her, but she had protected them and controlled her frightened horse, "sawing on the reins till her arms were sore." Perhaps it was the first time she had ever welcomed home a spectacular Pamela.

Jane said to one and all that she was moving back home, which was hardly accurate, for Keokuk had seen little of her. But at least it was her regional home. She was grateful to be returning to the river she loved, to her old associations, to the stability of Orion's comparative poverty where a silver dollar looked as big as a cart wheel.

Annie was somewhat frightened at leaving Fredonia, for Charley's life in New York had already become hectic. He was now the fascinated factotum of her dynamic and irascible uncle.

She talked it over with Pamela, who exclaimed, and with Jane who kept still. She complained that though Uncle Sam had put Charley in charge of the Kaolatype Engraving Company and would name him head of the Webster Publishing Company, being formed to publish Mark Twain, he dictated Charley's every move. And he was already asking him to sell stock in something called the Paige typesetting machine which Charley had never heard of till recently. He was asking Charley to line up evidence for his lawsuits, to go to Hartford and oversee the remodeling of his house, and even to pick up and price things, "like traveling clocks at Tiffany's for Aunt Livy," Annie said, "and fire fenders for Mrs. Langdon at out-of-the-way places. Charley's expected to attend to Aunt Livy's ivory glove stretcher that's being mended at Hillaire's, mind you, while he sets up a Kao agency in Boston!"

"It's too bad the colored race was freed," Pamela said sarcastically. "Sam's always wanted a slave. Ever since we lost Sandy he's craved a faithful slave. He employs a gardener and a coachman and a butler and a cook, I noticed when I was there. Then there're a couple of laundresses and the German-speaking nurse, not to mention a wet nurse for baby Jean. His servants have servants. But none's quite the worshiper of him that Sandy was. He's got Dan Slote distributing his patent scrapbook, and a German mechanic inventing away at the engraving thing. Then there's Mr. Perkins who always sends the checks to Keokuk. Have I left out anybody, Annie?"

"Yes, Mother. The literary agent in London he doesn't trust."

"Now, now," Jane said. "Remember how generous Sam is. Everybody gets well paid. *Especially* Charley, let me remind you both!"

"We won't deny that," Pamela answered. "Just the same I'm thankful Sammy doesn't work for him."

"Well, if we're through berating Sam Clemens," Jane suggested, "let's get one of the bedrooms ready for Orion and Mollie."

Mr. and Mrs. Orion Clemens arrived in good spirits, proud of the opportunity to assist in this upheaval. Orion, under Mark Twain's often conflicting instructions, disposed of Pamela's business affairs with the genial dignity that was natural to him. Mollie was as efficient at packing as a quartermaster's sergeant, and at the first of September the four of them headed westward. Sam had advised that they make the journey partly by lake steamer, partly by train, for the sake of variety, but this was found to be impracticable because of the baggage—an important consideration when women are changing homes. Orion took it upon himself to route them by railroad all the way, and Jane's first message after their arrival in Keokuk assured Sam and Livy:

Our trunks came with us. . . . The cars we came in were very good, we could lie down or sit up as we felt like doing. I don't know how we would have got along without Orion and Mollie to help us.

They were quartered at Keokuk's best hotel, the Patterson House, at Sam's expense and would be there for several weeks, or as long as Pamela remained with them. Pamela was to start West from St. Louis after a stop in Hannibal. Jane would have asked to accompany her on those visits except that she was too tired. That was strange, she told Mollie; she would not be eighty years old till next June, at which time a person might be expected to let down a little.

Mollie's sharp eyes grew gentle. "Has it ever occurred to you, Ma," she asked, "that you've led a mighty hard life? It's not as if you'd sat on a satin pillow and never known trouble."

Orion rented a comfortable brick house—larger than the one he and Mollie had been occupying—with two downstairs bedrooms, and they moved in. Sam had provided for fixing up the house, as Mollie explained to everyone, and for hiring a girl. No pains were spared in making Jane's bedroom bright and comfortable.

A very alluring little cat was procured for her by Orion, and she expressed delight.

"It was no trouble at all, Ma," Orion assured her truthfully. He had been offered at least a dozen. She must have known that, but she praised him as highly for getting her the little pearl-gray cat with the white stomach as she had ever praised Sam for one of his books. Yet neither son would have called her partial. Toward Henry she had leaned a little, of course; but as between themselves, the scales balanced.

To Pamela in California went a listing of her blessings, especially the stove and lamp which kept her room cozy as winter came on:

I have a delightful stove. It is a base burner nickle plated all around. I will not describe it. . . . I have a small copper kittle that sits on the back of the stove [and holds] warm water all the time. Orion and Mollie have only to cross a narrow hall to get to the kettle of hot water. I have a swinging lamp that swings from the ceiling. I can pull it down and push it up. Rosa or Orion lights the lamp every night. Orion turns it low and pushes it up at bedtime.

As there were three unused rooms upstairs—all adequately furnished, thanks to Sam's conscience—Mollie immediately turned them to practical use. The two front rooms became the parlor and bedroom of a young couple from Illinois named Higby. The husband was a railway inspector of some sort. He did not wear a uniform but, as Jane reported to Mela and Sam Moffett: *he runs on the cars to St. Louis.* The rear bedroom was presently let to George Marshall, the science and Latin professor at the high school. He too was young, and remarkably keen besides. Jane thought it delightful to have these noisy young lodgers in the house. They all three took their meals at the Widow Daniels' select boardinghouse across the street.

Now and then the Clemenses too indulged in that luxury, Jane standing treat; she still enjoyed variety and gaiety when dining, and she found it at Mrs. Daniels'. Pamela was told: *Six young men and some ladies and children board there. . . . The widows daughters wait on the table sometimes at dinner and have on figured swiss dresses with pink ribbons at their necks and there is perfect politeness all round.*

Orion cheerfully looked after his lodgers, thankful for the additional income they brought him. For though somewhere along the line Sam had raised his pension to seventy-five dollars a month, and his mother paid twenty-five for board, and he had his small salary with the newspaper, it was not always easy for him to make ends meet. The long Iowa winters called for a great deal of kerosene for the lamps and coal for the coalbin; and Ma's base-burner

330

must be supplied with Pennsylvania hard coal to make the coals shine cozily through the isinglass. Then he must manage to secure decent clothes for himself and Mollie after the butcher and grocer and druggist were paid. Anxious to keep his roomers, he arose before dawn each morning to build a fire in the sitting room of the young Higbys, and in the littered bedroom of the young science teacher who kept spiders and worms in alcohol and stacked botany specimens on his bureau.

After that he made the downstairs fires, put the oatmeal to cook, waked Mollie, and dressed for his editorial job at the *Gate City*. No doubt he was neglecting the latter work somewhat, for he had an exciting new project. It had to do with an electric light plant for the city and he was promoting the stock. Too often, perhaps, he would leave his *Gate City* desk—(yes, he would soon be with WM. REES & Co., Printers and Paper Dealers, Sole Agents in Iowa for Hopkins Patent Roll)—and hurry to his small law office to meet a prospect. Ever hopeful of finding gilt-edged securities for Sam, he had written him about this rare opportunity to invest, but, so far, Sam had not responded. The town smiled at his oddities but respected his unfulfilled abilities. They knew, somehow, that Orion Clemens had "just missed it." His kindness, they took for granted, for they had known it so long. He was the man who would give a deprived boy his last dime to buy a top; who would walk through the sleet to fetch dry wheat for the birds.

32 ❖

It was Christmas again. The Congregational church had held its bazaar and oyster supper and Yule programs, Mollie and Orion taking part, for they had been welcomed to that broad-minded fellowship after Orion's expulsion by the Presbyterians. Snow covered southern Iowa, and wheeled vehicles had given way to runners. At the Clemens home, cedar and mistletoe had been hung. "Don't fret for Kentucky holly, Ma," Mollie scolded. "Don't you remember it won't grow here?" But the little cat wore a sleigh bell on a red ribbon.

Gifts had been exchanged with Sam's family. Orion and Mollie had shipped to Hartford their usual proud gift, a great bag of choice hickory nuts from the Illinois shore. Jane had sent Livy a tea cozy from the bazaar, and each child a pretty pair of knitted stockings with occasional dropped stitches. Hartford was just as aware of the Season. Livy had sent westward a box of charming and carefully chosen little gifts (the era of impressive gifts is not yet) which cost a great deal more than the innocent recipients suspected. Sam had mailed checks with affectionate greetings. He was too rushed to shop for presents, being almost beside himself with trying to finish *Life on the Mississippi* which he said had great gaps in it. Jane thought she knew why. It was not a book to be funny about.

After Christmas the days did not drag. There were socials and musicals, "at homes" and "readings" and spend-the-days. Jane had callers in profusion; if Mollie was helping Orion at his office, and the part-time servant was out, the front door would be left unlocked so that they might enter and find the still dressy octogenarian at her letterwriting or her knitting—two pursuits she kept at, though her sight was dimmer than she would admit to outsiders.

Her most urgent letter in the new year of 1883 was written on February 6, and it was to Sammy Moffett who had now established his mother and himself in a house he had bought near the university campus, a place with garden and orchard and vineyard. They would have their own strawberries very early, so Pamela had written; other fruits in season, and grapes galore. All she needed was a strong female servant to make her life complete, possibly an Oriental. But Jane disregarded the wonders of California to call Sammy to task for something she considered a grave error. It concerned the two work horses he had left at the Oakland ranch. She did it as tactfully as she could, for she knew her grandson had had more than his share of criticism:

Mela and Sam we received your welcome letters. . . . Sam you are good at management. But I am afraid you missed it, hiring your horses out. If they are scrub horses they can be worked down and not fed well. Don't think these men will take the care of them

332

you do. Poor horses. Across half a continent went her concern for a pair of drudging horses she had never seen, and she was obliged to speak out.

Pamela's stop in St. Louis had alerted their friends and relatives to Jane's return to the Valley. All wrote letters, welcoming her back. If there was a slight reserve in their messages, it was neither their fault nor hers; it was because Sam Clemens had become Mark Twain. They had followed his career from the beginning; they doted on his books. It was whispered that he hated St. Louis, but they tried to understand; they said it was because of his sorrow there when Henry died.

There came to Jane and Mollie in the new year a package letter from Katie Lampton, carrying Ella's picture. Katie said her mother could not get around now, could hardly leave her chair because of a crippling gout, but she sent her love to all. The letter was cheerful—touchingly so, for it came from a twenty-seven-year-old woman whose life had been blighted by an erring mother. Since James Andrew's death, Jane and Mollie knew, Ella and Katie had lived in boardinghouses; but as to Dr. McDowell's whereabouts, they could only wonder.

Jane and Mollie studied Ella's picture. "She is the fleshiest woman I ever saw!" Jane declared. "Yes, I never saw a larger woman than Ella Lampton has turned out to be."

"But well-preserved," Mollie said grudgingly. "She's nearly sixty. Someone told me her age and I had Orion write it in our family records. But when we were living in St. Louis, Ella got hold of my Bible and altered it. She changed 1824 to 1834 when I was out of the room one day."

"That's quite a reduction," Jane said, though mildly; she considered a woman's age her own business. They examined the photograph yet again. In spite of the fleshy neck and massive bosom, some of the former Ella remained intact. Her humorous wide mouth, her bold gray eyes, her glossy hair (dressed discreetly), and the complexion that still seemed free of wrinkles. They were glad she had become enormous and gotten the gout. "She can hardly snare another man now," Mollie commented.

Katie's letters continued to come. They were carefully written, free of errors. Orion and Mollie commented on their beautiful pen-manship and recalled that she was said to be an excellent secretary. No doubt her abilities exceeded her salary, for she was a mere woman, and unaggressive at that. Toward the end of April she wrote gratefully:

Cousin Sam is going to have Annie's husband send me a type-writer if I think I can master it. I believe I can. It will enable me to earn more, for there are very few type-writers in St. Louis. I am between situations now and will have time to practice. She concluded by declaring: *How I should like to see you again, Aunt Jane.*

"Poor little Katie," Jane said. "I think she wants to come and visit us, Mollie. How would you feel about it?"

"I'd be willing. I recall how she and Jennie used to play together. Never a quarrel. Do you realize, Ma, our Jennie would be a grown-up woman like Katie? Our little Jennie that was only eight when she died?"

"Don't, Mollie," Jane warned. "Don't tear yourself to pieces."

"Is there a way not to?" Mollie asked.

"There's this way. Do things for Katie for Jennie's sake. Write and invite her to come here toward the end of May. We'll give her a June party. I'll ask Sam for the money. I'll tell him it's important. It is."

Sam was finally concluding *The Adventures of Huckleberry Finn* when the request came, making great strides because of his pleasure in the absurdly relaxed comedy that followed its serious satire. He told his mother he was finding it as easy to write now as to lie. He sent a sizable check and said go to it.

When the event drew near, Jane wrote Sam and Livy of their plans, marred only by the illness of her cousin Robert Creel. It was possible his death might cause the postponement of the party, but not its cancellation. *Dear children. Katie is here. We are prepared to give her a party to introduce her to the young ladies and gentlemen. I requested Orion to send a carriage for us to deliver the invitations, according to the customs of this city. Katie and I sat still, Mollie went in and gave the invitations to about 16 or 17 ladies. Then, as the custom is here, Orion takes the list to* [that

334

many] *gentlemen, they select their ladies, so the ladies all know how they will get home. Mollie thinks she could fix three rooms to dance in. Mollie thought the ladies seemed pleased to come and meet Miss Lampton, and almost all promised to come.* (Orion's pen had added punctuation to the letter; there was this and other evidence that the party interested him greatly.)

The aged Mr. Creel delayed his passing, and Katie's party went off well. Her Lampton red hair was beautifully arranged by the town's best hairdresser, summoned by Jane; her dress was one of her mother's finest from better days, cut down; her manners were her customary ones, very gentle. Professor Marshall was attentive.

Jane seemed tired the following day, though in a satisfied way. She confessed she had not slept all night after the lights went out, thinking about one thing and another. "It occurred to me how nice it would be," she said to Orion and Mollie, "if Professor Marshall and Katie would fall in love." That seemed sensible enough to them, but her next observation caused them to look at each other in wonder, for she was only eighty years old, and alert. "I thought James Andrew looked very handsome last night when he danced with his daughter. And Patsy never looked lovelier. But I was surprised to see Andy Russell."

It was the first of her noticeable departures from the normal. They let it pass. Every so often it happened again: she would claim to have communicated with persons who had gone on. "They are trying to get through to me," she would say, using a term the professional spirit-summoners used, though she had tried the cult and found it wanting long ago in Hannibal. The Valley had been rife with séances in those days and she had occasionally attended one. But when a medium who had dirty fingernails and smelled of stale coffee claimed to have called up Benjamin Lampton, his disillusioned daughter announced on returning home, "I'm through with the whole business. My father wouldn't have given that woman more than a polite howdy-do if she'd cornered him."

Yet she felt, incurably, that a longing heart and a receptive mind could be her own key to the spirit world; and she was rewarded with a unique happiness: from the time of her sister's death, after the first shock had passed, she sometimes felt her pres-

335

ence, unsummoned and unannounced; she was the Patsy of Quarles farm. When Jane Clemens would now and then say through the years, "My sister often seems near me," a thoughtful listener might detect more than a platitude. Yet she tactfully discouraged probings into the gossamer situation.

Now that she had become elderly, the Patsy who came to her was a young person. It was Patsy Lampton, not Patsy Quarles encumbered with flesh and children and hysterical slaves. Jane talked this over with Orion and Mollie, for she had not lost her hold on reality. She wanted to reconcile the actual with the improbable. Orion looked at her sadly and urged her to rest more. They increased her servings at mealtime. Mollie, ever practical, advised her not to refer to her occult experiences, either in conversation or in writing. "Do watch yourself, Ma," she said. "People will think you're senile. You'll lose friends."

Jane did watch herself and certainly nothing could have been more earthy than a July letter she sent to Hartford—a letter whose envelope Sam designated: *Hens and ducks*. In it, she wooed them all, offering such bits of news as her condition afforded. Though she had once been described as "magnificently illiterate when holding a pen," her instincts now, as always, were those of a good dinner partner determined to entertain.

To the children. About the pictures. Where Jean is by herself she is the best looking one of all. It was a family witticism that Jean, or Jane Lampton as she had been named, when at her best resembled her grandmother; when stormy, her father. *Livy your hair is dressed so plain. I would not know you anywhere else* [but for] *the three children with you. . . . Sam you have got trash in your pocket. . . . I thank you all over and over* [for the pictures].

Now I must tell the children what I saw in the Park. A hen came down the hill with 8 or 10 little young ducks, they were covered with down but not a feather on their wings. The little ones ran before their mother & flew into the lake. The poor hen we all felt so sorry to see how she was distressed. She would call them they would swim up to her she would start up the hill calling

336

them & away they would swim in the lake like spoiled children
tantalising their mother.

I thank you all again for the pictures. All think them beautiful.
Now a reference to Charley and Annie Webster's new baby, Samuel Charles Webster, lately arrived in New York City: *Charlie*
will have to be watched he is so proud of that son. If the son
gives C. half as much trouble as he gave his father He will have
something. And that is all right. Livy there is one of our first
ladies here, if she sees or smells spirits of any kind she is almost
frantic. her husband sends her to some place to be cured but she
comes home not much better. She has grown daughters that keep
house. A son married last winter. Livy do you like the abominable
[new] *fashions. While I am writing a carriage drives up to my*
neighbors gate in front of my window. our wealthy people. The
young lady walked out to the gate dressed in white muslin or lawn
the dress sewed to the yoke hung loose down. In my young days
she could not have made that appearance. But so is the fashion.
I keep drinking the hot [mineral] *water. I find it very good for*
me. Orion and Mollie are as well as usual. Love to all. Ma &
Grand Ma.

But when winter came on, the mood changed. Some nostalgia
related to falling snow could not be suppressed. In southern Kentucky the great flakes, barely crystallized, had fallen so softly on
young people wild with pleasure. She must try not to let those
memories make her critical of the sharp and driving snows of
Iowa. Yet in a late November letter to Sam and Livy she broke off,
mid-page, to make some strange observations. She had been reporting lucidly her activities of the day before—a visit to the
Patterson House with Mollie:

Snow and cold keep me in doors. We were invited to spend the
day yesterday at Col Pattersons. He was an active business man
but now he only can walk with two crutches & the help of a
negro man to get him started. When the young people are about
he enjoys their fun. . . . I suppose the Hotel is doing a good
business. I see plenty of snow every where I look. I have to stop.
I find myself trying to think of something to be interesting to
write to my sister. That is strange. My sister had been dead many

337

years. That is strange to believe. As many others, her spirit is round me. O if I could see her spirit what Joy & comfort it would be to me. But to feel that her spirit is here, that is Joy I cannot [sic] *can not express.*

Jane Clemens.

Sam scrawled on the envelope containing this communication: *A pathetic letter.* But being who he was and what he was, he must have detected the simple triumph it conveyed, and coveted it.

Livy, whose own mother was aging in a more conventional way —via pain, luxury and apprehensions of reduced income—often failed to read her mother-in-law's letters. But sometimes Sam would direct her attention to one that contained an excerpt he especially wished her to see. As the one that carried this paragraph: *Sam in looking over your last letter this morning I see you are offering me more than any mother could expect. I feel it is as free from Livy as from yourself. Orion is just as kind as a son can be to his mother. Mollie comes in for her part as good two.*

Mark Twain, not realizing he was notating it for posterity, wrote on the envelope: *From Ma—read it, Livy.*

Mollie's fears of an incurable disease had been dislodged from her mind by Jane's persuasions; and her pains were allayed by Jane's advice to elevate the feet when resting, and by judicious doses of blackberry cordial, recommended by the same authority. She went about her duties now without the dread of approaching death, and she entered into Keokuk's simple social life with her former verve. A party which she sponsored was described by Jane in a letter to Sam's children.

Susie, Clara and Jean. I attended a funnie party last night. At Dr Cleavers. Called sheet and pillow case party. I had the curiosity to see what that meant. Two young ladies came across the street for Mollie to fix a mask on one of them. prof Marshall & Orion were trying to fix a sheet on Marshall in his room. I enjoyed the fun. I drove off all bad feeling and went to the party. The innocent goings-on afforded her great pleasure, for the actors all bowed to her before forming a figure and circling the room. As she sat with a friend of Mollie's whom she called Ret, she thought

338

some of the masked figures seemed amusingly grotesque: *I said to Ret,* continued her letter to her grandchildren, *that woman, pointing to the woman before us her bussle is two large & she looks two loose. I kept on with* [such] *remarks until Ret said that is a man. she put the gown to one side & there was the great boots.*

Orion and Mollie had been permitting Professor Marshall to hold debating sessions in their parlor and to produce comedies staged by his pupils. Those affairs had made many an evening enjoyable for Jane, and it whetted her appetite to see Sam and his children put on their plays and charades in his great hall at Hartford. Several times she had hinted for an invitation to visit them; and she concluded the mask affair letter with her first out-and-out, bold bid: *Sam and Livy I can be ready to go to your house any time you think it suits you. Let me know what suits you both. My breakfast is on the stand waiting.*

Though she was so eager to promote the idea that she allowed her eggs and coffee to cool, the invitation from Hartford was not forthcoming. Livy was too delicate and too encumbered to cope with the willing guest. Sam conveyed this message right tactfully by way of Mollie.

As 1884 neared its close a great excitement pervaded the house at Keokuk. They read in the newspapers that Mark Twain and a fellow writer, the popular George W. Cable of New Orleans, had begun a joint platform engagement that would last four months and bring them as far west as St. Louis. Each man would give readings from his own works. Their agent was J. B. Pond, a capable lyceum circuit manager.

To be in ignorance of Sam's schedule was intolerable to Jane and Orion and Mollie. They must, to use an old horse term, un-bear, or loosen the checkrein on their emotions. Orion pursued Sam with a flock of telegrams, beseeching information. Sam replied by a letter from Boston on November 15.

My Dear Bro—
Don't send telegrams to me—it wastes your money. I placed the matter in my agent's hands two days ago; & there I leave all such things. We have but 2 dates open in January—that is, we had

2 open; but it is quite possible that the N.Y. agency has filled them before this. We have no engagements on the river except St. Louis—not a single hall or theatre to be had, upon a convenient date, in any town from St. Louis to St. Paul.

Yrs
Sam

Not a word of hope for their yearnings, not even an invitation to come to St. Louis. But they would go down to St. Louis anyway, Orion decided, if Ma would produce the railway fare.

Oh she would, she said! A thousand times yes. They could stay with friends or relatives—that much would be cost-free. Mollie wailed that she could not wear her three-year-old hat to St. Louis, it was so out-of-date; and Jane said Mollie must have a new hat—some fur-topped galoshes like Livy's, too. They began a frantic search for St. Louis addresses which Jane had had and misplaced; particularly Cousin James Lampton's and Mrs. George Schroeter's. With the latter person, the wife of Will Moffett's business partner, Pamela had kept a close friendship through the years.

While this was going on there came a letter from Sam written on December 26 at Hartford where he was spending Christmas with his family. It contradicted his other letter very nimbly without actually saying so. It implied that of course they must have known he would have readings along the upper Mississippi.

"How could we have thought otherwise!" Mollie exclaimed sarcastically. "Where on earth would we have got such notions?"

Said Sam's letter which Orion read aloud:

"My Dear Bro—

"I am just starting off again. I ought to have answered you long ago, but am driven to death. We read in Hannibal the day before we read in Keokuk, & in Chicago the day after we are in Keokuk. Of course I shall strike for Keokuk by the first train from Hannibal; & after all shall get but little time with you, considering how far away Chicago is. I do not arrange my route myself, or I would have tried to get more time in Keokuk. I do not allow Mr. Pond to make suggestions about my end of the show, & so I do not allow myself to make suggestions about his end of it. These things cannot be mixed together & keep peace in the family.

340

"We are all well—everybody—& all send love to you all & the heartiest Xmas greetings.

"Affly Yr Bro
"Sam

"P.S. I am rushing, to clear off my letters today & leave a clear desk behind me. Livy has just sent up your letters. . . ."

Orion put on his hat and rushed downtown where he learned that Mark Twain's agent had just wired negotiations for Keokuk's Opera House for January 14. Orion was able to say to the manager, "I'm just inquiring for the details, sir. Of course I had the news of this Keokuk engagement direct from my brother himself."

It was a narrow squeak for his pride. Perhaps it was such deliverances as this in his harried life that convinced Orion there was, after all, a personal God who would meet him halfway. For he was resuming a simple faith in religion, try as he might to salute Mr. Ingersoll.

The Keokuk stand was a success. Almost everybody who could afford the admittance price attended. Jane delayed going to her seat until the house was well filled, still using the formula she had taught Patsy when they were girls: Always make a late entrance. As she went down the aisle on an usher's arm there were half-audible references to her erect carriage and beribboned evening cap. She would have preferred that this scene were being enacted in St. Louis with Barrets and wealthy Clemenses present, but such inordinate desires were presently driven from her mind by a simple pride in her remarkable son who could make all manner of people laugh and forget their cares. She knew that he was taking the same artistic pains here as he took for his audiences in New York and London. Her heart overflowed with love for him. She had not had such a good cry in years.

Cable and Pond retired to a hotel after the performance, but Sam held a handshaking session in the foyer. At Orion's, later, some kin and friends came to have coffee and cake with the celebrity. A boy in his teens, one of Professor Marshall's students, had brought his harmonica and he innocently began to play it, wishing to do his part. Jane Clemens lifted her skirts ankle-high and began to dance in a cleared place, stepping off a minuet and

341

then a waltz in time to the boy's music. She was flushed of face, happy, and erect. She was also aware that she was misbehaving. Sam and Orion were charmed. Mollie was not charmed but she was tolerant. "That's Ma for you," she said resignedly to one of her cousins.

Early next morning Cable and Pond boarded a train for Burlington to prepare for an engagement there that evening. Sam remained at Orion's, planning to follow on the afternoon train. It was an exhausting interval for Jane and Orion and Mollie, for Sam talked volcanically. He told of the elaborate theatrical production his family had put on for him at Christmas, Livy having dramatized *The Prince and the Pauper* for their own children and the neighbors' to play, and Karl Gerhardt, his sculptor protégé, having staged it. He told of his readings in St. Louis, and of the visit to him in his hotel suite of Cousin James Lampton, now whiteheaded and infirm, but still gallant in adversity (he had gracefully accepted some complimentary tickets) and still fantastically optimistic. Sam talked of his Historical Game which he had copyrighted but never marketed; of the Mark Twain Scrapbook, which was going very well; of his book sales, good and lagging; of a patented bed-clamp to hold the covers on a restless infant. He said it would sell for three dollars and a half in its de luxe form.

Jane was scandalized. "Three dollars and a half, Sam? That would feed a little child for weeks! Can't a woman keep her own child covered?"

All this talk reminded Sam that he had not prodded his young business manager lately, so they cleared a table for him and brought him the writing equipment he requested. In a routine way he cursed the pen and then fell to. Charles L. Webster in New York was presently to receive a stern letter about his shortcomings.

Keokuk, Jan. 15/85

Dear Charley:

Your letter is very blind. Bed-clamp man's "estimate of expense" is $1200 for year exclusive of advertising; "a salary" for him of "$1000 & expenses." Now who can guess what you mean

342

by that. Do you mean that the first year will cost $2200 & a double bill of "Expenses" added? Try again. . . .

Pond? I will fill no engagement after Feb. 28. I have said it already some 500,000 times.

You want to make a list like this, & stick it on the wall where you can see it when you go to bed & when you get up:

> *For weekly report: Concerning—*
> *Historical Game*
> *Perpetual Calendar*
> *Osgood's Quarterly Statement*
> *Am. Pub. Co.   "   "*
> *Slote & Co.—   "*
> *Bed-clamp man.*
> *Am. Exchange in Europe.*

Truly yours
S L Clemens

The afternoon train going north was late. Orion and Jane and Mollie kept vigil with him in the Keokuk depot while he awaited it. It gave him an opportunity to repeat to Mollie all of his instructions for her house-to-house canvass in the sale of *Huck Finn,* she having assumed the Keokuk agency, as she had done for *A Tramp Abroad* several years ago.

Woe betide! The train to Burlington continued to lose time, even with Mark Twain aboard and remonstrating with the crew. Cable had to lengthen his readings that night while the audience fretted for Twain. The family heard about this, straight from headquarters:

Chicago, Friday

My Dear Bro—

I wish to thank you heartily for a most pleasant sojourn in Keokuk—& of course I also thank Ma & Mollie—that goes without saying. I had a perfect 24 hours there, with the sort of social activity which produces rest instead of fatigue.

I don't like to think of the Burlington performance. Cable had been on the platform more than an hour & a half when I arrived; & so I did not dare to try to make the house listen an hour to me. I had to cut myself shorter than I wanted to, & I did not talk

343

well, anyway, because I felt myself so heavily handicapped by the hellish circumstances.

With great love to all of you

Sam

"What hellish circumstances?" Mollie asked Orion. "Oh, yes! The circumstances of his laying-over a day with his family."

"S-sh!" Jane warned. "Let's not pay any attention to Sam." She saw that Orion seemed worn out; spare him resentment.

33 ❖

Jane took a lively interest in the Mark Twain Historical Game when she and Orion and Mollie and their friends played it, though her remarks provided more laughter than solutions. Sam had sent them some English histories in connection with it; these, Orion often read aloud on Sunday afternoons. Jane found the beheadings to be absorbing, not worrying over the political implications. She thought it strange that Lady Jane Grey did not want to be prayed for after death; thought it a theological error, and a bleak one, on Lady Jane's part. But then, Lady Jane was a Presbyterian.

Jane herself, in spite of her belief in God's over-all planning, prayed for her dead. Something in her father's old prayer book had authorized it: *Remember thy servant, O Lord, according to the favour which thou bearest unto thy people, and grant that, increasing in knowledge and love of thee, he may go from strength to strength, in the life of perfect service in thy heavenly kingdom.* She recognized good and evil, personifying the latter as Milton's Satan, rather alluring, but her stands on Justification and the Atonement were shaky, God's justice being consumed in His mercy. She was unfitted for the Calvinistic niche in which Mark Twain so relentlessly placed her. One sees him dutifully trying to whitewash her to a semblance of that serene Presbyterian church-goer, his Mother Fairbanks; but surely he must have known that after Jane's Hannibal days, just as before her Hannibal days (little Benjamin's death, her turning point), she had been a religious vagrant. Pamela would have told him.

344

And now in Keokuk, for all her gratitude to the Congregational-ists who had befriended Orion, she avoided attending their services with every excuse at her command. Having, through circum-stances, been denied a ritualism which might have defined religion for her emotionally—even the glorious colors of the Church Sea-sons were lacking to her—she found boredom instead. Inadvert-ently she made a joke at the expense of Mollie's and Orion's well-meaning pastor. On being asked one Sunday afternoon, "Why are you so dressed up, Mrs. Clemens?" she replied, "Oh, I've been *somewhere* today. To church, I think."

Keokuk's synagogue, the Congregation of B'Nai Israel, had an outstanding men's chorus, and Jane had not overlooked the matter. Not long after Sam's visit to Keokuk, though her rheumatism was again assailing her beyond the help of her electric battery and applications of Colfax mineral water, she "dressed up and went to hear the Jews sing." Mrs. Isaac Stern, a friend and near neighbor, escorted her there. It was Mollie's contention that "Ma's Jewish friends spoil her."

On the eve of her eighty-second birthday Orion and Mollie held a reception for her, and the ordeal of conversing with a house full of guests temporarily unsettled her. To receive one's guests gra-ciously was a responsibility too deeply ingrained to be taken lightly; right gladly would she have foregone the party except that Mollie and Orion set such store by it. How else could they have afforded to entertain? Jane's letter to Sam and Livy revealed this.

June 18, 1885

Dear children.
Sam you said you would send me money to do something with for the poor. Orion and Mollie wanted to give me a birth [sic] day party. I thought that was a good way to use that extra money you sent for the poor. Orion was to hold the money & keep accounts. Mollie was to have what she caled for. Help and everything. Well the table was full and beautiful. And every one ladies & gentle-men did full justice to the eatables. And expressed themselves well pleased. I never saw so many beautiful flowers before. My room this morning is full. It is raining. I cant go out. My mind is not

345

strait. I am admiring my many beautiful uncommon flowers. . . .
I am very much Oblieged for the extra money. Mother. & all of
the money I receive.

But she later resumed: *Sometimes I forget every thing. I said*
Mollie I am very sorry I did not speak to Judge Moore last night
here. Mollie said I had a long talk with Judge More. I then asked
Why she and Orion did not ask Dr. Bancroff & Mollie said they
were both here. I have no recollection of seeing them or Judge
Moor that evening. It was not because I was tired for they would
not let me do any thing. I forget every thing but I don't find my
mind is all rong. . . . I have a new set of teeth made in a new
way. I think I shall like them. Livy I am afraid you and Sam will
think they will not do. But I am delighted with them, I think
they will do. I have no teeth to hold them.

How rare in all history, Mark Twain may have thought, this
unqualified praise of new dentures! No doubt it made his payment
of Dr. Mill's bill a pleasure. Had Jane so intended?

Without complaint she moved to the upstairs front bedroom
so that Professor Marshall might be promoted to the lower floor,
an honor he deserved. He was about to become principal of the
high school. From this new vantage the neighbors, their children,
their pets and their lawns looked handsomer to her. Even the insects showed up well; that summer there came to her attention a
remarkable spider and she wrote about it to Sam Moffett and to
Sam Clemens, who labeled the envelope: *Ma's strange spider:*

There is an elm tree in Judge Moors yard. I can reach the
limbs with my hands from my window upstairs. I pulled a leaf
off one day. I told Orion to look and see what was in it. There
was a nest something like a silk worms. The spider had a black
head and large black eyes and looked you in the face. . . . Its
feet were red like a chicken or bird. Then its back was round
about the size of a marble and yellow with black spots and marks
over it. I think if it was grown it would have nails like a chicken
or bird. Mr. Marshall a teacher in the school has a room in this
house. He is a professor of science, he wanted the spider. I told
him if it died he should have it. Mr. Marshall had to wait, however. Jane proffered the spider water and crumbs and small dead

346

insects for several days, courteously turning her back while it dealt with the offerings, until it expired.

While she could see objects at a distance very well, her sight for closer range was failing and her reading was much curtailed. Sometimes she mentioned it in letters to her children, but so resignedly that they paid little attention. Did not all elderly persons make the same complaint? Jane Clemens had never used the term "my bad eye," and so her children seemed totally unaware that she had one. They still regarded the matter as she had pictured it to them in their formative years: *one* of Ma's eyes was *better* than the other.

But in the new year of 1886 she turned the tables. She used her disability for a bit of extortion when, at Mollie's instigation, she struck Sam for an increase of allowance. It came about through an item Mollie found in a Chicago newspaper and read aloud to her—an astounding piece of news relating to General Grant's memoirs just issued by Mark Twain's publishing house.

"'The Webster Publishing Company,'" quoted Mollie breathlessly to her erstwhile calm and contented mother-in-law, "'has just sent a U. S. National Bank check for two hundred thousand dollars to Mrs. Julia D. Grant, widow of the late General. The check was dated February 27th.'—Would you like to read this with your own eyes, Ma? Shall I get your magnifying glasses?"

"Yes, get them," Jane said, "and give me the piece." After she had studied it and adjudged it to be genuine she reached for her pen. Mrs. Julia D. Grant, indeed! She began to compose a brief letter, needing very few suggestions from Mollie:

Dear children. Sam I hear you are worth a million of dollars. if so I want to call for a larger sum. I will not say how much more. My health is very good but I fear I am losing my best eye. If I loose my eyes what will this world be to me. This is cold weather, but Orion has a comfortable house. My stove keeps my room warm day and night. There are very few old people here now that were here when you were here. Mollies father is living but very feeble. I am as well and strong as people are of my age. I think our friends and relatives are all in moderate health. Your Mother

Mollie then wrote blandly in a space reserved for her:

Dear Sam & Livy—Ma asks me to add a line. She is quite cheerful today. . . . She is not willing to venture out. Orion wanted her to go sleighing yesterday—as it was mild and good sleighing— but she would not consent. We are delighted with the Grant book. (Deduce from this, said Mollie's letter between the lines, how your mother is failing! How unlike her old self, to turn down a sleigh ride!) She then spoke of rereading *Huckleberry Finn* and praised its dialects and realism; concluded: *Orion's cough is alarming. I got Emulcion of Cod liver oil last night for him. It may be the best thing yet.*

We hope you are not going to give up your visit here. Love to all. Mollie

Oh, the fury of Sam against this woman who had dared to plague him through his mother! He would have written richer grotesqueries about her to Howells, except that he could not exceed his former efforts. He had already caricatured her as a "bald-headed" spinster, taboo socially, who had "snaffled" a reluctant Orion against his will in order to marry an editor. Yet Mollie had been only eighteen at the time, kin to the best of the Western settlers. And though she had a high forehead, which she dressed with a fringe of bangs carefully curled, she was blessed with as healthy a head of hair as was the average woman.

The brief rapier duel concerning Jane's allowance which Mollie had instigated was not followed up by her, for there was very little malice in her disposition. Her chief resentment against Sam was his assumption that the Langdons were unassailably important. "Does Sam Clemens ever inquire after my old father?" she had recently asked Orion to illustrate one cause for her umbrage. "No! Yet if Mr. or Mrs. Theodore Crane so much as break a toe we are told about it, so we can lament." No doubt it was her Scottish way of discovering Sam's weaknesses that had made her so unpopular with him. After he had thoughtlessly divulged some extravagance in house decoration or foreign travel that he and Livy had indulged in, Mollie would refer to it with such restraint that they were compelled to see her raised eyebrows. She had annoyed Livy through the years, no end, and for this Sam would have her hide, if only in monstrous sarcasm and hyperbole.

The visit referred to in Mollie's letter materialized in July. It was a family reunion in honor of Pamela Moffett who had returned from California in March and had spent most of her time with her daughter in New York. The young Websters now owned a handsome three-story house on 126th Street, a rural area made accessible by the new elevated railroad. They were en route to Europe at this time, Charley having been chosen by Mark Twain to go to Rome and arrange for the American publication of Pope Leo XIII's biography. Their children were being cared for in Fredonia.

Sam and Livy and their three children reached Keokuk by lake steamer between Buffalo and Chicago, with railway stretches at each end. Keokuk was agog with interest. The McElroy family lent guest rooms, and so every one was well quartered. But the weather was so hot and humid as to be almost intolerable. It was the Valley at its most sullen and dreaded. Storms brewed but never broke, clothing clung to the daintiest skins. Sam and Pamela were soon bickering over national politics and certain aspects of California: since both had lived in California, both felt qualified to eulogize and detract. The Clemens children were wearied by attentions. Clara and little Jean wept from the weather's discomforts, and Jean added to every one's trials by injuring her arm so painfully that Dr. Jenkins, adept with children, must be summoned. Jane was patient. Livy was self-controlled, and Susie, her budding counterpart, remained angelic.

Mollie, busy with her staff of two, tried valiantly to secure enough ice to cool the tea, the lemonade and the Scotch required by the visitors, still holding back enough to keep the butter from running. Orion was annoyingly genial. The lodger, George Edward Marshall, interested Sam Clemens by always appearing immaculate in a white cotton or linen suit, the first Northern man Sam had ever seen wearing such. "I do it to be clean and comfortable," the young professor explained. "These suits tub nicely. It takes courage to wear them, though. Some people are inclined to stare." Did Livy, ever watchful, see a speculative look in her husband's eyes?

Such was the visit. Sam's thank-you letter said in part:

We came home very comfortably indeed. The Chicago railroad men came to see me, & advised against a special car; & they were right; it was not needed. I took the stateroom (because I wanted to smoke in it,) & 4 sections. Everybody had a lower berth but me; & all had abundance of room & air; & the expense from Chicago to Elmira was less by $240 than it would have been if we had taken a special car.

The remainder of the letter carried an apology to Pamela for hurting her feelings, and a postscript describing their being waited on in their Chicago hotel suite by the wealthy and charming Erasmus Moffett family.

The postscript caused Mollie to ask, "Aren't the Erasmus Moffetts richer than the Langdons, Pamela?"

"Oh, yes, the Moffetts are millionaires," Pamela answered. "But what are you getting at?"

Jane knew, in a general way. "Tch, tch, Mollie!" she reproved sternly. "If I still wore a thimble I'd use it on you."

34 ❖

Jane walked a good deal that autumn, for there was a lack in her life after her children departed. Pamela had returned to New York to hear the wonders of the young Websters' trip to Rome. Sam, in Hartford, was starting a book that fascinated him; *A Yankee in King Arthur's Court,* he intended to call it. When this was not occupying him, he was dashing over to the busy Pratt Whitney shops in that city to see how his Paige typesetter was coming along. One called it his because he had already invested tens of thousands of dollars in it and he expected it to reap him a fortune. When he sang its praises by letter, Orion and Mollie became reverently impressed but Jane grew merely restless. She would put

350

on her hat and go for a call or a walk. Too often from Lamptons and Clemenses she had heard such siren songs.

It was during this period that she thought she encountered her old love along the leaf-strewn paths at the edge of town. Mollie later heard about it from her cousin Mary Ann Patterson Creel, in whom Jane had confided. Mrs. Creel had found the confidence very interesting, for she knew a good deal about Jane's girlhood through her late husband.

What Jane had said to Mrs. Creel—she and Mrs. Creel were examining a beautiful old quilt at the time—was this: "I think Dr. Richard Barret has moved here. I see him sometimes when I'm walking and he bows to me very stately. He sends his sisters to see me. Long ago they disdained me, but now they are kind."

"But Dr. Barret is dead," Mrs. Creel objected.

Jane quickly changed the subject, looking as if she had cast her pearls before swine.

She stuck to her story when Mollie questioned her some months later. Indeed, Mollie catching her in one of her vaguer moods, she wove a yet more fantastic story about the Barrets and her several encounters with them.

Mollie, in several letters to Sam, was pleased to tell all this, for she wanted the Mark Twains to know what a difficult charge they must now deal with. They had all heard last year about the Lampton-Barret romance; for Jane, with emotion, had told her pent-up story to Pamela soon after her arrival from California. It was as if she had withheld it too long from her only daughter and must now have it out. Pamela had lost no time in confiding it to Sam, who did not take it lightly. The long-ago romance and its subsequent sorrows so filled Mark Twain with pity that he must quickly relate it to Howells, with all stops out. He had added to it an ingredient not entirely accurate.

There had been a Tri-State Old Settlers reunion in Keokuk in September 1885, and Jane had seen Richard A. Barret's name among those attending. She was aware that this was a son of Richard F. Barret—the son whose education she had coveted for Henry—and she felt an urge to meet him. She had asked Orion to take her to his hotel so that she might introduce herself and

351

talk to him about his father. Orion humored her, but when they reached the desk they were told that Mr. Barret had just left for his home in St. Louis. Jane was strangely disappointed. After brooding for several days she had told Orion of her blighted romance and her loveless marriage to his father. In the bruiting about of this news among Jane's astonished children, it was agreed that she had gone to the hotel expecting to see her former lover. They underrated her sanity. She had gone to see his son; her Richard's son. It was merely an old lady's nostalgic whim, almost conventional.

Now, however, it was a different story. Richard F. Barret himself, too long suppressed, had come to join the roster of her occasional visitors.

Jane seemed to give little thought to her own mortality in the ensuing years, and when she spoke of the matter at all it was in an unemotional and practical way. She was concerned with the disposal of her amethyst ring and her two brooches; the one that held Orion's miniature would of course go to Mollie; but the antique piece enshrining her ruffled-shirted father was sometimes bequeathed to one child, sometimes to another; it rather depended on how they had been behaving toward her. She wished to be buried in "a muslin shroud," she instructed, because she wanted no cherished clothes of hers to end up in the grave. "It would be just like Sam to order me dressed in my finest," she reminded Mollie. "Watch for that. I want all my clothes given to people who will enjoy them. I know several who hanker for my black velvet right now."

She was not to be spared the pains of old age, for she had a worsening rheumatism and a maddening eczema called salt rheum. Some of the hot applications she must use for her sore muscles and joints had a way of bringing out rashes that tortured her when the weather was humid. But she took a determined stand against the medical profession. In her last years, which were now upon her, she managed to resist, unless temporarily tuckered out, the combined efforts of Mollie and Orion to call in Dr. Bancroft or any of his cohorts. If a physician succeeded in reaching her side she evaded a discussion of symptoms and reduced him to

352

a social caller. The doctor always ended by declaring her "in a remarkable condition for a woman of her age." Once Dr. Bancroft won a notable victory. She had been coughing in a very weakening way, and he left some powders which he promised her would keep her from hearing the clock strike. They did, and she praised them highly.

On April 20, 1886, Jane wrote a letter to Hartford which Mark Twain must have regarded as poignant, for he scrawled on the envelope: *Longing after the school-mates of 70 years ago.* There were, however, several other angles to it, rather revealing:

Dear children all. This is a pleasant warm day. I don't know much to write. I have been very closely confined in the house for some time. I am rather tired of Keokuk but I don't know any better place to go to. At Columbia I think most of my relations of all colours have gone home. Here was revealed a compatibility with the dark race more profound than Uncle Tomism, and a nostalgia to match that felt for her blood kin . . . *I think all of Uncle Green's family are gone. All of my aunts about there are gone. Andy Russle and Betsy Acles* [Echols] *are gone. . . . How sad I can't go & see the old faces. This is a busy City. Buildings all over the city going up. Every man or woman can own their own house. But I can't persuade my son here to do like other men when I know he could if he would try. I think it is because you find fault of his writings. I tell him you don't write like any person else. and you can't read like any person else. My son I fear you wrong your brother finding fault unnessaryly. give him a fair chance & he will write as well as other men that write in his style. . . . Confusion. I wrote this some time ago & lost it. but don't scold. Love to all.*

Her eagerness for Orion to own a house of his own was due to the uncertainties of their living under a rented roof—the landlord's always threatening to sell the house and so on; but the wished-for security would not be attained until Mollie had received her inheritance from her father two years hence and would purchase the long desired home. Undoubtedly Sam was tired of being urged by Jane to spare poor Orion. Understandably he may have given the plaguing exhortions of this letter only an impatient

353

glance. If so, he missed a succinct proof of his mother's clear understanding of two diverse literary styles.

When the weather was good they could not prevent her from walking abroad and making impulsive calls on persons she liked, and Mollie spent a good deal of time correcting her inaccuracies. She once related that Pamela, when a baby, was stolen from her by Indians. It was an absurd story, yet so touchingly told that her audience was moved. Like Jane herself, the listening woman wept.

She had a yearning for molasses taffy that had been pulled till brittle-white, and she often bought a sack of it at her favorite store. Orion was pleased to share it with her, and to share the memories it evoked. Once Mollie asked him enviously, "What was there so special about those candy pulls on Hill Street, Orion?"

"I don't know," he answered honestly. "I really don't know. It was some magic of Ma's, I reckon."

If Jane heard of anyone's making lemon pie in the neighborhood she could not resist hinting for a piece. Mollie and Pamela were in agreement on the hazards of lemon pie for Ma. "If she eats lemon pie," Mollie told Pamela, "and gets sick afterward, she will lay it to anything. She will even lay it to a piece of apple she ate yesterday."

Pamela's reply was vigorous. "She was always wild for lemon pie. Pa often cautioned her against giving it to us children. If I should eat a piece of lemon pie even today, I'd be ill from it."

The more they closed in on her, the more she made a country of her own. Some days she gave Orion and Mollie a hard time, forgetting where she was and who surrounded her. She often thought she was a girl again and would accuse Orion and Mollie of neglecting Patsy, their house guest. "Patsy comes here to dine," she once accused Orion and Mollie, "and you drive her away with cold looks. If my sister is treated so again, I'll go with her." Patsy came and went, but only her doting sister saw her.

Jane would often put on her purple velvet dress and her watch and chain and ask to be taken for rides in the parks and along the levee, thinking she was in St. Louis; and Orion would hire a hack and take her about, using the money Sam had supplied for such emergencies. She would complain at times of the intense pain that

354

afflicted her neck, a pain that was hard to bear, yet she would throw open a window near her bed on chilly nights, determined never to be shut in. She would tolerate her dyspepsia with bad grace and try to cure it by eating only buttered crackers and chocolate for days at a time—chocolate, the wonderful product of the Amazon that Sam used to praise so, saying a man could walk all day and never get tired if he but consumed a few cacao beans.

She would talk sometimes of "going home" as a thing to be desired above all else; but "home," when they questioned her, though it seemed to be Heaven, was not a place but a time. She had envisioned the fourth dimension ahead of science and had found it to be satisfactory; in that dimension she would find waiting for her all that she had ever lost, including her youth. But in the meantime she begged to buy a little house where she and Patsy, in their teens, could live without being bothered by tiresome Keokukians; and she would cause Orion to send off her letters to Sam, whom she knew to be rich, demanding such an establishment. . . . Sometimes there would come lucid hours when she was herself: considerate, patient, optimistic, sassy. Her mind, her personality, all of her was there, actually, when not sidetracked by the tired body.

When the autumn of 1888 came on, and thereafter, she had to be watched for her own safety. Orion and Mollie were hard pressed to care for her with but one servant. There was talk of hiring an attendant, Sam authorizing the expenditure. But while a suitable companion was being sought, there came a letter from Sam regarding the Paige typesetter, bewailing his heavy expenses in perfecting the machine and saying only eighty-five more days would see them through. Sam, of course, was thinking in terms of thousands of dollars, sums too great to be affected by the little crisis in Keokuk, but patient Orion responded in the terms of a poor man, which was the only way he knew. He wrote to say that he and Mollie could hold out three months longer without a nurse for Ma, for during the winter she would not be wandering out-of-doors. Yes, he and Mollie could certainly do without extra help until the typesetter was perfected; they could spare him that expense at such a crucial time. Sam's reply might have shattered a post office:

Nov. 29, '88.
Jesus Christ!—*It is perilous to write such a man. You can go crazy on less material than anybody that ever lived. What in hell has produced all these maniacal imaginings? You told me you had hired an attendant for ma. Now hire one instantly, and stop this nonsense of wearing Mollie and yourself out trying to do that nursing yourselves. Hire the attendant, and tell me her cost so that I can instruct Webster & Co. . . . hell and damnation! You see I've read only the first page of your letter; I wouldn't read the rest for a million dollars.*

Yr Sam.

The nurse was procured, and Jane liked her very well. At least she accepted her courteously. She would not begin in her eighty-sixth year to find fault with someone who was attached to her. She often wondered aloud to the neighbors about the possible duration of this guest's visit. "Mollie's new woman seems right fond of me," she told Mrs. Dr. Jenkins. "She follows me about so. She's moved her cot into my room, and she's taken the bureau drawer I let the cat sleep in."

In 1889 Jane contributed to the town's lore by appropriating a child's tricycle, the kind resembling a little phaeton, and propelling herself cautiously about. "I've always wanted one," she explained to Orion. It was as hard to separate her from the vehicle as it had been to separate her from an organ-grinder's monkey that she had taken a fancy to in Fredonia; a fancy that was reciprocated, for the little creature had clung to her, and she to it; there had been profanity from the Italian, just as there were protests now from the ten-year-old girl who owned the tricycle.

In the following August, Jane had a stroke. Orion summoned Sam who was vacationing with Livy and the children at Tannersville in the Catskills. As Pamela was living again with Sammy Moffett in California, there was only Sam to come. Jane rallied on seeing him, and they joked gently together. He was soon able to

356

return to his family. He had rarely been more needed at home; Livy's mother was in her last illness at Elmira and little Jean had the beginnings of a disturbing malady.

On the 27th of October, 1890, at half-past eight in the evening, Jane Clemens went home. Sam hurried directly to Hannibal, where the burial was to be. There was a eulogy at the Presbyterian Church—Jane would not have recognized herself—and then the town's entire output of hacks and carriages, drawn by the handsomest horses available, carried relatives and friends and mere acquaintances to the cemetery. It was not the dreary little burying ground where her dead had first been interred. Some years before, they had secured a lot in the new cemetery on the hill; and later, John Robards, their friend, had attended to the moving of John M. Clemens' body, and little Benjamin's and Henry's, to this spot.

Jane was laid beside her husband. The spaces beyond her were reserved for Orion and Mollie.

Afterward, those who stood and mingled told one another things that Jane Clemens had said and done. The lore had begun. You heard a good deal of laughter for such a serious occasion. "She could certainly soothe you," said a woman who had known her slightly. "Once I was caught in a downpour standing in the doorway of Simmons' store, and she beside me. I was carrying on frightful because I'd left all my windows open at home, and she said, 'You've got nothing at all to worry about. It's coming straight down.' And sure enough, it was."

They moved toward Mark Twain, who was shaking hands, right and left. A man doesn't bury a mother every day, and the drama of it excited him. He reminisced warmly, tenderly, brilliantly. He was enjoying himself profoundly. Jane would not have had it otherwise.

BIBLIOGRAPHY

Anderson, Frederick. *Concerning Cats.* An introductory essay to two of Mark Twain's stories. Book Club of California, San Francisco, 1959. Edition limited to 450 copies.

————. *See also* Smith, Henry Nash.

Barret, Richard Ferrell. Medical thesis. Transylvania University Library, Lexington, Kentucky, 1827.

Bellamy, Gladys Carmen. *Mark Twain as a Literary Artist.* University of Oklahoma Press, Norman, Oklahoma, 1950.

Brashear, Minnie M. *Mark Twain, Son of Missouri.* University of North Carolina Press, Chapel Hill, North Carolina, 1934.

————. With Robert M. Rodney. *The Art, Humor, and Humanity of Mark Twain.* University of Oklahoma Press, Norman, Oklahoma, 1959. Introduction by Edward Wagenknecht.

Brooks, Van Wyck. *The Ordeal of Mark Twain.* Revised edition. E. P. Dutton and Company, New York, 1933.

Burdette, Ruth Paull, genealogist. Unpublished data of Adair County and Green County, Kentucky, since their foundings.

Carrico, Paul. A sketch of Ann Hancock Saunders, half sister of John M. Clemens, and the Hancock-Saunders family, from the Notre Dame thesis of Paul Carrico.

Casey, Mrs. Joseph Montgomery. Recollections; and the Bible of Mary Eleanor Stotts Clemens, with data. Fort Madison, Iowa.

Clemens, Mary Eleanor. Memoirs concerning her mother's girlhood in Adair County, unpublished. Her Bible, with family records. "Molly Clemens's Notebook," *The Palimpsest,* October 1929, Fred W. Lorch.

Clemens, Orion. Census of Keokuk. Two editions, 1856, 1857; Ben Franklin Job Printing, Keokuk, Iowa; an inclusion of the first edition: *History of the Half Breed Tract.*

————. Letters to a St. Louis newspaper from Tennessee, 1867, signed "Cumberland."

Clemens, Samuel Langhorne. All of his published writings. Harper & Brothers, New York and London.

Clift, G. Glenn. *The Corn Stalk Militia of Kentucky;* and further compilations of the militia of the War of 1812. Kentucky Historical Society, Frankfort, Kentucky, 1957.

————. (editor). *The Private War of Lizzie Hardin,* a Civil War diary. Kentucky Historical Society, Frankfort, Kentucky, 1963.

Coleman, J. Winston, Jr. *Slavery Times in Kentucky.* University of North Carolina Press, Chapel Hill, North Carolina, 1940.

Collins, Lewis. *History of Kentucky.* First edition; for the Montgomery massacre, the life of Colonel William Casey, the Hardin family, and General Benjamin Logan. James & Company, Stereotypers, Cincinnati, Ohio, 1847.

Columbia-Union Presbyterian Church, *Shiloh.* Its history in Adair County, 1803–1956. A brochure by the membership. Columbia, Kentucky.

Crocker, Elizabeth L. *Yesterdays.* Sketches of early Fredonia, New York, and Chautauqua County. Fredonia *Censor.* 1960–61–62–63.

De Voto, Bernard. *Mark Twain's America.* Little, Brown and Company, Boston, 1932.

————. Introduction, *Mark Twain in Eruption.* Harper & Brothers, New York, 1940.

————. *Mark Twain at Work.* Harvard University Press, Cambridge, 1942.

Fatout, Paul. *Mark Twain on the Lecture Circuit.* Indiana University Press, Bloomington, Indiana, 1960.

Filson Club, The. Genealogical files for McDowell family in Kentucky and Missouri, and data relating to Lampton and Clemens families. Various issues, *The Filson Club History Quarterly.* Louisville, Kentucky.

Foner, Philip S. *Mark Twain, Social Critic.* International Publishers Company, Inc., New York, 1958.

Gara, Larry. *The Liberty Line: The Legend of the Underground Railroad.* University of Kentucky Press, Lexington, Kentucky, 1961.

Garrison, Raymond E. Writings pertaining to Keokuk, Iowa, including *Goodbye My Keokuk Lady.* Privately printed. Keokuk, 1962.

Glazier, Captain Willard. *Down the Great River.* Hubbard Brothers, Publishers, Philadelphia, 1889.

Gibson, William M. Coeditor with Henry Nash Smith. *Mark Twain-Howells Letters.* Harvard University Press, Cambridge, Massachusetts, 1960.

Goodpasture, A. V. *Mark Twain Southerner.* Tennessee Historical Magazine, second series I (1931), Nashville, Tennessee.

Hardin, Parker Calhoun. Recollections, unpublished. Sketch of his life under Adair County; Perrin, Battle, Kniffin, *A History of Kentucky.* Louisville and Chicago, 1880. Eighth edition, 1888.

Herdman, Mrs. Mary Quarles. Genealogy of the Quarles family and some facts relating to Patsy Lampton Quarles. Waco, Texas.

Hogue, Albert R. *History of Fentress County, Tennessee.* Nashville, 1916.

Horine, Emmet Field, M.D. *Daniel Drake (1785–1852), Pioneer Physician of the Midwest.* University of Pennsylvania Press, Philadelphia, 1961.

Howells, W. D. *My Mark Twain.* Harper & Brothers, New York and London, 1910.

Hurt, Judge Rollin, alias John Avroe Steele. *The Permanent Settlement of Adair County, Kentucky. Adair County News,* 1919.

Keith, Clayton. A Sketch of the Lampton Family in America. St. Louis, Missouri, 1914.

Kendrick, William Carnes. *Reminiscences of Old Louisville. The Courier-Journal,* Louisville, Kentucky, 1937.

Lambton, John George, First Earl of Durham. *See* Reid, Stuart J.

Lampton, The Rev. Eugene J.; Memoirs, unpublished, Pike County, Missouri.

Little, Lucius P. *Ben Hardin: His Times and Contemporaries.* Louisville, Kentucky, 1887.

Lorch, Fred W. Sketches of Orion Clemens. *The Palimpsest,* October 1929.

Lowe, Mary Lucy. Some Quarles and Clemens Tennessee anecdotes.

McBrayer, Sophia (Hardin). Recollections, unpublished.

Meltzer, Milton. *Mark Twain Himself,* pictorial. Thomas Y. Crowell Company, New York, 1960.

Mississippi Panorama, pictorial. City Art Museum of St. Louis. Caledonia Press, 1950.

Missouri Historical Review. Published quarterly by the State Historical Society of Missouri. Columbia, Missouri. Various issues.

"Moorman Family in Virginia." *William and Mary College Quarterly,* second series XII.

Neider, Charles (editor). *The Autobiography of Mark Twain,* with inclusions. Harper and Brothers, New York, 1959.

———. (editor). *Mark Twain: Life As I Find It.* Doubleday & Company, Inc., 1961.

Paine, Albert Bigelow. *Mark Twain, A Biography.* 4 volumes. Harper and Brothers, New York and London, 1912.

———. *Mark Twain's Letters.* 2 volumes. Harper and Brothers, New York and London, 1917.

Paullin, C. O. *Mark Twain's Virginia Kin. William and Mary College Quarterly,* second series XV, 1935.

Reid, Stuart J. *Life and Letters of the First Earl of Durham.* Longmans, Green & Company, London, New York, and Bombay, 1906.

Rice, Father David, first Presbyterian minister in the wilderness. "Philanthropos"; *Slavery Inconsistent with Justice.* Kentucky *Gazette,* Lexington, Kentucky, January 1792.

Rideing, William H. *Many Celebrities and a Few Others.* Doubleday, Page & Company. Garden City, New York, 1912.

Rodney, Robert M., with M. M. Brashear. *The Art, Humor, and Humanity of Mark Twain.* University of Oklahoma Press, Norman, Oklahoma, 1959.

Saint Louis, Encyclopedia of the History of. Edited by William Hyde and Howard L. Conrad. The Southern History Company, New York, Louisville, St. Louis, 1899. Biography of James Clemens, Jr., and his family; of the Berkeley families; of the Barret family; of Dr. Joseph Nash McDowell.

Saint Louis, History of City and County of, by John Thomas Scharf. Louis H. Everts & Co., Philadelphia, Pennsylvania, 1883. Biography of Dr. Richard F. Barret of St. Louis, industrialist.

Saunders, Xantippe. Her description of Jane Lampton Clemens to various persons; including a letter to Albert Bigelow Paine, June 6, 1907. Mark Twain Papers.

Sewell, Mrs. Jennie Anderson. Unpublished information regarding the Montgomery, Casey, and Anderson families. Copies of the portraits of Jane Montgomery Casey, John Montgomery and his wife Anne Casey Montgomery, Peggy Casey Lampton, and Green Casey.

Smith, Henry Nash, Literary Editor of the Mark Twain Estate and custodian of the Mark Twain Papers. *Mark Twain-Howells Letters* with William M. Gibson and assisted by Frederick Anderson. The Belknap Press of Harvard University Press, Cambridge, 1960.

————. *Mark Twain: The Development of a Writer.* The Belknap Press of Harvard University Press, Cambridge, 1962.

The Twainian, published bimonthly by the Mark Twain Research Foundation, Inc., Perry, Missouri. Various issues.

Varble, Captain Pinkney. His obituaries; newspapers of Louisville, Kentucky. A listing of his steamboats. April 2, 1892.

Wagenknecht, Edward. *Mark Twain: The Man and His Work.* Revised. University of Oklahoma Press, Norman, Oklahoma, 1961.

Webster, Annie Moffett. Memoirs, published and unpublished.

Webster, Samuel Charles. *Mark Twain Business Man.* Little, Brown and Company. Boston, 1946.

Webster, Samuel and Doris. "Whitewashing Jane Clemens." *The Bookman* LXI (1925) 531–35.

Wecter, Dixon. *Mark Twain to Mrs. Fairbanks* (editor). Huntington Library Press, San Marino, California, 1949.

———. *The Love Letters of Mark Twain* (editor). Harper & Brothers, New York, 1949.

———. *Sam Clemens of Hannibal.* Houghton Mifflin Company, Boston, 1952.

Wheat, M. T. *Wheat's Philosophy of Slavery*—"Advantages Enumerated and Explained." Stereotyped in Louisville, Kentucky, 1862.

Newspapers of the era, including those of Hannibal, made available to me at the Missouri Historical Society, Columbia, Missouri, and at the Public Library of St. Louis.

Order books, court records, deed books, will books of counties in Virginia, Kentucky, Tennessee, Missouri.

Tavern books of charge accounts. Inventories of sales.

Tradition, lore, gossip.

364

1–7, 9, 11, 13; a "born listener," 54; childhood, early days, 17, 24 ff, 40, 45 ff; cobbling, 51, 86, 124, 206, 259, 299; dancing of, 52, 53, 57, 58, 66, 109, 160, 341–42; and death, reaction to, attitude towards, 17, 144–45, 188, 196–99, 235–40, 265–67, 344; death and burial of, 357; dramatic ability, mimicry, 67–68, 70, 103, 123, 142, 156–57; and dressmaking, clothes, 47, 53, 58, 109, 152, 160, 203, 254–55; education, 37, 52, 54, 58; eyesight, 17–18, 25, 51, 254, 347; and faith healing, 181–82; illness, 320, 345, 352–57; imagination, wit, odd streaks of, 45, 54, 101–2, 103, 123–24, 136, 140, 195, 278–79, 298, 313, 356; joins temperance crusade, 180; kindness, love of people, fun, living, 57–58, 59, 63, 82, 89, 93–94, 109, 114–15, 136, 189, 199; letters, 107, 173, 263, 303–4, 307, 319–21, 330–39 *passim,* 345–46, 353; and members of family, friends, specific people (*See* by name); "miscalculates" her age, 212, 213, 282; and Mississippi River, fondness for, 127, 128, 132, 185, 327; near ninety, rides tricycle, 356; and Parker Hardin, 66–72, 81–82, 183–86; portraits, photos of, 242, 326; "practices" medicine, 123–24, 157, 195–96, 217; recalls past, 319; refuses to eat veal, 278–79; religious attitudes, beliefs, 42–43, 88, 101–2, 117, 153–54, 187, 194, 205, 227–28, 240, 317, 344–45; reveals her marriage was loveless, 352; and Richard F. Barret, 59–60, 62, 67, 68, 70–73, 75–80, 85–88, 97–98, 113–14, 185, 351–52; and silkworm culture, interest in, 156–57, 298; and slavery, attitudes on, 62, 69, 138–40, 189, 226; smokes a pipe, 180–81; sociability, gregariousness of, 25, 52, 55–57, 58–63, 113–14, 152, 159, 160, 187–88, 216, 221, 224, 225–26, 338; "spider letter," 346–47; and spiritualism, 208, 239–40, 335–36; tea set incident, 178–79, 180; and walking, exercise, love of, 140, 153, 350

Clemens, Jean, 336, 349, 357
Clemens, Jennie, 231, 233, 254, 260; death in Nevada of, 263–64
Clemens, Jeremiah, 132
Clemens, John Marshall, 21, 22–24, 38, 68, 210; business and financial ventures, failures, 105 ff, 132, 133, 135 ff, 143–44, 148 ff, 159, 162–65,

166, 174–76, 198, 206; character, habits, manner, 94–97, 102, 103, 133–35; and daughter Pamela, 161, 169, 209; in Florida, Mo., 115–27; and Hannibal (brother), 99, 109, 127, 131; in Hannibal, Mo., 127, 128–33, 135–72 *passim;* illness, death, 166, 168–72, 177–78, 357; inventions, 100, 110, 111; religion, 154, 169; and wife, JLC, 39–40, 60–63, 73–74, 82–93 ff, 99 ff, 111 ff, 127–71 *passim*

Clemens, Mrs. John Marshall. *See* Clemens, Jane Lampton
Clemens, Dr. John Marshall, 127, 275, 288, 291
Clemens, Langdon, 297, 308
Clemens, Margaret, 109, 116, 127
Clemens, Orion, 149, 180, 198, 199, 213–14 ff, 221, 231, 233, 238, 264, 272–77, 290–91, 316–17 ff; birth, education, early days, 101–24 *passim;* in Civil War, 249, 257; as clerk in father's store, 126, 132–33, 135, 136–37; described, 206, 212; edits *Journal,* 204, 205–11, 215; expelled by Presbyterian church, 316–17; and father, 168, 177–78, 302; in Hartford, 286, 301–3, 305; and inventions, 166, 281, 303–4; and James Clemens, 150–51; in Keokuk, 221 ff, 269 ff, 306–7, 312–13, 327, 328–57 *passim;* meets, marries Mary Stotts (Mollie), 218–19 ff; in Nevada Territory, 249–51, 255–56, 261–68, 269; as printing apprentice, 137, 141, 146, 149, 166, 172; and Sam Clemens, 199–200, 205–6 ff, 222–23, 229–30, 240–42, 247, 250, 270–71, 272, 280–81, 303–7, 312, 319–22, 330, 331, 353; studies, practices law, 166, 236, 244–45, 265, 312; with Ustick printing office, 150–51, 161, 186; as writer, 275–76, 304, 314, 316, 317, 319–21, 353

Clemens, Mrs. Orion (Mary "Mollie" Stotts), 218–19, 220, 221, 231, 233, 240–42, 249–50, 253–55, 272, 273–77, 283 ff, 322; in Hartford, 301–3, 305; illness, 322–23, 338; and Jane Clemens, 270, 277–78, 280, 320; marriage, 218 ff; in Nevada, 260, 261–68; notebook, 251; and Sam Clemens, 348

Clemens, Pamela (Mela). *See* Moffett, Mrs. Will
Clemens, Pleasants, 21, 22, 62, 99, 122
Clemens, Pleasants Hannibal, 108
Clemens, Samuel, 21–22

365

Duncan, Mrs. Nancy, 90
Dunkirk, 291, 295, 299
Durham, Earl of, 3, 140–41

Eagle House, 29, 30, 31, 32, 34, 57, 64, 66, 75
Ealer, George: Sam Clemens trains as pilot under, 240
Echols, Elizabeth, 81
Eddy, Mary Baker, 182
"Eleven Locust Street, Upstairs" (St. Louis), 200
Elgin, Colonel, 194
Elmira, N.Y., 297, 315
England. *See* Great Britain
Episcopalians, 50
Erie, Lake, 299
Esmeralda mines, 257
Established Church, 22, 77
Evening News, St. Louis, 213, 219
Evening Post, New York, 303
Ewers, James, 60
Express, Buffalo, 281, 283

Fairbanks, Mary Mason, 281–82, 285, 344
Falls of the Ohio, 23, 32
Farmer's Library, The, 5
Fayette County, Ky., 2
Fentress County, Tenn., 102, 105, 109, 206
Field, Mr. and Mrs. John, 74, 83–84, 95, 96, 97
Field and Creel store, 74
Field and St. Clair (family theatre troupe), 224
52nd Regiment, Kentucky Militia, 31
First Presbyterian Church, St. Louis, 226
Florida, Mo., 115, 119, 125; Academy, 125
Flowers' Ferry, Green River, 80
Flyaway mine, 257
Forks of Wolf, 111
Fort Donelson, 257, 258
Fort Jefferson, 246
France, 7, 8, 9, 27
Fredonia, N.Y., 312, 313 ff; Academy, 300; JLC moves to, 286, 287, 291–94 ff; Sam Clemens visits, 308–11, 314
Fugitive Slave Law, 215
Fuqua, Widow, 187
Fuqua, Andy, 266, 267

Gainesboro, Tenn., 99, 100, 102, 216, 262

Gaither, Dr. Nathan, 17, 33, 41, 91–92, 157
Gaither, Mrs. Nathan (Martha Morrison), 91–92
Garnett, William, 60
Garnett, Mrs. William (Emily Willis), 60
Garth, Mr. and Mrs., 160
Gate City, Keokuk, 261, 270, 320, 331
Gazette (Cincinnati), 166
Gazette (Hannibal), 137, 162
Gazette (Kentucky), 20
Gerhardt, Karl, 342
Ghent, Treaty of, 34
Gilded Age, The, 29, 85, 229
Gill, Mrs. Alexander (Polly Goggin), 21
Gilmer, Thomas, 38
Glasgow, Ky., 30
Godey's Lady's Book, 179, 203, 254
Goggin, Pamela ("Permelia"; formerly Mrs. Samuel Clemens). *See* Hancock, Mrs. Simon
Goggin, Polly, 21
Goggin, Thomas, 21, 23
Golden Era (steamboat), 220
Golden Era, The: Sam Clemens writes for, 180, 264
Goodall, Judge, 236
Grady, Peachy, 61–62
Grady, Susan, 61–62
Grant, Dr. and Mrs. Orville, 163–66 ff, 172, 176
Grant, Julia D. (Mrs. Ulysses S.), 347
Grant, Ulysses S., 258, 265, 347
Grass Valley, 270
Gray, Mr. and Mrs. David, 308
Gray, John A., printing firm: Sam Clemens employed by, 214
Great Britain, 27; War of 1812, 31–35
Green (slave), 138–39
Green County, Ky., 4, 73, 89, 206, 258
Greening, Mr., 245
Greening, Mrs. (Tabitha "Puss" Quarles), 120, 245, 288
Green River, 2, 39, 80, 117
Green River Bridge, battle of, 259
Greensburg, Ky., 6, 8
Grey, Lady Jane, 344
Grissom, John, 75

Halley's Comet, 122
Halleck, Fitz-Greene, 311
Halloway family, 93–94
Hamilton, Alexander, 10
Hancock, Ann. *See* Saunders, Mrs. William
Hancock, Polly, 116, 130, 275

75, 93, 104, 115, 142–43, 179–80; born, 12; death of, 196–99; described, 26, 36, 54, 58, 59, 64, 120, 173; in Florida, Mo., 118 ff; marriage, 101; and sister, JLC, 25–26, 42, 46 ff, 58 ff, 72, 85–86, 96, 104, 120–21, 135, 147–48, 173, 186, 196–99, 336–38

Quarles, John Polk, 173
Quarles, Margaret, 109, 180
Quarles, Martha, 180
Quarles, Sara, 147
Quarles, Tabitha "Puss." *See* Greening, Mrs.
Quarles, William Pennington, 101
Quarry Farm, 297, 308

Rachel (slave), 92
Raisin, River, battle at, 32, 36, 225
Ralls, Colonel, 248
Ralls County, Mo., 119, 124, 158, 162, 248
Randolph, William, 50
Raymond, Sam, 192
Reason (slave), 109
Red Dog (mining camp), 270
Redpath, Mr.: Sam Clemens lectures for, 281
Red Ribbon Hall, Keokuk, 317
Rees, George, 230
Rees, Wm., and Co., 331
Renneau, Mr., 112, 116
Rice, Father, 20
Richmond, Va., 176, 195
Robards, Archibald, 187, 192, 210
Robards, John, 357
Robertson, Rev. Samuel B., 39, 58, 93
Robertson's Academy, 37, 54, 58
Robins family, 256–57
Rock Castle Farm, 76
Rome, Websters in, 349, 350
Rush, Benjamin, 254
Roughing It, 303, 312
Russell, Mr. and Mrs., 290
Russell, Andrew, 70, 81, 290
Russell, Orion, 290, 291
Russell Creek, 71, 98

Sacramento Union, 267
St. George's (church), 261
St. Joseph, Mo., 210, 251
St. Joseph's church, 117
St. Louis, Mo., 119, 128, 130, 204, 211–14, 219, 221, 228, 235, 246, 248, 259; *Evening News*, 213, 219
St. Paul, 210
Salt River, 115, 119, 124–25; Navigation Company, 125, 127
"Sam Clemens Bay," 256

Samuel (slave), 92
Sand Springs, Tenn., 102, 103
Sandwich Islands. *See* Hawaiian Islands
Sandy (slave), 159, 164, 165, 178, 186, 189–90, 209, 328
San Francisco, 262, 264, 269–70, 322; *Morning Call,* 264
Sangamon County, Ill., 262
Sarah (slave), 53, 55, 64, 92
Saturday Post, Keokuk, 230
Saturday Press, New York, 267
Saunders, Mary Ann Pamela Xantippe Bryon (Tip), 131, 275, 288
Saunders, William, 130–32, 275, 288, 289
Saunders, Mrs. William (Ann Hancock), 116, 130–31, 275
Saunders, Mrs. William (Polly Hancock), 275, 288
Schooler (Schuyler), Martha, 5, 12, 27, 157
Schroeter, George, 182, 245, 247, 259, 265–67, 340
Schroeter, Mrs. George, 340
Schuyler (Schooler) family, 5
Scotland County, Mo., 121, 244–45
Scots' Club, 218
Sebastian, Benjamin, 8
Selby, Mr. and Mrs. Lingan, 100, 110, 111
Sellers, Colonel Mulberry, 29, 85, 229
Selmes, T. R., 176
Sexton, Mrs., 149, 152, 261
Sexton, Margaret, 149, 152, 261
Shelby County, 220
Shenandoah Valley, 5, 49
Shiloh, battle of, 258
Shiloh Church, 6, 39, 93
Shirley, John Warfield, 33
Shocking Events (play), 224
Silas (slave), 18, 109
Simmons and Company, 187
"Sketch of the Black Hawk War and History of the Half Breed Tract," 222
Slavery, 5, 12, 18–20, 38, 92, 111, 258; Fugitive Slave Law, 215; JLC's attitude towards, 62, 69, 138–40, 189–90, 226
Slote, Dan, 328
Small, Mr., 257, 287
Smarr, Sam, 188
Smith, Mrs. Betsey, 242
Smith, Edith, 199
Smith, Josephine, 206
"Snodgrass" letters, 230
South Carolina, 246

372

G10

Jane's mother, Peggy Casey Lampton, who died when Jane was fourteen.

Portrait of Jane's grandmother, Jane Montgomery Casey, painted in 1811. The artist is unknown.

This is where Jane and John Clemens spent their honeymoon. The house still stands in Columbia, Kentucky. Drawing by Walter H. Kiser.